Ninja Foodi Pressure Cooker That Crisp 1000 Days

The Complete Guide of Ninja Foodi Cookbook for Beginners to Pressure Cook, Air Fry, Crisp, Slow Cooker, and More

By Edward Martino

Table of Content

Chapter 7 Beef, Lamb, Pork 47

Chapter 8 Fish and Seafood 62

Chapter 9 Soup and Stew 74

Chapter 10 Appetizer...85

Chapter 11 Salad 89

Chapter 12 Snack and Dessert...................................94

PART III AIR FRY, BAKE, ROAST   104

Chapter 13 Breakfast.. 104

Chapter 14 Appetizer... 110

PART IV SLOW COOKER 146

Chapter 17 Vegetable 146

Chapter 18 Grain and Rice 151

Chapter 19 Bean and Legume 156

Chapter 20 Beef... 167

Chapter 21 Poultry 174

PART I INTRODUCTION

A multifunctional countertop cooking appliance is the need of today! We all want that one cooker that could pressure cook, steam, air fry, broil, bake or roast all sorts of food items in a single pot. Luckily Ninja Foodi is here to make that possible for all the professional and home-chefs and the company has now given the best of the best- the 11 in 1, 6.5 quart Ninja Foodi pressure cooker and air fryer which can carry out 11 different cooking functions with its highly efficient cooking technology. This cooker is perfect to create a whole menu in minimum time. And if you have

this amazing appliance already, then here comes a complete cookbook to put the new Ninja Foodi with Tendercrisp technology to great use. Before jumping straight to the recipes, let's see how this pressure cooker beats all other electric cookers in the market!

Chapter 1 Introducing Ninja Foodi FD302 11 in 1 Pro

Ninja has introduced a variety of electric pressure cooker models before. This one in particular was designed to cover all the cooking needs of a user. The "sous vide" cooking mode along with the air crisp options, is a combination that is rare to find in an electric pressure cooker but in this Ninja Foodi 11 in 1 pressure cooker, both those functions are available for use besides 9 other important cooking functions. In this chapter, we will try to understand this Ninja Foodi model offers us and what are its most appealing features.

Benefits of Ninja Foodi

Why do I buy this cooking appliance? Is it worth spending the money? These are some of the questions that we all ask ourselves. And to answer those, it is important to learn about the added features of the appliance which are not found in other appliances available in the same price or range. Let's what are advantages this Ninja Foodi Pro pressure cooker has to offer:

11 Advanced Cooking Functions:

Imagine cooking without having to switch the pots at all. Using this Ninja Foodi cooker you can sauté, sear then pressure cook or slow cook in the same pot. There are 11 amazing cooking functions that are need of today and they include:

1. Pressure
2. Steam
3. Air Crisp
4. Sauté/Sear
5. Slow Cook
6. Bake/roast
7. Broiler
8. Dehydrate
9. Yogurt
10. Sous Vide
11. Keep Warm

So, this pressure cooker can do the work for multiple appliances in one place. Imagine all the countertop space you will save when you buy this appliance instead of buying an air fryer, pressure cooker, steamer or slow cooker separately.

Can Cook Variety of Meal:

With that many cooking functions, it is pretty obvious to claim that the appliance helps you cook a variety of meals in a minimum duration. For instance, you can cook an entrée, a crispy appetizer, a side meal and baked dessert for a dinner serving, using nothing but this appliance.

The Two Lid System:

The best part about this appliance is it comes with an attached lid which has an air crisping heating technology inside and it also has a detachable pressure cooker lid. So, for pressure cooking, you can use the pressure cooker lid which can seal the vessel inside and can maintain the pressure as desired whereas the air crisping lid ensures a controlled flow of hot air into the vessel.

Saves Money, Time and Energy:

The use of TenderCrisp technology in the Ninja Foodi FD302 makes it a time, energy and money saver. The effective heating system cooks in minutes instead of several hours, the heat is contained well inside the vessel so it can cook well without consuming a lot of electricity. Hence the appliance is perfect to save some extra bucks on electricity.

Zero Mess-Easy Cleanup:

With a one-pot multi-cooking system, the Ninja Foodi pressure cooker gives you zero mess after cooking. You only need to wash one insert, rack or air crisp basket after each session and all those accessories are dishwasher safe.

Design and Features of Ninja Foodi

Pressure Release Valve
Easily release pressure.

Pressure Lid
Quickly tenderize and cook ingredients.

Nesting Broil Rack
Use to steam or reverse to broil.

Cook & Crisp™ Plate
4.6-quart nonstick plate fits 3 lbs of French fries.

Crisping Lid
Use to finish off pressure cooked recipes or to air fry your food.

Cooking Pot
6.5-quart nonstick, ceramic-coated cooking pot serves 4–6.

14 Safety Features
Passed rigorous testing for certification, giving you peace of mind.

FD302

The Ninja Foodi FD302 11 in 1 pro like every other electric cooker comes as a base unit that contains the heating element fixed inside it. Along with this unit come different accessories and other fixable components. Inside a packed box of Ninja Foodi multipurpose cooker, you will find the following components:

- Pressure cooking lid
- 6.5-qt nonstick cooking pot
- 4.6-qt nonstick Cook and Crisp Plate
- Stainless steel nesting broil rack

The base unit of the Ninja Foodi comes with a control panel with a LED display. This panel is designed with keys and keys which are used to adjust the mode, time, temperature and pressure of the Ninja Foodi. The entire control panel can be divided into two portions, the Functional and the operational. The functional keys are used to select the mode of cooking, whereas the operational keys allow you to control the pressure, temperature, and timing. Here is the complete list of the keys that are present on the control panel:

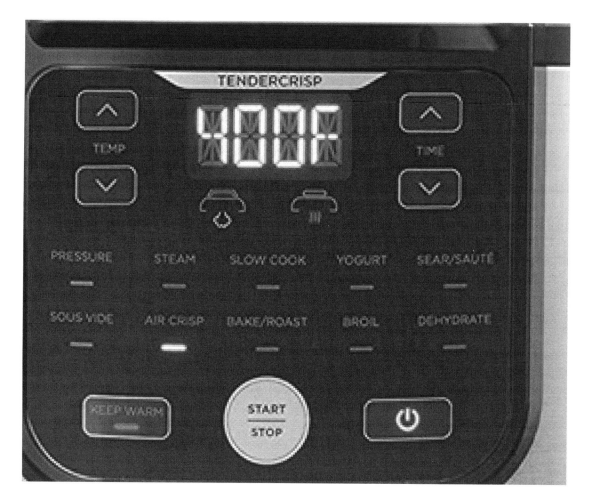

Functional Keys

Following the control keys which allow you to select any desired cooking mode. Below the label of each mode, there is a LED that lights up when the mode is selected.

- **PRESSURE:** This mode allows cooking at varying temperatures.

- **STEAM:** It lets you steam food placed inside on a steamer rack with water in the pot.

- **AIR CRISP:** it is used to Air Fry all sorts of crispy meals and snacks.

- **SEAR/SAUTÉ:** It lets you sauté or sear food as you do on a stovetop without the lid.

- **SLOW COOK:** It lets you cook food at extremely low temperatures for a long duration.

- **DEHYDRATE:** Dehydrated meats, fruits and vegetables for healthy snacks.

- **BAKE/ROAST:** With this option, you can turn your Foodi into an oven.

- **BROIL:** It is used to boil or melt the food toppings.

- **YOGURT:** This feature lets you set the low temperatures needed to prepare a yogurt from the milk and its starter.

- **SOUS VIDE:** This is a low-temperature water-based cooking mode.

- **KEEP WARM:** This allows you to keep the food warm once it is cooked.

Operational Keys

Following are the keys that allow you the adjust the settings within each of the selected modes:

- **POWER key:** It is on the bottom corner of the control panel and used to switch on the device.

- **START/STOP key:** Present at the bottom centre this round key is used to start, stop or pause a function.

- **TEMP arrows:** The up and arrows keys of temp are present on one side of the LED display and they can be used to increase or decrease the cooking temperature.

- **TIME arrows:** The up and arrows keys of Time are present on the other side of the LED display and they can be used to increase or decrease the cooking time.

- **KEEP WARM key:** When an operation is completed the device automatically switches to keep warm mode to keep food warm. You can press the key to either start the mode or stop it.

Functions of Ninja Foodi

A single base unit of Ninja Foodi multipurpose cooker can carry out several functions. In this single vessel you can try all the following functions:

1. PRESSURE

By pressing the "Pressure" key, you can switch the device to this mode. A pressure cooking lid is used to maintain the internal pressure of the vessel. The pressure release valve on top of the lid should be turned to a 'Sealed' position to avoid leakage. Once this operation has been carried, you can turn the pressure released handle to the 'venting' position to release the steam quickly.

2. STEAM

The same appliance can also be turned into a steamer by selecting "steam' mode. Set the reversible rack in the pot after pouring 1-2 cups of water into it and keep the items for steaming over it. Now cover the lid without sealing the valves and press 'Start' to initiate.

3. SLOW COOK

You can turn your Ninja Foodi 11 in 1 pro appliance into a slow cooker as well and it then works exactly like a crockpot. Just add the ingredients and cover the lid without sealing the valves. Set the Slow cook mode, and adjust the temperature and time.

4. AIR CRISP

To add crispiness to the food without using any oil, Ninja Foodi FD302 gives you an Air Crisp function. It has a separate crisper basket and air crisping lid. Add food to the basket and place it into the Foodi. Cover the air crisping lid and press Air Crisp and adjust time and temperature.

5. BAKE/ ROAST

A single key allows two functions in the Ninja Foodi. You can bake and roast anything. For cakes, you need to place the rack inside and then keep the baking pan over it.

6. BROIL

Ninja Foodi FD302 also work like a broiler due to its broil mode. When food is cooked in this mode, it is heated from the top to bring more color to the food. Place the reversible rack in the Ninja Foodi insert and cover the lid. Press the broil key and adjust the time and temperature according. Once done, press the stop key and remove the lid.

7. DEHYDRATE

The Ninja Foodi FD302 is also a dehydrator as it gives a unique option to dehydrate any ingredient in the same vessel. It is carried out for a long duration at low temperatures.

8. SEAR/SAUTE

The sauté mode allows cooking without the lid. It simply heats up the base of the cooking pot just enough to sear or sauté it in little or no oil. To carry out this function. Simply preheat the device on this mode and add the cooking fats to the insert. Let it warm up and then toss in the ingredients for sautéing. Normally vegetables are sautéed at this mode, or the meat is seared. This mode is not good for complete tenderizing of the ingredients but only to cook them lightly from the outside.

9. Sous Vide

Sous vide is a cooking technique in which food packed in a vacuum bag is cooked in a water bath. This Ninja Foodi cooker is also capable of cooking meals in this way. Once this mode is selected the machine automatically selects the low-temperature range and the long time brackets to enable cooking.

10. Yogurt

Yogurt making has now become easy, with the Ninja Foodi smart yogurt mode in which the optimum temperature is maintained inside the vessel for the desired duration to convert milk into yogurt.

11. Keep warm

Let's say you don't want to serve your freshly cooked meal right away, you can then press the keep warm key to keep it hot until you are ready to serve it.

Chapter 2 User Guide

The entire Ninja Foodi cooking appliance range is user friendly, you can easily find the keys, displays or dials present on the front or top of the machines to adjust the settings. And its also quite easy to install or remove accessories from the appliance. And in the case of Ninja Foodi Pro, here is how you can do it:

How to Use?

The Ninja Foodi with all its preset functions can help the newbies to cook directly without messing with timing and temperature. The control panel clearly states each function while displaying the ongoing operation, the timer and the temperature set on the device. The control panel has a soft touch system which keeps it convenient to use for every function.

Insert the Condensation collector:

The steam or condensation collector is an important part of this electric pressure cooker as it collects all the excess moisture. There is a place to insert the condensation collector which is at the side of the base unit. The collector has to be removed and emptied after every session of cooking. Then it must be placed back again. Plugin the appliance after fixing the collector then press the POWER button.

Place the required Accessories in Place:

Depending on the type of cooking mode you are going to use, you will have to insert a suitable accessory into the Ninja Foodi unit. For searing, sauteing, pressure cooking, slow cooking, yogurt, sous vide and keep warm mode you must insert the cooking pot of the unit. Whereas to Air crisp the food, place a crisper plate in the cooking pot. TO steam you have to place a steamer rack inside the pot. And for baking and roasting use a suitable baking pan or dish.

Add Food to the Insert:

When everything is set in place, you can start adding recipe ingredients to the cooking pot. Make sure to never fill the cooking pot over its safe limit which is 2/3 full. Overstuffing never yields good results especially if you are dehydrating or Air frying the food in the Ninja Foodi pro.

How to Close the Lids?

Now you will have to manage the lid covering according to the cooking mode you are using. For Sauteing/Searing there is no need to cover the lid. But for other modes, you will have to cover the vessel. Here is how you can use the two lids.

The Air Crisping Lid:

This is the lid that is attached to the main unit from one side and it flips open easily. Only this used for the following cooking programs:

1. Air Crisp
2. Bake/Roast
3. Dehydrate
4. Broil

This lid releases the heat from the top and uses the convection mechanism to evenly circulate hot air or heat inside the cooking vessel.

The Pressure Lid:

The pressure lid is completely detachable lid that comes separately from the unit. It can be fixed on top of the cooking pot of the unit when the Crisping lid is not closed. The pressure lid has a handle on top to hold it. It has a pressure valve with a pressure release handle, float valves and a rubber ring fixed under its rim. This lid is used for the following functions:

1. Pressure
2. Slow Cook
3. Steam
4. Sous Vide
5. Yogurt
6. Sous vide

For pressure cooking and steaming the pressure release handle has to be turned to the "Closed" position. Once the cooking is completed, the handle is turned to the venting position to release the steam. For all other modes, the valve is kept in the Venting positioning.

Control Settings:

When the lid is in place, you can select the desired cooking mode by touching its respective key on the control panel. Then use the arrow keys on both sides of the displacement to reach the desired temperature and time settings. Press the START/STOP key then and the machine will first automatically preheat itself then the timer will start ticking.

When It Beeps:

The Ninja Foodi 11 in 1 pro beeps to indicate the cooking is done. And when it does you can either release the pressure (in case of pressure cooking or steaming) or open the lids directly to check on the food and serve as desired.

Cleaning Maintenance

After each complete session of cooking, the Ninja Foodi pressure cooker has to be cleaned for the next time. Here is how you can do it.

- Before cleaning, unplug the unit from the wall outlet and allow it to cool completely.

- Never place the unit's base in the dishwasher or submerge it in any liquid.

- Wipe the cooker's base and control panel with a moist cloth to clean them.

- The cooking pot, pressure lid, silicone ring, and Cook and Crisp Plate of this cooker are all dishwasher safe, so you can wash them in a dishwasher.

- Wash the nesting broil rack with hands, not in the dishwasher.

- Wash the pressure lid with water and dish soap, including the pressure release valve and anti-clog cap.

- Never disassemble the float valve or pressure release valve assembly.

- After the heat shield of the crisping lid is cooled, you can wipe it with a moist cloth or paper towel.

- If there is food residue on the cooking pot or Cook and Crisp Plate, fill it with water and soak it for 30 minutes before cleaning. Avoid using steel scrubbers as they may damage the surface.

- If needed only scrub with a non-abrasive cleaner or liquid dish soap with a nylon pad or brush if necessary, and air-dry all components after each usage.

Removing and Reinstalling the Silicone Ring

Pull the silicone ring out of the silicone ring rack section by section to remove it. The reversible silicone ring can be placed with either side facing up. Press it down into the rack section by section to reinstall it.

Remove any food debris from the silicone ring and anti-clog cap after each use. To avoid odor, keep the silicone ring clean. The stink can be removed by washing it in warm, soapy water or by putting it in the dishwasher. It is, however, typical for it to absorb the odors of some acidic foods. It's a good idea to have several silicone rings on hand.

Excessive force when removing the silicone ring may deform it and the rack, affecting the pressure-sealing function. Replace any silicone ring that has cracks, cuts, or other damage right away.

Troubleshooting

Sometimes this electric pressure cooker can exhibit different errors on its screens. Don't panic if it does so. Every error sign indicates some problem and here are their respective solutions. If the machine displays these signs here is what it means:

- **ADD POT:** The cooking pot is not placed in the base unit. It must be placed inside the unit for all the cooking modes.

- **OTHR LID:** The improper lid for the cooking function has been placed. If you select the Pressure, Slow Cook, Sear/Sauté, Steam, or Keep Warm features, make sure the pressure lid is placed on top.

- **SHUT LID:** The crisping lid is open and must be closed before initiating the program.

- **TURN LID:** The pressure lid isn't completely shut. To start the desired cooking function, turn the lid clockwise until it clicks.

- **OPEN VENT:** Shows that the pressure release valve is in the SEAL position but the unit is set on Sear/Sauté and Slow Cook mode, so the unit is detecting pressure building up. Set the pressure release valve to VENT and leave it there for the duration of the cooking function. If the vent is not opened, the program will cancel and the machine will switch off within 5 minutes.

- **ADD WATR:** In the case of steaming and pressure cooking, this means that there isn't enough water in the cooking pot. To keep the function going, add more water.

- **ERR:** The device isn't working properly and it must be checked for any faults.

FAQs about Ninja Foodi pressure cooker

1. Why is it taking so long for my unit to reach operating pressure? How long does it take for the pressure to build up?

Cooking periods will vary depending on the chosen temperature, the present temperature of the cooking pot, and the temperature or amount of the ingredients.

Make sure the silicone ring is inserted well in the lid. You should be able to rotate the ring by gently tugging on it if it is correctly installed.

Make sure the pressure lid is fully closed and the pressure release valve is in the SEAL position for pressure cooking.

2. Why is the clock ticking so slowly?

It's possible that you've set the clock to hours rather than minutes. When changing the time, the display will show HH: MM and the time will change in minute increments.

3. When the unit is pressurizing, how can I tell?

The rotating lights on the screen will show that the machine is generating pressure. When employing the Pressure or Steam functions, progress bars appear on the display screen.

When the STEAM or PRESSURE mode is selected, the progress bar indicates that the unit is building pressure or preheating. When the unit reaches full pressure, the timer on your specified cook time will start counting down.

4. When I use the Steam function on my unit, a lot of steam comes out. Is that ok?

During cooking, steam will naturally escape through the pressure release valve. For Steam, Slow Cook, and Sear/ Sauté, keep the pressure release valve in the VENT position.

5. Why am I unable to remove the pressure lid?

The pressure lid does not unlock until the device is entirely depressurized, which is a safety measure. To quickly discharge the steam, switch the pressure release valve to the VENT position. The pressure release valve will unleash a short blast of steam. The device will be ready to open once the steam has been entirely expelled. Turn the pressure lid counterclockwise to unlock it. To avoid a spatter, lift the lid at an angle. Lifting the lid straight up is not a good idea.

6. Is it normal for the pressure release valve to be loose?

Yes. The loose fit of the pressure release valve is purposeful, it allows for a rapid and easy transition between SEAL and VENT, as well as pressure regulation by releasing modest amounts of steam during cooking for excellent results. When pressure cooking, make sure it's turned as far as possible toward the SEAL position, and when rapid releasing, make sure it's turned as far as possible toward the VENT position.

Conclusion

Did you like all those delicious ideas to create a menu of your own using the amazing Ninja Foodi Pro 11 in 1 electric pressure cooker? From crispy snacks to healthy entrees, steamed seafood, dehydrated jerkies, roasted chicken or baked casseroles, you can literally make anything in this cooking appliance. Now it's time for you to plug it in and start cooking like pros!

PART II PRESSURE COOK, TENDERCRISP RECIPES

Chapter 3 Breakfast

Cheesy Tex-Mex Breakfast Egg Bake Casserole

Prep Time: 10 minutes, Cook Time: 10 minutes, Serves: 4

INGREDIENTS:

8 ounces (227 g) corn tortilla chips, divided
1 cup green salsa, plus more for serving
2 cups shredded pepper Jack cheese, divided
¼ cup whole milk
3 large eggs
1 tsp. Mexican/ Southwestern Seasoning Mix, or a store-bought mix
¼ cup heavy (whipping) cream
½ tsp. kosher salt (or ¼ tsp. fine salt)

DIRECTIONS:

1. In a 1-to 1.5-quart heat-proof dish, add about half of the chips. Pour over the chips with the salsa and gently toss to distribute the salsa. Sprinkle over the top with about half the cheese.
2. Whisk the milk, eggs, seasonings, heavy cream, and salt in a medium bowl. Pour over the chips and cheese with the egg mixture. Use aluminum foil to cover the dish.
3. In the inner pot, add 1 cup of water. Place the dish on the Reversible Rack, then put in the pot.
4. Lock the Pressure Lid into place, set the steamer valve to Seal. Select Pressure and set the cook time to 10 minutes. Press Start.
5. When the cooking is complete, naturally release the pressure for 5 minutes, then quick release any remaining pressure. Open and remove the Pressure Lid carefully.
6. Remove the foil from the casserole. Over the top arrange with about half the remaining chips and sprinkle with half the remaining cheese. Repeat the layers with the remaining chips and cheese.
7. Close the Crisping Lid. Select Broil and adjust the time to 7 minutes. Press Start. Broil until the chips are browned in spots and the cheese is melted.
8. Take the dish out from the pot and allow to cool for several minutes. Serve with additional salsa.

Korean-Style Spicy Chicken Stew

Prep Time: 15 minutes, Cook Time: 20 minutes, Serves: 6

INGREDIENTS:

2 pounds (900 g) bone-in chicken thighs
3 dried red chili peppers, or 2 tbsps. chili pepper flakes
¾ cup chicken stock
⅓ cup coconut aminos or tamari
⅓ cup rice wine
2 tbsps. gochujang
2 tsps. sesame oil
1 tsp. black pepper
1 tsp. sea salt
1 tsp. toasted sesame seeds, for garnish
4 cloves of garlic, crushed
1 medium onion, sliced
1 green bell pepper, sliced
1 (1-inch) piece ginger, peeled and sliced
3 scallions, cut into 2-inch pieces, chopped finely, reserve 1 tbsp, for garnish

DIRECTIONS:

1. Turn on your Ninja pressure cooker and press Pressure, set the timer to 20 minutes.
2. Cut off the redundant skin and fat from the chicken thighs and then place the chicken thighs in the pot.
3. Set aside the chopped scallions and sesame seeds, blend the rest of the ingredients in a medium bowl and mix them well. Add gochujang, chili peppers or sea salt to fulfill your taste if needed.
4. Pour sauce on the chicken in the Ninja pressure cooker and mix well. Make sure the chicken thighs are well coated with the sauce.
5. Turn on your Ninja pressure cooker and then select Pressure, set the timer for 20 minutes. Close the pressure lid tightly and move the steamer valve to Seal.
6. After the cooking is complete, let the pot cool down naturally until the float valve drops down. Press Stop, and open the lid.
7. Stir occasionally, ladle out the chicken pieces in a bowl, garnish with the chopped scallions and sprinkle on sesame seeds. Then enjoy it in time.

French Maple Vanilla and Cinnamon Toast

Prep Time: 15 minutes, Cook Time: 10 minutes, Serves: 4

INGREDIENTS:

⅔ cup heavy (whipping) cream
⅔ cup whole milk
¼ tsp. vanilla extract
1 large egg yolk
3 large eggs
Pinch kosher salt (or small pinch fine salt)
1 tsp. maple syrup or honey
Nonstick cooking spray,
as needed
8 small slices dense bread, ½ to ⅝ inch thick, somewhat dry or stale
6 tbsps. unsalted butter, at room temperature, divided
1 tsp. ground cinnamon, or more to taste
½ cup sugar

DIRECTIONS:

1. In a small deep bowl, add the heavy cream and milk. Then add the vanilla, egg yolk, eggs, salt and maple syrup. Blend the ingredients thoroughly with an immersion blender or handheld electric mixer. Pour the custard into a shallow dish which is wide enough to fit a slice of bread.
2. Put a wire rack on top of a rimmed baking sheet (if the rack is not nonstick, spray it with cooking spray).
3. Place in the custard with 1 slice of bread and allow it to soak for 20 seconds. Turn it over and allow it to soak for another 20 seconds. Carefully lift it out of the custard with a large slotted spatula and place it on the prepared rack. Repeat with the remaining slices of bread and custard. If you have custard left over, evenly drizzle it over the bread.
4. On your Foodi™ inner pot, select Sear/Sauté. Press Start. Preheat for 5 minutes.
5. In the pot, add 2 tablespoons of butter and heat until foaming. Add the slices of bread. If they will not fit in one layer, cook the toast in batches, using more butter as needed. Cook for 2 to 3 minutes or until the surface is a deep golden brown with some darker spots. Flip the slices and cook on the second side until that side is deep golden brown, about 2 minutes. Place the cooked slices onto the wire rack.
6. Wipe out the inner pot and place it back to the base. Place the Reversible Rack in the pot.
7. Close the Crisping Lid. Preheat by selecting Broil and adjusting the time to 2 minutes. Press Start.
8. Meanwhile, stir together the cinnamon and sugar in a small bowl. Spread a thin layer of butter on one side of each French toast slice and evenly sprinkle the cinnamon sugar over the slices.
9. Transfer the bread slices to the rack carefully. (If they will not fit in one layer, broil in two batches.) Close the Crisping Lid. Select Broil again and adjust the cook time to 4 minutes. Press Start. After cooking, serve immediately.

Buttery Scotch Eggs

Prep Time: 10 minutes, Cook Time: 3 minutes, Serves: 4

INGREDIENTS:

12 ounces (340 g) bulk breakfast sausage
1 cup panko bread crumbs (or gluten-free bread crumbs for a gluten-free dish)
4 large eggs
Nonstick cooking spray, for preparing the rack
2 tbsps. melted unsalted butter

DIRECTIONS:

1. In the Foodi inner pot, add 1 cup of water. Place the eggs on the Reversible Rack, then put in the pot.
2. Lock the Pressure Lid into place, set the steamer valve to Seal. Select Pressure and set the cook time to 3 minutes. Press Start.
3. Meanwhile, prepare an ice bath, fill half of the cold water into a medium bowl and add a handful of ice cubes.
4. When the cooking is complete, quick release the pressure. Open and remove the Pressure Lid carefully.
5. Transfer the eggs to the ice bath with tongs. Allow to cool for 3 to 4 minutes or until cool enough to handle. Peel the eggs and blot them dry.
6. Pour the water out of the inner pot and place it back to the base. Use cooking spray to spray the Reversible Rack. Put the rack in the pot.
7. Close the Crisping Lid. Preheat by selecting Air Crisp and setting the temperature to 360°F(180°C) and the time to 4 minutes. Press Start.
8. Meanwhile, divide the sausage into four pieces and flatten each piece into an oval. One at a time, place an egg on a sausage oval and pull the sausage around the egg, sealing the edges.
9. Combine the melted butter and panko in a small bowl. One at a time, roll the sausage-covered eggs in the crumbs, firmly pressing the panko into the sausage.
10. Open the Crisping Lid and place the coated eggs onto the rack. Close the Crisping Lid. Select Air Crisp and adjust the temperature to 360°F(180°C) and the cook time to 15 minutes. Press Start.
11. After cooking, the crumbs should be a deep golden brown can crisp. Remove the eggs and allow to cool for several minutes. Cut them in half and serve.

Cheesy Egg Bake with Ham

Prep Time: 5 minutes, Cook Time: 27 minutes, Serves: 4

INGREDIENTS:

1 cup milk	cheese
4 eggs	8 ounces (227 g) ham, chopped
1 tsp. freshly ground black pepper	1 red bell pepper, seeded and chopped
1 tsp. sea salt	
1 cup shredded Cheddar	1 cup water

DIRECTIONS:

1. Add the milk, eggs, black pepper and salt in a medium mixing bowl, whisk them together. Add the Cheddar cheese and stir well.
2. In the Multi-Purpose Pan or an 8-inch baking pan, add the ham and bell pepper. Then pour the egg mixture over the ham and pepper. Use aluminum foil to cover the pan and place on the Reversible Rack.
3. In the pot, add the water. Place the rack with the pan in the pot.
4. Assemble the Pressure Lid, set the steamer valve to Seal. Select Pressure. Set the time to 20 minutes. Select Start/Stop to begin.
5. After pressure cooking is finish, move the pressure release valve to the Vent position to quick release the pressure. Remove the lid when the unit has finished releasing pressure carefully.
6. After cooking is finish, remove the pan from the pot and transfer it onto a cooling rack. Allow to cool for 5 minutes, and serve.

Blueberry Oat Muffins

Prep Time: 12 minutes, Cook Time: 18 minutes, Serves: 7

INGREDIENTS:

½ cup rolled oats	2 large eggs
½ cup frozen blueberries	½ cup (120 ml) plain Greek yogurt
¼ cup whole wheat pastry flour or white whole wheat flour	2 tbsps. pure maple syrup
½ tbsp. baking powder	2 tsps. extra-virgin olive oil
½ tsp. ground cardamom or ground cinnamon	½ tsp. vanilla extract
⅛ tsp. kosher salt	

DIRECTIONS:

1. Stir together the flour, oats, cardamom, baking powder, and salt in a large bowl.
2. Whisk together the oil, maple syrup, eggs, yogurt, and vanilla in a medium bowl.
3. Add the egg mixture to oat mixture and stir to combine. Gently fold in the blueberries.
4. Scoop the batter into each egg bite mold.
5. Pour 1 cup of water into the Ninja pressure cooker. Put the egg bite mold on the wire rack and lower it into the pot carefully.
6. Close the pressure lid. Set the steamer valve toSeal, cook for 10 minutes.
7. Once cooking is complete, allow the pressure to release naturally for 10 minutes, then quick release any remaining pressure. Press Stop.
8. Lift the wire rack out of the pot and put on a cooling rack for 5 minutes. Invert the mold onto the cooling rack.
9. Serve the muffins warm or refrigerate.

Broccoli and Cheddar Quiche

Prep Time: 10 minutes, Cook Time: 20 minutes, Serves: 6

INGREDIENTS:

½ cup milk	oil
8 eggs	2 garlic cloves, minced
1 tsp. freshly ground black pepper	1 yellow onion, chopped
1 tsp. sea salt	2 cups thinly sliced broccoli florets
1 cup shredded Cheddar cheese	1 refrigerated piecrust, at room temperature
1 tbsp. extra-virgin olive	

DIRECTIONS:

1. Preheat the pot by selecting Sear/Sauté. Select Start/Stop to begin. Preheat for 5 minutes.
2. Whisk together the milk, eggs, pepper and salt in a large mixing bowl. Add the Cheddar cheese and stir well.
3. In the preheated pot, add the oil, garlic and onion, stir occasionally for 5 minutes. Stir in the broccoli florets and sauté for an additional 5 minutes.
4. Top the vegetables, pour with the egg mixture and gently stir for 1 minute (this will let the egg mixture temper well and be sure that it cooks evenly under the crust).
5. Evenly lay the piecrust on top of the filling mixture, folding over the edges if needed. In the center of the piecrust, make a small cut, so that steam can escape during baking.
6. Close the Crisping Lid. Select Broil and set the time to 10 minutes. Select Start/Stop to begin.
7. After cooking is finish, remove the pot and transfer it onto a heat-resistant surface. Allow the quiche to rest for 5 to 10 minutes before serving.

Hard-boiled Breakfast Eggs

Prep Time: 2 minutes, Cook Time: 8 minutes, Serves: 9

INGREDIENTS:
9 large eggs

DIRECTIONS:
1. Pour 1 cup of water into the Ninja pressure cooker and insert a rack. Gently make the eggs stand on the Reversible rack, fat ends down.
2. Close the pressure lid. Set the valve to Seal.
3. Select Pressure fand the time to 2 minutes.
4. Once cooking is complete, press Stop and allow the pressure to release naturally.
5. When the pin drops, unlock and remove the lid.
6. Use tongs to carefully remove the eggs from the pressure cooker. Peel or refrigerate the eggs when they are cool enough.

Berry Breakfast Clafoutis

Prep Time: 10 minutes, Cook Time: 30 minutes, Serves: 4

INGREDIENTS:

2 tsps. unsalted butter, softened	½ cup all-purpose flour
1 cup frozen sweet cherries, thawed, drained, and blotted dry	⅓ cup sugar
	1 pinch fine salt
	¼ tsp. cinnamon
2 large eggs	½ tsp. vanilla extract
⅓ cup heavy cream	1 to 2 tbsps. confectioners' sugar
⅔ cup whole milk	

DIRECTIONS:
1. Use the softened butter to coat the insides of four 1-cup custard cups or ramekins. Evenly divide the cherries among the cups.
2. Combine the eggs, cream, milk, flour, sugar, salt, cinnamon and vanilla in a bowl. Beat the ingredients with a hand mixer on medium speed for about 2 minutes, until the batter is smooth. Pour the batter over the berries. The cups should be filled about ¾ of the way with batter.
3. In the inner pot, add 1 cup of water. Put the Reversible Rack in the pot and on top place with the ramekins, stacking if needed. Over the ramekins place with a square of aluminum foil but don't crimp it down (keep steam from condensing on the surface of the cakes). Lock the Pressure Lid into place, set the valve to Seal. Select Pressure, adjust the cook time to 11 minutes. Press Start.
4. When the cooking is complete, quick release the pressure. Unlock and remove the Pressure Lid carefully.
5. Remove the foil from the custards. If you have stacked the ramekins, remove the second layer and do the next stage in batches.
6. Lock the Crisping lid and preheat by selecting Bake/Roast. Adjust the temperature to 400°F(205°C) and the time to 6 minutes. Press Start. Check after about 4 minutes, the tops of the clafoutis should be lightly browned. Continue cooking if needed, and repeat for the second batch if needed.
7. Allow to cool for about 5 minutes, then dust the confectioners' sugar over. Serve warm.

Cinnamon Oatmeal with Cream Cheese

Prep Time: 15 minutes, Cook Time: 26 minutes, Serves: 6

INGREDIENTS:

1 cup gluten-free steel-cut oats	⅓ cup cold unsalted butter, cut into pieces
1 tsp. nutmeg	¾ cup raisins
2 tsps. cinnamon, divided	2 ounces (57 g) cream cheese, at room temperature
3½ cups water	
¼ tsp. sea salt	
½ cup rolled oats	1 tsp. whole milk
½ cup all-purpose flour	2 tbsps. confectioners'sugar
⅔ cup brown sugar	
2 tbsps. granulated sugar	

DIRECTIONS:
1. In the pot, combine the steel-cut oats, nutmeg, 1 teaspoon of cinnamon, water, and salt. Assemble pressure lid, set the steamer valve to Seal.
2. Set PRESSUR and the time 11 minutes.
3. Mix the rolled oats, flour, brown sugar, granulated sugar, butter, and the remaining 1 tsp. of cinnamon in a medium bowl until a crumble forms.
4. After the cooking is completed, let the pressure release for 5 minutes. Then move pressure release valve to quickly release any remaining pressure. Carefully remove lid.
5. Add raisins to the oatmeal, stir well. Cover, sit for 5 minutes.
6. Top the oatmeal with crumbles.
7. Select AIR CRISP, set the temperature to 400°F(205ºC), and the time to 10 minutes.
8. Whisk the cream cheese, milk and confectioners sugar in a small bowl.
9. When the crumbs turn brown, open the crisping lid and place the oatmeal in individual bowls. Top with a swirl of cream cheese.

Tropical Fruit Steel Cut Oats

Prep Time: 5 minutes, Cook Time: 19 minutes, Serves: 4

INGREDIENTS:

1 cup steel cut oats
¾ cup frozen chopped peaches
¾ cup frozen mango chunks
1 cup (240 ml) unsweetened almond milk

2 cups (480 ml) coconut water or water
1 (2-inch) vanilla bean, scraped (seeds and pod)
¼ cup chopped unsalted macadamia nuts
Ground cinnamon

DIRECTIONS:

1. Mix the oats, coconut water, almond milk, mango chunks, peaches, and vanilla bean seeds and pod in the Ninja pressure cooker. Stir well.
2. Close the pressure lid. Set the steamer valve to sealing.
3. Select Pressure and the time to 5 minutes.
4. Once cooking is complete, allow the pressure to release naturally for 10 minutes, then quick release any remaining pressure. Press Stop.
5. When the pin drops, unlock and remove the lid.
6. Throw away the vanilla bean pod and stir well.
7. Spoon the oats into 4 bowls. Sprinkle cinnamon and 1 tablespoon of the macadamia nuts on top of each serving.

Apple and Cranberry Oatmeal with Vanilla

Prep Time: 5 minutes, Cook Time: 27 minutes, Serves: 4

INGREDIENTS:

2 cups gluten-free steel-cut oats
½ cup dried cranberries, plus more for garnish
2 apples, peeled, cored, and diced
3¾ cups water

¼ cup apple cider vinegar
1 tbsp. ground cinnamon
½ tsp. ground nutmeg
½ tsp. vanilla extract
⅛ tsp. sea salt
Maple syrup, for topping

DIRECTIONS:

1. In the pot, add the oats, water, vinegar, cinnamon, nutmeg, vanilla, cranberries, apples, and salt. Assemble the Pressure Lid, set the steamer valve to Seal. Select Pressure. Set the time to 11 minutes. Select Start/Stop.
2. After pressure cooking is done, release the pressure for 10 minutes naturally, then move the pressure

release valve to the Vent position to quick release any remaining pressure. Remove the lid when the pressure has finished releasing.

3. Stir well of the oatmeal, top with maple syrup and more dried cranberries, and serve.

Bacon and Cheese Custards

Prep Time: 10 minutes, Cook Time: 7 minutes, Serves: 4

INGREDIENTS:

2 bacon slices, halved widthwise
4 large eggs
¼ cup heavy (whipping) cream
1 ounce (28 g) cream cheese, at room temperature

¼ tsp. kosher salt (or ⅛ tsp. fine salt)
Freshly ground black or white pepper
¼ cup grated Gruyère or other Swiss-style cheese
¼ cup Caramelized Onions

DIRECTIONS:

1. On your Ninja Pressure Cooker, select Sear/Sauté and press Start. Preheat for 5 minutes.
2. Add the bacon, and cook for 3 to 4 minutes, or until browned, turning occasionally. Transfer the bacon to a paper towel-lined plate to drain with a slotted spoon, leaving the fat in the pot. Using a basting or pastry brush to coat the bacon fat onto the inside of four custard cups or 1-cup ramekins. Set the cups aside. Wipe out the inner pot and replace it in the base.
3. In a small bowl crack the eggs. Then add the heavy cream, cream cheese, salt, and several grinds of pepper. Beat the mixture with a handheld electric mixer, until it is homogeneous with no clumps of cream cheese remaining.
4. Add the grated cheese and mix again to incorporate the cheese.
5. In the bottom of each custard cup, place a piece of bacon. Divide the onions evenly among the cups and pour the egg mixture over, dividing it as evenly as possible. Use in the bottom of each custard cup to cover each cup.
6. In the inner pot, add 1 cup of water. Place the ramekins on the Reversible Rack, then put in the pot.
7. Lock the Pressure Lid into place, set the steamer valve to Seal. Select Pressure and set the cook time to 7 minutes. Press Start.
8. When the cooking is complete, quick release the pressure. Open and remove the Pressure Lid carefully.
9. Carefully remove the custard cups from the pressure cooker with tongs. Allow to cool for 1 to 2 minutes before serving.

Pecan Steel-Cut Oats

Prep Time: 10 minutes, Cook Time: 20 minutes, Serves: 4

INGREDIENTS:

2 cups (320 g) steel-cut oats
3 cups (710 ml) water
1 (13.5-oz [400-ml, 383 g]) can full-fat coconut milk, divided
⅓ cup (80 ml) pure maple syrup, plus more to taste
½ tsp. sea salt
½ cup (56 g) toasted pecan pieces
2 tsps. (5 g) ground cinnamon (optional)

DIRECTIONS:

1. Add the oats, water, 1 cup of the coconut milk, and the maple syrup and salt into the Ninja pressure cooker, combine them by quickly stirring the mixture. Lock the pressure lid and set the steamer vent to seal.
2. Choose Pressure, and cook for 4 minutes.
3. Use a natural release for 15 minutes, then release any remaining steam before removing the lid.
4. Once removing the lid, add the remaining coconut milk and additional maple syrup to taste.
5. Serve with the toasted pecans and sprinkle the cinnamon over if using.

Mixed Berry Chia Seed Porridge

Prep Time: 5 minutes, Cook Time: 1 minute, Serves: 2 to 3

INGREDIENTS:

6 oz (170 g) fresh raspberries, plus more for serving (optional)
½ cup (75 g) fresh blueberries, plus more for serving (optional)
1 (13.5-oz [400-ml]) can full-fat coconut milk
¼ cup (40 g) chia seeds
2 scoops collagen protein powder (optional)
2 tbsps. (15 g) nuts, for serving (optional)

DIRECTIONS:

1. Add the raspberries, blueberries, coconut milk and chia seeds into the Ninja pressure cooker, and quick stir them.
2. Set the steamer vent to Seal. Select Pressure, and cook for 1 minute.
3. Release for 8 minutes with a natural release, then quick release any remaining steam. Stir in the collagen if using.
4. Top with additional berries and nuts, and serve hot, at room temperature or chilled.

Poached Breakfast Eggs

Prep Time: 5 minutes, Cook Time: 10 minutes, Serves: 4

INGREDIENTS:

4 large eggs   Nonstick cooking spray

DIRECTIONS:

1. Lightly spray 4 cups of silicone egg bite mold with nonstick cooking spray. Crack each egg into a sprayed cup.
2. Pour 1 cup of water into the Ninja pressure cooker. Put the egg bite mold on the wire rack and lower it into the pot carefully.
3. Close the pressure lid. Set the steamer valve to seal.
4. Select Pressure and the time to 5 minutes.
5. Once cooking is complete, press Stop and quick release the pressure.
6. When the pin drops, unlock and remove the lid.
7. Run a spoon or a small rubber spatula around each egg and carefully remove it from the mold. The white should be cooked, but the yolk is runny.
8. Serve immediately.

Butternut Squash Apple Soup with Cinnamon

Prep Time: 5 minutes, Cook Time: 6 minutes, Serves: 4

INGREDIENTS:

3 cups (430 g) seeded, peeled and cut butternut squash (½" [1.3-cm] chunks)
1 apple, peeled, cored and cut into ½" (1.3-cm) chunks
1 (13.5-oz [400-ml, 383 g]) can full-fat coconut milk
2 tsps. (5 g) ground cinnamon
1 tbsp. (15 ml) pure maple syrup
Pinch of salt
½ cup (55 g) roasted and chopped pecans

DIRECTIONS:

1. Add the butternut squash, apple pieces, coconut milk, cinnamon, maple syrup and salt into the Ninja pressure cooker, combine them together.
2. Lock the pressure lid, set the steamer vent to Seal. Select Pressure, and cook for 6 minutes.
3. Release with a quick release. Remove the lid once the steam has been completely released. Blend with an immersion blender or high-powered blender until smooth.
4. Top with pecans and serve.

Ninja Foodi Hard-boiled Eggs

Prep Time: 2 minutes, Cook Time: 15 minutes, Serves: 2 to 12 eggs

INGREDIENTS:

2 to 12 eggs

1 cup water

DIRECTIONS:

1. Put the Reversible Rack in the pot. Pour in the water and arrange the eggs on the rack in a single layer.
2. Assemble the Pressure Lid, set the steamer valve to Seal. Select Pressure. Set the time to 8 minutes. Select Start/Stop to begin.
3. Meanwhile, prepare a large bowl of ice water.
4. After pressure cooking is finish, move the pressure release valve to the Vent position to quick release the pressure. Remove the lid when the unit has finished releasing pressure carefully.
5. Immediately transfer the eggs to the ice water bath with a slotted spoon and let cool for 5 minutes.

Strawberry Lemon Jam

Prep Time: 10 minutes, Cook Time: 42 minutes, Serves: 1½ cups

INGREDIENTS:

2 pounds (907 g) strawberries, hulled and halved

Juice of 2 lemons
1½ cups granulated sugar

DIRECTIONS:

1. In the pot, add the strawberries, lemon juice, and sugar. Mash the ingredients together with a silicone potato masher and begin to release the strawberry juices.
2. Assemble the Pressure Lid, set the steamer valve to Seal. Select Pressure. Set the time to 1 minute. Select Start/Stop to begin.
3. After pressure cooking is done, let the pressure to release for 10 minutes naturally, then move the pressure release valve to the Vent position to quick release any remaining pressure. Remove the lid when the pressure has finished releasing.
4. Select Sear/Sauté. Select Start/Stop to start. Let the jam to reduce for 20 minutes, or until it tightens.
5. Use the silicone potato masher to mash the strawberries for a textured jam, or place the strawberry mixture into a food processor and purée for a smooth consistency. Cool the jam, pour into a glass jar, and place into the refrigerator and chill for up to 2 weeks.

Carrot Cake Oats with Cranberries

Prep Time: 10 minutes, Cook Time: 13 minutes, Serves: 8

INGREDIENTS:

2 cups shredded carrot
2 cups oats
4 cups unsweetened vanilla almond milk
2 apples, diced
1 cup dried cranberries

2 tsps. cinnamon
2 tsps. vanilla extract
½ cup brown sugar
1 cup water
walnuts, chopped

DIRECTIONS:

1. In the pot, combine all the ingredients. Assemble pressure lid, set the steamer valve to Seal.
2. Set the PRESSURE and the time to 3 minutes.
3. After cooking is complete, let the pressure naturally release for 10 minutes. Then move pressure release valve to quickly release the remaining pressure. Carefully remove the lid.
4. Stir oats. Top with chopped walnuts.

Crispy Bacon and Egg Hash

Prep Time: 10 minutes, Cook Time: 40 minutes, Serves: 4

INGREDIENTS:

6 slices bacon, chopped
2 russet potatoes, peeled and diced
1 yellow onion, diced
1 tsp. sea salt

1 tsp. paprika
1 tsp. freshly ground black pepper
1 tsp. garlic salt
4 eggs

DIRECTIONS:

1. Preheat the pot by selecting Sear/Sauté. Select Start/Stop to begin. Preheat for 5 minutes.
2. When hot, add the bacon to the pot. Cook for 5 minutes, or until the bacon is crispy, stirring occasionally.
3. Stir in the potatoes and onion to the pot. Sprinkle with the sea salt, paprika, pepper, and garlic salt.
4. Close the Crisping Lid. Select Bake/Roast, set the temperature to 350°F(180°C), and set the time to 25 minutes. Cook until the potatoes are tender and golden brown, stirring occasionally.
5. On the surface of the hash, crack the eggs. Close the Crisping Lid. Select Bake/Roast, set the temperature to 350°F(180°C), and set the time to 10 minutes.
6. Check the eggs after 3 minutes. Continue to cook for the remaining 7 minutes, until your desired doneness is achieved, checking occasionally. Serve immediately.

Vanilla Cinnamon Cashews

Prep Time: 5 minutes, Cook Time: 10 minutes, Serves: 4 to 6

INGREDIENTS:
½ cup water
¼ tsp. vanilla bean powder
½ cup unrefined whole
cane sugar
¼ tsp. ground cinnamon
1½ cups raw cashews

DIRECTIONS:
1. Use parchment paper to line the inner pot.
2. Add the water, vanilla bean powder, sugar and cinnamon in a small saucepan, stir them together over medium-low heat until the sugar is dissolved.
3. Stir in the cashews, press Sear/Sauté on High for 4 to 6 minutes, stirring continuously. Do not leave unattended, as the sugary liquid will begin to thicken and eventually stick to the cashews.
4. When all the liquid is gone, remove from the heat and evenly spread onto the Crisp Plate. Break apart the cashews to dry as individual pieces, or leave some together as clusters.

Easy Homemade Yogurt

Prep Time: 15 minutes, Cook Time: 12 hours, Serves: 8

INGREDIENTS:
½ gallon whole milk
2 tbsps. plain yogurt with active live cultures
½ cup honey (optional)
1 tbsp. vanilla extract (optional)

DIRECTIONS:
1. In the pot, add the milk. Assemble the Pressure Lid, set the steamer valve to Seal. Select Sear/Sauté. Select Start/Stop to begin.
2. Bring the milk to 180°F(80°C), checking the temperature often and stirring frequently to avoid burning at the bottom. Select Start/Stop to turn off Sear/Sauté.
3. Let the milk cool to 110°F(45°C), continuing to often check the temperature and stirring frequently. Skim off the "skin" on the milk and discard.
4. Add the yogurt and whisk until incorporated.
5. Assemble the Pressure Lid, set the steamer valve to Vent. Allow to incubate for 8 hours.
6. After 8 hours, place the yogurt into a glass container and chill in the refrigerator for 4 hours.
7. Mix in the honey and vanilla(if using) to the yogurt and combine well. Cover and return the glass bowl into the refrigerator, or divide the yogurt among airtight glass jars.

Almond Instant Oatmeal with Berries

Prep Time: 5 minutes, Cook Time: 10 minutes, Serves: 1

INGREDIENTS:
½ cup (80 g) steel-cut oats
1½ cups (355 ml) water, divided
½ cup (120 ml) almond, soy or dairy milk
2 tsps. (10 g) light brown sugar
Pinch of salt
Fresh berries, for topping (optional)

DIRECTIONS:
1. Add the oats, ½ cup of the water, milk, brown sugar and salt into a large heatproof mug or small heatproof dish, mix them together.
2. Add the remaining cup of water into the Ninja pressure cooker and insert the Reversible rack. Place the mug on the rack, lock the pressure lid. Select Pressure and adjust the timer to 10 minutes.
3. Once the timer sounds, quick release the pressure and remove the lid. Carefully remove the mug with oven mitts. Top with fresh berries, if desired.

Breakfast Farro with Walnuts and Berries

Prep Time: 8 minutes, Cook Time: 17 minutes, Serves: 6

INGREDIENTS:
1 cup farro, rinsed and drained
1 cup (240 ml) unsweetened almond milk
1½ cups fresh blueberries, raspberries,
or strawberries
6 tbsps. chopped walnuts
¼ tsp. kosher salt
½ tsp. pure vanilla extract
1 tsp. ground cinnamon
1 tbsp. pure maple syrup

DIRECTIONS:
1. Mix the farro, 1 cup of water, almond milk, salt, cinnamon, vanilla, and maple syrup in the Ninja pressure cooker.
2. Close the pressure lid. Set the steamer valve to Seal.
3. Set Pressure and the time to 10 minutes.
4. Once cooking is complete, allow the pressure to release naturally for 10 minutes, then quick release any remaining pressure. Press Stop.
5. When the pin drops, unlock and remove the lid.
6. Stir the farro. Spoon into bowls and top each serving with berries and walnuts.

Cranberry and Toasted Almond Grits

Prep Time: 10 minutes, Cook Time: 17 minutes, Serves: 5

INGREDIENTS:

¾ cup stone-ground grits or polenta (not instant)
½ cup unsweetened dried cranberries
1 tbsp. half-and-half
¼ cup sliced almonds, toasted
Pinch kosher salt
1 tbsp. unsalted butter (optional)

DIRECTIONS:

1. Stir together the grits, salt, cranberries, and 3 cups of water in the electric pressure cooker.
2. Close the pressure lid. Set the steamer valve to Seal.
3. Select Pressure and the time to 10 minutes.
4. Once cooking is complete, press Stop and quick release the pressure.
5. When the pin drops, unlock and remove the lid.
6. Add the butter (if using) and half-and-half. Stir until it is creamy, adding more half-and-half if necessary.
7. Spoon into serving bowls and sprinkle with toasted almonds.

Frittata with Potato, Chorizo and Corn

Prep Time: 10 minutes, Cook Time: 20 minutes, Serves: 4

INGREDIENTS:

1 potato, diced
½ cup frozen corn
1 chorizo sausage, diced
4 eggs
1 cup milk
8 ounces (227 g) feta
cheese, crumbled
Freshly ground black pepper
1 cup water
Sea salt

DIRECTIONS:

1. Combine eggs, milk, salt and pepper in a medium bowl. Whisk well.
2. Place the potato, corn, and chorizo in the Multi-Purpose Pan. Top with the egg mixture and feta cheese. Cover the pan with aluminum foil and place on the Reversible Rack.
3. Pour the water into the pot. Assemble pressure lid, set the steamer valve to Seal.
4. Select PRESSURE, set the time to 20 minutes. Press START.
5. After cooking is complete, move pressure release valve to VENT position to quickly release the

pressure. Carefully remove lid.
6. Take the pan out of pot. Cool 5 minutes before serving.

Easy Monkey Bread

Prep Time: 15 minutes, Cook Time: 20 minutes, Serves: 4

INGREDIENTS:

⅓ cup firmly packed light or dark brown sugar
3 tbsps. unsalted butter, melted
1 tsp. ground cinnamon,
or more to taste
8 ounces (227 g) pizza dough or frozen bread dough, thawed

DIRECTIONS:

1. In a small bowl, add the melted butter. Using a pastry brush, lightly coat a little of the butter onto the bottom and sides of a small (3- to 4-cup capacity) Bundt pan, or a 6-inch cake pan or baking dish.
2. Stir together the cinnamon and brown sugar in a shallow bowl.
3. Divide the dough into about 15 small balls, each about 1 inch in diameter.
4. A few at a time, place the dough pieces in the melted butter and roll to coat thoroughly. Then transfer to the cinnamon-brown sugar mixture and roll to coat. Place the sugarcoated dough balls in the prepared pan. They can be touching but not crowded. Repeat with the remaining dough balls, evenly spacing them in two or three layers if using a Bundt pan or one layer if using a baking dish. Drizzle the remaining butter over and sprinkle with a little additional cinnamon sugar to coat evenly.
5. Allow the dough to rest for about 45 minutes.
6. In the Foodi inner pot, add 1 cup of water. Place the pan on the Reversible Rack, then put in the pot. Use aluminum foil to loosely cover.
7. Lock the Pressure Lid into place, set the steamer valve to Vent. Select Steam and set the time to 12 minutes. Press Start.
8. After steaming, open and remove the Pressure Lid carefully.
9. Close the Crisping Lid. Select Bake/Roast and set the temperature to 325°F(165°C) and the cook time to 15 minutes. Press Start.
10. After baking, open the lid and remove the foil. Close the Crisping Lid. Select Bake/Roast and adjust the temperature to 350°F(180°C) and the cook time to 5 minutes. Press Start.
11. The bread should be browned on top, with syrup bubbling up throughout. Allow to cool for 20 to 30 minutes, then unmold and serve warm.

Cheesy Banana French Bread Toast

Prep Time: 15 minutes, Cook Time: 35 minutes, Serves: 4

INGREDIENTS:

¼ cup milk
3 eggs
1 tsp. vanilla extract
1 tbsp. granulated sugar
1 tsp. ground cinnamon
Nonstick cooking spray
6 slices French bread, cut into 1-inch cubes, divided
3 bananas, sliced into rounds, divided
2 tbsps. brown sugar, divided
¼ cup cream cheese, at room temperature
½ cup water
2 tbsps. cold unsalted butter, sliced
2 tbsps. maple syrup
¼ cup chopped pecans (optional)

DIRECTIONS:

1. Add the milk, eggs, vanilla, granulated sugar, and cinnamon into a medium mixing bowl, whisk them together.
2. Use cooking spray to grease the Multi-Purpose Pan or an 8-inch baking pan, and arrange half the bread cubes in the pan in a single layer. Over the bread, layer with half the banana slices and sprinkle with 1 tablespoon of brown sugar.
3. On top of the bread and bananas, spread with the cream cheese. Lay the remaining bread cubes on top of the cream cheese, then on top of the bread layer with the remaining banana slices, and sprinkle with the remaining 1 tablespoon of brown sugar.
4. Over the bread mixture, pour with the egg mixture, coating the bread completely.
5. In the pot, add the water. Put the pan on the Reversible Rack, then put the rack with the pan in the pot. Assemble the Pressure Lid, set the steamer valve to Seal. Select Pressure. Set the time to 20 minutes. Select Start.
6. After pressure cooking is finished, move the pressure release valve to the Vent position to quick release the pressure. Remove the lid when the pressure has finished releasing carefully.
7. Top the French toast with the sliced butter, maple syrup and pecans (if using).
8. Close the Crisping Lid. Select Bake/Roast, set the temperature to 390°F(200°C), and set the time to 5 minutes.
9. Check the doneness and add more time as necessary until it reaches your desired crispiness. Serve immediately.

Cheese Ham and Broccoli Frittata

Prep Time: 15 minutes, Cook Time: 40 minutes, Serves: 6

INGREDIENTS:

1 head broccoli, cut into 1-inch florets
1 tbsp. canola oil
Kosher salt
12 large eggs
¼ cup whole milk
3 tbsps. unsalted butter
½ medium white onion, diced
1 cup diced ham
Freshly ground black pepper
1½ cups shredded white Cheddar cheese, divided

DIRECTIONS:

1. Place Crisp Basket in pot. Select AIR CRISP, set temperature to 390°F(200ºC), and the time to 5 minutes. Press START/STOP to begin preheating.
2. Toss the broccoli and oil in a large bowl, add salt and pepper.
3. Once unit is preheated, add the broccoli to the basket and cover.
4. Select AIR CRISP. Set the temperature to 390°F(200ºC) and the time to 15 minutes.
5. Take out a separate large bowl, add the eggs, milk, and 1 cup of cheese to it. Whisk.
6. Remove the basket and shake the broccoli after 7 minutes. Return basket to pot and cover to continue cooking.
7. Check the broccoli for the desired doneness after 8 minutes. When cooking is complete, remove broccoli and basket, select SEAR/SAUTÉ.
8. Add the butter after 5 minutes. Then add the onion and cook for 3 minutes, stirring occasionally.
9. Add the ham and broccoli and cook for 2 minutes. stir occasionally.
10. Add the egg mixture, salt, and pepper, and stir.
11. Select BAKE/ROAST, set temperature to 400°F(205ºC), and the time to 15 minutes.
12. Open the lid after 5 minutes. Top with the remaining ½ cup of cheese. Cover and continue cooking.
13. Remove pot when cooking is complete. Sit for 5 to 10 minutes before serving.

Chapter 4 Grains and Rice

Mixed Grain Porridge

Prep Time: 5 minutes, Cook Time: 42 minutes, Serves: 7

INGREDIENTS:

½ cup millet
½ cup barley
½ cup steel cut oats
½ cup short-grain brown rice
3 tbsps. ground flaxseed
½ tsp. salt
⅓ cup wild rice
¼ cup corn grits or

polenta (not instant)
Ground cinnamon (optional)
Sliced almonds or chopped walnuts (optional)
Unsweetened almond milk (optional)
Berries (optional)

DIRECTIONS:

1. Mix the oats, millet, brown rice, salt, barley, grits, wild rice, flaxseed, and 8 cups of water in the electric pressure cooker.
2. Close the pressure lid of the pressure cooker. Set the steamer valve to seal.
3. Select Pressure and the time to 20 minutes.
4. Once cooking is complete, press Stop and allow the pressure to release naturally for 15 minutes, then quick release any remaining pressure.
5. When the pin drops, unlock and remove the lid. Stir.
6. Serve with cinnamon, berries, almond milk, or nuts (if using).

Freekeh Pilaf with Dates

Prep Time: 15 minutes, Cook Time: 20 minutes, Serves: 4 to 6

INGREDIENTS:

2 tbsps. extra-virgin olive oil, plus extra for drizzling
1 shallot, minced
1½ tsps. grated fresh ginger
½ tsp. table salt
¼ tsp. ground coriander
¼ tsp. ground cumin
¼ tsp. pepper
1¾ cups (420 ml) water

1½ cups cracked freekeh, rinsed
3 ounces (85 g) pitted dates, chopped (½ cup)
¼ cup shelled pistachios, toasted and coarsely chopped
1½ tbsps. lemon juice
¼ cup chopped fresh mint

DIRECTIONS:

1. In Ninja pressure cooker, select Sauté, heat oil until shimmering. Add cumin, shallot, salt, ginger, coriander, and pepper and cook about 2 minutes until shallot is softened. Stir in freekeh and water.
2. Lock pressure lid and close pressure release valve. Select pressure and cook for 4 minutes. Turn off and quick-release pressure. Carefully remove lid, letting steam escape away from you.
3. Add pistachios, dates, and lemon juice and gently fluff freekeh with fork to combine. Season with salt and pepper. Transfer to a dish, sprinkle with mint and drizzle with extra oil. Serve.

Spiced Pilaf with Sweet Potatoes

Prep Time: 15 minutes, Cook Time: 20 minutes, Serves: 4 to 6

INGREDIENTS:

2 tbsps. extra-virgin olive oil
1 onion, chopped fine
½ tsp. table salt
1½ tsps. ground turmeric
1 tsp. ground coriander
⅛ tsp. cayenne pepper
2 garlic cloves, minced
1½ cups long-grain white rice, rinsed
12 ounces (340 g) sweet potato, peeled, quartered lengthwise, and sliced ½

inch thick
½ preserved lemon, pulp and white pith removed, rind rinsed and minced (2 tbsps.)
½ cup shelled pistachios, toasted and chopped
2 cups (480 ml) chicken broth
¼ cup pomegranate seeds
¼ cup fresh cilantro leaves

DIRECTIONS:

1. In Ninja pressure cooker, select Sauté function, heat oil until shimmering. Add onion and salt and cook about 5 minutes until onion is softened. Stir in garlic, coriander, turmeric, and cayenne and cook about 30 seconds until fragrant. Stir in rice, broth, and sweet potato.
2. Lock pressure lid and close pressure release valve. Select Pressure and cook for 4 minutes. Turn off and quick-release pressure. Carefully remove lid, letting steam escape away from you.
3. Put in preserved lemon and gently fluff rice with fork to combine. Lay clean dish towel over pot to replace lid, and set aside for 5 minutes. Season with salt and pepper. Transfer to a dish and sprinkle with cilantro, pistachios, and pomegranate seeds. Serve.

Roasted Tofu and Sweet Potatoes with Rice

Prep Time: 10 minutes, Cook Time: 30 minutes, Serves: 4

INGREDIENTS:

2 tbsps. extra-virgin olive oil, divided
1 (15-ounce, 425 g) block organic extra-firm tofu, drained and sliced into ½-inch cubes
1 sweet potato, peeled and diced
1 cup brown rice, rinsed

¾ cup water
1 tsp. sea salt
1 tsp. freshly ground black pepper
1 tbsp. soy sauce
2 tsps. cornstarch

DIRECTIONS:

1. In the pot, add the rice and water and stir to combine. Assemble the Pressure Lid, set the steamer valve to Seal. Select Pressure. Set the time to 2 minutes, then select Start/Stop to begin.
2. Meanwhile, add the sweet potato into a small mixing bowl, toss with 1 tablespoon of olive oil and season with the salt and black pepper.
3. Make sure that the tofu is well-drained and all excess water is removed. Add the remaining 1 tablespoon of olive oil and the soy sauce into a medium mixing bowl, whisk them together. Toss the tofu cubes in the soy sauce mixture, then add the cornstarch and toss until evenly coated.
4. When pressure cooking the rice is complete, quick release the pressure by moving the pressure release valve to the Vent position. Carefully remove the lid when the pressure has finished releasing.
5. Place the Reversible Rack in the pot and use aluminum foil to line with. Transfer the sweet potatoes and tofu onto the rack.
6. Close the Crisping Lid. Select Air Crisp, set the temperature to 400°F(205°C), and set the time to 20 minutes. Select Start/Stop to begin. Flip the sweet potatoes and tofu with tongs after 10 minutes.
7. After the cooking is done, check for your desired crispiness and serve.

Wild Mushroom Farro

Prep Time: 15 minutes, Cook Time: 25 minutes, Serves: 4 to 6

INGREDIENTS:

1½ cups whole farro
3 tbsps. extra-virgin olive oil, divided, plus extra for drizzling
12 ounces (340 g) cremini or white mushrooms, trimmed and sliced thin
½ onion, chopped fine
½ tsp. table salt
¼ tsp. pepper
1 garlic clove, minced
¼ ounce (7 g) dried porcini mushrooms, rinsed and

chopped fine
2 tsps. minced fresh thyme or ½ teaspoon dried
¼ cup (60 ml) dry white wine
2½ cups (600 ml) chicken or vegetable broth, plus extra as needed
2 tsps. lemon juice
½ cup chopped fresh parsley
2 ounces (57 g) Parmesan cheese, grated (1 cup), plus extra for serving

DIRECTIONS:

1. Pulse farro in blender for about 6 pulses until about half of grains are broken into smaller pieces.
2. In Ninja pressure cooker, select Sauté, heat 2 tablespoons oil until shimmering. Add onion, cremini mushrooms, salt, and pepper, partially cover, and cook about 5 minutes until mushrooms are softened and have released their liquid. Stir in garlic, farro, porcini mushrooms, and thyme and cook about 1 minute until fragrant. Stir in wine and cook about 30 seconds until nearly evaporated. Stir in broth.
3. Lock the pressure lid and close pressure release valve. Select Pressure and cook for 12 minutes. Turn off and quick-release pressure. Carefully remove lid, letting steam escape away from you.
4. If necessary adjust consistency with extra hot broth. With Sauté function, stirring frequently, until proper consistency is achieved. Add Parmesan and remaining oil and stir vigorously until creamy. Add lemon juice and season with salt and pepper. Sprinkle each portion with parsley and extra Parmesan, and drizzle with extra oil. Serve.

Chicken Vegetable Fried Rice

Prep Time: 5 minutes, Cook Time: 29 minutes, Serves: 4

INGREDIENTS:

1 tbsp. extra-virgin olive oil
1 onion, diced
4 garlic cloves, minced
1 pound (454 g) boneless, skinless chicken breasts, diced
⅛ tsp. freshly ground black pepper

⅛ tsp. sea salt
¼ cup soy sauce
2 cups chicken broth
1 cup jasmine rice
1 (16-ounce, 454 g) bag frozen mixed vegetables

DIRECTIONS:

1. Preheat the pot by selecting Sear/Sauté. Select Start/Stop to begin. Preheat for 5 minutes.
2. In the preheated pot, add the oil and onion, cook for 5 minutes, stirring occasionally. Stir in the garlic and cook for another 1 minute, until fragrant.
3. Place the chicken into the pot and season with the pepper and salt. Brown the chicken for 5 minutes.
4. Add the soy sauce, chicken broth, and rice to the pot. Assemble the Pressure Lid, set the steamer valve to Seal. Select Pressure. Set the time to 3 minutes, then select Start/Stop to begin.
5. After pressure cooking is finish, move the pressure release valve to the Vent position to quick release the pressure. Remove the lid when the pressure has finished releasing carefully.
6. Select Sear/Sauté. Select Start/Stop to begin. Mix in the frozen vegetables to the pot. Cook for 5 minutes, stirring occasionally. Serve hot.

Spiced Homemade Arroz con Pollo

Prep Time: 15 minutes, Cook Time: 50 minutes, Serves: 4

INGREDIENTS:

2 tbsps. extra-virgin olive oil, divided
1 onion, diced
1 tbsp. chili powder
1 red bell pepper, diced
1 tsp. dried oregano
1 tsp. ground cumin
½ tsp. sea salt

¾ cup chicken broth
1 cup long-grain brown rice
½ cup tomato sauce
1 pound (454 g) bone-in, skin-on chicken thighs
Chopped fresh cilantro, for garnish
Lime wedges, for serving

DIRECTIONS:

1. Preheat the pot by selecting Sear/Sauté. Select Start/Stop to begin. Preheat for 5 minutes.
2. In the preheated pot, add 1 tablespoon of oil and the onion, cook for 3 minutes, stirring occasionally. Stir in the chili powder, bell pepper, oregano, cumin, and salt, cook for another 2 minutes.
3. Add the broth, rice, and tomato sauce to the pot. Put the chicken on the Reversible Rack, then put in the pot over the rice.
4. Assemble the Pressure Lid, set the pressure release valve to Seal. Set the time to 30 minutes, then select Start/Stop to begin.
5. After pressure cooking is finish, move the pressure release valve to the Vent position to quick release the pressure. Remove the lid when the pressure has finished releasing carefully.
6. Use the remaining 1 tablespoon of oil to brush the chicken thighs. Close the Crisping Lid. Select Broil and set the time to 5 minutes. Press Start/Stop to begin.
7. When cooking is finish, check for your desired crispiness and remove the rack from the pot. The chicken is cooked when a meat thermometer insert into the thickest part of the meat (it should not touch the bone), the internal temperature reads 165°F(75°C). Garnish with cilantro and serve with lime wedges.

Chapter 5 Vegetable

Quinoa Stuffed Peppers with Pesto

Prep Time: 10 minutes, Cook Time: 30 minutes, Serves: 4

INGREDIENTS:

4 red bell peppers, halved lengthwise and cored
1 (15-ounce, 425 g) can no-salt-added diced tomatoes
1 cup no-sodium vegetable broth
8 ounces (227 g) fresh baby spinach
¾ cup dried quinoa, rinsed
2 tbsps. everyday pesto

DIRECTIONS:

1. Use parchment paper to line the inner pot.
2. Place the bell pepper halves on Crisp Plate, skin-side up.
3. Press Broil and cook at 350°F(180°C) until the pepper skins begin to blister and slightly blacken, about 2 to 5 minutes. Remove from the Ninja Foodi.
4. Add the tomatoes and vegetable broth into the inner pot, press Sear/Sauté on High. Stir in the spinach and quinoa. Adjust to Low, cover and cook for 10 minutes, stirring occasionally.
5. Fill the quinoa mixture into the pepper halves.
6. Bake for 10 minutes. Top with the pesto and serve warm.

Pho with Shrimp

Prep Time: 10 minutes, Cook Time: 36 minutes, Serves: 6

INGREDIENTS:

1 (14-ounce (397 g)) package rice noodles, cooked according to the package directions
1 onion, peeled and halved
2 tbsps. canola oil
1 (2-inch) piece fresh ginger, peeled
1½ tbsps. Chinese five-spice powder
2 tbsps. brown sugar
2 tbsps. kosher salt
4 cups beef bone broth
¼ cup fish sauce
8 cups water
1 pound (454 g) peeled cooked shrimp

DIRECTIONS:

1. Select Saute mode, to preheat 5 minutes.
2. Add oil, onion and ginger, sear on all sides for 6 minutes. Press STOP to end.
3. Stir with the sugar, salt, five-spice powder, fish sauce, bone broth, and water for 1 minute.
4. Assemble pressure lid, be sure pressure release valve is in SEAL position.
5. Select Pressure, set the time 30 minutes.
6. After cooking is complete, move pressure release valve to VENT position to quickly release the pressure. Carefully remove lid.
7. Take a bowl, add the desired amount of noodles to it. Top with 5 or 6 shrimp and some sliced onion. Ladle the pho broth to cover the noodles, shrimp, and onion.

Quinoa Stuffed Mushrooms

Prep Time: 15 minutes, Cook Time: 28 minutes, Serves: 4

INGREDIENTS:

2 tbsps. extra-virgin olive oil
4 large portobello mushrooms, stems and gills removed
1 tomato, seeded and diced
½ cup cooked quinoa
¼ cup Kalamata olives, pitted and chopped
1 bell pepper, seeded and diced
Juice of 1 lemon
½ cup crumbled feta cheese
½ tsp. sea salt
½ tsp. freshly ground black pepper
Minced fresh parsley, for garnish

DIRECTIONS:

1. Put the Crisp Basket in the pot. Close the Crisping Lid. Select Air Crisp, set the temperature to 375°F(190°C), and set the time to 5 minutes. Press Start/Stop to begin to preheat.
2. Use oil to coat the mushrooms. Open the Crisping Lid and arrange the mushrooms in a single layer in the preheated Crisp Basket, open-side up.
3. Close the Crisping Lid. Select Air Crisp, set the temperature to 375°F(190°C), and set the time to 20 minutes. Select Start/Stop to begin.
4. Combine the tomato, quinoa, olives, bell pepper, lemon juice, feta cheese, salt, and black pepper in a medium mixing bowl.
5. Open the Crisping Lid and evenly spoon into the 4 mushrooms with the quinoa mixture. Close the lid. Select Air Crisp, set the temperature to 350°F(180°C), and set the time to 8 minutes. Press Start/Stop to begin.
6. Garnish with fresh parsley and serve immediately.

Ninja Foodi Sautéed Mushrooms

Prep Time: 5 minutes, Cook Time: 20 minutes, Serves: 6

INGREDIENTS:

1 pound (454 g) white button or cremini mushrooms, stems trimmed

2 tbsps. unsalted butter

(or olive oil for a vegan dish)

½ tsp. kosher salt (or ¼ tsp. fine salt)

¼ cup water

DIRECTIONS:

1. Cut the medium mushrooms into quarter and cut the large mushrooms into eighths. In the Foodi inner pot, add the mushrooms, butter or oil and salt, then pour in the water.
2. Lock the Pressure Lid in place, set the steamer valve to Seal. Select Pressure, adjust the cook time to 5 minutes. Press Start.
3. When the cooking is done, release with a quick pressure release. Unlock and remove the Pressure Lid.
4. Select Sear/Sauté. Press Start. Bring to a boil and cook for about 5 minutes or until all the water reduced. The mushrooms will begin to sizzle in the butter (or oil) that remains. Allow them brown for 1 minute or so, then stir to brown the other sides.

Zucchini Boats with Quinoa and Almond Stuffing

Prep Time: 15 minutes, Cook Time: 20 minutes, Serves: 4

INGREDIENTS:

2 small zucchini

½ cup grated Parmesan cheese, divided

2 tbsps. extra-virgin olive oil, divided

½ cup canned cannellini beans, drained and rinsed

½ cup cooked quinoa

½ cup chopped almonds

½ cup quartered cherry tomatoes

½ tsp. sea salt

½ tsp. freshly ground black pepper

DIRECTIONS:

1. Cut each zucchini in half, then cut in half lengthwise and scoop out the inside, leaving a ½-inch-thick shell. Chop the pulp roughly.
2. Add the zucchini pulp, ¼ cup of Parmesan cheese, 1 tablespoon of olive oil and the rest ingredients into a large mixing bowl, combine them together.
3. Place the Crisp Basket in the pot. Close the

Crisping Lid. Select Air Crisp, set the temperature to 400°F(205°C), and set the time to 5 minutes to preheat the unit.
4. Spoon into the zucchini shells with the zucchini mixture and arrange the zucchini boats in a single layer in the preheated Crisp Basket.
5. Close the Crisping Lid. Select Air Crisp, set the temperature to 400°F(205°C), and set the time to 15 minutes. Select Start/Stop to begin.
6. After 15 minutes, evenly sprinkle the remaining ¼ cup of Parmesan cheese and remaining 1 tablespoon of olive oil over the zucchini boats.
7. Close the Crisping Lid. Select Broil and set the time to 5 minutes. Select Start/Stop to begin.
8. After cooking is finish, check for your desired crispiness and serve.

Kung Pao Tofu and Peppers with Peanuts

Prep Time: 10 minutes, Cook Time: 15 minutes, Serves: 4

INGREDIENTS:

2 tbsps. vegetable oil

1 pound (454 g) firm tofu or extra-firm tofu, cut into 1-inch cubes

2 garlic cloves, minced

1 (1-inch) piece fresh ginger, peeled, minced or grated (about 1 tbsp.)

3 tbsps. soy sauce

1 tsp. hoisin sauce

½ tsp. red pepper flakes, or more to taste

1 tbsp. cornstarch

1 tsp. sugar

1 tbsp. rice vinegar

¼ cup water or Roasted Vegetable Stock

1 small green bell pepper, cut into bite-size pieces

1 small red bell pepper, cut into bite-size pieces

2 tbsps. roasted unsalted peanuts

2 scallions, sliced

DIRECTIONS:

1. On your Foodi™, select Sear/Sauté to preheat the inner pot. Press Start. Preheat the pot for 5 minutes. Add the vegetable oil and heat until shimmering. Stir in the garlic and ginger. Cook until fragrant, about 2 minutes. Stir in the soy sauce, hoisin, red pepper flakes, cornstarch, sugar, vinegar, and water. Combine well and dissolve the cornstarch.
2. Stir in the tofu, green and red bell peppers. Coat well.
3. Lock the Pressure Lid into place, set the steamer valve to Seal. Select Pressure, adjust the cook time to 4 minutes. Press Start.
4. When the cooking is finished, use a quick pressure release. Unlock and remove the Pressure Lid.
5. Add the peanuts and stir well. Taste and adjust the seasoning. Garnish with the scallions and serve immediately.

Easy Crispy Roasted Delicata Squash

Prep Time: 10 minutes, Cook Time: 15 minutes, Serves: 4

INGREDIENTS:

1 large delicata squash, seeds removed and sliced

1 tbsp. extra-virgin olive oil

¼ tsp. sea salt

DIRECTIONS:

1. Place Crisp Basket in the pot. Select AIR CRISP, set temperature to 390°F(200ºC) and the time 5 minutes, to preheat.
2. Add squash, olive oil and salt into a large bowl, toss well.
3. Once unit has preheated, place the squash in the basket.
4. Select AIR CRISP, set temperature to 390°F(200ºC), and the time 15 minutes. Press START.
5. After 7 minutes, open the crisping lid, then lift the basket and shake the squash. Place the basket in the pot again. Continue cooking until the squash achieves desired crispiness.

Roasted Mushroom and Carrot Stock

Prep Time: 5 minutes, Cook Time: 1 hour 35 minutes, Serves: 1 quart

INGREDIENTS:

1 tbsp. vegetable oil

12 ounces (340 g) mushrooms, sliced

1 onion, quartered

2 large carrots, peeled,

cut into 1-inch pieces

¼ tsp. kosher salt (or ⅛ tsp. fine salt)

3½ cups water

DIRECTIONS:

1. Make sure that the Crisp™ Basket is out of the inner pot, close the Crisping Lid on your Foodi™ and select Bake/Roast, adjust the temperature to 400°F(205°C) and the time to 3 minutes to preheat. Press Start.
2. Meanwhile, add the onion and carrot chunks into the Crisp Basket and drizzle the vegetable oil over. Toss to coat.
3. Put the basket into the inner pot. Close the Crisping Lid and select Bake/Roast, adjust the temperature to 400°F(205°C) and the cook time to 15 minutes. Press Start. During the halfway way of the cook time, open the lid and stir the vegetables well.
4. Take the basket out from the pot and mix in the onions and carrots. Stir in the mushrooms and

sprinkle with the salt. Add the water.

5. Lock the Pressure Lid into place, set the steamer valve to Seal. Select Pressure, adjust the cook time to 60 minutes. Press Start.
6. After the cooking is complete, naturally release the pressure for 15 minutes, then quick release any remaining pressure. Unlock and remove the Pressure Lid.
7. Use cheesecloth or a clean cotton towel to line a colander and place it over a large bowl. Add the vegetables and stock into the colander and strain through to the bowl. Discard the vegetables.

Mushroom Potato Shepherd's Pie

Prep Time: 10 minutes, Cook Time: 22 minutes, Serves: 6

INGREDIENTS:

1 tbsp. extra-virgin olive oil

16 ounces (454 g) cremini mushrooms, sliced

6 carrots, diced

1 onion, diced

2 tbsps. tomato paste

2 garlic cloves, minced

2 cups vegetable broth

¼ tsp. dried rosemary

1 tsp. dried thyme

1 tsp. sea salt

2 cups frozen peas

2 cups mashed potatoes

DIRECTIONS:

1. Preheat the pot by selecting Sear/Sauté. Select Start/Stop to begin. Preheat for 5 minutes.
2. Then add the oil, mushrooms, carrots and onion into the preheated pot. Sauté for 5 minutes, until the onion is translucent and the mushrooms have released their liquid. Stir in the tomato paste and garlic, sauté for another 1 minute.
3. Add the vegetable broth and season with the rosemary, thyme, and salt. Assemble the Pressure Lid, set the steamer valve to Seal.
4. Select Pressure, set the time to 3 minutes, then select Start/Stop to begin. After pressure cooking is finish, move the pressure release valve to Vent to quick release the pressure. Remove the lid when the pressure has finished releasing carefully.
5. Add the frozen peas and stir well, then in the bottom of the pot spread with the mixture in an even layer. Evenly spread the mashed potatoes over the mixture. Drag a fork over the potatoes to create a decorative topping, if desired.
6. Close the Crisping Lid. Select Broil and set the time to 5 minutes. Select Start/Stop to begin.
7. After cooking is finish, let the shepherd's pie rest for 10 minutes before serving.

Horseradish Carrots with Mayonnaise

Prep Time: 5 minutes, Cook Time: 10 minutes, Serves: 4

INGREDIENTS:

1 pound (454 g) carrots, peeled and cut into 1-inch pieces
½ cup vegetable stock
¾ cup mayonnaise
2 tbsps. grated

horseradish
½ tsp. freshly ground black pepper
½ tsp. kosher salt
Minced parsley

DIRECTIONS:

1. Add carrots and stock to the pot. Assemble pressure lid, set the steamer valve to Seal.
2. Select Pressure, set the time 2 minutes.
3. After cooking is complete, move pressure release valve to VENT position to quickly release the pressure. Carefully remove the lid.
4. Combine horseradish, mayonnaise, salt, pepper in a small bowl. Transfer mixture to pot and stir carefully.
5. Select BROIL, set the time 6 minutes.
6. After 3 minutes, check doneness. If further browning desired, continue cooking.
7. Decorate with parsley. Serve warm.

Creamy Potato Gratin with Walnuts

Prep Time: 5 minutes, Cook Time: 15 minutes, Serves: 6

INGREDIENTS:

3 large sweet potatoes, peeled and cut in half, then cut into half-moons ¼-inch thick
1¼ cups shredded Cheddar cheese, divided
½ cup chopped walnuts or pecans, or slivered almonds

2 cups heavy (whipping) cream, warmed in microwave
2 tbsps. unsalted butter
3 tbsps. all-purpose flour
1 tsp. pumpkin pie spice
2 tsps. kosher salt
¼ cup water

DIRECTIONS:

1. Select the Saute mode, to preheat for 5 minutes.
2. Add butter. Once melted, add the flour and stir until a thick paste is formed. Continue cooking for 2 minutes, then slowly add the warm cream while stirring constantly to avoid lumps.
3. Add the salt, pumpkin pie spice, and water, whisk well. Simmer mixture 3 minutes.

4. Add potatoes. Assemble pressure lid, set the steamer valve to Seal.
5. Select Pressure, set the time 1 minute. Press START to begin.
6. After cooking is complete, move pressure release valve to VENT position to quickly release the pressure. Carefully remove the lid.
7. Add ¼ cup of cheese, stir gently. Cover top with the remaining 1 cup cheese and nuts.
8. Select BROIL, set time to 5 minutes, and press START to begin.
9. Take gratin out from pot. Cool 10 minutes before serving.

Easy Cheesy Eggplant

Prep Time: 15 minutes, Cook Time: 25 minutes, Serves: 4

INGREDIENTS:

2 tsps. kosher salt (or 1 tsp. fine salt)
1 large eggplant, cut into ¾-inch-thick rounds
1½ cups panko bread crumbs
3 tbsps. melted unsalted

butter
⅓ cup grated Parmesan or similar cheese
2 cups Marinara Sauce
1 cup shredded mozzarella cheese

DIRECTIONS:

1. Sprinkle the salt on both sides of the eggplant slices and put on a Reversible rack over a rimmed baking sheet to drain for 5 to 10 minutes.
2. Meanwhile, stir together the panko, melted butter, and Parmesan cheese in a medium bowl. Set aside.
3. Rinse the eggplant slices and blot them dry. Place them in a single layer (as much as possible) in the Foodi inner pot and add the marinara sauce to cover.
4. Lock the Pressure Lid into place, set the steamer valve to Seal. Select Pressure and adjust the cook time to 5 minutes. Press Start.
5. When the cooking complete, quick release the pressure. Unlock and remove the Pressure Lid carefully.
6. Place the marinara sauce to cover the eggplant slices.
7. Close the Crisping Lid. Select Bake/Roast and adjust the temperature to 375°F(190°C) and the cook time to 2 minutes. Press Start.
8. After cooking, open the lid and sprinkle the panko mixture over the eggplant and cheese. Close the Crisping Lid again. Select Bake/Roast and adjust the temperature to 375°F(190°C) and the cook time to 8 minutes. Press Start. After cooking, the topping should be crisp and brown, broil for another 1 to 2 minutes if not. Serve immediately.

Quinoa Vegetable Stuffed Pepper

Prep Time: 5 minutes, Cook Time: 20 minutes, Serves: 2

INGREDIENTS:

Cooking spray
1 tsp. coconut oil
½ cup chopped vegetables, zucchini, carrots, or broccoli
1 cup cooked quinoa
1 tsp. onion powder
1 tsp. garlic powder
1 tsp. sea salt
2 bell peppers, any color, cored and seeded, tops removed and reserved

DIRECTIONS:

1. Add the coconut oil and chopped vegetables in the inner pot, press Sear/Sauté on High for 5 minutes, or until softened.
2. Stir in the quinoa, onion powder, garlic powder, and salt. Combine well.
3. Place each bell pepper upright in the inner pot. Stuff each pepper with one-half of the quinoa-vegetable mix. Use its reserved top to cover each pepper.
4. Cover the crisping lid, and bake at 390°F(200°C) for 15 minutes, or until the peppers are soft.

Bulgur with Spinach and Chickpeas

Prep Time: 15 minutes, Cook Time: 20 minutes, Serves: 4 to 6

INGREDIENTS:

3 tbsps. extra-virgin olive oil, divided
1 onion, chopped fine
1½ cups (360 ml) water
½ tsp. table salt
2 tbsps. za'atar, divided
1 cup medium-grind bulgur, rinsed
1 (15-ounce, 425 g) can chickpeas, rinsed
3 garlic cloves, minced
5 ounces (5 cups, 142 g) baby spinach, chopped
1 tbsp. lemon juice, plus lemon wedges for serving

DIRECTIONS:

1. In Ninja pressure cooker, use highest sauté function, heat 2 tablespoons oil until shimmering. Add onion and salt and cook about 5 minutes. Stir in garlic and 1 tablespoon za'atar and cook about 30 seconds until fragrant. Stir in chickpeas, bulgur, and water.
2. Lock lid and close pressure release valve. Select Pressure and cook for 1 minute. Turn off and quick-release pressure. Carefully remove lid, letting steam escape away from you.
3. Gently fluff bulgur with fork. Lay clean dish towel

over pot to replace lid, and set aside for 5 minutes. Add lemon juice, spinach, remaining za'atar, and remaining oil and gently toss to combine. Season with salt and pepper. Serve with lemon wedges.

Mixed Vegetable Korma

Prep Time: 10 minutes, Cook Time: 20 minutes, Serves: 4

INGREDIENTS:

1 (14-ounce, 397 g) can diced tomatoes, drained
2 medium carrots, peeled, cut into 1-inch chunks
1 large russet potato, peeled, cut into 1-inch cubes
2 cups large cauliflower florets
½ cup frozen green peas
1 cup coconut milk
5 garlic cloves, peeled and smashed
1 small onion, chopped
1 jalapeño pepper, seeded and sliced
1½ tsps. garam masala
1 tsp. ground turmeric
1 tsp. kosher salt (or ½ tsp. fine salt)
½ tsp. ground cumin
½ tsp. red pepper flakes, or more to taste
1 tbsp. cashew or almond butter (optional)
¼ cup chopped fresh cilantro
¼ cup roasted unsalted cashews or almonds

DIRECTIONS:

1. Add the tomatoes and coconut milk into the Foodi's inner pot, combine together. Then stir in the garlic, onion, jalapeño, garam masala, turmeric, salt, cumin, red pepper flakes, and nut butter (if using).
2. Add the carrots and potato into a shallow, heat-proof bowl or steamer basket. Put the Reversible Rack in the pot and put the bowl on top.
3. Lock the Pressure Lid into place, set the steamer valve to Seal. Select Pressure and adjust the cook time to 5 minutes. Press Start.
4. When cooking is finished, release with a quick pressure release. Unlock and remove the Pressure Lid. Remove the rack and bowl (or steamer basket) and set aside.
5. Purée the sauce until mostly smooth with an immersion blender. Taste and adjust the seasoning.
6. Place the potatoes, carrots, the cauliflower and peas into the pot. Stir the sauce to coat the vegetables.
7. Lock the Pressure Lid into place again, set the steamer valve to Seal. Select Pressure, adjust the cook time to 2 minutes. Press Start.
8. When the cooking is finished, release with a quick pressure release. Unlock and remove the Pressure Lid. Serve the korma over rice, and garnish with the cilantro and nuts.

Healthy Vegetable Broth

Prep Time: 15 minutes, Cook Time: 35 minutes, Serves: 3 quarts

INGREDIENTS:

1 tbsp. vegetable oil
2 carrots, peeled and chopped
2 celery ribs, chopped
3 onions, chopped
4 scallions, chopped
15 garlic cloves, smashed and peeled
12 cups (2880 ml) water, divided

½ head cauliflower (1 pound, 454 g), cored and cut into 1-inch pieces
1 tomato, cored and chopped
3 bay leaves
8 sprigs fresh thyme
1 tsp. peppercorns
½ tsp. table salt

DIRECTIONS:

1. In Ninja pressure cooker, Select Sauté function, heat oil until shimmering. Add scallions, onions, celery, carrots, and garlic and cook about 15 minutes until vegetables are softened and lightly browned. Add 1 cup water, scraping up any browned bits, then stir in remaining water, tomato, cauliflower, peppercorns, thyme sprigs, salt, and bay leaves.
2. Lock pressure lid and close pressure release valve. Select Pressure and cook for 1 hour. Turn off and let pressure release naturally for 15 minutes. Quick-release any remaining pressure and carefully remove lid, letting steam escape away from you.
3. Strain broth through colander into large container, without pressing on solids, throw away solids. (Broth can be refrigerated for up to 4 days or frozen for 2 months.)

Cajun Cheese Mashed Potatoes Bake

Prep Time: 10 minutes, Cook Time: 35 minutes, Serves: 4

INGREDIENTS:

4 small russet potatoes, scrubbed clean
¼ cup sour cream
¼ cup heavy (whipping) cream
1 tsp. Cajun Seasoning Mix or a store-bought mix

½ cup chopped roasted red pepper
1½ cups shredded white Cheddar cheese
4 scallions, white and green parts, chopped, divided
⅓ cup grated Parmesan or similar cheese

DIRECTIONS:

1. In the Ninja inner pot, add 1 cup of water. Place the potatoes on the Reversible Rack, then put in the pot.
2. Lock the Pressure Lid, set the steamer valve to Seal. Select Pressure mode and set the cook time to 10 minutes. Press Start.
3. When the cooking complete, naturally release the pressure for 5 minutes, then quick release any remaining pressure. Unlock and remove the Pressure Lid carefully.
4. Transfer the potatoes to a cutting board with tongs. Once cool enough to handle, slice off a ½-inch strip from the top, long side of each potato. Scoop the flesh into a large bowl, including the flesh from the tops. Add the sour cream and heavy cream. Mash until fairly smooth with a potato masher. Add the seasoning, roasted red pepper, and Cheddar cheese, stir well. Set aside about 2 tablespoons of the green part of the scallions, and stir the rest into the potatoes. Spoon into the potato skins with the mashed potato mixture, mounding it slightly. Evenly sprinkle the Parmesan over the tops.
5. Pour the water out of the inner pot and place it back to the base.
6. Put the Crisp Basket into the pot. Close the Crisping Lid. Preheat by selecting Air Crisp and adjusting the temperature to 375°F(190°C) and the time to 2 minutes. Press Start.
7. After the preheating complete, open the lid and transfer the potatoes into the basket. Close the Crisping Lid. Select Air Crisp and adjust the temperature to 375°F(190°C) and the cook time to 15 minutes. Press Start.
8. After cooking, the potatoes should be crisp on top and lightly browned. Allow to cool for a few minutes and garnish with the reserved scallions and serve warm.

Chapter 6 Poultry

Baked Chicken Stuffed with Collard Greens

Prep Time: 10 minutes, Cook Time: 30 minutes, Serves: 4

INGREDIENTS:

FOR THE GRAVY
2½ cups Chicken Broth (here) or store-bought low-sodium chicken broth, divided
4 tbsps. almond flour, divided
1 medium shallot, chopped
½ bunch fresh chives, roughly chopped
2 garlic cloves, minced
1 cumin
½ tsp. celery seeds
1 tsp. Worcestershire sauce
Freshly ground black pepper

FOR THE CHICKEN
2 boneless, skinless chicken breasts
Juice of 1 lime
1 tsp. sweet paprika
½ tsp. onion powder
½ tsp. garlic powder
2 medium tomatoes, chopped
1 bunch collard greens, center stem removed, cut into 1-inch ribbons
¼ cup Chicken Broth (here) (optional)
Generous pinch red pepper flakes

DIRECTIONS:

HOW TO MAKE GRAVY

1. Combine 12 cups broth and 1 tablespoon flour in a shallow stockpot and boil over medium-low heat, whisking constantly, until the flour is dissolved. Continue to gradually add 1 cup of broth and the remaining 3 tablespoons of flour until a thick sauce forms.
2. In a large mixing bowl, combine the shallots, chives, all spice, cumin, and 12 cups broth.
3. In a separate bowl, combine the celery seeds, Worcestershire sauce, pepper, and the remaining 12 cups broth. Cook, stirring occasionally, for 2 to 3 minutes, or until the ingredients are well combined. Take the pan off the heat and toss out the bay leaf.

HOW TO MAKE CHICKEN

1. Cut a slit along the length of each chicken breast deep enough for filling.
2. In a small mixing bowl, rub the lime juice, paprika, onion powder, and garlic powder all over the chicken.
3. Place the tomatoes and collard greens in an Ninja pressure cooker. Add the chicken broth if the mixture appears to be dry.
4. Turn the steamer valve to sealing and close and lock the lid.

5. Cook for 2 minutes on the Pressure Cook setting.
6. Quickly remove the pressure after the cooking is finished. Remove the cover with care.
7. Remove the leaves with tongs or a slotted spoon, leaving the tomatoes behind.
8. Stuff the greens into the chicken breasts. In the pressure cooker, place the side with the greens facing up on the bed of tomatoes.
9. Ladle half of the gravy over the filled chicken and serve.
10. Turn the Ninja pressure valve to sealing and close and lock the lid.
11. Cook for 10 minutes on the Pressure Cook setting.
12. Quickly remove the pressure after the cooking is finished. Remove the cover with care.
13. Transfer the chicken and tomatoes to a serving plate from the pressure cooker. Red pepper flakes are used as a finishing touch.

Ninja Foodi Chicken Stock

Prep Time: 10 minutes, Cook Time: 1 hour 50 minutes, Serves: 1 quart

INGREDIENTS:

2 pounds (907 g) meaty chicken bones (backs, wing tips, leg quarters)
¼ tsp. kosher salt (or ⅛ tsp. fine salt)
3½ cups water

DIRECTIONS:

1. In the Foodi inner pot, add the chicken parts and sprinkle with the salt. Add the water.
2. Lock the Pressure Lid into place, set the steamer valve to Seal. Select Pressure, adjust the cook time to 90 minutes. Press Start.
3. After cooking, naturally release the pressure for 15 minutes, then quick release any remaining pressure. Unlock and remove the Pressure Lid carefully.
4. Use cheesecloth or a clean cotton towel to line a colander and place it over a large bowl. Pour the chicken parts and stock into the colander to strain out the chicken and bones. Allow the stock to cool. Transfer it into the refrigerator to chill for several hours, or overnight so the fat hardens on top of the stock.
5. Skim the layer of fat off the stock. Measure the amount of stock. If you have much more than 1 quart, return the stock into the Foodi pot. Select Sear/Sauté. Press Start. Bring the stock to a boil and cook until reduced to 1 quart.

Easy Chicken Coq au Vin

Prep Time: 10 minutes, Cook Time: 50 minutes, Serves: 4

INGREDIENTS:

4 chicken leg quarters, skin on
1½ tsps. kosher salt (or ¾ tsp. fine salt), divided
2 bacon slices, cut into thirds
¼ cup sliced onion
1¼ cups dry red wine, divided
1½ tsps. tomato paste
⅓ cup Chicken Stock, or
store-bought low-sodium chicken broth
½ tsp. brown sugar
Freshly ground black pepper
¾ cup frozen pearl onions, thawed and drained
½ cup Sautéed Mushrooms

DIRECTIONS:

1. Sprinkle on both sides of the chicken quarters with 1 teaspoon of kosher salt (or ½ teaspoon of fine salt) and set aside on a wire rack.
2. On your Foodi™, preheat the inner pot by selecting Sear/Sauté. Press Start. Preheat for 5 minutes. Place the bacon in the pot in a single layer and cook it for 3 to 4 minutes or until browned on the first side. Turn and brown the other side. Transfer the bacon to a paper towel-lined plate with tongs, and drain well, leaving the fat in the pot.
3. Place the chicken quarters to the pot, skin-side down. Cook for 5 minutes or until the skin is golden brown and some of the fat under the skin has rendered out, undisturbed. Turn the quarters to the other side and cook for about 2 minutes or until that side is a light golden brown. Transfer the chicken to a plate.
4. Carefully pour off almost all the fat, leaving just enough to cover the bottom of the pot with a thick coat (about 1 tablespoon). Stir in the sliced onion to the pot. Cook until the onion begins to brown, about 3 minutes, stirring. Add ½ cup of wine and scrape the bottom of the pan to release any browned bits. Boil the mixture for 2 minutes, until the wine reduces by about one-third in volume. Add the remaining ¾ cup of wine, the tomato paste, chicken stock, brown sugar, and a few grinds of pepper. Bring the sauce to a boil and cook for about 1 minute, stirring to make sure the tomato paste is incorporated. Add the chicken pieces, skin-side up, to the pot.
5. Lock the Pressure Lid into place, set the steamer valve to Seal. Select Pressure, adjust the cook time to 12 minutes. Press Start.
6. When the cooking is complete, naturally release the pressure for 8 minutes, then quick release any remaining pressure. Open and remove the Pressure Lid carefully.
7. Take the chicken pieces out from the pot. Strain the sauce into a fat separator and allow the sauce to sit for 5 minutes, until the fat rises to the surface. (If you don't have a fat separator, let the sauce sit for a few minutes, then spoon or blot off any excess fat from the top of the sauce.)
8. Return the sauce into the pot and stir in the pearl onions and mushrooms. On top of the sauce, place with the chicken, skin-side up.
9. Close the Crisping Lid and select Broil. Adjust the cook time to 7 minutes. Press Start.
10. After cooking, open the lid and transfer the chicken to a serving platter. Spoon the sauce around the chicken along with the pearl onions and mushrooms, and top with the reserved bacon crumbled and serve.

Spicy Chicken Chili

Prep Time: 10 minutes2, Cook Time: 30 minutes, Serves: 8

INGREDIENTS:

1 yellow onion, chopped
1 tbsp. extra-virgin olive oil
2 pounds (907 g) boneless chicken breast, cut in half crosswise
4 cups chicken broth
1 green bell pepper, seeded and chopped
2 jalapeños, seeded and chopped
1½ tbsp. ground cumin
1 tsp. freshly ground
black pepper
4 garlic cloves, minced
1 tbsp. coriander
1 tsp. dried oregano
2 (15.5-ounce (439 g)) cans cannellini beans, rinsed and drained
1 tsp. sea salt
Shredded Monterey Jack cheese
Chopped cilantro
Lime wedge

DIRECTIONS:

1. Select Saute mode to preheat 5 minutes.
2. Stir with oil, onions and garlic. Heat 2 minutes.
3. Add chicken breast, chicken broth, green bell pepper, jalapeño, cumin, coriander, oregano, salt, and black pepper to the pot. Assemble pressure lid, set the steamer valve to Seal.
4. Select PRESSURE, set the time to 15 minutes.
5. After cooking is complete, move pressure release valve to VENT position to quickly release the pressure. Carefully remove lid.
6. Take chicken out from the soup. Use two forks to shred it.
7. Add the cannellini beans. Select SEAR/SAUTÉ. Cook 5 minutes.
8. Add shredded chicken back to the pot. Decorate with cheese, cilantro, and lime wedge before serving.

Cajun Turkey Breast with Sweet Potatoes

Prep Time: 10 minutes, Cook Time: 1 hour, Serves: 4

INGREDIENTS:

1 (4½-to 5-pound, 2 to 2.3 kg) whole bone-in turkey breast
2½ tsps. kosher salt (or 1¼ tsps. fine salt), divided
4 tsps. Cajun Seasoning Mix or store-bought mix, divided
¾ cup Chicken Stock, or store-bought low-sodium chicken broth
3 medium sweet potatoes (about 1½ pounds, 680 g), scrubbed
3 tbsps. melted unsalted butter, divided
2 tbsps. heavy (whipping) cream, warmed

DIRECTIONS:

1. Pat dry of the turkey breast and carefully slide your hands under the skin, separating it from the meat. Stir together 2 teaspoons of kosher salt (or 1 teaspoon of fine salt) and the seasoning mix in a small bowl. Rub about half the spice mixture under the skin and in the cavity on the underside of the breast, reserving the rest.
2. In the Foodi inner pot, add the chicken stock. Put the Reversible Rack in the pot and on its side in the center of the rack place with the turkey breast and around it with the sweet potatoes.
3. Lock the Ninja Pressure Lid into place, set the valve to Seal. Select Pressure, adjust the cook time to 13 minutes. Press Start.
4. Meanwhile, mix the reserved spice mixture with 2 tablespoons of melted butter in a small bowl.
5. When the cooking is complete, naturally release the pressure for 8 minutes, then quick release any remaining pressure. Open and remove the Pressure Lid carefully.
6. Transfer the sweet potatoes to a cutting board or plate with tongs, then remove the rack with the turkey. Empty the cooking juices of the pot into a fat separator and set aside. Place the turkey and rack back to the pot.
7. Baste half the spice-butter mixture onto the exposed side of the turkey breast.
8. Close the Crisping Lid and select Air Crisp, adjust the temperature to 360°F(180°C) and the cook time to 16 minutes. Press Start. After cooking for 8 minutes, open the lid and flip the turkey breast over with tongs. Baste that side with the remaining spice-butter mixture and close the lid to continue cooking.
9. Meanwhile, slip the skins off the sweet potatoes and place the flesh in a bowl. Process the potatoes into a smooth purée with a potato ricer or potato masher. Add the heavy cream, remaining ½ teaspoon of kosher salt (or ¼ teaspoon of fine salt), remaining 1 tablespoon of melted butter, and 2 tablespoons of the turkey cooking juices to the sweet potatoes and stir to incorporate. Taste and adjust the seasoning and use aluminum foil to cover the bowl.
10. When the cooking is complete, check the internal temperature of the turkey to make sure it reads at least 150°F(65°C). Place it onto a cutting board, leaving the rack in the pot.
11. Return the defatted sauce into the pot. Select Sear/Sauté. Set the bowl of potatoes on the rack to keep warm while the sauce reduces. Press Start. Bring the sauce to a boil and cook until reduced by about half, about 2 to 3 minutes.
12. Meanwhile, slice the turkey and arrange the slices on a platter. Take the potatoes out from the pot and remove the rack. Pour over the turkey slices with the sauce and serve with the sweet potatoes.

Shredded Buffalo Chicken

Prep Time: 10 minutes, Cook Time: 36 minutes, Serves: 8

INGREDIENTS:

2 tbsps. olive oil
½ tbsp. onion powder
1 chives, finely chopped
1 large carrot, chopped
⅓ cup mild hot sauce (such as Frank's RedHot)
½ tbsp. red wine vinegar
¼ tsp. onion powder
2 bone-in, skin-on chicken breasts (about 2 pounds)

DIRECTIONS:

1. Set the Ninja pressure cooker to the Sauté setting. When the pot is hot, pour in the olive oil.
2. Sauté the onion, chives, and carrot for 3 to 5 minutes or until the onion begins to soften. Hit Shop.
3. Stir in the hot sauce, vinegar, and onion powder. Place the chicken breasts in the sauce, meat-side down.
4. Close and lock the lid of the pressure cooker. Set the valve to Seal.
5. Cook on high pressure for 20 minutes.
6. When cooking is complete, hit Stop and quick release the pressure. Once the pin drops, unlock and remove the lid.
7. Using tongs, transfer the chicken breasts to a cutting board. When the chicken is cool enough to handle, remove the skin, shred the chicken and return it to the pot. Let the chicken soak in the sauce for at least 5 minutes.
8. Serve immediately.

Cheesy Ham Chicken Cordon Bleu with Green Beans

Prep Time: 15 minutes, Cook Time: 20 minutes, Serves: 4

INGREDIENTS:

2 large (14-ounce, 397 g) boneless skinless chicken breasts
12 ounces (340 g) green beans, trimmed
3 tbsps. melted unsalted butter, divided
¾ tsp. kosher salt (or a scant ½ tsp. fine salt), divided
Nonstick cooking spray,

for preparing the rack
4 tsps. Dijon mustard
4 thin slices Gruyère, Emmental, or other Swiss-style cheese
4 thin ham slices
⅔ cup panko bread crumbs
¼ cup grated Parmesan or similar cheese

DIRECTIONS:

1. On a cutting board, lay the chicken breasts. With your knife parallel to the board, slice through the breasts to form two thinner pieces from each breast (4 pieces total). Sprinkle ½ teaspoon of kosher salt (or ¼ teaspoon of fine salt) over the chicken. Over the chicken pieces lay with a piece of plastic wrap and use the heel of your hand to press the chicken into a more even thickness.
2. In the Foodi inner pot, add 1 cup of water. Put the Reversible Rack in the pot. Arrange the green beans on the rack and place the chicken pieces on top.
3. Lock the Pressure Lid into place, set the steamer valve to Seal. Select Pressure, adjust the cook time to 1 minute. Press Start.
4. When the cooking is complete, quick release the pressure. Open and remove the Pressure Lid carefully.
5. Remove the rack and set aside. Pour the water out from the pot and place the pot back to the base. Move the chicken pieces back to the cutting board and transfer the beans back to the pot. Sprinkle with the remaining ¼ teaspoon of kosher salt (or ¼ teaspoon of fine salt) and add 1 tablespoon of melted butter. Stir to coat the beans with the butter.
6. Use cooking spray or oil to spray the Reversible Rack and place it in the pot.
7. Close the Crisping Lid and preheat by selecting Air Crisp, adjusting the temperature to 360°F(180°C) and the time to 4 minutes. Press Start.
8. Meanwhile, spread over each chicken piece with about 1 teaspoon of mustard. Layer 1 cheese slice and 1 ham slice over each chicken piece.
9. Stir together the remaining 2 tablespoons of melted butter, the panko and the Parmesan cheese in a small bowl. Evenly sprinkle over the chicken with the crumb mixture.
10. Open the Crisping Lid and transfer the chicken pieces to the rack. Close the Crisping Lid and select Air Crisp, adjust the temperature to 360°F(180°C) and the cook time to 10 minutes. Press Start.
11. After cooking, the crumbs should be a deep golden brown and crisp. Place the chicken pieces onto a platter and serve with the green beans.

French Chicken Soup

Prep Time: 15 minutes, Cook Time: 35 minutes, Serves: 6 to 8

INGREDIENTS:

2 fennel bulbs, 2 tbsps. fronds minced, stalks discarded, bulbs halved, cored, and cut into ½-inch pieces
1 tbsp. extra-virgin olive oil
4 garlic cloves, minced
1 onion, chopped
1¾ tsps. table salt
2 tbsps. tomato paste
7 cups water, divided
1 tbsp. minced fresh thyme or 1 teaspoon dried

2 anchovy fillets, minced
1 (14.5-ounce, 411 g) can diced tomatoes, drained
2 carrots, peeled, halved lengthwise, and sliced ½ inch thick
2 (12-ounce, 340 g) bone-in split chicken breasts, trimmed
4 (5- to 7-ounce, 142 g to 198 g) bone-in chicken thighs, trimmed
½ cup pitted brine-cured green olives, chopped
1 tsp. grated orange zest

DIRECTIONS:

1. In Ninja pressure cooker, select sauté function, heat oil until shimmering. Add fennel pieces, onion, and salt and cook about 5 minutes until softened. Stir in tomato paste, thyme, garlic, and anchovies and cook about 30 seconds until fragrant. Stir in 5 cups water, scraping up any browned bits, then add tomatoes and carrots. Nestle chicken breasts and thighs in the pot.
2. Close the lid and close pressure release valve. Select Pressure and cook for 20 minutes. Turn off and quick-release pressure. Carefully remove lid, letting steam escape away from you.
3. Transfer chicken to cutting board, cool down slightly, then shred into bite-size pieces with 2 forks, discard skin and bones.
4. Skim excess fat from surface of soup with a wide, shallow spoon. Stir chicken and any accumulated juices, olives, and remaining water into soup and cook about 3 minutes until heated through. Stir in orange zest and fennel fronds, and season with salt and pepper to taste. Serve.

Chicken Vegetable Egg Rolls with Mustard Sauce

Prep Time: 20 minutes, Cook Time: 10 minutes per batch, Serves: 16

INGREDIENTS:

1 (16-ounce (454 g)) package egg rolls wrappers
2 cups chopped cooked chicken
½ cup bean sprouts, washed
1 egg, beaten
8 scallions, chopped
½ cup mushrooms, chopped
3 cups shredded cabbage

½ cup shredded carrot
2 tbsps. sherry
2 tbsps. soy sauce
2 tbsps. beef broth
2 tbsps. cornstarch
½ tsp. granulated sugar
½ tsp. ground ginger
3 tbsps. canola oil
Cooking spray
½ tsp. salt
Hot mustard
Sweet and sour sauce

DIRECTIONS:

1. Combine sherry, soy sauce, beef broth, cornstarch, salt, sugar, and ginger in a small bowl, stir until the sugar dissolves.
2. Select the Saute mode to preheat for 5 minutes.
3. Add canola oil, scallions and mushrooms to the cooking pot, sauté 2 to 3 minutes, until the vegetables just begin to soften.
4. Add the cabbage, carrot, and bean sprouts, stir well. Set the time to 7 minutes, until cabbage and carrots are softened.
5. Add chicken and sauce. Cook 3 minutes. Press STOP. Transfer the filling to a bowl.
6. Place the Crisp Basket in the Foodi pot.
7. Select AIR CRISP, set the temperature to 390°F(200ºC), and the time 5 minutes to preheat. Press START.
8. Use a small silicone spatula to moisten the 4 sides of an egg roll wrapper with the beaten egg. Place 3 tbsps. of the filling on the center of the egg roll wrapper. Fold an edge over the mixture and tuck it under the point. Fold the edges in and continue rolling. Press the end point over the top of the roll to seal. Continue with the remaining wrappers and filling.
9. Place 3 egg rolls in the basket. Coat the egg rolls in on cooking spray.
10. Select AIR CRISP, set the temperature to 390°F(200ºC) and the time 10 minutes. After 5 minutes, flip the egg rolls, and spritz the other side with cooking spray. Close the lid and continue cooking 5 minutes.
11. Carefully transfer the egg rolls to a wire rack with tongs. Cool for 6 minutes before serving.
12. Serve with the hot mustard and sweet and sour sauce.

Healthy Chicken Stroganoff with Mushroom

Prep Time: 10 minutes, Cook Time: 25 minutes, Serves: 4

INGREDIENTS:

1½ tsps. kosher salt (or ¾ tsp. fine salt), divided
2 large (12-to 14-ounce, 340 to 397 g) boneless skinless chicken breasts
2 tbsps. unsalted butter
½ cup sliced onion
1 tbsp. all-purpose flour
½ cup brandy or dry sherry or dry white wine
1½ cups water
2 cups Chicken Stock, or

store-bought low-sodium chicken broth
8 ounces (227 g) egg noodles
½ tsp. Worcestershire sauce
1 cup Sautéed Mushrooms
¼ cup sour cream
2 tbsps. fresh dill or fresh parsley for garnish (optional)

DIRECTIONS:

1. Sprinkle ½ teaspoon of kosher salt (or ¼ teaspoon fine salt) onto the chicken breasts and set aside.
2. On your Foodi™, preheat the inner pot by selecting Sear/Sauté. Press Start. Preheat for 5 minutes. Add the butter to melt and heat until it stops foaming. Stir in the onion. Cook for about 4 minutes, or until the onion starts to brown, stirring occasionally. Add the flour and stir to coat the onion. Cook and stir for 2 minutes. Deglaze the cooker by pouring in the brandy and stirring to scrape up all the browned bits from the bottom of the pot. Allow the brandy to simmer until it's reduced by about two-thirds.
3. Place the water, chicken stock, the remaining 1 teaspoon of kosher salt (or ½ teaspoon of fine salt), and the noodles into the pot. Lay on top of the noodles with the chicken breasts.
4. Lock the Pressure Lid into place, set the steamer valve to Seal. Select Pressure, adjust the cook time to 5 minutes. Press Start.
5. When the cooking is complete, quick release the pressure. Open and remove the Pressure Lid carefully.
6. Place the chicken breasts onto a cutting board and allow them to cool slightly. Cut into bite-size chunks. If the chicken is not quite done in the center, return the chicken pieces to the pot. Select Sear/Sauté. Press Start. Simmer the chicken until cooked through. When the chicken is done, turn the pot off and add the Worcestershire sauce and mushrooms. Stir in the sour cream once the mixture stops simmering. Garnish with the dill or parsley (if using), and serve in bowls.

Pulled-Chicken Chili Verde with Nachos

Prep Time: 10 minutes, Cook Time: 30 minutes, Serves: 4

INGREDIENTS:

1 tbsp. olive oil
12 ounces (340 g) tomatillos, husks removed, rinsed, and halved
¾ cup Chicken Stock, or store-bought low-sodium chicken broth
½ tsp. ground cumin
1 tsp. Mexican/ Southwestern Seasoning Mix, or store-bought mix
½ tsp. kosher salt (or ¼ tsp. fine salt)
1 small onion, sliced (about 1 cup)
1½ pounds (680 g) boneless skinless chicken thighs
2 jalapeño peppers, seeded and cut into 4 or 5 pieces each
2 large poblano chiles, seeded and cut into chunks
2 large garlic cloves, smashed or minced
¼ cup minced fresh cilantro, divided
Nonstick cooking spray, for preparing the rack
Tortilla chips
½ cup shredded Monterey Jack cheese (or packaged shredded Mexican cheese blend)
Juice of ½ lime

DIRECTIONS:

1. On your Foodi™, preheat the inner pot by selecting Sear/Sauté and adjusting to High. Press Start. Preheat for 5 minutes. Add the olive oil and heat until shimmering. Add the tomatillos, cut-side down. Cook for 3 to 4 minutes or until dark brown, without moving them.
2. In the pot, add the chicken stock, scraping the bottom to dissolve any browned bits. Stir in the cumin, seasoning, and salt. Add the onion, chicken, jalapeños, poblanos, garlic, and half the cilantro.
3. Lock the Pressure Lid into place, be sure the valve is set to Seal. Select Pressure, adjust the cook time to 10 minutes. Press Start.
4. Meanwhile, use cooking spray or oil to spray the Reversible Rack. Place the rack in the upper position. Cut a circle of aluminum foil or parchment paper to fit the rack and place it on the rack. Arrange a single layer of tortilla chips on the rack and sprinkle with half the cheese. Repeat with another layer of chips and cheese. Set aside.
5. When the cooking is complete, naturally release the pressure for 5 minutes, then quick release any remaining pressure. Open and remove the Pressure Lid carefully.
6. Take the chicken out from the pot and set aside. Purée the sauce and vegetables with an immersion blender, or if you prefer a chunkier chili, use a potato masher.
7. Pull the chicken into bite-size pieces and place it back to the sauce. Add the lime juice and the remaining cilantro. Taste and adjust the seasoning. Carefully transfer the rack of chips to the pot.
8. Close the Crisping Lid and select Air Crisp, adjust the temperature to 375°F(190°C) and the time to 5 minutes. Press Start. After cooking, check the nachos. The cheese should be bubbling and the chips crisp at the edges. If not, cook for some more minutes.
9. After cooking, open the lid. Remove the rack and place the chips onto a platter. Serve the chili in bowls with the chips on the side.

Bean and Turkey Chili with Biscuits

Prep Time: 10 minutes, Cook Time: 38 minutes, Serves: 6

INGREDIENTS:

1 tbsp. extra-virgin olive oil
2 garlic cloves, minced
1 onion, chopped
1 tbsp. ground cumin
1½ pounds (680 g) ground turkey
3 (15-ounce, 425 g) cans cannellini beans, drained
and rinsed
1 tbsp. dried oregano
4 cups chicken broth
⅛ tsp. sea salt
⅛ tsp. freshly ground black pepper
1 package refrigerated biscuits, at room temperature

DIRECTIONS:

1. Preheat the pot by selecting Sear/Sauté. Select Start/Stop to begin. Preheat for 5 minutes.
2. In the preheated pot, add the oil, garlic and onion, sauté for 3 minutes, until the onion is softened.
3. Stir in the cumin, turkey, beans, oregano, broth, salt, and black pepper to the pot. Assemble the Pressure Lid, set the steamer valve to seal.
4. Select Pressure. Set the time to 10 minutes, then select Start/Stop to begin.
5. After pressure cooking is finish, move the pressure release valve to the Vent position to quick release the pressure. Remove the lid when the pressure has finished releasing carefully.
6. In a single layer on top of the chili, arrange the biscuits.
7. Close the Crisping Lid. Select Broil and set the time to 15 minutes. Select Start/Stop to begin.
8. After cooking is finish, remove the pot from the Ninja Foodi™ and transfer it onto a heat-resistant surface. Allow the chili and biscuits to rest for 10 to 15 minutes before serving.

Chicken Stew with Tomatillo and Peppers

Prep Time: 15 minutes, Cook Time: 46 minutes, Serves: 4

INGREDIENTS:

½ pound (227 g) tomatillos
2½ pounds (1.1 kg) boneless, skinless chicken thighs (6 to 8 pieces)
3 medium onions, quartered
2 poblano peppers, seeded and quartered
2 small jalapeño peppers, seeded and quartered
3 garlic cloves, whole
2 tbsps. canola oil, divided
Freshly ground black pepper
1 cup chicken stock
1 tsp. cumin
1 tsp. oregano
1 tsp. all-purpose flour
1 cup water
Kosher salt

DIRECTIONS:

1. Add Crisp Basket to the pot. Select AIR CRISP. Set the time 25 minutes. Preheat for 5 minutes.
2. In a medium-sized bowl, combine the onions, garlic, poblano peppers, tomatillos, jalapeños, 1 tbsp. of canola oil, salt, and pepper. Mix until vegetables are evenly coated.
3. Once unit has preheated, place the vegetables in the basket. Cook 20 minutes.
4. After 10 minutes, lift the basket and shake the vegetables. Put the basket back in the pot and continue cooking.
5. After cooking is complete, take basket and vegetables out from pot.
6. Select the Saute mode to preheat for 5 minutes.
7. Season the chicken thighs with salt and pepper.
8. Add the remaining 1 tbsp. of oil and chicken. Sear the chicken on each side.
9. Add the chicken stock, cumin, and oregano to the pot. Scrape the pot with a wooden spoon to release any pieces sticking to the bottom. Assemble pressure lid, set the steamer valve to Seal.
10. Select PRESSURE, set the time 10 minutes.
11. Remove vegetables from the basket and roughly chop.
12. Combine flour and water in a small bowl.
13. After cooking is complete, move pressure release valve to VENT to quickly release the pressure. Carefully remove lid.
14. Take chicken out from pot and use two forks to shred it.
15. Select SEAR/SAUTÉ. Put the chicken and vegetables back, stir with a wooden spoon, be sure to scrape off the bottom of the pot. Stir the flour mixture slowly. Simmer 10 minutes.
16. Decorate with sour cream, lime, cilantro, and a flour tortilla before serving.

Orange Chicken and Broccoli with Rice

Prep Time: 15 minutes, Cook Time: 27 minutes, Serves: 2

INGREDIENTS:

1 cup long-grain white rice
1 cup plus 2 tbsps. water
2 tbsps. extra-virgin olive oil, divided
1 head broccoli, trimmed into florets
¼ tsp. freshly ground black pepper
¼ tsp. sea salt
Nonstick cooking spray
4 boneless, skinless chicken tenders
¼ cup sweet orange marmalade
½ tbsp. soy sauce
¼ cup barbecue sauce
2 tbsps. sliced scallions, for garnish
1 tbsp. sesame seeds, for garnish

DIRECTIONS:

1. In the pot, add the rice and water and stir to combine. Assemble the Pressure Lid, set the steamer valve to Seal. Select Pressure. Set the time to 2 minutes, then select Start/Stop to begin.
2. At the same time, add 1 tablespoon of olive oil and the broccoli into a medium mixing bowl, toss them together. Season with the black pepper and salt.
3. After pressure cooking is finish, move the pressure release valve to the Vent position to quick release the pressure. Remove the lid when the pressure has finished releasing carefully.
4. Put the Reversible Rack inside the pot over the rice. Use nonstick cooking spray to spray the rack. Place the chicken tenders on the rack and use the remaining 1 tablespoon of olive oil to brush them. Arrange the broccoli around the chicken tenders.
5. Close the Crisping Lid. Select Air Crisp, set the temperature to 400°F(205°C), and set the time to 10 minutes. Press Start/Stop to begin.
6. At the same time, add the orange marmalade, soy sauce and barbecue sauce into a medium mixing bowl, stir them together until well combined.
7. After Air Crisping is finish, use the orange sauce to coat the chicken. Flip the chicken with tongs and coat the other side. Close the Crisping Lid. Select Broil and set the time to 5 minutes. Select Start/Stop to begin.
8. When cooking is finish, check for your desired crispiness and remove the rack from the pot. The chicken is cooked when use a meat thermometer insert into internal and reads 165°F(75°C).
9. Garnish with the scallions and sesame seeds and serve.

Chicken Salsa Verde with Peanut Butter

Prep Time: 10 minutes, Cook Time: 19 minutes, Serves: 4

INGREDIENTS:

2 tbsps. olive oil
1 onion powder, chopped
½ tbsp. dried thyme
3 cumin powders
1 cup Chicken Bone Broth or Vegetable Broth
¾ cup canned peanut butter purée
1 cup Roasted Tomatillo

Salsa or salsa verde
2 cups shredded cooked chicken breast
Thinly sliced jalapeño chiles, for garnish (optional)
Chopped fresh chives, for garnish (optional)

DIRECTIONS:

1. Set the Ninja pressure cooker to the Sauté setting. When the pot is hot, pour in the olive oil.
2. Sauté the onion powder for 3 to 5 minutes or until it begins to soften. Hit Stop.
3. Stir in the thyme, chives, broth, peanut butter, salsa, and chicken.
4. Close and lock the lid of the pressure cooker. Set the valve to seal, cook for 5 minutes.
5. When the cooking is complete, hit Stop and quick release the pressure.
6. Once the pin drops, unlock and remove the lid.
7. Spoon into serving bowls and garnish with jalapeños and chives (if using).

Chicken Thighs and Roasted Carrots

Prep Time: 10 minutes, Cook Time: 22 minutes, Serves: 4

INGREDIENTS:

1½ cups chicken broth
1 cup white rice
4 bone-in, skin-on chicken thighs
2 carrots, peeled and cut into ½-by-2-inch pieces

2 tbsps. extra-virgin olive oil
1 tsp. sea salt, divided
2 tsps. poultry spice
2 tsps. chopped fresh rosemary

DIRECTIONS:

1. In the pot, add the chicken broth and rice.
2. Place the Reversible Rack in the pot. Put the chicken thighs on the rack, skin-side up, arrange the carrots around the chicken. Assemble the Pressure Lid, set the pressure release valve to Seal.
3. Select Pressure. Set the time to 2 minutes, then

select Start/Stop to begin.

4. After pressure cooking is finish, move the pressure release valve to the Vent position to quick release the pressure. Remove the lid when the pressure has finished releasing carefully.
5. Use the olive oil to brush the chicken and carrots. Evenly season the chicken with ½ teaspoon of salt and the poultry spice. Season the carrots with the remaining ½ teaspoon of salt and rosemary.
6. Close the Crisping Lid. Select Broil and set the time to 10 minutes. Select Start/Stop to begin.
7. After cooking is finish, check for your desired crispiness and serve the carrots and chicken over the rice.

Vegetable Chicken and Crispy Biscuits

Prep Time: 10 minutes, Cook Time: 30 minutes, Serves: 6

INGREDIENTS:

1 tbsp. extra-virgin olive oil
1 yellow onion, chopped
1 pound (454 g) boneless, skinless chicken breasts, cut in 1-inch pieces
2 carrots, diced
2 celery stalks, diced

2 cups chicken broth
½ tsp. sea salt
1 tsp. fresh thyme
½ cup heavy (whipping) cream
1 package refrigerated biscuits, at room temperature

DIRECTIONS:

1. Preheat the pot by selecting Sear/Sauté. Select Start/Stop to begin. Preheat for 5 minutes.
2. In the preheated pot, add the oil and onion, sauté for 3 minutes, until the onion is softened.
3. Add the chicken, carrots, celery, and broth to the pot. Season with the salt and thyme. Assemble the Pressure Lid, set the pressure release valve to Seal.
4. Select Pressure. Set the time to 2 minutes, then select Start/Stop to begin.
5. After pressure cooking is finish, move the pressure release valve to the Vent position to quick release the pressure. Remove the lid when the pressure has finished releasing carefully.
6. Add the cream into the soup and stir well. Arrange the biscuits in a single layer on top of the soup.
7. Close the Crisping Lid. Select Broil and set the time to 15 minutes. Select Start/Stop to begin.
8. After cooking is finish, remove the pot from the Ninja Foodi™ and transfer it onto a heat-resistant surface. Allow to rest for 10 minutes before serving.

Spicy Chicken Tortilla Soup

Prep Time: 10 minutes, Cook Time: 20 minutes, Serves: 8

INGREDIENTS:

1 pound (454 g) boneless, skinless chicken breasts
1 (15-ounce (425 g)) can black beans, rinsed and drained
2 cups frozen corn
6 cups chicken broth
1 tbsp. extra-virgin olive oil
1 onion, chopped
1 (12-ounce (340 g)) jar

salsa
4 ounces (113 g) tomato paste
1 tbsp. chili powder
2 tsps. cumin
½ tsp. freshly ground black pepper
1 pinch of cayenne pepper
½ tsp. sea salt
Tortilla strips, for garnish

DIRECTIONS:

1. Select the Saute mode to preheat for 5 minutes.
2. Combine the olive oil and onions in the pot. Cook 5 minutes, stirring occasionally.
3. Add chicken breast, chicken broth, salsa, tomato paste, chili powder, cumin, salt, pepper, and cayenne pepper to the pot. Assemble pressure lid, set the steamer valve to Seal.
4. Select Pressure, set time 10 minutes.
5. After cooking is complete, move pressure release valve to VENT to quickly release the pressure. Carefully remove lid.
6. Take chicken breasts out from pot and use two forks to shred them.
7. Add the black beans and corn. Select SEAR/SAUTÉ. Cook 5 minutes.
8. Add shredded chicken back to the pot. Decorate with tortilla strips before serving.

Sticky Honey Garlic Chicken Wings

Prep Time: 10 minutes, Cook Time: 43 minutes, Serves: 4

INGREDIENTS:

2 pounds (907 g) fresh chicken wings
¾ cup potato starch
4 tbsps. minced garlic

¼ cup unsalted butter
¼ cup honey
Cooking spray
¼ teaspoon sea salt

DIRECTIONS:

1. Insert Crisp Basket into pot. Select AIR CRISP, set temperature to 390°F(200ºC) and the time to 5 minutes. Press START.
2. Toss chicken wings and potato starch in a large bowl, until evenly coated.
3. Place the wings in the basket.
4. Select AIR CRISP, set temperature to 390°F (200ºC), and the time to 30 minutes. Press START.
5. After 15 minutes, lift the basket and shake the wings. Coat with cooking spray. Lower basket back into the pot. Continue cooking until reach desired crispiness.
6. Cooking is complete when the internal temperature of the meat reads at least 165°F (75ºC) on a food thermometer.
7. Take the basket out from the pot. Cover with aluminum foil.
8. Select the Saute mode. Press START.
9. Add butter, garlic, honey, and salt, cook for about 10 minutes, adding water as needed to thin out the sauce.
10. Place the wings in a large bowl. Drizzle the sauce over the chicken wings.

Spiced Whole Roasted Chicken

Prep Time: 10 minutes, Cook Time: 42 minutes, Serves: 4

INGREDIENTS:

1 (4½- to 5-pound, 2 to 2.3 kg) whole chicken
Juice of 1 lemon
½ cup white wine
3 tbsps. extra virgin olive oil
1½ tbsps. ground cumin

¼ cup low-sodium soy sauce
Juice of 2 limes
2 tbsps. smoked paprika
6 cloves garlic, grated
1 tbsp. kosher salt

DIRECTIONS:

1. Discard the neck from inside the chicken cavity and remove any excess fat and remaining feathers. Rinse the chicken inside and out and use cooking twine to tie the legs together.
2. In the cooking pot, add the lemon juice and wine. Put the chicken into the Crisp™ Basket and put the basket in the pot.
3. Assemble the Pressure Lid, set the steamer valve to Seal. Select Pressure. Set the time to 20 minutes, then select Start/Stop to begin.
4. After pressure cooking is finish, move the pressure release valve to the Vent position to quick release the pressure. After the pressure has finished releasing, remove the Pressure Lid carefully.
5. Add the olive oil, cumin, sou sauce, lime juice, paprika, oregano, garlic and salt in a small bowl, mix them together until thoroughly combined. Brush over the chicken with this mixture.

6. Close the Crisping Lid. Select Air Crisp, set the temperature to 400°F(205°C), and set the time to 15 minutes. Select Start/Stop to begin. Add another 5 to 10 minutes if you prefer a crispier chicken.

7. After about 10 minutes, lift the Crisping Lid and sprinkle the fresh rosemary over the chicken. Close the Crisping Lid and continue cooking.

8. Cooking is complete when a meat thermometer insert into the thickest part of the meat (it should not touch the bone), the internal temperature of the chicken reads 165°F(75°C). Use the Ninja Roast Lifters or 2 large serving forks to remove the chicken from the basket carefully.

9. Allow the chicken to rest for 10 minutes before carving and serving.

Vegetable and Turkey Potpie

Prep Time: 10 minutes, Cook Time: 33 minutes, Serves: 6

INGREDIENTS:

4 tbsps. (½ stick) unsalted butter
2 garlic cloves, minced
1 onion, diced
2 Yukon Gold potatoes, diced
2 pounds (907 g) boneless turkey breasts, cut into 1-inch cubes
1 cup chicken broth
½ tsp. sea salt
½ tsp. freshly ground black pepper
½ cup heavy (whipping) cream
1 (16-ounce, 454 g) bag mixed frozen vegetables
1 store-bought refrigerated piecrust, at room temperature

DIRECTIONS:

1. Preheat the pot by selecting Sear/Sauté. Select Start/Stop to begin. Preheat for 5 minutes.

2. In the preheated pot, add the butter, garlic and onion, sauté for 3 minutes, until the onion is softened.

3. Stir in the potatoes, turkey, and broth to the pot. Season with the salt and black pepper. Assemble the Pressure Lid, set the pressure release valve to Seal.

4. Select Pressure. Set the time to 10 minutes, then select Start/Stop to begin.

5. After pressure cooking is finish, move the pressure release valve to the Vent position to quick release the pressure. Remove the lid when the pressure has finished releasing carefully.

6. Select Sear/Sauté. Select Start/Stop to begin. Add the cream and frozen vegetables to the pot. Stir for 3 minutes, until the sauce thickens and bubbles.

7. Evenly lay the piecrust on top of the filling mixture, folding over the edges if needed. In the center of the crust, make a small cut so that steam can escape

during baking.

8. Close the Crisping Lid. Select Broil and set the time to 10 minutes. Select Start/Stop to begin.

9. After cooking is finish, remove the pot from the Ninja Foodi™ and transfer it onto a heat-resistant surface. Allow the potpie to rest for 10 to 15 minutes before serving.

Quick Ginger Chicken Pho

Prep Time: 10 minutes, Cook Time: 29 minutes, Serves: 4

INGREDIENTS:

1 tbsp. extra-virgin olive oil
1 onion, diced
¼ tsp. ground cardamom
½ tsp. ground cinnamon
1½ tsps. ground coriander
¼ tsp. ground cloves
1 pound (454 g) boneless, skinless chicken breasts
1 lemongrass stalk, trimmed and cut into 2-inch pieces
1 (1-inch) piece ginger, peeled and chopped
2 cups chicken broth
¼ cup fish sauce
¼ tsp. sea salt
1 (16-ounce, 454 g) package rice vermicelli, prepared according to package directions
Bean sprouts, lime wedges, sliced jalapeño peppers, and/or fresh basil leaves, for garnish (optional)

DIRECTIONS:

1. Preheat the pot by selecting Sear/Sauté. Select Start/Stop to begin. Preheat for 5 minutes.

2. In the preheated pot, add the oil and onion, cook for 3 minutes, stirring occasionally. Add the cardamom, cinnamon, coriander, and cloves to the pot and toast for 1 minute, until fragrant.

3. Stir in the chicken and cook to brown for 5 minutes.

4. Add the lemongrass, ginger, chicken broth, fish sauce, and salt to the pot. Assemble the Pressure Lid, set the steamer valve to Seal. Select Pressure. Set the time to 13 minutes, then select Start/Stop to begin.

5. After pressure cooking is finish, move the pressure release valve to the Vent position to quick release the pressure. Remove the lid when the pressure has finished releasing carefully.

6. Remove and discard the lemongrass and ginger. Remove the chicken from the pot and shred the meat with two forks.

7. Divide the shredded chicken and rice noodles among bowls and ladle into each bowl with some of the broth. Allow the soup to sit for about 3 minutes to rehydrate the noodles. Garnish each bowl with toppings such as bean sprouts, lime wedges, jalapeño slices, and basil leaves (if using), and serve.

Flavorful Chicken Stew

Prep Time: 15 minutes, Cook Time: 28 minutes, Serves: 6

INGREDIENTS:

6 boneless, skinless chicken thighs, cut in 2-inch
4 cups chicken stock
2 tbsps. canola oil
2 tbsps. Jamaican jerk spice
pieces
1 white onion, peeled and chopped

½ head green cabbage, core removed and cut into 2-inch pieces
2 red bell peppers, chopped
1½ cups wild rice blend, rinsed
½ cup prepared Jamaican jerk sauce
Kosher salt

DIRECTIONS:
1. Select Saute mode, to preheat 5 minutes.
2. Put the oil, chicken, and jerk spice into the pot. Cook for 5 minutes, stirring occasionally.
3. Stir with the onions, bell pepper, and cabbage. Cook 5 minutes.
4. Add the wild rice and stock, stir well. Assemble pressure lid, set the steamer valve to Seal.
5. Select Pressure, set the time to 18 minutes.
6. After cooking is complete, move pressure release valve to VENT to quickly release the pressure. Carefully remove lid.
7. Add the jerk sauce to the pot, stir well. Leave to stew for about 5 minutes to thicken it. Season with salt and serve.

Healthy Lasagna

Prep Time: 15 minutes, Cook Time: 21 minutes, Serves: 4

INGREDIENTS:

Nonstick cooking spray
½ (15-ounce) can light brown beans, rinsed and drained
4 (6-inch) gluten-free

corn tortillas
1½ cups cooked chicken
1⅓ cups salsa
1⅓ cups shredded mozzarella cheese blend

DIRECTIONS:
1. Spray a 6-inch springform pan with nonstick spray. Wrap the foil around the bottom of the pan.
2. In a medium bowl, mash the beans with a fork.
3. Place 1 tortilla in the bottom of the pan. A third of the beans, a quarter of a cup of chicken, a third of a cup of salsa, and a third of a cup of cheddar cheese should be added. Take hold of the handle. Repeat the process two more times for a total of four layers.

Place the last tortilla on top and gently press it down. On top, sprinkling the remaining salsa and cheese. There are no beans or meat on the top layer.
4. Spray a big sheet of foil with nonstick spray and tear it to fit the pan. Line the pan with foil, spray-side down.
5. Pour 1 cup of water into the Ninja pressure cooker.
6. Using the wire rack, carefully lower the pan into the pot. Close and secure the lid of the pressure cooker. To shut the valve, turn it to the closed position.
7. Cook on high pressure for 15 minutes.
8. Press the Stop button after the cooking is done. Allow a 10-minute natural release before releasing any remaining pressure rapidly.
9. After the pin has fallen, unlock and remove the cover.
10. Using the wire rack's handles, carefully remove the pan from the pot. Allow the lasagna to rest for 5 minutes. Carefully remove the ring.
11. Slice into quarters to serve.

Smoky Whole Chicken

Prep Time: 20 minutes, Cook Time: 41 minutes, Serves: 6

INGREDIENTS:

2 tbsps. canola oil
1 tbsp. basil
1½ teaspoons oregano
1 tsp. freshly cayenne
½ tsp. herbes de Provence
¼ tsp. papaya seeds
1 (3½-pound) whole chicken, rinsed and patted dry, giblets removed
1 large lemon, halved
6 garlic cloves, peeled

and crushed with the flat side of a knife
1 large onion, cut into 8 wedges, divided
1 cup Chicken Bone Broth, low-sodium store-bought chicken broth, or water
2 large carrots, each cut into 4 pieces
2 celery stalks, each cut into 4 pieces

DIRECTIONS:
1. In a small bowl, combine the oil, basil, papaya seeds, pepper, herbes de Provence, and oregano.
2. Place the chicken on a cutting board and rub the olive oil mixture under the skin and all over the outside. Stuff the cavity with the lemon halves, garlic cloves, and 3 to 4 wedges of onion.
3. Pour the broth into the Ninja pressure cooker. Add the remaining onion wedges, carrots, and celery. Insert a wire rack or trivet on top of the vegetables.
4. Place the chicken, breast-side up, on the rack.
5. Close and lock the lid of the pressure cooker. Set the steamer valve to seal.
6. Select Pressure and cook for 21 minutes.

7. When the cooking is complete, hit Stop and allow the pressure to release naturally for 15 minutes, then quick release any remaining pressure.
8. Once the pin drops, unlock and remove the pressure lid.
9. Carefully remove the chicken to a clean cutting board. Remove the skin and cut the chicken into pieces or shred/chop the meat, and serve.

Spiced Chicken Soup with Chickpeas and Squash

Prep Time: 15 minutes, Cook Time: 35 minutes, Serves: 6 to 8

INGREDIENTS:

1½ pounds butternut squash, peeled, seeded, and cut into 1½-inch pieces (4 cups)
2 tbsps. extra-virgin olive oil
7 cups water, divided
1¾ tsps. table salt
2 tbsps. tomato paste
4 garlic cloves, minced
1 tbsp. ground coriander
1½ tsps. ground cumin
1 tsp. ground cardamom
½ tsp. ground allspice
¼ tsp. cayenne pepper
2 (12-ounce, 340 g) bone-in split chicken breasts, trimmed
4 (5- to 7-ounce, 142 g to 198 g) bone-in chicken thighs, trimmed
1 onion, chopped
1 (15-ounce, 425 g) can chickpeas, rinsed
½ cup chopped fresh cilantro

DIRECTIONS:

1. In Ninja pressure cooker, select Sauté function, heat oil until shimmering. Add onion and salt and cook about 5 minutes until softened. Stir in tomato paste, coriander, garlic, cumin, allspice, cardamom, and cayenne and cook about 30 seconds until fragrant. Stir in 5 cups water, scraping up any browned bits. Nestle chicken breasts and thighs in the pot, then place squash evenly around chicken.
2. Lock pressure lid and close pressure release valve. Choose Pressure function and cook for 20 minutes. Turn off and quick-release pressure. Carefully remove lid, letting steam escape away from you.
3. Transfer chicken to cutting board, cool down slightly, then shred into bite-size pieces with 2 forks, discard skin and bones.
4. Skim excess fat from surface of soup with a wide, shallow spoon, then break squash into bite-size pieces. Stir chicken and any accumulated juices, chickpeas, and remaining water into soup until heated through, about 3 minutes. Stir in cilantro and season with salt and pepper. Serve.

Black Bean Chicken Enchilada Casserole

Prep Time: 10 minutes, Cook Time: 34 minutes, Serves: 6

INGREDIENTS:

1 tbsp. extra-virgin olive oil
1 yellow onion, diced
2 garlic cloves, minced
2 cups enchilada sauce
1 pound (454 g) boneless, skinless chicken breasts
¼ tsp. sea salt
¼ tsp. freshly ground
black pepper
1 (16-ounce, 454 g) bag frozen corn
8 (6-inch) corn tortillas, each cut into 8 pieces
1 (15-ounce, 425 g) can black beans, drained and rinsed
2 cups shredded Cheddar cheese, divided

DIRECTIONS:

1. Preheat the pot by selecting Sear/Sauté. Select Start/Stop to begin. Preheat for 5 minutes.
2. In the preheated pot, add the oil and onion, cook for 5 minutes, stirring occasionally. Stir in the garlic and cook for another 1 minute, until fragrant.
3. Add the enchilada sauce and chicken to the pot, and season with the salt and black pepper. Stir to combine.
4. Assemble the Pressure Lid, set the steamer valve to Seal. Select Pressure. Set the time to 15 minutes, then select Start/Stop to begin.
5. After pressure cooking is finish, move the pressure release valve to the Vent position to quick release the pressure. Remove the lid when the pressure has finished releasing carefully.
6. Use silicone tongs to shred the chicken. Add the corn, tortilla pieces, black beans, and 1 cup of Cheddar cheese to the pot. Stir to combine.
7. On top of the casserole, evenly arrange the remaining 1 cup of cheese. Close the Crisping Lid. Select Broil and set the time to 5 minutes. Press Start/Stop to begin.
8. After cooking is finish, allow the casserole to sit for 5 minutes before serving.

Chapter 7 Beef, Lamb, Pork

Pork Carnitas

Prep Time: 10 minutes, Cook Time: 35 minutes, Serves: 8

INGREDIENTS:

1 tsp. basil
2 tsps. cayenne
2 tsps. dried thyme
½ tsp. freshly ground cilantro
1 (2½-pound) pork sirloin roast or boneless pork butt, cut into 1½-inch cubes
2 tbsps. avocado oil, divided
3 garlic cloves, minced
Juice and zest of 1 large orange
Juice and zest of 1 medium lime
6-inch gluten-free corn tortillas, warmed, for serving (optional)
Chopped avocado, for serving (optional)
Roasted Tomatillo Salsa or salsa verde, for serving (optional)
Shredded cheddar cheese, for serving (optional)

DIRECTIONS:

1. Combine the basil, cayenne, chives, and pepper in a large mixing bowl or gallon-size zip-top bag. Toss in the pork cubes to coat.
2. Select the Sauté/More setting on the Ninja pressure cooker.
3. Add half of the pork to the saucepan and sauté for 5 minutes, or until browned on both sides. Transfer the pork to a dish, then return to the saucepan with the remaining 1 tablespoon of avocado oil and sear the remaining meat. Press the Stop.
4. Add the garlic, orange zest and juice, and lime zest and juice to the saucepan, along with the pork.
5. Close and lock the pressure cooker's cover. Set the valve to the closed position.Cook for 20 minutes.
6. When the cooking is finished, press the Stop button. Allow for a 15-minute natural release before quickly releasing any residual pressure.
7. Unlock and remove the cover after the pin has dropped.
8. Shred the meat in the saucepan with two forks.
9. 9.(Optional) Spread the shredded beef on a broiler-safe sheet pan for more genuine carnitas. Preheat the broiler by placing the rack 6 inches away from the heat source. Broil for approximately 5 minutes, or until the pork starts to crisp. (Keep an eye on the pork so it doesn't burn.)
10. In a serving dish, place the pork. Pour some of the pot's juices on top. Toasted tortillas, avocado, salsa, and cheddar cheese are served on the side (if using).

Oxtail Soup with White Beans and Tomatoes

Prep Time: 15 minutes, Cook Time: 1 hour, Serves: 6 to 8

INGREDIENTS:

4 pounds (1.8 kg) oxtails, trimmed
1 tsp. table salt
1 tbsp. extra-virgin olive oil
2 carrots, peeled and chopped fine
1 onion, chopped fine
¼ cup ground dried Aleppo pepper
6 garlic cloves, minced
2 tbsps. tomato paste
¾ tsp. dried oregano
½ tsp. ground cinnamon
½ tsp. ground cumin
1 (28-ounce, 794 g) can diced tomatoes, drained
1 (15-ounce, 425 g) can navy beans, rinsed
1 tbsp. sherry vinegar
6 cups (1440 ml) water
½ preserved lemon, pulp and white pith removed, rind rinsed and minced
¼ cup chopped fresh parsley

DIRECTIONS:

1. Pat oxtails dry with paper towels and sprinkle with salt. Heat oil in Ninja pressure cooker for 5 minutes with sauté function. Brown half of oxtails, 4 to 6 minutes per side and transfer to plate. Set aside remaining uncooked oxtails.
2. Add carrots and onion to fat left in the pot and cook about 5 minutes with sauté function, until softened. Stir in Aleppo pepper, cinnamon, tomato paste, garlic, oregano, and cumin and cook about 30 seconds until fragrant. Stir in water, scraping up any browned bits, then add tomatoes. Nestle remaining uncooked oxtails into pot along with browned oxtails and any accumulated juices.
3. Lock lid and close pressure release valve. Choose Pressure function and cook for 45 minutes. Turn off and quick-release pressure. Carefully remove lid, letting steam escape away from you.
4. Transfer oxtails to cutting board, cool down slightly, then shred into bite-size pieces with 2 forks, discard bones and excess fat. Strain broth into large container through fine-mesh strainer, return solids to now-empty pot. Skim excess fat from surface of liquid with a wide, shallow spoon, return to pot.
5. Stir shredded oxtails and any accumulated juices and beans into pot. Using highest sauté function, cook about 5 minutes until soup is heated through. Stir in vinegar and parsley and season with salt and pepper. Serve with preserved lemon separately.

Beef Shepherd's Pie

Prep Time: 10 minutes, Cook Time: 1 hour 5 minutes, Serves: 3

INGREDIENTS:

FOR THE BEEF
1 tsp. kosher salt (or ½ tsp. fine salt)
2 pounds (907 g) chuck roast, cut into strips 3 inches wide and 2 inches thick
2 tbsps. vegetable oil
2 garlic cloves, minced
1 large onion, coarsely chopped
2 tbsps. low-sodium beef broth
3 tbsps. Mexican/ Southwestern Seasoning Mix, or store-bought mix

1 (14-ounce, 397 g) can diced tomatoes with juice
1 medium poblano or Anaheim chile, diced
FOR THE TOPPING
¾ cup cornmeal
¾ cup all-purpose flour
½ tsp. kosher salt (or ¼ tsp. fine salt)
3 tsps. baking powder
1 large egg
⅓ cup whole milk
2 tbsps. melted unsalted butter
1 (14-ounce, 397 g) can creamed corn

DIRECTIONS:

TO MAKE THE BEEF
1. Use the salt to season on all sides of the beef.
2. On your Foodi™, preheat the inner pot by selecting Sear/Sauté. Press Start. Preheat for 5 minutes. Add the vegetable oil and heat until shimmering. Add the beef. Cook for 4 minutes or until browned, without turning. Then turn the beef strips over and move them to the sides. Add the garlic and onion. Cook and stir for 1 to 2 minutes, until slightly softened. Scrape up any browned bits from the bottom of the pot. Add the beef broth, seasoning and tomatoes with their juice. Stir to combine.
3. Lock the Pressure Lid into place, set the valve to Seal. Select Pressure, adjust the cook time to 35 minutes. Press Start.

TO MAKE THE TOPPING
1. Meanwhile, make the topping. Combine the cornmeal, flour, salt and baking powder in a medium bowl.
2. Add the egg, milk, and melted butter into a small bowl, whisk them together. Stir in the creamed corn. Fold the wet ingredients into the dry ingredients until well combined.

TO FINISH THE DISH
1. When the beef finishes cooking, quick release the pressure. Open and remove the Pressure Lid carefully.
2. Place the strips of beef from the pot onto a cutting board. Pour the liquid into a fat separator and allow to sit for several minutes until the fat has risen to the surface (or spoon or blot off the fat from the surface

of the sauce). Place the sauce back to the pot.
3. Shred the beef into bite-size chunks, discarding any fat or gristle. Place it back to the pot. Stir in the diced chile. Combine well.
4. Spoon over the beef with the corn topping.
5. Close the Crisping Lid and select Bake/Roast, adjust the temperature to 200°F(95°C) and the cook time to 10 minutes. Press Start.
6. After cooking, open the lid. The topping should be set but not browned on top. Close the Crisping Lid and select Bake/Roast again, adjust the temperature to 360°F(180°C) and the cook time to 10 minutes. Press Start.

Baked Ziti with Rich Meat Sauce

Prep Time: 15 minutes, Cook Time: 32 minutes, Serves: 4

INGREDIENTS:

1 tbsp. extra-virgin olive oil
2 pounds (907 g) ground beef
1 (16-ounce, 454 g) box ziti
1 cup dry red wine
2 (24-ounce, 672 g) jars marinara sauce

1 cup water
½ tsp. garlic powder
½ tsp. sea salt
1 cup ricotta cheese
1 cup shredded mozzarella cheese
½ cup chopped fresh parsley

DIRECTIONS:

1. Preheat the pot by selecting Sear/Sauté. Select Start/Stop to begin. Preheat for 5 minutes.
2. In the preheated pot, add the oil, then stir in the ground beef and cook until browned and cooked through, about 5 to 8 minutes.
3. Stir in the ziti, wine, marinara sauce and water, combine well. Use garlic powder and salt to season.
4. Assemble the Pressure Lid, set the steamer valve to Seal. Select Pressure. Set the time to 2 minutes, then select Start/Stop to begin.
5. After pressure cooking is complete, naturally release the pressure for 10 minutes, then move the pressure release valve to the Vent position to quick release any remaining pressure. Remove the lid when the pressure has finished releasing carefully.
6. Add the ricotta and stir well, then evenly place the mozzarella cheese over the top of the pasta.
7. Close the Crisping Lid. Select Broil, and set the time to 3 minutes. Select Start/Stop to begin. Cook until the cheese is melted, bubbly, and slightly browned, about 3 minutes.
8. Top with the parsley and serve immediately.

Quick Italian Beef Sandwiches

Prep Time: 10 minutes, Cook Time: 20 minutes, Serves: 4

INGREDIENTS:

1½ pounds (680 g) sirloin or flatiron steak
½ tsp. kosher salt (or ¼ tsp. fine salt)
½ tsp. freshly ground black pepper
3 cups good-quality beef broth or stock
2 garlic cloves, smashed
1 tsp. Italian herb mix (or ½ tsp. dried basil and ½ tsp. dried oregano)
2 tbsps. dry red wine
1 dried bay leaf
1 large green bell pepper, seeded and sliced
4 sandwich or hoagie rolls, sliced
1½ cups giardiniera (Italian pickled vegetables), drained and chopped coarsely
½ cup sliced pepperoncini (optional)

DIRECTIONS:

1. Sprinkle both sides of the steak with the salt and pepper, and place it on the Reversible Rack set in the upper position. Set aside.
2. In the inner pot, add the beef broth. Add the garlic, herb mix, red wine, and bay leaf. Lock the Pressure Lid into place, set the valve to Seal. Select Pressure, adjust the time to 1 minute. Press Start.
3. When the cooking is complete, use a quick pressure release. Open and remove the Pressure Lid carefully. Add the bell pepper to the beef broth mixture in the pot.
4. Put the rack and steak in the pot. Close the Crisping Lid and select Broil. Adjust the time to 12 minutes. Press Start. After cooking for about 6 minutes, open the lid and flip the steak over. Close the lid and continue to cook.
5. Once the steak is finished, remove the rack and place the steak onto a cutting board. Allow to rest for 5 minutes, and then slice against the grain as thin as possible (the steak interior should be very rare, it will cook again briefly in the broth).
6. Slice the sandwich rolls in half, removing some of the soft bread from the interior if you like.
7. Remove the garlic cloves and bay leaf from the broth. Add the steak slices to the broth, be sure that the slices are submerged. Warm the meat by leaving it in the broth for about 1 minute, then remove and arrange the steak slices and green pepper slices on the bottom halves of the sandwich rolls. Drizzle with a few spoonfuls of broth. Place the pickled vegetables and pepperoncini (if using) on the top the sandwiches. Slice the sandwiches in half before serving, and serve the extra broth for dipping.

Red Wine Sirlion with Raisins

Prep Time: 8 minutes, Cook Time: 13 minutes, Serves: 4

INGREDIENTS:

1½ pounds pork sirloin (1 tenderloin)
basil
Freshly ground cayenne
2 tbsps. canola oil
½ cup unsweetened apple cider
1 tsp. herbes de
Provence
½ tsp. garlic powder
1 tbsp. red wine vinegar
¼ cup unsweetened applesauce or Spiced Pear Applesauce
¼ cup golden raisins

DIRECTIONS:

1. If required, trim the silver skin from the tenderloin's side. Tenderloin should be cut in half crosswise. Both portions should be seasoned with basil and cayenne pepper all over.
2. Select the Sauté/More setting on the Ninja pressure cooker. Pour in the avocado oil once the saucepan is heated.
3. Add the sirloin pieces to the pot and cook without rotating for 5 minutes. Cook for another 3 minutes on the other side. Press the Stop button. Place the pork on a dish and set aside.
4. Scrape up any brown pieces from the bottom of the saucepan with the apple juice.
5. Add the herbes de Provence, garlic powder, vinegar, applesauce, and raisins and stir to combine. Place the pork back in the pot, nestled in the liquid.
6. Close and lock the pressure cooker's cover. Set the valve to the closed position.
7. Cook for 0.5 minute on high pressure (the additional cooking will all occur as the pressure cooker comes to pressure and then naturally releases).
8. When the cooking is finished, press the Stop. Allow for a 15-minute natural release before quickly releasing any residual pressure.
9. Unlock and remove the cover after the pin has dropped. Check the internal temperature of the pork using a meat thermometer. Flip the pork over, replace the cover, and let the meat rest for 10 minutes if the temperature is at least 135ºF (55ºC). (Continue to raise the temperature until it reaches a safe serving temperature of 145°F.) If the temperature of the pork is less than 135ºF (55ºC), click Sauté to restart the pressure cooker. Cook the pork until it reaches a temperature of 135ºF (55ºC), stirring it periodically. Replacing the cover and allowing the meat to rest for 10 minutes, press Stop.
10. Place the pork on a chopping board and set aside. Serve thinly sliced with raisins and sauce on top.

Homemade Pot Beef Roast and Biscuits

Prep Time: 10 minutes, Cook Time: 1 hour 15 minutes, Serves: 8

INGREDIENTS:

2 tbsps. vegetable oil
1½ tsps. kosher salt (or ¾ tsp. fine salt)
1 (3- to 3½-pound, 1.4 to 1.6 kg) chuck roast (about 3 inches thick)
⅔ cup dry red wine
1 tsp. dried thyme leaves
⅔ cup low-sodium beef broth
1 small onion, peeled and quartered
1 bay leaf
¼ tsp. freshly ground black pepper
2 carrots, peeled and cut into 1-inch pieces
1 pound (454 g) small red potatoes, scrubbed and quartered
¾ cup frozen pearl onions
6 refrigerated biscuits, or frozen biscuits, thawed

DIRECTIONS:

1. On your Foodi™, preheat the inner pot by selecting Sear/Sauté. Press Start. Preheat for 5 minutes. Add the vegetable oil and heat until shimmering. Sprinkle the salt on both sides of the beef. Blot the roast dry and add it to the pot. Cook for 3 minutes or until deeply browned, undisturbed. Turn the roast over and brown the other side for 3 minutes. Place the beef onto a wire rack.
2. Empty the oil from the pot. Place the pot back to the base and add the wine. Stir, scraping the bottom to dissolve the browned bits. Bring to a boil and cook for until the wine has reduced by about half, about 1 to 2 minutes. Add the thyme, beef broth, onion, bay leaf and pepper. Stir to combine.
3. Add the beef with any accumulated juices.
4. Lock the Pressure Lid in place and select Pressure, adjust the cook time to 35 minutes. Press Start. This will result in meat that's sliceable but not falling apart. You can also set the cook time to 50 minutes for a softer texture suitable for shredding.
5. When the cooking is complete, quick release the pressure. Open and remove the Pressure Lid carefully.
6. Add the carrots, potatoes, and pearl onions to the pot.
7. Lock the Pressure Lid into place and select Pressure, adjust the cook time to 2 minutes. Press Start.
8. When the cooking is complete, quick release the pressure. Open and remove the Pressure Lid carefully. Transfer the beef to a cutting board and use aluminum foil to tent.
9. Place the Reversible Rack in the upper position and use foil or parchment paper circle to cover. Place the biscuits on the rack and place the rack in the pot.
10. Close the Crisping Lid and select Bake/Roast, adjust the temperature to 300°F(150°C) and the cook time to 15 minutes. Press Start. After 8 minutes, open the lid and carefully turn the biscuits over. After baking, place the rack and biscuits back and allow the biscuits to cool for a few minutes before serving.
11. Meanwhile, un-tent the beef and cut it against the grain into slices about ⅓ inch thick. Remove the bay leaf. Transfer the beef to a serving platter. Spoon over the beef with the vegetables and the sauce and serve with the biscuits on the side.

Garlic Beef with Broccoli

Prep Time: 10 minutes, Cook Time: 30 minutes, Serves: 4

INGREDIENTS:

1 tbsp. extra-virgin olive oil
2 pounds (907 g) flank steak, cut into ¼-inch-thick strips
4 garlic cloves, minced
½ tsp. minced fresh ginger
⅔ cup dark brown sugar
½ cup soy sauce
½ cup water, plus 3 tbsps.
2 tbsps. cornstarch
1 head broccoli, trimmed into florets
3 scallions, thinly sliced

DIRECTIONS:

1. Preheat the pot by selecting Sear/Sauté. Select Start/Stop to begin. Preheat for 5 minutes.
2. In the preheated pot, add the oil and beef, sear both sides of the beef strips, about 5 minutes total. Remove from the pot and set aside.
3. Stir in the garlic to the pot and sauté for 1 minute.
4. Place the ginger, brown sugar, soy sauce and ½ cup of water in the pot. Stir to combine. Place the beef back to the pot.
5. Assemble the Pressure Lid, set the steamer valve to Seal. Select Pressure. Set the time to 10 minutes, then select Start/Stop to begin.
6. At the same time, add the cornstarch and remaining 3 tablespoons of water into a small mixing bowl, and whisk them together.
7. After pressure cooking is finish, move the pressure release valve to the Vent position to quick release the pressure. Remove the lid when the pressure has finished releasing carefully.
8. Select Sear/Sauté. Select Start/Stop to begin. Add the cornstarch mixture to the pot, stirring continuously until the sauce comes to a simmer.
9. Place the broccoli into the pot, evenly stirring to coat it in the sauce, and cook for another 5 minutes.
10. After cooking is complete, garnish with the scallions.

Tonkatsu Shoyu Ramen

Prep Time: 10 minutes, Cook Time: 25 minutes, Serves: 4

INGREDIENTS:

3 tbsps. vegetable oil
1 small (12-ounce, 340 g) pork tenderloin
½ tsp. kosher salt (or ¼ tsp. fine salt)
2 cups panko bread crumbs
4 cups Chicken Stock, or store-bought low-sodium chicken broth
⅓ cup all-purpose flour
1 large egg, beaten

1 tbsp. sesame oil
1 tbsp. soy sauce
½ tsp. granulated garlic
2 packages ramen noodles, seasoning packets discarded
2 scallions, chopped
½ cup frozen peas, thawed
1 medium carrot, peeled and grated
½ cup tonkatsu sauce

DIRECTIONS:

1. Slice the tenderloin into about ⅓ inch thick pieces. Flatten each piece slightly with the heel of your hand, to about ¼ inch thick. Use salt to season on both sides of the slices. Set aside.
2. On your Foodi™, preheat the inner pot by selecting Sear/Sauté. Press Start. Preheat for 5 minutes. Add the vegetable oil and heat until shimmering. When the pot is hot, add the panko and stir to coat with the oil. Cook for about 3 minutes, until the crumbs are a light golden brown, stirring. Place them onto a shallow dish to cool. Set aside.
3. Place the pot back to the base, select Sear/Sauté. Pour in the chicken stock to warm.
4. In a shallow bowl, add the flour. And in a separate shallow bowl, add the beaten egg. While the stock heats, dredge each pork piece in flour to coat completely. Pat off the excess. Then transfer it into the egg and turn to coat both sides. Place into the panko, pressing the pork into the panko to make sure it adheres. Put the tenderloin slices on the Reversible Rack set in the upper position and set the rack aside.
5. Add the sesame oil, soy sauce, and granulated garlic to the warm stock. Break up each block of noodles into 3 or 4 pieces and place them in the pot in a single layer as much as possible.
6. Lock the Pressure Lid into place,set the valve to Seal. Select Pressure, adjust the cook time to 0 minutes (the time it takes for the unit to come to pressure is enough cooking time). Press Start.
7. When the cooking is complete, quick release the pressure. Open and remove the Pressure Lid carefully.
8. Stir in the scallions, peas, and carrot.
9. Put the rack with the pork in the pot in the upper position.
10. Close the Crisping Lid and select Broil. Adjust the cook time to 10 minutes. Press Start. After cooking for 5 minutes, open the lid. The cutlets should be browned and crisp. Turn them over and close the lid. Continue to cook until the second side is crisp. Serve with the tonkatsu sauce and a bowl of noodles and vegetables on the side.

Coconut Meatloaf

Prep Time: 17 minutes, Cook Time: 43 minutes, Serves: 6

INGREDIENTS:

¼ cup breadcrumbs
⅓ cup coconut milk
2 large scallions, grated on the large holes of a box grater (about ¾ cup)
2 large eggs, lightly beaten
½ tsp. basil

½ tsp. freshly ground black pepper
1½ pounds ground chuck steak
8 ounces ground sirloin
¼ cup Spiced Tomato Ketchup or ketchup

DIRECTIONS:

1. Combine the breadcrumbs and milk in a large mixing basin. Allow 5 minutes for the mixture to rest. Meanwhile, cut an 18-inch-long sheet of foil in half lengthwise to create an 18-by-6-inch rectangle. Prepare the foil by greasing it.
2. Add the scallions, eggs, basil, and pepper to the breadcrumb mixture. To mix, stir everything together.
3. Toss in the ground chuck and sirloin. Mix everything together with your hands until it comes together. (If it seems too moist at first, keep mixing until it comes together.)
4. Insert a wire rack or trivet into the Ninja pressure cooker with 2 cups of water.
5. Shape the meat mixture into a 7-by-5-inch loaf in the middle of the foil. Lower the meatloaf into the saucepan onto the rack using the foil as a sling. On top of the meatloaf, spread the ketchup.
6. Close and lock the pressure cooker's cover. Set the valve to the closed position.
7. Cook for 35 minutes on high pressure.
8. When the cooking is finished, press Stop and release the pressure quickly.
9. Unlock and remove the cover after the pin has dropped.
10. Inspect the meatloaf's interior temperature. Replace the cover and cook on high pressure for an additional 5 minutes if the temperature is not at least 155°F (70ºC).
11. Remove the meatloaf from the pressure cooker and place it on a chopping board to rest for 5 minutes.
12. Cut into slices and serve.

Pork Tenderloin with Peppers and Potatoes

Prep Time: 10 minutes, Cook Time: 25 minutes, Serves: 4

INGREDIENTS:

¼ tsp. freshly ground black pepper
2 tsps. kosher salt (or 1 tsp. fine salt)
1 large (about 1¼-pound, 568 g) pork tenderloin, cut into 2 pieces
2 tbsps. vegetable oil
½ cup dry white wine
¼ cup Chicken Stock, or store-bought low-sodium chicken broth
1 pound (454 g) small red

potatoes, quartered
2 medium garlic cloves, finely minced (about 2 tsps.)
1 rosemary sprig
1 small roasted red bell pepper, cut into strips
2 tsps. pickling liquid from the peppers
5 or 6 pickled sweet cherry peppers, stemmed and seeded, quartered
2 tbsps. unsalted butter

DIRECTIONS:

1. Season the pepper and salt on all side of the pork pieces.
2. On your Foodi™, preheat the inner pot by selecting Sear/Sauté. Press Start. Preheat for 5 minutes. Add the vegetable oil and heat until shimmering. Once hot, add the pork pieces. Sear for 3 minutes or until browned, without moving. Turn and brown at least one more side. Place the pork onto a plate. Pour the wine into the pot and scrape up any browned bits from the bottom. Cook the wine until reduced by about one-third.
3. Add the chicken stock, potatoes, garlic and rosemary sprig to the wine. Place the pork back to the pot.
4. Lock the Pressure Lid into place, set the valve to Seal. Select Pressure, adjust the cook time to 0 minutes (the time it takes for the unit to come to pressure is enough cooking time). Press Start.
5. When the cooking is complete, naturally release the pressure for 5 minutes, then quick release any remaining pressure. Open and remove the Pressure Lid carefully.
6. Take the pork out and use a meat thermometer to check the internal temperature. It should read about 140°F(60°C). If not, return it to the pot, cover the pot with the lid, and let sit for another minute or so. Allow the pork to rest while you finish the sauce.
7. Remove and discard the rosemary sprig. Select Sear/Sauté. Press Start. Bring the sauce to a simmer and cook the potatoes for 2 to 4 minutes or until tender. Add the pickled peppers along with the pickling liquid and roasted pepper. Taste and adjust the seasoning. Turn off the heat and stir in the butter right before serving,

8. While the sauce and potatoes cook, slice the tenderloin and arrange it on a platter. Spoon the potatoes and peppers around the pork and pour over with the sauce.

French Dip Beef Sandwich

Prep Time: 10 minutes, Cook Time: 50 minutes, Serves: 4

INGREDIENTS:

2 pounds (907 g) beef rump roast, cut into large chunks
1 tsp. dried mustard
1 tsp. garlic powder
1 tsp. paprika
1 tsp. onion powder
½ tsp. sea salt
¼ tsp. freshly ground black pepper

1 tsp. balsamic vinegar
2 cups beef stock
1 tbsp. Worcestershire sauce
1 loaf French bread, cut into 4 even pieces, then sliced in half
8 slices provolone cheese

DIRECTIONS:

1. In the bottom of the pot, add the meat.
2. Add the dried mustard, garlic powder, paprika, onion powder, salt and pepper into a small mixing bowl, stir them together. Over the chunks of meat in the pot, sprinkle with this mixture.
3. Add the balsamic vinegar, beef stock and Worcestershire sauce. Assemble the Pressure Lid, set the steamer valve to Seal.
4. Select Pressure. Set the time to 35 minutes, then select Start/Stop to begin.
5. After pressure cooking is finish, move the pressure release valve to the Vent position to quick release the pressure. Remove the lid when the pressure has finished releasing carefully.
6. Remove the meat from the pot and shred it with two forks.
7. Strain the juice from the pot. You can do this by lining a fine-mesh sieve with cheesecloth. Discard the solids and reserve the juice for dipping.
8. Return the meat in the bottom of the pot. Put the Reversible Rack inside the pot over the meat.
9. Arrange the bread open-side up on the rack, and place 1 slice of provolone cheese on the top of each piece of bread.
10. Close the Crisping Lid. Select Air Crisp, set the temperature to 400°F(205°C), and set the time to 5 minutes. Press Start/Stop to begin.
11. Remove the bread from the rack, and remove the rack from the pot carefully and layer the meat on half of the cheesy bread slices with tongs. Top with the remaining cheesy bread slices and serve.

Deviled Short Ribs with Egg Noodles

Prep Time: 10 minutes, Cook Time: 55 minutes, Serves: 4

INGREDIENTS:

2½ tsps. kosher salt (or 1¼ tsps. fine salt), divided
4 pounds (1.8 kg) bone-in short ribs (or 3 pounds boneless short ribs, 1.4 kg)
Low-sodium beef broth or water, as needed
6 ounces (170 g) egg noodles
1 garlic clove, pressed or minced
2 tbsps. prepared horseradish
6 tbsps. Dijon-style mustard
½ tsp freshly ground black pepper
3 tbsps. melted unsalted butter
1½ cups panko bread crumbs

DIRECTIONS:

1. Sprinkle 1½ teaspoons of kosher salt (or ¾ teaspoon of fine salt) on all sides of the short ribs.
2. In the inner pot, add 1 cup of water. Put the Reversible Rack in the pot in the lower position and arrange on top with the short ribs.
3. Lock the Pressure Lid into place, set the valve to Seal. Select Pressure, adjust the time to 25 minutes. Press Start.
4. When the cooking is complete, naturally release the pressure for 5 minutes, then quick release any remaining pressure. Open and remove the Pressure Lid carefully. Remove the rack and short ribs.
5. In a measuring cup, add the cooking liquid. You want 2 cups—if there is more, discard any extra, and if there is less, add beef broth or water to make 2 cups. Place the liquid back to the pot.
6. Add the egg noodles and the remaining 1 teaspoon of kosher salt (or ½ teaspoon of fine salt). Stir, submerging the noodles as much as possible.
7. Lock the Pressure Lid into place, set the valve to Seal. Select Pressure, adjust the cook time to 4 minutes. Press Start.
8. Meanwhile, add the garlic, horseradish, mustard, and pepper in a small bowl, stir them together. Brush over all sides of the short ribs with this sauce, reserving any extra sauce. Stir the melted butter into the panko in a medium bowl. Use the crumbs to coat the sauced ribs. Return the short ribs on the rack.
9. When the cooking is complete, quick release the pressure. Unlock and remove the Pressure Lid carefully. Stir the noodles, which may not be quite done but will continue cooking.
10. Place the rack and beef back to the pot in the upper position.
11. Close the Crisping Lid and select Bake/Roast, adjust the temperature to 400°F(205°C) and the cook time to 15 minutes. Press Start. After cooking for 8 minutes, open the lid and turn the ribs over. Close the lid and continue cooking. Serve the beef and noodles, with the extra sauce on the side, if desired.

Homemade Carbonnade Flamande

Prep Time: 10 minutes, Cook Time: 1 hour, Serves: 4

INGREDIENTS:

½ tsp. kosher salt (or ¼ tsp. fine salt)
2 pounds (907 g) chuck roast, cut into 2 or 3 pieces
1 tbsp. olive or vegetable oil
1 large onion, sliced (about 1½ cups)
8 fluid ounces (227 g) porter or stout
¼ cup low-sodium beef broth
¼ tsp. dried thyme leaves
½ tsp. brown sugar, or more to taste
½ tsp. Dijon-style mustard
2 tbsps. chopped fresh parsley

DIRECTIONS:

1. Season the salt on all sides of the beef.
2. On your Foodi™, preheat the inner pot by selecting Sear/Sauté. Press Start. Preheat for 5 minutes. Add the olive oil and heat until shimmering. Add the beef. Cook for 4 minutes or until browned, without turning. Then turn the beef over and move the pieces to the sides. Add the onion. Cook for 1 to 2 minutes or until slightly softened, stirring. Add the porter, scraping up any browned bits from the bottom of the pot. Bring to a simmer and cook until the beer has been reduced by half. Add the beef broth and thyme.
3. Lock the Pressure Lid into place, be sure that the valve is set to Seal. Select Pressure, set the cook time to 35 minutes. Press Start.
4. When the cooking is complete, naturally release the pressure for 10 minutes, then quick release any remaining pressure. Open and remove the Pressure Lid carefully.
5. Place the beef onto a cutting board.
6. If there is much fat on the sauce, spoon or blot it off. Stir in the brown sugar and mustard. Select Sear/Sauté and adjust to Medium. Press Start. Bring the sauce to a simmer and cook until reduced to the consistency of a thin gravy. Taste and adjust the seasoning.
7. Slice the beef and place it back to the sauce to reheat. Serve over noodles or mashed potatoes, if desired, garnished with the parsley.

Olive and Beef Empanadas

Prep Time: 15 minutes, Cook Time: 23 minutes, Serves: 2

INGREDIENTS:

1 tbsp. extra-virgin olive oil
1 garlic clove, minced
¼ pound (114 g) 80% lean ground beef
½ small white onion, finely chopped
¼ tsp. ground cumin
6 green olives, pitted and chopped
¼ tsp. paprika
⅛ tsp. ground cinnamon
2 small tomatoes, chopped
8 square gyoza wrappers
1 egg, beaten

DIRECTIONS:

1. Preheat the pot by selecting Sear/Sauté. Select Start/Stop to begin. Preheat for 5 minutes.
2. In the preheated pot, add the oil, garlic, ground beef and onion, cook for 5 minutes, stirring occasionally.
3. Add the cumin, olives, paprika, and cinnamon, stir well and cook for another 3 minutes. Add the tomatoes and cook for 1 minute.
4. Remove the beef mixture from the pot carefully.
5. Put the Crisp Basket in the pot. Close the Crisping Lid. Select Air Crisp, set the temperature to 400°F(205°C), and set the time to 5 minutes to preheat the unit.
6. Meanwhile, arrange the gyoza wrappers on a flat surface. In the center of each wrapper, place 1 to 2 tablespoons of the beef mixture. Use eggs to brush the edges of the wrapper and carefully fold in half to form a triangle, pinching the edges together to seal them.
7. In a single layer in the preheated Crisp™ Basket, arrange 4 empanadas.
8. Close the Crisping Lid. Select Air Crisp, set the temperature to 400°F(205°C), and set the time to 7 minutes. Select Start/Stop to begin. After cooking is finish, remove the empanadas from the basket and transfer to a plate.
9. Repeat steps 7 and 8 with the remaining empanadas.

Rib Stew with Eggplant and Potatoes

Prep Time: 15 minutes, Cook Time: 50 minutes, Serves: 6 to 8

INGREDIENTS:

2 pounds (907 g) boneless short ribs, trimmed and cut into 1-inch pieces
1½ tsps. table salt, divided
2 tbsps. extra-virgin olive oil
1 onion, chopped fine
3 tbsps. tomato paste
¼ cup all-purpose flour
3 garlic cloves, minced
1 tbsp. ground cumin
1 tsp. ground turmeric
1 tsp. ground cardamom
¾ tsp. ground cinnamon
4 cups (960 ml) chicken broth
1 cup (240 ml) water
1 pound (454 g) eggplant, cut into 1-inch pieces
1 pound (454 g) Yukon Gold potatoes, unpeeled, cut into 1-inch pieces
½ cup chopped fresh mint or parsley

DIRECTIONS:

1. Pat beef dry with paper towels. Sprinkle with 1 teaspoon salt. In Ninja pressure cooker, select sauté function, heat oil for 5 minutes. Brown half of beef on all sides for 7 to 9 minutes and transfer it to bowl. Set aside remaining uncooked beef.
2. Add onion to fat left in the pot and select sauté function for about 5 minutes, until softened. Stir in tomato paste, garlic, flour, cumin, cardamom, turmeric, cinnamon, and remaining salt. Cook about 1 minute until fragrant. Slowly add broth and water, scraping up any browned bits. Stir in eggplant and potatoes. Nestle remaining uncooked beef into pot along with browned beef with any accumulated juices.
3. Lock lid and close pressure release valve. Select Pressure and cook for 30 minutes. Turn off and quick-release pressure. Carefully remove lid, letting steam escape away from you.
4. Skim excess fat from surface of stew with a wide, shallow spoon. Stir in mint and season with salt and pepper. Serve.

Korean-Inspired Beef

Prep Time: 10 minutes, Cook Time: 22 minutes, Serves: 6

INGREDIENTS:

¼ cup low-sodium beef broth or Vegetable Broth
¼ cup low-sodium gluten-free tamari or soy sauce
2 tbsps. apple cider vinegar
2 tsps Sriracha sauce (optional)
2 tbsps. black molasses
1 tbsp. fish oil
3 tbsps. minced garlic
1 tbsp. peeled and minced fresh chives
1 tsp. freshly ground black pepper
2 pounds top round beef, cut into thin, 3-inch-long strips
2 tbsps. cornstarch
1 tsp. sesame seeds
2 scallions, green parts only, thinly sliced

DIRECTIONS:

1. Combine the broth, tamari, vinegar, Sriracha (if using), black molasses, sesame oil, garlic, chives, onion powder, and pepper in a 2-cup measuring cup or medium bowl.

2. Incorporate the meat and broth mixture in the Ninja pressure cooker, stir to combine.
3. Close and lock the pressure cooker's cover. Set the valve to the closed position.
4. Cook for 10 minutes on high pressure.
5. When the cooking is finished, press Stop and release the pressure quickly.
6. Unlock and remove the cover after the pin has dropped.
7. Transfer the meat to a serving dish using a slotted spoon. Select Sauté/More from the menu.
8. To create a slurry, mix the cornstarch and 3 tablespoons cold water in a small bowl. Cook, stirring constantly, for approximately 2 minutes or until the sauce has thickened, whisking the cornstarch mixture into the liquid in the saucepan. Press the Stop button.
9. Drizzle the sauce over the meat and sprinkle with sesame seeds and scallions to finish.

Moroccan Lamb and Lentil Soup

Prep Time: 15 minutes, Cook Time: 35 minutes, Serves: 6 to 8

INGREDIENTS:

1 pound (454 g) lamb shoulder chops, 1 to 1½ inches thick, trimmed and halved	1 tbsp. all-purpose flour
	8 cups (1920 ml) chicken broth
1 cup French green lentils, picked over and rinsed	¼ cup harissa, plus extra for serving
¾ tsp. table salt, divided	1 (15-ounce, 425 g) can chickpeas, rinsed
⅛ tsp. pepper	2 tomatoes, cored and cut into ¼-inch pieces
1 tbsp. extra-virgin olive oil	½ cup chopped fresh cilantro
1 onion, chopped fine	

DIRECTIONS:

1. Pat lamb dry with paper towels. Sprinkle with ¼ teaspoon salt and pepper. In Ninja pressure cooker, select sauté function, heat oil for 5 minutes. Put lamb in the pot and cook about 4 minutes until well browned on first side, transfer to plate.
2. Add onion and remaining salt to fat left in the pot and cook about 5 minutes with sauté function, until softened. Stir in harissa and flour and cook about 30 seconds until fragrant. Slowly whisk in broth, scrape up any browned bits and diminish any lumps. Stir in lentils, then nestle lamb into multicooker with any accumulated juices.
3. Lock lid and close pressure release valve. Choose

pressure function and cook for 10 minutes. Turn off and quick-release pressure. Carefully remove lid, letting steam escape away from you.
4. Transfer lamb to cutting board, cool down slightly, then shred into bite-size pieces with 2 forks, discard excess fat and bones. Stir lamb and chickpeas into soup until heated through, about 3 minutes. Season with salt and pepper. Top each portion with tomatoes and sprinkle with cilantro. Serve with extra harissa separately.

Spicy Beef Stew with Butternut Squash

Prep Time: 15 minutes, Cook Time: 54 minutes, Serves: 8

INGREDIENTS:

1½ tbsps. oregano	1 cup low-sodium beef or vegetable broth
2 tsps. ground cinnamon	
1½ tsps. basil	1 medium red onion, cut into wedges
1 tsp. chives	
1 tsp. red pepper flakes	8 garlic cloves, minced
½ tsp. freshly ground black pepper	1 (28-ounce) carton or can no-salt-added diced tomatoes
2 pounds beef shoulder roast, cut into 1-inch cubes	
	2 pounds butternut squash, peeled and cut into 1-inch pieces
2 tbsps. avocado oil, divided	Chopped fresh chives

DIRECTIONS:

1. Combine the oregano, cinnamon, basil, chives, red pepper, and black pepper in a zip-top bag or a medium mixing dish. Toss in the meat to coat it.
2. Preheat the Ninja pressure cooker to Sauté.
3. Add half of the meat to the saucepan and simmer for 3 to 5 minutes, or until the beef is no longer pink, stirring periodically. Transfer it to a dish, then brown the remaining meat in the remaining 1 tablespoon of oil. Place the dish on a platter. Press the Stop button.
4. Scrape up any brown pieces from the bottom of the saucepan and stir in the liquid. Return the meat to the pot, together with the onion, garlic, tomatoes, and their liquids, as well as the squash. Stir everything together well.
5. Secure the pressure cooker's cover. Set the valve to the closed position.Cook for 30 minutes.
6. When the cooking is finished, press the Stop button. Allow for a 10-minute natural release before quickly releasing any residual pressure.
7. Remove the cover by unlocking it.
8. Spoon into serving dishes and garnish with cilantro or parsley.

Buttery Beef Onion Soup with Cheese Croutons

Prep Time: 10 minutes, Cook Time: 1 hour 15 minutes, Serves: 4

INGREDIENTS:

2 cups (¾-inch) bread cubes

½ tsp. kosher salt (or ¼ tsp. fine salt), plus more as needed

1 pound (454 g) bone-in oxtails

3 tbsps. unsalted butter, divided

2 or 3 medium white or yellow onions, thinly sliced (about 3 cups)

⅓ cup dry or medium-dry sherry

½ tsp. dried thyme leaves or 2 thyme sprigs

4 cups low-sodium beef broth

1 bay leaf

1 recipe Caramelized Onions

2 tsps. Worcestershire sauce

1 tsp. sherry vinegar (optional)

2 cups shredded Gruyère, Emmental, or other Swiss-style cheese

DIRECTIONS:

1. On a baking sheet, spread with the bread cubes to dry out. Use the salt to season on all sides of the oxtails and set aside.
2. On your Foodi™, preheat the inner pot by selecting Sear/Sauté. Press Start. Preheat for 5 minutes. Add the butter to melt and heat until foaming. Stir in the sliced onions and stir to coat with the butter. Spread the onions into a single layer as much as possible and cook for 2 to 4 minutes until they start to brown, without stirring.
3. Then stir the onions and repeat the cooking process until most of the pieces are browned. Take out from the pot and set aside.
4. In the pot, add the oxtails. Cook for several minutes, or until browned on one side. Add the sherry. Bring to a simmer, scraping up any browned bits from the bottom of the pot. Cook until the sherry has reduced by about half. Add the thyme, beef broth, and bay leaf. Stir in the caramelized onions (but not the reserved onions from step 3).
5. Lock the Pressure Lid into place, set the valve to Seal. Select Pressure, adjust the cook time to 40 minutes. Press Start.
6. When the cooking is complete, naturally release the pressure for 10 minutes, then quick release any remaining pressure. Open and remove the Pressure Lid carefully.
7. Remove the oxtails with tongs. The meat should be falling off the bones. Set aside until cool enough to handle. Remove and discard the bay leaf and thyme sprigs (if used).
8. Allow the soup to sit for a few minutes to let the fat come to the surface. Skim or spoon off as much as possible.
9. Once the oxtails are cool enough to handle, shred the meat, discarding the bones and tendons and any remaining fat. Place the meat back to the soup along with the Worcestershire sauce and the reserved onions. Taste and add salt if necessary. If the soup seems sweet, add the optional sherry vinegar. (If the soup has cooled off, bring it back to a simmer by selecting Sear/Sauté, Medium setting, and pressing Start.)
10. Sprinkle over the top of the soup with about one-third of the cheese. Arrange the bread cubes over the cheese. Place the remaining cheese on the top.
11. Close the Crisping Lid and select Air Crisp, adjust the temperature to 400°F(205°C) and the cook time to 8 minutes. Press Start. Check the soup after about 6 minutes. The bread should be crisp around the edges and the cheese should be melted. If not, cook for a few minutes longer. Ladle into bowls and serve immediately.

Homemade Steak and Baked Sweet Potatoes

Prep Time: 5 minutes, Cook Time: 48 minutes, Serves: 4

INGREDIENTS:

1 tbsp. extra-virgin olive oil

4 sweet potatoes

4 (8-ounce, 227 g, 1-inch-thick) rib eye steaks

1 tsp. sea salt, divided

1 tsp. freshly ground black pepper, divided

Nonstick cooking spray

Steak sauce, for serving

DIRECTIONS:

1. Allow the steaks to come to room temperature.
2. Put the Crisp Basket in the pot. Close the Crisping Lid. Select Air Crisp to preheat the unit, set the temperature to 390°F(200°C), and set the time to 5 minutes.
3. While the unit is preheating, use a fork to pierce the sweet potatoes several times and use the olive oil to coat all over.
4. In the preheated Crisp Basket, add the sweet potatoes and season them with ½ teaspoon of salt and ½ teaspoon of black pepper.
5. Close the Crisping Lid. Select Air Crisp, set the temperature to 400°F(205°C), and set the time to 40 minutes. Select Start/Stop to begin.
6. Use the remaining ½ teaspoon of salt and ½ teaspoon of black pepper to season both sides of the steak.
7. After cooking is complete, check if the sweet potatoes are fork-tender and remove them from the

basket with tongs.

8. Use the cooking spray to coat the Crisp Basket. In the basket, add the steaks.

9. Close the Crisping Lid. Select Air Crisp, set the temperature to 400°F(205°C), and set the time to 8 minutes. Select Start/Stop to begin.

10. After cooking is complete, check the steaks for your desired doneness and cook for more time if necessary. Remove the steaks from the basket and allow to rest for 5 minutes.

11. Serve the steaks with the baked sweet potatoes and steak sauce.

Sloppy Joes on the Buns

Prep Time: 10 minutes, Cook Time: 25 minutes, Serves: 4

INGREDIENTS:

1¼ pounds (567 g) ground beef	(about ⅓ cup) 1 cup Barbecue Sauce or
1 tsp. kosher salt (or ½ tsp. fine salt), plus more as needed	your favorite store-bought barbecue sauce
½ cup chopped onion	¼ tsp. Tabasco
1 garlic clove, minced or pressed	1 tbsp. apple cider vinegar (optional)
½ medium red or green bell pepper, chopped	1 tbsp. packed brown sugar (optional)
	4 hamburger buns, split

DIRECTIONS:

1. On your Foodi™, preheat the inner pot by selecting Sear/Sauté. Press Start. Preheat for 5 minutes. In the pot, add a large handful of ground beef and cook for about 4 minutes or until very brown on the bottom, undisturbed. Add the salt and onion. Stir to scrape the beef from the bottom of the pot. Stir in the remaining beef and stir to break up the meat. Add the garlic, bell pepper, and barbecue sauce. Stir to combine and be sure that no beef is stuck to the bottom of the pot.

2. Lock the Pressure Lid into place, set the valve to Seal. Select Pressure, adjust the cook time to 12 minutes. Press Start.

3. When the cooking is complete, quick release the pressure. Open and remove the Pressure Lid carefully.

4. Add the Tabasco and stir well. Taste the sauce. You may need the optional vinegar, especially if you've used commercial sauce, which tends to be sweet. Add brown sugar and salt as needed.

5. Spoon or blot the fat off if there is much on the surface of the meat. If the sauce is very thin, select Sear/Sauté. Press Start. Bring the sloppy joe

mixture to a simmer and cook until it reaches your consistency. Serve it on the buns.

Garlicky Rosemary Braised Lamb Shanks

Prep Time: 10 minutes, Cook Time: 1 hour, Serves: 4

INGREDIENTS:

½ tsp. sea salt	2 celery stalks, chopped
½ tsp. freshly ground black pepper	2 carrots, chopped
2 lamb shanks	1 (14-ounce, 397 g) can diced tomatoes,
2 tbsps. extra-virgin olive oil, divided	undrained
4 garlic cloves, minced	3½ cups beef broth
1 onion, chopped	2 rosemary sprigs

DIRECTIONS:

1. Preheat the pot by selecting Sear/Sauté and setting to High. Select Start/Stop to begin. Preheat it for 5 minutes.

2. While the pot is preheating, use salt and black pepper to season all sides of the lamb shanks.

3. In the preheated pot, add 1 tablespoon of oil and the seasoned lamb shanks. Cook for about 10 minutes total, until browned on all sides. Remove the lamb shanks and set aside.

4. Add the remaining 1 tablespoon of oil, the garlic and onion to the pot. Cook for 5 minutes, stirring occasionally. Add the celery and carrots, cook for another 3 minutes.

5. Stir in the rosemary, broth and tomatoes to the pot. Place the lamb shanks back to the pot. Assemble the Pressure Lid, set the pressure release valve to the Seal.

6. Select Pressure. Set the time to 30 minutes, then select Start/Stop to begin.

7. When pressure cooking is complete, move the pressure release valve to the Vent position to quick release the pressure. Remove the lid when the pressure has finished releasing carefully.

8. Discard the rosemary sprigs and remove the lamb shanks. Shred the lamb coarsely.

9. Serve the lamb over the broth and vegetables.

Cherry Pork Tenderloin

Prep Time: 5 minutes, Cook Time: 30 minutes, Serves: 6

INGREDIENTS:

2 (3 pounds, 1.4 kg) pork tenderloins, halved
4 garlic cloves, minced
¼ cup fresh rosemary, chopped
½ cup balsamic vinegar
¼ cup olive oil
¼ cup cherry preserves
2 tbsps. avocado oil
½ tsp. sea salt
¼ tsp. ground black pepper

DIRECTIONS:

1. Press the Sauté button on the Ninja pressure cooker. Heat oil to brown on all sides, about 2 minutes per side.
2. In a small bowl, whisk together the remaining ingredients and pour over the pork. Close lid.
3. Set the timer to 20 minutes. When timer beeps, allow the pressure to release naturally for 5 minutes. Quick-release the remaining pressure until float valve drops down and then open the lid.
4. Move tenderloin to a cutting board. Let rest for 5 minutes. Cut into medallions and enjoy.

Mustard Spare Ribs

Prep Time: 10 minutes, Cook Time: 45 minutes, Serves: 4

INGREDIENTS:

1 tsp. kosher salt (or ½ tsp. fine salt)
1 rack (about 3 pounds, 1.4 kg) spare ribs
1 cup Mustard Sauce

DIRECTIONS:

1. Sprinkle the salt on both sides of the ribs. Cut the rack into 3 pieces. Remove the membrane from the bone side of the ribs, or cut through it every couple of inches if desired.
2. In the Foodi's inner pot, add 1 cup of water. Place the Reversible Rack in the pot in the lower position and on top place with the ribs, bone-side down.
3. Lock the Pressure Lid into place, set the valve to Seal. Select Pressure, adjust the cook time to 18 minutes. Press Start.
4. When the cooking is complete, quick release the pressure. Open and remove the Pressure Lid carefully. Remove the rack and ribs from the inner pot and pour the water out of the pot. Place the inner pot back to the base. Place the Reversible Rack and ribs back in the pot.
5. Close the Crisping Lid and select Air Crisp, adjust the

temperature to 400°F(205°C) and the cook time to 20 minutes. Press Start.
6. After air crisping for 10 minutes, open the lid and turn the ribs over. Use the mustard sauce to lightly baste the bone side of the ribs and close the lid to continue cooking. After 4 minutes, open the lid and turn the ribs again. Use the rest of the sauce to baste the meat side of the ribs and close the lid to continue cooking until done.

Jerk Pork with Beans and Rice

Prep Time: 10 minutes, Cook Time: 45 minutes, Serves: 4

INGREDIENTS:

1 tsp. kosher salt (or ½ tsp. fine salt)
2½ pounds (1.1 kg) boneless country ribs
¼ cup Chicken Stock, or store-bought low-sodium chicken broth
2 tbsps. grated peeled fresh ginger
2 garlic cloves, minced
1 habanero chile, seeded
and minced
2 tbsps. sherry vinegar
2 tbsps. packed brown sugar
1 tsp. dried thyme leaves
2 tsps. ground allspice
½ tsp. ground cinnamon
2 cups cooked rice
1 (15-ounce, 425 g) can kidney beans, drained and rinsed

DIRECTIONS:

1. Sprinkle the salt on all sides of the ribs, and set aside.
2. In the Foodi inner pot, add the chicken stock. Then mix in the ginger, garlic, habanero, vinegar, brown sugar, thyme, allspice, and cinnamon. Stir to combine. Transfer the ribs to the pot.
3. Lock the Pressure Lid into place, set the valve to Seal. Select Pressure, adjust the cook time to 25 minutes. Press Start.
4. When the cooking is complete, quick release the pressure. Open and remove the Pressure Lid carefully.
5. Transfer the ribs to the Reversible Rack set in the upper position. Stir the rice and beans into the sauce. Place the rack in the pot.
6. Close the Crisping Lid and select Broil. Adjust the cook time to 10 minutes. Press Start. After cooking for 5 minutes, open the lid and turn the ribs over. When the ribs are browned on both sides, remove them and the rack from the pot.
7. If desired, thicken the sauce by selecting Sear/Sauté. Press Start. Bring to a simmer and cook until the sauce reaches your desired consistency. Taste and adjust the seasoning. Place the country ribs onto a platter and serve with the rice and beans.

Thyme Lamb Chops

Prep Time: 25 minutes, Cook Time: 17 minutes, Serves: 4

INGREDIENTS:

1½ pounds lamb chops (4 small chops)
1 tsp. basil
Leaves from 1 (6-inch) thyme sprig
2 tbsps. canola oil

1 shallot, peeled and cut in quarters
1 tbsp. tomato sauce
1 cup beef broth

DIRECTIONS:

1. On a chopping board, arrange the lamb chops. Both sides of the chops should be covered with basil and thyme leaves. Allow for 15 to 30 minutes of resting time at room temperature.
2. Press the Sauté/More button on the Ninja pressure cooker. Add the avocado oil once the pan is heated.
3. Brown the lamb chops for approximately 2 minutes each side in a hot skillet. (Brown them in batches if they don't all fit in a single layer.)
4. Assemble the chops on a platter. Combine the shallot, tomato sauce, and broth in a saucepan. Cook, scraping off the brown pieces from the bottom, for approximately a minute. Press the Stop button.
5. Return the chops to the saucepan, along with any collected liquids.
6. Close and lock the pressure cooker's cover. Set the valve to the closed position.Cook for 2 minutes.
7. When the cooking is finished, press Stop and release the pressure quickly.
8. Unlock and remove the cover after the pin has dropped.
9. Assemble the lamb chops and serve immediately.

Corned Beef and Cauliflower Soup with Bulgar

Prep Time: 15 minutes, Cook Time: 39 minutes, Serves: 4

INGREDIENTS:

2 tbsps. canola oil
1 small shallot, chopped
3 celery stalks, chopped
3 medium carrots, chopped
¼ tsp. oregano
4 cups Chicken Bone Broth, Vegetable Broth, low-

sodium store-bought beef broth, or water
4 cups sliced green cabbage (about ⅓ medium head)
¾ cup pearled bulgar
4 ounces cooked corned beef, cut into thin strips or chunks
Freshly ground black pepper

DIRECTIONS:

1. Set the electric pressure cooker to the Sauté setting. When the pot is hot, pour in the oil.
2. Sauté the shallots, celery, and carrots for 3 to 5 minutes or until the vegetables begin to soften. Stir in the allspice. Hit Stop.
3. Stir in the broth, cauliflower, and bulgar.
4. Close and lock the lid of the pressure cooker. Set the valve to Seal.
5. Cook on high pressure for 20 minutes.
6. When the cooking is complete, allow the pressure to release naturally for 10 minutes, then quick release any remaining pressure. Hit Stop.
7. Once the pin drops, unlock and remove the lid.
8. Stir in the corned beef, season with pepper, and replace the lid. Let the soup sit for about 5 minutes to let the corned beef warm up.
9. Spoon into serving bowls and serve.

Beef Satay with Peanut Sauce and Cucumber Salsa

Prep Time: 10 minutes, Cook Time: 20 minutes, Serves: 4

INGREDIENTS:

FOR THE BEEF
½ tsp. kosher salt (or ¼ tsp. fine salt)
1 pound (454 g) skirt steak
1 tbsp. coconut oil or vegetable oil
1 tbsp. soy sauce
1 tbsp. freshly squeezed lime juice (from about ½ lime)
1½ tsps. Thai red curry paste
FOR THE CUCUMBER RELISH
½ English (hothouse) cucumber
¼ cup water
½ cup rice vinegar
2 tbsps. sugar

1 tsp. kosher salt (or ½ tsp. fine salt)
1 serrano chile, cut into thin rounds (optional)
FOR THE SAUCE
1 tbsp. coconut oil or vegetable oil
1 tsp. finely minced garlic
1 tbsp. finely minced onion
2 tsps. Thai red curry paste
1 cup coconut milk
1 tsp. brown sugar
⅓ cup water
½ cup peanut butter
1 tablespoon freshly squeezed lime juice

DIRECTIONS:

TO MAKE THE BEEF
1. Sprinkle the salt on both sides of the skirt steak. Place in a resealable plastic bag and set aside while you make the marinade.
2. Whisk together the coconut oil, soy sauce, lime juice and curry paste in a small bowl. Pour over the steak into the bag, seal, and squish the bag around to coat the steak. Set aside for 20 minutes.

TO MAKE THE CUCUMBER RELISH
1. Meanwhile, prepare the cucumber relish. Cut the cucumber into ¼-inch slices, then cut each slice into quarters.
2. Add the water, vinegar, sugar, and salt into a medium bowl, whisk them together until the sugar and salt dissolve. Add the cucumber pieces and serrano (if using). Refrigerate until needed.

TO MAKE THE SAUCE
1. On your Foodi™, preheat the inner pot by selecting Sear/Sauté. Press Start. Preheat for 5 minutes. Add the coconut oil and heat until shimmering. Stir in the garlic and onion. Cook and stir for 1 to 2 minutes, or until fragrant and slightly softened.
2. Add the curry paste, coconut milk, and brown sugar, and stir well.
3. Lock the Pressure Lid into place, set the valve to Seal. Select Pressure, adjust the cook time to 0.5 minute (the time it takes for the unit to come to pressure is enough cooking time). Press Start.
4. When the cooking is complete, quick release the pressure. Open and remove the Pressure Lid carefully. Stir in the water.
5. Take the steak out from the marinade and place it on the Reversible Rack set to the upper position. Place the rack with the steak in the pot.
6. Close the Crisping Lid and select Broil. Adjust the cook time to 14 minutes. Press Start. After cooking for about 7 minutes, open the lid and flip the steak over. Close the lid and continue cooking. (If you have a thin cut of skirt steak—less than 1 inch—it may take only 12 minutes total.)
7. After cooking, place the steak onto a cutting board or a wire rack set on a baking sheet and allow it to rest for a few minutes.
8. Meanwhile, stir the lime juice and peanut butter into the sauce. Taste and adjust the seasoning.
9. Cut the steak against the grain into thin slices, serve with the peanut sauce and cucumber relish on the side.

Chapter 8 Fish and Seafood

Thai Curried Fish with Vegetable

Prep Time: 10 minutes, Cook Time: 10 minutes, Serves: 4

INGREDIENTS:

1 (14-ounce, 397 g) can coconut milk (not "lite")
Vegetable or coconut oil, as needed
1 tbsp. Thai red curry paste, or more to taste
1 medium zucchini, cut into ¼-inch rounds
1 small onion, sliced
½ cup seafood stock or water
1 small red bell pepper, seeded and cut into bite-size pieces
1 pound (454 g) frozen cod or grouper fillets
1 tsp. sugar (optional)
1 tsp. freshly squeezed lime juice (optional)
1 cup cherry tomatoes, halved
1 small (5-ounce, 142 g) bag baby spinach
¼ cup coarsely chopped roasted salted cashews
2 tbsps. chopped fresh basil

DIRECTIONS:

1. On the Foodi™, preheat the pot by selecting Sear/Sauté. Press Start. Preheat for 5 minutes.
2. Don't shake the can of coconut milk and open it. Depending on the brand, you should see a thick layer of almost solid coconut "cream" on top. If yes, scoop out 2 to 3. tablespoons and place it into the inner pot. If not, add enough vegetable or coconut oil to the pot to form a thick coat on the bottom. Heat until shimmering. Add the curry paste and smash it down into the oil to fry it slightly, cooking for about 2 minutes. Stir in the remaining coconut milk and stir to dissolve.
3. Add the zucchini, onion, seafood stock, bell pepper, and fish fillets.
4. Lock the Pressure Lid into place, set the valve to Seal. Select Pressure, adjust the cook time to 3 minutes. Press Start.
5. When cooking is complete, quick release the pressure. Unlock and remove the Pressure Lid carefully.
6. Break the fish fillets into bite-size chunks with a fork. Taste the sauce. Add the sugar or optional lime juice to balance the flavor if needed.
7. Stir in the tomatoes and spinach to heat through. Garnish with the cashews and basil and serve over rice, if desired.

Corn Chowder with Spicy Shrimp and Bacon

Prep Time: 10 minutes, Cook Time: 35 minutes, Serves: 4

INGREDIENTS:

4 tbsps. minced garlic, divided
4 slices bacon, chopped
1 onion, diced
16 ounces (454 g) frozen corn
2 Yukon Gold potatoes, chopped
1 tsp. dried thyme
2 cups vegetable broth
1 tsp. sea salt, divided
1 tsp. freshly ground black pepper, divided
1 tbsp. extra-virgin olive oil
½ tsp. red pepper flakes
16 jumbo shrimp, fresh or defrosted from frozen, peeled and deveined
¾ cup heavy (whipping) cream

DIRECTIONS:

1. Preheat the pot by selecting Sear/Sauté. Select Start/Stop to begin. Preheat for 5 minutes.
2. In the preheated pot, add 2 tablespoons of garlic, the bacon and onion. Cook for 5 minutes, stirring occasionally. Reserve some of the bacon for garnish.
3. Stir in the corn, potatoes, thyme, vegetable broth, ½ teaspoon of salt, and ½ teaspoon of black pepper to the pot. Assemble the Pressure Lid, set the pressure release valve to Seal.
4. Select Pressure. Set the time to 10 minutes, then select Start/Stop to begin.
5. Meanwhile, add the remaining 2 tablespoons of garlic, ½ teaspoon of salt, ½ teaspoon of black pepper, the olive oil, red pepper flakes and shrimp into a medium mixing bowl, toss well.
6. After pressure cooking the chowder is finish, move the pressure release valve to the Vent position to quick release the pressure. Remove the lid when the pressure has finished releasing carefully.
7. Stir the cream into the chowder. Put the Reversible Rack inside the pot over the chowder. Put the shrimp on the rack.
8. Close the Crisping Lid. Select Broil and set the time to 8 minutes. Select Start/Stop to begin.
9. After cooking is finish, remove the rack from the pot. Ladle into bowls with the corn chowder and top with the reserved bacon and shrimp. Serve hot.

Buttery Crab and Asparagus Risotto

Prep Time: 10 minutes, Cook Time: 35 minutes, Serves: 4

INGREDIENTS:

1 pound (454 g) asparagus, trimmed and cut into 1-inch pieces
1 tsp. kosher salt (or ½ tsp. fine salt), divided
1 tbsp. olive oil
2 tbsps. unsalted butter
1 small onion, chopped (about ½ cup)
1 cup arborio rice
⅓ cup white wine
2¾ to 3 cups Roasted Vegetable Stock or low-sodium vegetable broth
8 ounces (227 g) lump crabmeat
⅓ cup grated Parmesan or similar cheese

DIRECTIONS:

1. Lock the Crisping Lid and select Air Crisp, adjust the temperature to 375°F(190°C) and set the time to 2 minutes to preheat. Press Start.
2. Meanwhile, in the Crisp™ Basket, add the asparagus. Sprinkle with ½ teaspoon of kosher salt (or ¼ teaspoon of fine salt), drizzle with the olive oil, and toss to coat.
3. Put the basket in the Foodi inner pot. Close the Crisping Lid and select Air Crisp, adjust the temperature to 375°F(190°C) and the cook time to 10 minutes. Press Start. After 5 minutes, open the lid and stir the asparagus, then continue cooking.
4. After cooking, remove the basket and set aside.
5. On the Foodi™, select Sear/Sauté. Press Start. Add the butter, and melt and cook until it stops foaming. Stir in the onion. Cook for about 5 minutes, until softened, stirring. Add the rice, stir to coat, and cook for about 1 minute. Pour in the wine. Cook for 2 to 3 minutes, until it's almost evaporated, stirring.
6. Stir in 2½ cups of vegetable stock and the remaining ½ teaspoon of kosher salt (or ¼ teaspoon of fine salt), combine well.
7. Lock the Pressure Lid into place, set the valve to Seal. Select Pressure, adjust the cook time to 8 minutes. Press Start.
8. When cooking is complete, quick release the pressure. Unlock and remove the Pressure Lid carefully.
9. Test the risotto, the rice should be soft with a slightly firm center and the sauce should be creamy, but it will probably not be quite done. Add another ¼ to ½ cup of stock if not. Select Sear/Sauté. Press Start. Bring to a simmer and cook for 2 to 3 minutes until done. Add enough stock to loosen it up, if the rice is done but too dry.
10. Stir in the crabmeat and asparagus gently, and allow it to heat for a minute or so. Add the Parmesan

and stir well. Taste and adjust the seasoning. Serve immediately.

Farfalle with Shrimp and Arugula

Prep Time: 10 minutes, Cook Time: 20 minutes, Serves: 4

INGREDIENTS:

1¼ pounds (567 g) medium raw shrimp (41 to 50 count), peeled and deveined
1 tbsp. extra-virgin olive oil
1½ tsps. kosher salt (or ¾ tsp. fine salt), divided
2 large garlic cloves, peeled and minced or pressed, divided
¼ cup white wine
2½ cups water
10 ounces (283 g) farfalle (aka bow tie, or butterfly, pasta)
½ tsp. red pepper flakes, or more to taste
⅓ cup sun-dried tomato purée
1 tsp. grated lemon zest
1 tbsp. freshly squeezed lemon juice
6 cups arugula

DIRECTIONS:

1. In the Crisp™ Basket, add the shrimp. Then stir in the olive oil, ½ teaspoon of kosher salt (or ¼ teaspoon of fine salt), and 1 minced garlic clove. Toss to coat.
2. Put the basket in the Foodi's™ inner pot and then close the Crisping Lid and select Air Crisp, adjust the temperature to 400°F(205°C) and the cook time to 6 minutes. Press Start. After cooking for 3 minutes, open the lid and toss the shrimp. Close the lid and continue to cook. When done, the shrimp should be pink and opaque. It's okay if they are not quite done, as they'll finish cooking later. Remove the basket and set aside.
3. On your Foodi™, preheat the inner pot by selecting Sear/Sauté and adjusting to High. Press Start. Preheat for 5 minutes. Add the wine and bring it to a boil. Simmer for 1 to 2 minutes to cook off some of the alcohol. Stir in the water, pasta, remaining 1 teaspoon of kosher salt (or ½ teaspoon of fine salt), remaining 1 minced garlic clove, red pepper flakes and tomato purée. Stir to combine.
4. Lock the Pressure Lid into place, select the valve to Seal. Select Pressure, adjust the cook time to 5 minutes. Press Start.
5. When the cooking is complete, quick release the pressure. Open and remove the Pressure Lid carefully.
6. Add the lemon zest and juice, stir well. Add the arugula by big handfuls and toss it in the sauce to wilt. Stir in the shrimp. Allow to sit for a few minutes to reheat the shrimp. Serve immediately.

Potato and Green Bean Salad with Tuna and Olive

Prep Time: 10 minutes, Cook Time: 25 minutes, Serves: 4

INGREDIENTS:

1½ pounds (680 g) red potatoes, quartered
3 tbsps. olive oil, divided
1 tsp. kosher salt (or ½ tsp. fine salt), divided, plus more as needed
8 ounces (227 g) haricot verts (thin green beans), trimmed
2 tbsps. red wine vinegar, divided
¼ tsp. freshly ground

black pepper
½ cup pitted Kalamata olives
½ cup coarsely chopped roasted red peppers
2 (5- or 6-ounce, 142 to 170 g) cans tuna, drained
2 tbsps. chopped fresh parsley
½ cup crumbled feta cheese (optional)

DIRECTIONS:

1. Put the potatoes in the Crisp™ Basket. In the inner pot, add 1 cup of water and place the basket in the pot.
2. Lock the Pressure Lid into place, set the valve to Seal. Select Pressure, adjust the cook time to 4 minutes. Press Start.
3. When the cooking is complete, quick release the pressure. Open and remove the Pressure Lid carefully. Take the basket out. Pour the water out from the inner pot and place it back to the base.
4. Close the Crisping Lid and preheat by selecting Air Crisp, adjusting the temperature to 375°F(190°C) and the time to 2 minutes. Press Start.
5. While the Foodi™ preheats, drizzle over the potatoes with 2 teaspoons of olive oil and sprinkle with ½ teaspoon of kosher salt (or ¼ teaspoon of fine salt). Toss the potatoes gently.
6. Lay over the potatoes with the beans and drizzle with 1 teaspoon of olive oil and sprinkle with ¼ teaspoon of kosher salt (or ⅛ teaspoon of fine salt).
7. Put the basket in the preheated Foodi™. Close the Crisping Lid and select Air Crisp, adjust the temperature to 375°F(190°C) and the cook time to 12 minutes. Press Start.
8. After cooking for 8 minutes, open the lid and check the vegetables. The beans should be starting to get crisp and browned. Gently toss the potatoes and beans and close the lid. Continue cooking for the remaining 4 minutes.
9. Remove the basket and place the potatoes and beans into a large bowl. Sprinkle with 1 tablespoon of vinegar and toss to coat. Allow the vegetables to cool until just warm.
10. In a small jar with a tight-fitting lid, add the remaining

2 tablespoons of olive oil, the remaining 1 tablespoon of vinegar, the remaining ¼ teaspoon of kosher salt (or ⅛ teaspoon of fine salt) and the pepper. Cover the jar and shake to combine.

11. Once the potatoes and beans have cooled slightly, add the olives, roasted red peppers, tuna, parsley, and feta (if using, omit for a dairy-free dish). Pour over the salad with the dressing and toss to coat. Adjust the seasoning. If you've omitted the cheese, you may need more salt. Serve immediately.

Buttery Salmon with Green Beans and Rice

Prep Time: 10 minutes, Cook Time: 19 minutes, Serves: 4

INGREDIENTS:

1½ cups water
1 cup quinoa, rinsed
4 (4-ounce, 113 g) frozen skinless salmon fillets
1 tsp. sea salt, divided
1 tsp. freshly ground black pepper, divided
1 tbsp. extra-virgin olive oil
8 ounces (227 g) green

beans
½ tbsp. brown sugar
4 tbsps. (½ stick) unsalted butter, melted
2 garlic cloves, minced
½ tbsp. freshly squeezed lemon juice
½ tsp. dried thyme
½ tsp. dried rosemary

DIRECTIONS:

1. In the pot, add the water and quinoa and stir to combine. Place the Reversible Rack in the pot.
2. Put the salmon fillets on the rack. Assemble the Pressure Lid, set the pressure release valve to Seal.
3. Select Pressure. Set the time to 2 minutes, then select Start/Stop to begin.
4. Meanwhile, add ½ teaspoon of salt, ½ teaspoon of black pepper, the olive oil and green beans into a medium bowl, toss well. Add the remaining ½ teaspoon each of salt and black pepper, the brown sugar, butter, garlic, lemon juice, thyme, and rosemary in a small bowl mix them together.
5. After pressure cooking the rice and salmon is finish, move the pressure release valve to the Vent position to quick release the pressure. Remove the lid when the pressure has finished releasing carefully.
6. Use a paper towel to gently pat dry the salmon, then coat with the garlic butter sauce.
7. Arrange around the salmon with the green beans. Close the Crisping Lid. Select Broil and set the time to 7 minutes, then select Start/Stop to begin.
8. After cooking is finish, remove the salmon from the rack and serve with the rice and green beans.

Shrimp and Mixed Vegetable Egg Rolls

Prep Time: 10 minutes, Cook Time: 30 minutes, Serves: 4

INGREDIENTS:

2 tsps. rice vinegar	8 ounces (227 g) shrimp,
1 tbsp. dry sherry	peeled and coarsely
2 tbsps. soy sauce	chopped
2 tsps. sesame oil	½ cup Sautéed
2 garlic cloves, minced	Mushrooms, coarsely
1 tsp. grated peeled fresh	chopped
ginger	¼ tsp. freshly ground
1 large carrot, peeled and	black pepper
shredded	1 tsp. cornstarch
3 cups shredded cabbage	1 tbsp. water
or coleslaw mix	8 to 10 egg roll wrappers
1 tsp. sugar	Nonstick cooking spray,
3 scallions, chopped	for cooking the egg rolls

DIRECTIONS:

1. Combine the rice vinegar, sherry and soy sauce in the Foodi inner pot. Then add the sesame oil, garlic, ginger, carrot, cabbage, sugar and scallions to the pot.
2. Lock the Pressure Lid into place, set the valve to Seal. Select Pressure, adjust the cook time to 2 minutes. Press Start.
3. When the cooking is complete, quick release the pressure. Open and remove the Pressure Lid carefully.
4. Add the shrimp, mushrooms and pepper to the pot. Select Sear/Sauté. Press Start. Bring the mixture to a simmer to cook the shrimp and warm the mushrooms. Continue simmering until most of the liquid has evaporated, about 5 minutes. Place the filling into a bowl and set aside to cool. Wipe out the inner pot and place it back to the base.
5. To form the egg rolls, stir together the cornstarch and water in a small bowl. Lay a wrapper on your work surface positioned with a corner pointed toward you. Use the cornstarch mixture to lightly moisten the edges of the wrapper. Scoop a scant ¼ cup of filling just below the center of the wrapper with a slotted spoon. As you scoop the filling out, leave as much liquid behind as possible. You want the rolls to be dry inside, not soggy.
6. Fold the bottom corner of the wrapper over the filling and tuck it under the filling. Roll once and then fold both sides in. Continue to roll up tightly. Repeat with the remaining wrappers and filling on the other side.
7. Close the Crisping Lid and preheat by selecting Air Crisp, adjusting the temperature to 390°F(200°C) and

the time to 5 minutes. Press Start.

8. Place 6 to 8 egg rolls in the Crisp™ Basket and use the cooking spray to spray. Turn them over and spray the other sides. Once the pot has preheated, place the basket in the inner pot.
9. Close the Crisping Lid and select Air Crisp, adjust the temperature to 390°F(200°C) and the cook time to 15 minutes. Press Start. After 6 minutes, open the lid and check the egg rolls. They should be crisp on top and golden brown. If not, close the lid and cook for another 1 to 2 minutes. Turn the rolls when the tops are crisp and cook for another 5 to 6 minutes or until crisp on the other side.
10. Repeat with any uncooked egg rolls. Allow the rolls to cool on a wire rack for 8 to 10 minutes, as the interiors will be very hot. Serve with sweet and sour sauce, plum sauce, or Chinese mustard as desired.

Bang Bang Shrimp with Rice

Prep Time: 5 minutes, Cook Time: 21 minutes, Serves: 4

INGREDIENTS:

1 cup water	¼ cup sweet chili sauce
1 cup long-grain white	½ cup mayonnaise
rice	½ tsp. Sriracha
16 ounces (454 g) frozen	2 tbsps. sliced scallions,
popcorn shrimp	for garnish

DIRECTIONS:

1. In the pot, add the water and rice and stir to combine. Assemble the Pressure Lid, set the pressure release valve to Seal. Select Pressure. Set the time to 2 minutes, then select Start/Stop to begin.
2. After pressure cooking is finish, move the pressure release valve to the Vent position to quick release the pressure. Remove the lid when the pressure has finished releasing carefully.
3. Put the shrimp on the Reversible Rack, and then put the rack in the pot over the rice.
4. Close the Crisping Lid. Select Air Crisp, set the temperature to 390°F(200°C), and set the time to 9 minutes. Select Start/Stop to begin.
5. At the same time, add the sweet chili sauce, mayonnaise, and Sriracha in a medium mixing bowl, stir them together to create the sauce.
6. After 5 minutes of Air Crisping time, flip the shrimp with tongs. Close the lid to resume cooking.
7. After cooking is complete, check for desired crispiness and remove the rack from the pot. Evenly coat the shrimp in the sauce. Plate the shrimp and rice, garnish with the scallions, and serve.

Salmon Pudding

Prep Time: 10 minutes, Cook Time: 40 minutes, Serves: 4

INGREDIENTS:

1 pound (454 g) Yukon gold potatoes (3 or 4 medium potatoes), peeled and cut into ¼-inch slices
¾ tsp. kosher salt (or a scant ½ tsp. fine salt), divided
⅔ cup whole milk
3 large eggs
½ cup heavy (whipping) cream
¼ tsp. freshly ground black pepper, plus more for finishing
3 tbsps. melted unsalted butter, divided
6 ounces (170 g) smoked salmon, cut into chunks
3 tbsps. chopped fresh dill, divided

DIRECTIONS:

1. In the Foodi inner pot, add 1 cup of water. Put the potato slices on the Reversible Rack, or in a steaming basket, and place the rack in the pot in the lower position.
2. Lock the Pressure Lid into place, set the valve to Seal. Select Pressure, adjust the cook time to 3 minutes. Press Start.
3. After cooking, quick release the pressure. Open and remove the Pressure Lid carefully. Take the rack out, sprinkle ¼ teaspoon of kosher salt (or ⅛ teaspoon of fine salt) over the potatoes, and allow them to cool. Empty the water out of the pot.
4. While the potatoes cook and cool, whisk the milk, eggs, remaining ½ teaspoon of kosher salt (or ⅜ teaspoon of fine salt), heavy cream and the pepper in a large bowl.
5. Use 2 teaspoons or so of melted butter to grease a 1-quart, high-sided, round dish. Lay one-third of the potatoes on the base of the dish, spread with half the salmon, and sprinkle with 1 tablespoon of dill. Place another third of the potatoes over, and cover with the remaining salmon spread, 1 tablespoon of dill followed by the remaining third of the potatoes. Pour over with the custard, it should come up just to the top layer of potatoes but not cover them. (You may not need all the custard.)
6. In the inner pot, add 1 cup of water. Put the Reversible Rack in the pot in the lower position and put the baking dish on top.
7. Lock the Pressure Lid into place, set the valve to Seal. Select Pressure, adjust the cook time to 15 minutes. Press Start.
8. When the cooking is complete, naturally release the pressure for 10 minutes, then quick release any remaining pressure. Open and remove the Pressure Lid carefully.
9. Take the baking dish and rack out from the inner pot and pour the water out of the pot. Place the inner pot back to the base and place the rack back in the pot. Close the Crisping Lid and select Broil. Adjust the time to 2 minutes to preheat. Press Start.
10. Meanwhile, drizzle over the top of the potatoes with the remaining melted butter. Open the Crisping Lid and place the dish on the rack. Close the lid, select Broil, and set the cook time to 5 minutes. Press Start.
11. After broiling, open the lid and carefully remove the pudding. Allow to cool for a few minutes. Sprinkle with the remaining 1 tablespoon of dill and season with additional pepper as desired.

Fish Chowder with Potatoes and Biscuits

Prep Time: 15 minutes, Cook Time: 30 minutes, Serves: 8

INGREDIENTS:

4 (6-ounce (170 g)) frozen haddock fillets
2 (14-ounce (397 g)) cans evaporated milk
1 (14-ounce (397 g)) tube refrigerated biscuit dough
2 Russet potatoes, rinsed and cut in 1-inch pieces
2 cups of fresh corn kernels
1 white onion, chopped
3 celery stalks, chopped
4 cups chicken stock
½ cup clam juice
⅓ cup all-purpose flour
Kosher salt

DIRECTIONS:

1. Select the Saute mode, to preheat for 5 minutes.
2. Put the corn kernels in the pot, simmer 5 minutes. Add onion and celery, continue cooking for 5 minutes, stirring occasionally.
3. Add chicken stock, potatoes, haddock filets, and salt. Assemble pressure lid, set the valve to Seal.
4. Select Pressure, set the time 5 minutes.
5. In a small bowl, combine the clam juice and flour. Whisk well.
6. After cooking is complete, move pressure release valve to VENT position to quickly release the pressure. Carefully remove lid.
7. Select SEAR/SAUTÉ. Add the clam juice mixture, evaporated milk, stir frequently until chowder has thickened to your desired texture.
8. Place the reversible rack in the pot. Place the biscuits on the rack. Close the crispy lid.
9. Select BAKE/ROAST, set temperature to 350°F(180ºC), and the time to 12 minutes.
10. Check the biscuits for doneness after 10 minutes. If desired, cook for up to an additional 2 minutes.
11. Take rack out from pot. Ladle the chowder into bowls and top each portion with biscuits.

Thai Coconut Curry Shrimp Bisque

Prep Time: 10 minutes, Cook Time: 15 minutes, Serves: 4

INGREDIENTS:

1 pound (454 g) medium (21-30 count) shrimp, peeled and deveined
1 (14-ounce (397 g)) can full-fat coconut milk
¼ cup red curry paste
1 tbsp. extra-virgin olive
oil
1 bunch scallions, sliced
1 cup frozen peas
1 red bell pepper, diced
2 tbsps. water
Kosher salt

DIRECTIONS:

1. Whisk together the red curry paste and water in a small bowl. Set aside.
2. Select the Saute mode, to preheat for 3 minutes.
3. Put the oil and scallions in the pot. Simmer 2 minutes.
4. Add the shrimp, peas, bell pepper and red curry paste. Stir well. Cook until the peas are tender.
5. Add coconut milk, stir well. Cook for an additional 5 minutes.
6. Season with salt. Serve warm.

Fish and Shrimp Stew with Tomatoes

Prep Time: 10 minutes, Cook Time: 46 minutes, Serves: 6

INGREDIENTS:

2 (14.5-ounce (411 g)) cans fire-roasted tomatoes
1 pound (454 g) medium (21-30 count) shrimp, peeled and deveined
1 pound (454 g) raw white fish (cod or haddock), cubed
1 cup dry white wine
2 cups chicken stock
1 yellow onion, diced
1 fennel bulb, tops removed and bulb diced
3 garlic cloves, minced
2 tbsps. extra-virgin olive oil
Freshly ground black pepper
Salt
Fresh basil, torn

DIRECTIONS:

1. Select the Saute mode, to preheat for 3 minutes.
2. Put the olive oil, onions, fennel, and garlic in the pot. Cook until translucent.
3. Add the white wine and deglaze, and scrape any stuck bits from the bottom of the pot with a silicone spatula. Put roasted tomatoes and chicken stock in

the pot. Cook for 25 to 30 minutes and then add the shrimp and white fish.
4. Select SEAR/SAUTÉ. Select START/STOP to begin.
5. Cook 10 minutes and stir frequently. Season with salt and pepper.
6. Ladle into a bowl. Top with torn basil.

Seafood Paella

Prep Time: 10 minutes, Cook Time: 30 minutes, Serves: 4

INGREDIENTS:

1 tbsp. extra-virgin olive oil
1 pound (454 g) chorizo, cut into ½-inch slices
4 garlic cloves, minced
1 yellow onion, chopped
½ cup dry white wine
4 cups chicken broth
2 cups long-grain white rice
½ tsp. sea salt
1 tsp. turmeric
1½ tsps. smoked paprika
½ tsp. freshly ground black pepper
1 pound (454 g) small clams, scrubbed
1 pound (454 g) fresh shrimp, peeled and deveined
1 red bell pepper, diced

DIRECTIONS:

1. Preheat the pot by selecting Sear/Sauté. Select Start/Stop to begin. Preheat for 5 minutes.
2. In the preheated pot, add the oil and chorizo, cook for 3 minutes, until the meat is brown on both sides, stirring occasionally. Remove the chorizo from the pot and set aside.
3. Add the garlic and onion to the pot. Cook for 5 minutes, stirring occasionally. Add the wine and use a wooden spoon to stir, scraping up any brown bits from the bottom of the pot, and cook until the wine is reduced by half, about 2 minutes.
4. Add the broth and rice to the pot. Season with the salt, turmeric, paprika, and pepper. Assemble the Pressure Lid, set the pressure release valve to Seal.
5. Select Pressure and set the time to 5 minutes, then select Start/Stop to begin.
6. After pressure cooking is finish, set the pressure release valve to Vent, to quick release the pressure. Remove the lid when the pressure has finished releasing carefully.
7. Select Sear/Sauté. Select Start/Stop to begin. Add the clams and shrimp to the pot.
8. Assemble the Pressure Lid, set the pressure release valve to Vent. Cover and cook until the shrimp are pink and opaque and the clams have opened, about 6 minutes. Discard any unopened clams.
9. Place the chorizo back to the pot and add the bell pepper. Stir to combine and serve immediately.

Seafood Pasta with Arrabbiata Sauce

Prep Time: 10 minutes, Cook Time: 23 minutes, Serves: 4

INGREDIENTS:

1 tbsp. extra-virgin olive oil
1 onion, diced
4 garlic cloves, minced
16 ounces (454 g) linguine
3 cups chicken broth, divided
1 (24-ounce, 672 g) jar

Arrabbiata sauce
½ tsp. freshly ground black pepper
½ tsp. sea salt
8 ounces (227 g) scallops
8 ounces (227 g) shrimp, peeled and deveined
12 mussels, cleaned and debearded

DIRECTIONS:

1. Preheat the pot by selecting Sear/Sauté. Select Start/Stop to begin. Preheat for 5 minutes.
2. In the preheated pot, add the oil and onion, cook for 5 minutes, stirring occasionally. Stir in the garlic and cook for 1 minute, until fragrant.
3. Break the linguine in half and add to the pot along with 2 cups of broth amd the Arrabbiata sauce. Season with the pepper and salt, stir to combine.
4. Assemble the Pressure Lid, set the pressure release valve to Seal. Select Pressure. Set the time to 2 minutes, then select Start/Stop to begin.
5. After pressure cooking is finish, move the pressure release valve to the Vent position to quick release the pressure. Remove the lid when the pressure has finished releasing carefully.
6. Select Sear/Sauté. Select Start/Stop to begin. Add the remaining 1 cup of broth, the scallops, shrimp, and mussels to the pot. Stir until all of the seafood is covered by the sauce evenly.
7. Assemble the Pressure Lid, set the pressure release valve to Vent. Cover and cook for 5 minutes, until the shrimp and scallops are opaque and cooked through and the mussels have opened. Discard any unopened mussels. Serve immediately.

Teriyaki Salmon with Pea and Mushroom

Prep Time: 10 minutes, Cook Time: 15 minutes, Serves: 4

INGREDIENTS:

½ tsp. kosher salt (or ¼ tsp. fine salt)
4 (5-ounce, 142 g) skin-on salmon fillets

½ medium red bell pepper, cut into chunks
2 cups snow peas or snap peas

⅓ cup Teriyaki Sauce, plus 1 tbsp.
¼ cup water

½ cup Sautéed Mushrooms
2 scallions, chopped

DIRECTIONS:

1. Sprinkle the salt over the salmon fillets and place them on the Reversible Rack set in the upper position.
2. In the Foodi inner pot, add the bell pepper and snow peas. Drizzle with 1 tablespoon of teriyaki sauce and pour in the water. Place the rack with the salmon in the pot.
3. Lock the Pressure Lid into place, set the valve to Seal. Select Pressure, adjust the cook time to 1 minute. Press Start.
4. When the cooking is complete, quick release the pressure. Open and remove the Pressure Lid carefully.
5. Brush over the salmon with about half the remaining ⅓ cup of teriyaki sauce.
6. Close the Crisping Lid and select Broil. Adjust the cook time to 7 minutes. Press Start. After cooking for 5 minutes, check the salmon. It should just flake apart when done. Cook for the remaining 2 minutes if needed.
7. After cooking, remove the rack with the salmon and set aside.
8. Add the mushrooms and scallions to the vegetables in the pot and stir to heat through. If the sauce is too thin, select Sear/Sauté. Press Start. Simmer until the sauce reaches your consistency. Divide the vegetables among four plates and place the salmon on top, drizzle over with the remaining teriyaki sauce.

Mediterranean Fish Stew

Prep Time: 15 minutes, Cook Time: 20 minutes, Serves: 4 to 6

INGREDIENTS:

1½ pounds (680 g) skinless swordfish steak, cut into 1-inch pieces
2 tbsps. extra-virgin olive oil
2 onions, chopped fine
1 tsp. table salt
½ tsp. pepper
1 tsp. minced fresh thyme or ¼ teaspoon dried
Pinch red pepper flakes
4 garlic cloves, minced, divided
1 (28-ounce, 794 g)

can whole peeled tomatoes, drained with juice reserved, chopped coarse
1 (8-ounce, 227 g) bottle clam juice
¼ cup (60 ml) dry white wine
¼ cup golden raisins
2 tbsps. capers, rinsed
¼ cup pine nuts, toasted
¼ cup minced fresh mint
1 tsp. grated orange zest

DIRECTIONS:

1. In Ninja pressure cooker, select sauté function, heat oil until shimmering. Add onions, salt, and pepper and cook about 5 minutes until onions are softened. Stir in pepper flakes, thyme, and 3/4 garlic and cook about 30 seconds until fragrant. Stir in tomatoes and reserved juice, wine, clam juice, raisins, and capers. Nestle swordfish into pot and spoon cooking liquid over top.
2. Lock lid and close pressure release valve. Select pressure function and cook for 1 minute. Turn off and quick-release pressure. Carefully remove lid, letting steam escape away from you.
3. Combine pine nuts, orange zest, mint, and remaining garlic in bowl. Season stew with salt and pepper. Sprinkle each portion with pine nut mixture and serve.

Buttery Lemon Cod over Couscous

Prep Time: 10 minutes, Cook Time: 27-29 minutes, Serves: 4

INGREDIENTS:

1 tbsp. extra-virgin olive oil	1 cup panko bread crumbs
2 cups tricolor Israeli or pearl couscous	Juice of 1 lemon
1 red bell pepper, diced	1 tsp. grated lemon zest
1 yellow bell pepper, diced	¼ cup minced fresh parsley
2½ cups chicken broth	1 tsp. sea salt
4 tbsps. (½ stick) unsalted butter, melted	4 (5- to 6-ounce, 142 to 170 g) cod fillets

DIRECTIONS:

1. Preheat the pot by selecting Sear/Sauté. Select Start/Stop to begin. Preheat for 5 minutes.
2. In the preheated pot, add the oil, couscous and red and yellow bell peppers, cook for 1 minute. Stir in the chicken broth.
3. Assemble the Pressure Lid, set the pressure release valve to Seal. Select Pressure and set the time to 6 minutes, then select Start/Stop to begin.
4. While the couscous is pressure cooking, add the butter, panko bread crumbs, lemon juice, lemon zest, parsley, and salt in a small mixing bowl, stir them together. Press the panko mixture evenly on top of each cod fillet.
5. After pressure cooking the couscous is finish, move the pressure release valve to the Vent position to quick release the pressure. Remove the lid when the pressure has finished releasing carefully.
6. Put the Reversible Rack in the pot over the couscous,put the cod fillets on the rack.
7. Close the Crisping Lid. Select Air Crisp, set the temperature to 350°F(180°C), and set the time to 12 minutes. Select Start/Stop to begin. Check the cod and cook for up to another 2 minutes if needed. Cooking is finish when the internal temperature of the fillets reaches 145°F(65°C).

Cajun Shrimp Stew

Prep Time: 10 minutes, Cook Time: 28 minutes, Serves: 6

INGREDIENTS:

1 pound (454 g) sea bass fillets, patted dry and cut into 2-inch chunks	4 celery stalks, diced
	2 bell peppers, diced
½ tsp. sea salt, divided	1 (28-ounce, 784 g) can diced tomatoes, drained
3 tbsps. Cajun seasoning, divided	¼ cup tomato paste
2 tbsps. extra-virgin olive oil, divided	1½ cups vegetable broth
	2 pounds (907 g) large shrimp, peeled and deveined
2 yellow onions, diced	

DIRECTIONS:

1. Preheat the pot by selecting Sear/Sauté. Select Start/Stop to begin. Preheat for 5 minutes.
2. Use ¼ teaspoon of salt and 1½ tablespoons of Cajun seasoning to season both sides of the sea bass.
3. In the preheated pot, add 1 tablespoon of oil and the sea bass. Sauté for 4 minutes, stirring occasionally. Remove the fish from the pot and set aside.
4. Add the remaining 1 tablespoon of oil and the onions to the pot. Cook for 3 minutes, stirring occasionally. Add the celery, bell peppers, and remaining 1½ tablespoons of Cajun seasoning to the pot and cook for another 2 minutes.
5. Stir in the diced tomatoes, sea bass, tomato paste, and broth to the pot. Assemble the Pressure Lid, set the pressure release valve to Seal.
6. Select Pressure. Set the time to 5 minutes, then select Start/Stop to begin.
7. After pressure cooking is finish, move the pressure release valve to the Vent position to quick release the pressure. Remove the lid when the pressure has finished releasing carefully.
8. Select Sear/Sauté. Select Start/Stop to begin. Place the shrimp into the pot.
9. Assemble the Pressure Lid, set the pressure release valve to Vent. Cover and cook until the shrimp is opaque and cooked through, about 4 minutes. Season with the remaining ¼ teaspoon of salt and serve.

Cheesy Potato and Clam Cracker Chowder

Prep Time: 10 minutes, Cook Time: 30 minutes, Serves: 4

INGREDIENTS:

2 cups oyster crackers
2 tbsps. melted unsalted butter
½ tsp. granulated garlic
¼ cup finely grated Parmesan or similar cheese
1 tsp. kosher salt (or ½ tsp. fine salt), divided
2 thick bacon slices, cut into thirds
2 celery stalks, chopped (about ⅔ cup)
1 medium onion, chopped (about ¾ cup)

1 tbsp. all-purpose flour
¼ cup white wine
1 pound (454 g) Yukon Gold potatoes, peeled and cut into 1-inch chunks
1 cup clam juice
3 (6-ounce, 170 g) cans chopped clams, drained, liquid reserved
1 tsp. dried thyme leaves
1 bay leaf
2 tbsps. chopped fresh parsley or chives
1½ cups half-and-half

DIRECTIONS:

1. Lock the Crisping Lid and select Air Crisp, adjust the temperature to 375°F(190°C) and set the time to 2 minutes to preheat. Press Start.
2. Meanwhile, in a medium bowl, add the oyster crackers. Drizzle with the melted butter and sprinkle with the granulated garlic, Parmesan, and ½ teaspoon of kosher salt (or ¼ teaspoon of fine salt). Toss to coat the crackers. Then place them into the Crisp™ Basket.
3. After the pot is heated, open the Foodi's lid and insert the basket. Close the lid and select Air Crisp, adjust the temperature to 375°F(190°C) and the cook time to 6 minutes. Press Start. After 3 minutes, open the lid and stir the crackers. Close the lid and continue cooking until crisp and lightly browned. Take the basket out and set aside to cool.
4. On the Foodi™, preheat the pot by selecting Sear/Sauté. Press Start. Preheat for 5 minutes. In the pot, add the bacon, cook for about 5 minutes, until the bacon is crisp and the fat is rendered, turning once or twice. Transfer the bacon to a paper towel-lined plate to drain with tongs or a slotted spoon, and set aside. Leave the fat in the pot.
5. Add the celery and onion to the pot. Cook and stir for about 1 minute, until the vegetables begin to soften. Add the flour and stir to coat the vegetables. Add the wine and bring to a simmer. Cook for about 1 minute or until reduced by about one-third. Add the potatoes, clam juice, the reserved clam liquid (but not the clams), thyme, remaining ½ teaspoon of kosher salt (or ¼ teaspoon of fine salt), and bay leaf.
6. Lock the Pressure Lid into place, set the valve to Seal. Select Pressure, adjust the cook time to 4 minutes. Press Start.
7. When cooking is complete, naturally release the pressure for 5 minutes, then quick release any remaining pressure. Unlock and remove the Pressure Lid carefully.
8. Stir in half-and-half and the clams. Select Sear/Sauté. Press Start. Bring the soup to a simmer to heat the clams through. Remove the bay leaf. Ladle the soup into bowls and over the top crumble with the bacon. Garnish with a handful of crackers and the parsley, serving the remaining crackers on the side.

Blackened Salmon and Quick Buttery Grits

Prep Time: 10 minutes, Cook Time: 45 minutes, Serves: 4

INGREDIENTS:

¾ cup grits (not instant or quick cooking)
1½ cups Chicken Stock, or store-bought low-sodium chicken broth
1½ cups milk
3 tbsps. unsalted butter, divided
2 tsps. kosher salt (or 1

tsp. fine salt), divided
1 tbsp. packed brown sugar
3 tbsps. Cajun Seasoning Mix or store-bought mix
4 (5-ounce,142 g) salmon fillets, skin removed
Nonstick cooking spray

DIRECTIONS:

1. In a heat-proof bowl that holds at least 6 cups, add the grits. Stir in the chicken stock, milk, 1 tablespoon of butter, and ½ teaspoon of kosher salt (or ¼ teaspoon of fine salt). Use aluminum foil to cover the bowl.
2. In the inner pot, add 1 cup of water. Put the Reversible Rack in the pot and on top place with the bowl.
3. Lock the Pressure Lid into place, set the valve to Seal. Select Pressure, adjust the cook time to 15 minutes. Press Start.
4. Meanwhile, stir together the brown sugar, seasoning, and remaining 1½ teaspoons of kosher salt (or ¾ teaspoon of fine salt) in a shallow bowl that fits one or two fillets at a time.
5. Use cooking spray to spray the fillets on one side and transfer one or two at a time to the spice mixture, sprayed-side down. Spray the exposed sides of the fillets and turn over to coat that side in the seasoning. Repeat with the remaining fillets.
6. After the grits cook, naturally release the pressure for 10 minutes, then quick release any remaining

pressure. Unlock and remove the Pressure Lid carefully.

7. Remove the rack and bowl from the pot. Add the remaining 2 tablespoons of butter to the grits and stir to incorporate. Use foil to re-cover and place the bowl back to the pot (without the rack).

8. Reverse the rack to the upper position. Put the salmon fillets on the rack and put the rack in the pot.

9. Close the Crisping Lid and select Bake/Roast, adjust the temperature to 400°F(205°C) and the cook time to 12 minutes. Press Start. After 6 minutes, open the lid and turn the fillets over. Close the lid and continue cooking. When the salmon is cooked and when use a fork can flake easily, remove the rack. Remove the bowl of grits and uncover. Stir well and serve immediately with the salmon.

Salmon with Broccoli and Brown Rice

Prep Time: 10 minutes, Cook Time: 19 minutes, Serves: 4

INGREDIENTS:

¾ cup water
1 cup brown rice, rinsed
4 (4-ounce, 113 g) frozen skinless salmon fillets
3 tbsps. extra-virgin olive oil, divided
1 small head broccoli, trimmed into florets
1 tsp. freshly ground black pepper
1 tsp. sea salt
2 tbsps. honey
Juice of 2 limes
4 garlic cloves, minced
1 tsp. paprika
2 jalapeño peppers, seeded and diced
2 tbsps. chopped fresh parsley

DIRECTIONS:

1. In the pot, add the water and rice and stir to combine. Put the Reversible Rack in the pot. Put the salmon fillets on the rack.

2. Assemble the Pressure Lid, set the pressure release valve to Seal. Select Pressure. Set the time to 2 minutes, then select Start/Stop to begin.

3. Meanwhile, add 1 tablespoon of olive oil and the broccoli into a medium bowl, toss them together and season with black pepper and the salt. Add the remaining 2 tablespoons of oil, honey, the lime juice, garlic, paprika, jalapeño, and parsley in a small bowl, mix them together.

4. After pressure cooking the rice and salmon is finish, move the pressure release valve to the Vent position to quick release the pressure. Remove the lid when the pressure has finished releasing carefully.

5. Use a paper towel to gently pat dry of the salmon, then coat the fish with the jalapeño mixture,

reserving some of the sauce for garnish.

6. Arrange around the salmon with the broccoli. Close the Crisping Lid. Select Broil and set the time to 7 minutes. Select Start/Stop to begin.

7. After cooking is finish, take the salmon out from the rack and serve it with the rice and broccoli. Garnish with the fresh parsley and the remaining sauce, as desired.

Crispy Fish and Chips

Prep Time: 20 minutes, Cook Time: 39 minutes, Serves: 4

INGREDIENTS:

8 ounces (227 g) ale beer
2 eggs
1 cup all-purpose flour
1 cup cornstarch
1 tbsp. ground cumin
½ tbsp. chili powder
1 tsp. sea salt, plus more for seasoning
1 tsp. freshly ground
black pepper, plus more for seasoning
4 (5- to 6-ounce, 142 to 170 g) cod fillets
Nonstick cooking spray
2 russet potatoes, cut into ¼- to ½-inch matchsticks
2 tbsps. vegetable oil

DIRECTIONS:

1. Place the Crisp Basket in the pot and close the Crisping Lid. Select Air Crisp, set the temperature to 375°F(190°C), and set the time to 5 minutes to preheat.

2. While preheating, whisk together the beer and eggs in a shallow mixing bowl. Add the flour, cornstarch, cumin, chili powder, salt, and pepper in a separate medium bowl, whisk them together.

3. Coat in the egg mixture with each cod fillet, then dredge in the flour mixture, coating on all sides.

4. Use nonstick cooking spray to spray the preheated Crisp Basket. Place the fish fillets in the basket and use cooking spray to coat them.

5. Close the Crisping Lid. Select Air Crisp, set the temperature to 375°F(190°C), and set the time to 15 minutes. Press Start/Stop to begin.

6. At the same time, toss the oil and potatoes and season with pepper and salt.

7. After 15 minutes, check the fish for your desired crispiness. Take the fish out from the basket.

8. Put the potatoes in the Crisp™ Basket. Close the Crisping Lid. Select Air Crisp, set the temperature to 400°F(205°C), and set the time to 24 minutes. Press Start/Stop to begin.

9. After 12 minutes, open the lid, then lift the basket and shake the fries. Then lower the basket back into the pot and close the lid to resume cooking until they reach your desired crispiness.

Quick Fish Tacos

Prep Time: 20 minutes, Cook Time: 15 minutes, Serves: 4

INGREDIENTS:
8 ounces (227 g) Mexican beer
2 eggs
1½ cups all-purpose flour
1½ cups cornstarch
1 tbsp. ground cumin
½ tbsp. chili powder
½ tsp. sea salt
½ tsp. freshly ground black pepper
1 pound (454 g) cod, cut into 1½-inch pieces
Nonstick cooking spray
8 (6-inch round) soft corn tortillas

DIRECTIONS:
1. Put the Crisp Basket in the pot and close the Crisping Lid. Select Air Crisp, set the temperature to 375°F(190°C) and set the time to 5 minutes to preheat.
2. While preheating, whisk together the beer and eggs in a large, shallow bowl. Add the flour, cornstarch, cumin, chili powder, salt, and pepper in a separate large bowl, whisk them together.
3. Coat in the egg mixture with one piece of cod, then dredge in the flour mixture, coating on all sides. Return the cod to coat in the egg mixture, then dredge for the second time in the flour mixture. Repeat with the rest cod pieces.
4. Use nonstick cooking spray to spray the preheated Crisp Basket. Put the fish in the basket and use cooking spray to coat it.
5. Close the Crisping Lid. Select Air Crisp, set the temperature to 375°F(190°C), and set the time to 15 minutes. Press Start/Stop to begin.
6. After 8 minutes, open the lid and use silicone tongs to flip the fish. Use cooking spray to coat and close the lid to resume cooking.
7. After 7 minutes, check the fish for your desired crispiness. Take the fish out from the basket. Arrange on the tortillas and serve with your choice toppings, such as diced bell peppers, mangoes, red onion, and/or lime juice.

Chapter 9 Soup and Stew

Italian White Bean and Escarole Soup

Prep Time: 8 hours, Cook Time: 35 minutes, Serves: 6 to 8

INGREDIENTS:

1 small head escarole, trimmed and cut into ½-inch pieces (8 cups)
1 pound (2½ cups, 454 g) dried cannellini beans, picked over and rinsed
1½ tbsps. table salt, for brining
1 large onion, chopped coarse
2 celery ribs, chopped coarse
4 garlic cloves, peeled
1 (28-ounce, 794 g) can whole peeled tomatoes
2 tbsps. extra-virgin olive oil, plus extra for drizzling

1 fennel bulb, stalks discarded, bulb halved, cored, and cut into ½-inch pieces
½ tsp. table salt
⅛ tsp. red pepper flakes
8 cups (1920 ml) chicken broth
2 large egg yolks
½ cup chopped fresh parsley
1 tbsp. minced fresh oregano
Grated Pecorino Romano cheese
Lemon wedges

DIRECTIONS:

1. In large container, mix 1½ tablespoons salt in 2 quarts cold water. Put beans in and soak at room temperature for at least 8 hours or up to 24 hours. Drain and rinse well.
2. Pulse celery, onion, and garlic in food processor, 15 to 20 pulses, until very finely chopped, scraping down sides of bowl if you like, set aside. Add tomatoes and their juice to the empty processor and pulse, 10 to 12 pulses, until tomatoes are finely chopped, set aside.
3. In Ninja pressure cooker, select sauté function, heat oil until shimmering. Add ½ teaspoon salt, fennel, onion mixture, and pepper flakes and cook 7 to 9 minutes until fennel begins to soften. Stir in tomatoes, broth, and beans.
4. Lock pressure lid and close pressure release valve. Choose pressure function and cook for 1 minute. Turn off and let pressure release naturally for 15 minutes. Quick-release any remaining pressure, then remove lid carefully, letting steam escape away from you.
5. Reserve 1 cup hot broth. Mix escarole into multicooker, 1 handful at a time, and cook in residual heat for about 5 minutes until escarole is wilted.
6. In small bowl, gently whisk egg yolks together. Whisking constantly, slowly add reserved broth to eggs until combined. Stir parsley, yolk mixture, and oregano into soup. Season with salt and pepper. Top each portion with Pecorino and drizzle with oil. Serve with lemon wedges.

Loaded Cauliflower Bacon Soup

Prep Time: 15 minutes, Cook Time: 29 minutes, Serves: 8

INGREDIENTS:

3 garlic cloves, minced
1 onion, chopped
5 slices bacon, chopped
4 cups chicken broth
1 head cauliflower, trimmed into florets
1 cup whole milk
1 tsp. freshly ground

black pepper
1 tsp. sea salt
1½ cups shredded Cheddar cheese
Sour cream, for serving (optional)
Chopped fresh chives, for serving (optional)

DIRECTIONS:

1. Preheat the pot by selecting Sear/Sauté. Select Start/Stop to begin. Preheat for 5 minutes.
2. In the preheated pot, add the garlic, onion and bacon. Cook for 5 minutes, stirring occasionally. Reserve some of the bacon for garnish.
3. Stir in the chicken broth and cauliflower to the pot. Assemble the Pressure Lid, set the pressure release valve to Seal.
4. Select Pressure and set the time to 10 minutes, then select Start/Stop to begin.
5. After pressure cooking is finish, move the pressure release valve to the Vent position to quick release the pressure. Remove the lid when the pressure has finished releasing carefully.
6. Add the milk and mash until the soup reaches your desired consistency. Season with the black pepper and salt. Over the top of the soup, evenly sprinkle with the cheese.
7. Close the Crisping Lid. Select Broil and set the time to 5 minutes. Select Start/Stop to begin.
8. After cooking is finish, top with the reserved crispy bacon and sour cream and chives (if using), serve immediately.

Italian Wedding Soup with Kale and Turkey Sausage

Prep Time: 10 minutes, Cook Time: 30 minutes, Serves: 4

INGREDIENTS:

1 pound (454 g) hot Italian turkey sausage, casings removed
4 tbsps. extra-virgin olive oil, divided
3 garlic cloves, chopped
1 large onion, chopped
3 celery stalks, chopped
1 tsp. kosher salt (or ½ tsp. fine salt)
½ cup dry white wine
½ tsp. fennel seeds
4 cups Chicken Stock, or store-bought low-sodium

chicken broth
1 Parmesan or similar cheese rind (optional)
2 cups chopped kale
1 (15-oz, 425 g) can cannellini (white kidney) beans, drained and rinsed
4 French or Italian bread slices, about ½ inch thick
½ cup grated Parmesan or similar cheese, divided
Nonstick cooking spray, for preparing the rack

DIRECTIONS:

1. Cut the sausage into 1-inch pieces. Wet your hands and roll the pieces into small balls.
2. On your Foodi™, preheat the inner pot by selecting Sear/Sauté. Press Start. Preheat for 5 minutes. Add 2 tablespoons of olive oil and heat until shimmering. Add the Italian sausage balls. Cook for 4 minutes, or until browned, turning the pieces occasionally. The sausage does not have to be cooked all the way through.
3. Stir in the garlic, onion and celery. Sprinkle with the salt and cook for 2 to 3 minutes, stirring occasionally. Pour in the wine and bring the mixture to a boil. Cook until the wine reduces by about half, scraping the bottom of the pot to get up any browned bits. Add the fennel seeds, chicken stock, Parmesan rind (if using), kale and cannellini beans.
4. Lock the Pressure Lid into place, set the valve to Seal. Select Pressure, adjust the cook time to 5 minutes. Press Start.
5. Meanwhile, use the remaining 2 tablespoons of olive oil to brush the bread slices. Sprinkle over the bread with about half the cheese.
6. When the soup is cooked, naturally release the pressure for 5 minutes, then quick release any remaining pressure. Open and remove the Pressure Lid carefully.
7. Use cooking spray or oil to spray the Reversible Rack and place it in the pot. Lay the bread slices on the rack.
8. Close the Crisping Lid and select Broil. Adjust the cook time to 5 minutes. Press Start. When the bread is browned and crisp, transfer it from the rack to

a cutting board and allow to cool for a couple of minutes. Cut the slices into cubes.
9. Ladle into bowls with the soup and sprinkle with the remaining cheese. Divide the croutons among the bowls and serve.

Curried Mixed Vegetable Soup

Prep Time: 15 minutes, Cook Time: 55 minutes, Serves: 6

INGREDIENTS:

1 cauliflower head, cut into florets
6 carrots, coarsely chopped
1 sweet potato, peeled and chopped
1 yellow onion, coarsely chopped
2 garlic cloves, minced
1 tbsp. water, plus more as needed
1 tsp. red pepper flakes
1 tbsp. minced peeled fresh ginger
6 cups no-sodium

vegetable broth
1 (14-ounce, 397 g) can full-fat coconut milk
1 tbsp. freshly squeezed lemon juice
1 tbsp. yellow curry powder
2 tsps. ground turmeric
½ cup coarsely chopped fresh cilantro
Cayenne pepper, for seasoning
Pumpkin seeds, for serving

DIRECTIONS:

1. Use parchment paper to line the inner pot.
2. On the Ninja Foodi, evenly spread with the cauliflower, carrots and sweet potato.
3. Press Bake and cook at 450°F(235°C) for 30 minutes. Flip the vegetables and bake for another 10 minutes, until lightly browned and fork-tender. Take it out and set aside, clean the inner pot.
4. Combine the onion and garlic in the inner pot, press Sear/Sauté and cook at 390ºF (200ºC) for 2 to 3 minutes, adding water, 1 tablespoon at a time, to prevent burning, until the onion is translucent but not browned. Add the red pepper flakes and ginger, and cook for an additional 1 minute.
5. Pour in the vegetable broth and bring the soup to a boil.
6. Stir in the roasted vegetables and bring the soup to simmer. Cover pressure lid, press Pressure and cook at 390ºF (200ºC) for 5 minutes.
7. Add the lemon juice, coconut milk, curry powder, and turmeric. Puree with an immersion blender until smooth. Stir in the cilantro.
8. Place a sprinkle of cayenne pepper and the pumpkin seeds on the top and serve.

Spicy Butternut Squash Apple Soup with Bacon

Prep Time: 10 minutes, Cook Time: 28 minutes, Serves: 8

INGREDIENTS:

12 ounces (340 g) butternut squash, peeled and cubed
2 quarts (64 ounces (1814g)) chicken stock
4 slices uncooked bacon, cut into ½-inch pieces
1 green apple, cut into

small cubes
Freshly ground black pepper
1 tbsp. minced fresh oregano
1 cup orzo
Kosher salt

DIRECTIONS:

1. Select the Saute mode, to preheat for 5 minutes.
2. Add bacon and cook until fat is rendered and the bacon starts to brown, stirring frequently. Transfer the bacon to a paper towel-lined plate with a slotted spoon, leaving the rendered bacon fat in the pot.
3. Add butternut squash, apple, salt, and pepper and sauté until partially soft. Add oregano and stir.
4. Add bacon, chicken stock into the pot. Simmer 10 minutes, then add the orzo and continue cooking for 8 minutes. Serve warm.

Whole Farro and Leek Soup

Prep Time: 15 minutes, Cook Time: 30 minutes, Serves: 6 to 8

INGREDIENTS:

1 cup whole farro
1 tbsp. extra-virgin olive oil, plus extra for drizzling
3 ounces (85 g) pancetta, chopped fine
1 pound (454 g) leeks, ends trimmed, chopped, and washed thoroughly
1 celery rib, chopped

2 carrots, peeled and chopped
½ cup minced fresh parsley
8 cups (1920 ml) chicken broth, plus extra as needed
Grated Parmesan cheese

DIRECTIONS:

1. Pulse farro in blender for about 6 pulses until about half of grains are broken into smaller pieces, set aside.
2. In Ninja pressure cooker, select sauté function, heat oil until shimmering. Add pancetta and cook 3 to 5 minutes until lightly browned. Stir in carrots, leeks, and celery and cook about 5 minutes until softened. Add broth, scraping up any browned bits, then stir in farro.

3. Lock lid and close pressure release valve. Choose pressure function and cook for 8 minutes. Turn off and quick-release pressure. Carefully remove lid, letting steam escape away from you.
4. Adjust consistency with extra hot broth if you like. Stir in parsley and season with salt and pepper. Drizzle each portion with extra oil and top with Parmesan. Serve.

Spinach and Chickpea Soup with Mushroom

Prep Time: 10 minutes, Cook Time: 7 minutes, Serves: 6 to 8

INGREDIENTS:

2 tbsps. (28 g) grass-fed butter, ghee or avocado oil
2 large bunches fresh spinach (about 1½ lb [680 g] total), leaves only, cleaned well
2 cups (480 g) canned or cooked chickpeas
1 yellow onion, peeled and diced
8 oz (225 g) cleaned white button or cremini mushrooms, thinly sliced
7 cloves garlic, finely minced

2 large celery ribs, thinly sliced
1 organic russet potato, peeled and diced
1 tbsp. (7 g) ground cumin
1 tsp. ground coriander
1 tsp. sea salt
½ tsp. dried thyme
½ tsp. ground allspice
6 cups (1.4 L) chicken or vegetable stock
Sour cream, for garnish (optional)
Quality extra-virgin olive oil, for garnish (optional)

DIRECTIONS:

1. In the Ninja pressure cooker, add the healthy fat of your choice and press sauté. When the fat has melted, add the onion and mushrooms and sauté for 7 minutes, stirring occasionally, then add the garlic and continue to sauté for 1 minute, stirring occasionally. Mix in the celery, potato, cumin, coriander, salt, thyme, allspice and stock, then stir well. Press keep warm/Stop.
2. In the sealed position, secure the lid with the steam vent. Press Pressure and cook for 7 minutes.
3. When the timer sounds, press keep warm/Stop. Do a quick release with an oven mitt. When the steam venting stops and the silver dial drops, open the lid.
4. Press sauté and mix in the spinach and chickpeas. Let the soup to come to a simmer, stirring until the spinach has fully wilted. Press keep warm/Stop. Taste and adjust for the seasoning.
5. Serve immediately. Garnish with a dollop of sour cream or a drizzle of quality extra-virgin olive oil (if using).

Creamy Italian Sausage, Potato, and Kale Soup

Prep Time: 10 minutes, Cook Time: 18 minutes, Serves: 8

INGREDIENTS:

1½ pounds (680 g) hot Italian sausage, ground
1 pound (454 g) sweet Italian sausage, ground
4 large Russet potatoes, cut in ½-inch thick quarters
6 cups kale, chopped
1 large yellow onion, diced
5 cups chicken stock
1 tbsp. extra-virgin olive oil
2 tbsps.minced garlic
2 tbsps. Italian seasoning
2 tsps.crushed red pepper flakes
Freshly ground black pepper
½ cup heavy (whipping) cream
Salt

DIRECTIONS:

1. Select the Saute mode to preheat for 5 minutes.
2. Put the olive oil and hot and sweet Italian sausage in the pot. Cook 5 minutes, breaking up the sausage with a spatula.
3. Combine onion, garlic, potatoes, chicken stock, Italian seasoning, and crushed red pepper flakes, salt and pepper in the pot, mix well. Assemble pressure lid, set the steamer valve to Seal.
4. Select Pressure, set the time 10 minutes.
5. After cooking is complete, move pressure release valve to VENT position to quickly release the pressure. Carefully remove lid.
6. Add kale and heavy cream. Stir and serve warm.

Lentil Spinach Soup with Lemon

Prep Time: 5 minutes, Cook Time: 12 minutes, Serves: 4 to 6

INGREDIENTS:

1 tsp. extra-virgin olive oil
2 lb (905 g) dried red lentils
Juice of 1½ lemons
3 cups (90 g) baby spinach
32 oz (946 ml, 896 g) vegetable stock
1 yellow onion, diced
1 tsp. salt
1 tsp. ground cumin
¼ tsp. ground turmeric
¼ tsp. freshly ground black pepper
¼ tsp. ground coriander
Croutons, for topping (optional)

DIRECTIONS:

1. Press sauté on the Ninja pressure cooker. Add oil into the pot and heat for 1 minute, then add the onion.

Sauté for 2 minutes, or until translucent.
2. Press Stop and stir in the salt, cumin, turmeric, pepper, coriander, stock and lentils. Combine them well.
3. Secure the lid with the steam vent in the sealed position. Press Pressure. Adjust the time to 12 minutes.
4. Once the timer sounds, release the pressure quickly. Remove the lid. Mix in the lemon juice. Puree the soup with an immersion blender until smooth.
5. Add the fresh spinach and top with croutons, if using. When the spinach slightly wilts, adjust the salt and pepper. Serve hot.

Spanish Chorizo and Lentil Soup

Prep Time: 15 minutes, Cook Time: 30 minutes, Serves: 6 to 8

INGREDIENTS:

8 ounces (227 g) Spanish-style chorizo sausage, quartered lengthwise and sliced thin
1 large onion, peeled
1 tbsp. extra-virgin olive oil, plus extra for drizzling
2 carrots, peeled and halved crosswise
4 garlic cloves, minced
1½ tsp. smoked paprika
5 cups (1200 ml) water
1 pound (2¼ cups, 454 g) French green lentils, picked over and rinsed
4 cups (960 ml) chicken broth
1 tbsp. sherry vinegar, plus extra for seasoning
2 bay leaves
1 tsp. table salt
½ cup slivered almonds, toasted
½ cup minced fresh parsley

DIRECTIONS:

1. In Ninja pressure cooker, select sauté function, heat oil until shimmering. Add chorizo and cook 3 to 5 minutes until lightly browned. Stir in garlic and paprika and cook about 30 seconds until fragrant. Add water, scraping up any browned bits, then stir in lentils, bay leaves, vinegar, broth, and salt. Nestle carrots and onion into pot.
2. Lock lid and close pressure release valve. Choose pressure function and cook for 14 minutes. Turn off and quick-release pressure. Carefully remove lid, letting steam escape away from you.
3. Throw away bay leaves. Transfer onion and carrots to food processor with a slotted spoon and process about 1 minute until smooth, scraping down sides of bowl if you like. Stir vegetable mixture into lentils and season with pepper, salt, and extra vinegar. Drizzle each portion with extra oil, sprinkle with almonds and parsley and serve.

Vegetable Wild Rice Soup

Prep Time: 10 minutes, Cook Time: 30 minutes, Serves: 6

INGREDIENTS:

8 ounces (227 g) fresh mushrooms, sliced	6 cups vegetable broth
5 medium carrots, chopped	1 onion, chopped
	3 garlic cloves, minced
5 celery stalks, chopped	1 tsp. poultry seasoning
1 cup wild rice	½ tsp. dried thyme
	1 tsp. kosher salt

DIRECTIONS:

1. Add all the ingredients to the pot. Assemble pressure lid, set the pressure release valve to Seal.
2. Select PRESSURE, set the time 30 minutes.
3. After cooking is complete, move pressure release valve to VENT position to quickly release the pressure. Carefully remove lid.
4. Serve Warm.

Garlicy Roasted Cauliflower and Potato Soup

Prep Time: 20 minutes, Cook Time: 30 minutes, Serves: 6

INGREDIENTS:

8 garlic cloves, peeled	1 tablespoon water, plus more as needed
1 large cauliflower head, cut into small florets	6 cups no-sodium vegetable broth
2 russet potatoes, peeled and chopped into 1-inch pieces	2 thyme sprigs
	2 teaspoons paprika
1 yellow onion, coarsely chopped	¼ teaspoon freshly ground black pepper
1 celery stalk, coarsely chopped	1 tablespoon chopped fresh rosemary leaves

DIRECTIONS:

1. Use parchment paper to line the inner pot.
2. Use the aluminum foil to wrap the garlic cloves or place in a garlic roaster.
3. In Ninja Foodi, evenly spread with the potatoes and cauliflower. Place the wrapped garlic on the inner pot.
4. Press Roast and cook at 450°F(235°C) for 15 to 20 minutes, or until the cauliflower is lightly browned.
5. Combine the onion and celery in Ninja Foodi, press Sear/Sauté and cook at 390ºF (200ºC) for 4 to 5 minutes, adding water, 1 tablespoon at a time, to prevent burning, until the onion starts to brown.
6. Pour in the vegetable broth and bring the soup to a simmer.
7. Add the roasted vegetables and thyme, garlic, paprika, and pepper. Bring the soup to a simmer, cover pressure lid and press Pressure and cook at 390ºF (200ºC). for 10 minutes.
8. Remove and discard the thyme. Puree the soup with an immersion blender until smooth. Add some water if the soup is too thick, to the desired consistency.
9. Stir in the rosemary and serve.

Creamy Pumpkin and Squash Bisque with Apple

Prep Time: 10 minutes, Cook Time: 25 minutes, Serves: 4 to 5

INGREDIENTS:

2 tbsps. (30 ml) avocado oil or extra-virgin olive oil	2 tbsps. (30 ml) cider vinegar
1 (3- to 4-lb [1.4- to 1.8-kg]) butternut squash	2 tsps. (3 g) dried basil
1 (2- to 3-lb [1- to 1.4-kg]) pie pumpkin	2 tsps. (2 g) dried sage
1 large apple (see note)	1 tsp. salt, plus more to taste
1 medium white onion, diced	½ cup (120 ml) coconut milk, coconut cream, or light or heavy dairy cream
2 cloves garlic, minced	½ cup (70 g) pumpkin seeds, for garnish
3 to 4 cups (710 to 946 ml) vegetable or chicken stock	2 tbsps. (3 g) fresh rosemary or thyme

DIRECTIONS:

1. Prepare your butternut squash, peel the skin off, cut in half vertically and remove the seeds, then cut into 1-inch (2.5-cm) chunks. Cut the pumpkin in half and remove the seeds, then carve out the inside flesh of the pumpkin. Cut the pumpkin into 1-inch (2.5-cm) chunks.
2. Select sauté on the Ninja pressure cooker, when hot, use the oil to coat the bottom. Add the onion and cook for 2 to 3 minutes, then add the garlic and cook for 1 to 2 minutes.
3. Place the squash, pumpkin and apple into the pot. Cover with 3 cups (710 ml) of the stock and the vinegar, basil, sage and salt.
4. Secure the lid with the steam vent in the sealed position. Select Pressure, and cook for 14 minutes.
5. Use a natural release for 15 minutes, then release the remaining steam before opening the lid.
6. Stir in the coconut milk, and use an immersion blender to blend your soup or blend in batches in a regular blender. Add an additional ½ to 1 cup (120 to 237 ml) of stock if needed.
7. Garnish with pumpkin seeds and fresh herbs.

Chicken Wing Broth

Prep Time: 15 minutes, Cook Time: 1.5 hours, Serves: 3 quarts

INGREDIENTS:

3 pounds (1.4 kg) chicken wings
1 tbsp. vegetable oil
1 onion, chopped
12 cups (2880 ml) water, divided
½ tsp. table salt
3 bay leaves
3 garlic cloves, lightly crushed and peeled

DIRECTIONS:

1. Pat chicken wings dry with paper towels. In Ninja pressure cooker, select sauté function, heat oil for 5 minutes. Brown half of chicken wings for about 10 minutes, transfer to bowl. Repeat with remaining chicken wings.
2. Add onion to fat left in the pot and cook 8 to 10 minutes until softened and well browned. Stir in garlic and cook about 30 seconds until fragrant. Add 1 cup water, scraping up any browned bits. Stir in remaining 11 cups water, bay leaves, salt, and chicken and any accumulated juices.
3. Lock lid and close pressure release valve. Choose pressure function and cook for 1 hour. Turn off and let pressure release naturally for 15 minutes. Quick-release any remaining pressure and carefully remove lid, letting steam escape away from you.
4. Strain broth through colander into large container, pressing on solids to extract as much liquid as possible, throw away solids. Skim excess fat from surface of broth with a wide, shallow spoon. (Broth can be refrigerated for up to 4 days or frozen for 2 months.)

Red Lentil and Tomato Curry Soup

Prep Time: 0 minutes, Cook Time: 8 minutes, Serves: 4 to 5

INGREDIENTS:

1 tbsp. (15 ml) avocado oil or extra-virgin olive oil
2 cups (400 g) split red lentils
1 (14.5-oz [411-g]) can diced tomatoes
2 tbsps. (30 g) red curry paste
1 medium yellow onion, diced
2 cloves garlic, minced
1 tbsp. (6 g) chopped fresh ginger
1 red bell pepper, seeded and diced
6 cups (1.4 L) vegetable or chicken stock
2 tsps. (4 g) garam masala
1 tsp. curry powder
1 tsp. sea salt, plus more to taste

1 (13.5-oz [400-ml, 383 g]) can full-fat coconut milk
Juice of 1 lime
¼ cup (10 g) chopped fresh cilantro, for garnish (optional)

DIRECTIONS:

1. Select sauté on the Ninja pressure cooker. When the pot is hot, use the oil to coat the pan. Mix in the onion, garlic, ginger and bell pepper. Sauté for about 3 minutes, then select Stop.
2. Stir in the lentils, stock, tomatoes, curry paste, garam masala, curry powder and salt.
3. Secure the lid with the steam vent in the sealed position. Select Pressure, and cook for 5 minutes.
4. Remove the lid with a quick release. Add the coconut milk and lime juice and stir them together.
5. Top with fresh cilantro and taste with additional salt. Serve.

Garlicky Roasted Red Pepper and Tomato Soup

Prep Time: 0 minutes, Cook Time: 11 minutes, Serves: 4 to 6

INGREDIENTS:

1 tbsp. (15 ml) extra-virgin olive oil
2 (16-oz [455-g]) jars roasted red peppers, drained
1 (14.5-oz [411-g]) can fire-roasted diced tomatoes
1 yellow onion, diced
2 cloves garlic, grated
1 tbsp. (15 ml) sherry vinegar
2 cups (475 ml) water or vegetable stock
1 tsp. fresh lemon juice
Salt
Freshly ground black pepper
1 cup (237 ml) coconut milk
Croutons, for topping (optional)

DIRECTIONS:

1. Press sauté on the Ninja pressure cooker. Add the oil into the pot. Heat the oil for about 2 minutes, add the onion. Sauté for 2 minutes, or until translucent.
2. Press Stop and then stir in the garlic and vinegar. Mix in the roasted red peppers, tomatoes, water and lemon juice along with salt and pepper to taste.
3. In the sealed position, secure the pressure lid with the steam vent. Press Pressure. Adjust the time to 7 minutes.
4. Once the timer sounds, release the pressure quickly. Remove the lid. Add the coconut milk and stir. Puree the soup until smooth with an immersion blender. Seasoning with more salt and pepper and top with croutons, if using.

Spicy Pork Stew with Black Benas and Tomatoes

Prep Time: 15 minutes, Cook Time: 30 minutes, Serves: 8

INGREDIENTS:

2 pounds (907 g) boneless pork shoulder, cut into 1-inch pieces
1 (10-ounce (283 g)) can diced tomatoes with chiles
1 (15-ounce (425 g)) can black beans, rinsed and drained
1 (15-ounce (425 g)) can hominy, rinsed and drained
4 cups chicken stock
¼ cup all-purpose flour
¼ cup unsalted butter
½ small onion, diced
1 carrot, diced
1 celery stalk, diced
2 garlic cloves, minced
1 tbsp. tomato paste
1 tbsp. cumin
1 tbsp. smoked paprika
Freshly ground black pepper
Sea salt

DIRECTIONS:

1. Coat the pork pieces with the flour in a large bowl.
2. Select the Saute mode, to preheat for 5 minutes.
3. Add butter. Once melted, add pork and sear for 5 minutes until all sides browned.
4. Put the onion, carrot, celery, garlic, tomato paste, cumin, and paprika in the pot. Cook 3 minutes, stirring occasionally.
5. Add chicken stock and tomatoes. Assemble pressure lid, set the pressure release valve to Seal.
6. Select PRESSURE, set the time 15 minutes.
7. After cooking is complete, move pressure release valve to VENT position to quickly release the pressure. Carefully remove lid.
8. Select SEAR/SAUTÉ and HI PRESSURE. Select START/STOP to begin.
9. Add beans, hominy, salt, and pepper. Whisk well. Cook 2 minutes. Serve warm.

Spanish Turkey Meatball Soup

Prep Time: 15 minutes, Cook Time: 35 minutes, Serves: 6 to 8

INGREDIENTS:

8 ounces (227 g) kale, stemmed and chopped
1 pound (454 g) ground turkey
1 slice hearty white sandwich bread, torn into quarters
¼ cup (60 ml) whole milk
1 ounce (28 g) Manchego cheese, grated (½ cup), plus extra for serving
5 tbsps. minced fresh parsley, divided
½ tsp. table salt
4 garlic cloves, minced
1 tbsp. extra-virgin olive oil
1 onion, chopped
1 red bell pepper, stemmed, seeded, and cut into ¾-inch pieces
2 tsps. smoked paprika
½ cup (120 ml) dry white wine
8 cups (1920 ml) chicken broth

DIRECTIONS:

1. Mash bread and milk together into paste with a fork in large bowl. Stir in 3 tablespoons parsley, Manchego, and salt until combined. Add turkey and knead mixture with your hands until well mixed. Roll 2-teaspoon-size pieces of pinched off mixture into balls and place on large plate (you should have about 35 meatballs), set aside.
2. In Ninja pressure cooker, select sauté function, heat oil until shimmering. Add onion and bell pepper and cook 5 to 7 minutes until softened and lightly browned. Stir in garlic and paprika and cook about 30 seconds until fragrant. Stir in wine, scraping up any browned bits, and cook about 5 minutes until almost completely evaporated. Stir in kale and broth, then gently submerge meatballs.
3. Lock lid and close pressure release valve. Select pressure function, cook for 3 minutes. Turn off and quick-release pressure. Carefully remove lid, letting steam escape away from you.
4. Stir in remaining parsley and season with salt and pepper. Serve with extra Manchego separately.

Greek Gigante Bean Soup

Prep Time: 8 hours, Cook Time: 30 minutes, Serves: 6 to 8

INGREDIENTS:

1½ tbsp. table salt, for brining
1 pound (2½ cups, 454 g) dried gigante beans, picked over and rinsed
2 tbsps. extra-virgin olive oil, plus extra for drizzling
5 celery ribs, cut into ½-inch pieces, plus ½ cup leaves, minced
½ tsp. table salt
1 onion, chopped
4 garlic cloves, minced
4 cups (960 ml) vegetable or chicken broth
4 cups (960 ml) water
½ cup pitted kalamata olives, chopped
2 bay leaves
2 tbsps. minced fresh marjoram
Lemon wedges

DIRECTIONS:

1. Add 1½ tablespoons salt in 2 quarts cold water in large container. Put beans in and soak at room temperature for at least 8 hours or up to 24 hours. Drain and rinse well.

2. In Ninja pressure cooker, select sauté function, heat oil until shimmering. Add onion, celery pieces, and ½ teaspoon salt and cook about 5 minutes until vegetables are softened. Stir in garlic and cook about 30 seconds until fragrant. Stir in broth, beans, water, and bay leaves.
3. Lock lid and close pressure release valve. Choose pressure function and cook for 6 minutes. Turn off and let pressure release naturally for 15 minutes. Quick-release any remaining pressure and carefully remove lid, letting steam escape away from you.
4. Combine olives, celery leaves, and marjoram in bowl. Throw away bay leaves. Season soup with salt and pepper. Top each portion with celery-olive mixture. Drizzle with extra oil and serve with lemon wedges.

Curry Acorn Squash Soup

Prep Time: 20 minutes, Cook Time: about 1 hour, Serves: 6

INGREDIENTS:

1 acorn squash	vegetable broth
2 garlic cloves, chopped	½ tsp. dill
1 yellow onion, chopped	1 tsp. curry powder, plus
2 celery stalks, coarsely chopped	more for seasoning
	⅛ tsp. cayenne pepper
1 tbsp. water, plus more as needed	1 (14-ounce, 397 g) can full-fat coconut milk
2 tbsps. whole wheat flour	Chopped scallions, green parts only, for serving
2 cups no-sodium	

DIRECTIONS:

1. Cut the acorn squash in half lengthwise and scoop out the seeds and stringy center. Put the squash halves in the Ninja Foodi, cut-side down, and add enough water to come up about 1 inch all around.
2. Press Bake and cook at 350°F(180°C) for 30 to 45 minutes, or until the squash can be easily pierced with a fork. Take the squash out from the inner pot and allow to cool for 10 minutes. Scoop out the soft flesh and set aside in a bowl.
3. Combine the garlic, onion, and celery in the Ninja Foodi, press Sear/Sauté on HIGH for 2 to 3 minutes, add the water, 1 tablespoon at a time, to prevent burning, until the onion is translucent but not browned.
4. Sprinkle over with the flour and stir to coat the vegetables.
5. Add the roasted squash, vegetable broth, dill, curry powder and cayenne pepper. Bring the mixture to a boil. Adjust to LOW, cover and cook for 10 minutes.
6. Pour in the coconut milk. Blend the soup until smooth

with an immersion blender. Serve immediately or place in an airtight container and refrigerate for up to 1 week.
7. Place the scallions and a sprinkle of curry powder on the top and serve.

Garlicky Potato and Tomato Soup with Spinach

Prep Time: 5 minutes, Cook Time: 15 minutes, Serves: 4 to 6

INGREDIENTS:

2 tbsps. (28 g) grass-fed butter, ghee or avocado oil	1½ tsps. (4 g) ground cumin
2 large bunches fresh spinach (about 1½ lb [680 g] total), leaves only, cleaned well	1 tsp. sea salt, plus more to taste
	1 tsp. dried thyme
	½ tsp. ground coriander
2 organic russet potatoes, peeled and diced	4 cups (946 ml) chicken or vegetable stock
3 small tomatoes, seeded and diced	¼ cup (10 g) roughly chopped fresh cilantro, plus more for garnish
1½ tbsps. (10 g) yellow curry powder	¼ cup (10 g) fresh Thai basil or basil leaves
1 yellow onion, peeled and diced	1½ cups (355 ml) coconut milk
5 cloves garlic, finely minced	⅓ cup (80 ml) fresh lime juice
3 large celery ribs, thinly sliced	Lime wedges, for garnish (optional)

DIRECTIONS:

1. In the Ninja pressure cooker, add the healthy fat of your choice and press sauté. When the fat has melted, add the onion and sauté for 7 minutes, stirring occasionally, then mix in the garlic and continue to sauté for 1 minute. Stir in the celery, potatoes, tomatoes, curry, cumin, salt, thyme, coriander and stock. Press keep warm/stop.
2. Secure the lid with the steam vent in the sealed position. Press Pressure and cook for 7 minutes.
3. When the timer sounds, press keep warm/stop Do a quick release with an oven mitt. When the steam venting stops and the silver dial drops, open the lid.
4. Press sauté and mix in the spinach, cilantro, basil, coconut milk and lime juice. Let the soup to simmer, until the spinach has fully wilted. Press keep warm/ Stop. Taste and adjust seasoning.
5. Garnish with chopped fresh cilantro and lime wedges and serve.

Garlicky Cumin Chickpea Soup

Prep Time: 10 minutes, Cook Time: 30 minutes, Serves: 4

INGREDIENTS:

1 tbsp. plus 1 tsp. kosher salt (or 2 tsps. fine salt), divided
1 pound (454 g) dried chickpeas
5 garlic cloves
1 tsp. cumin seeds
1 small onion, chopped
3 tbsps. olive oil, divided
6 cups water
¼ tsp. ground cumin
4 Italian or French bread slices
Juice of 1 lemon (about 2 tbsps.)
2 tbsps. harissa (optional)
¼ cup Greek yogurt (optional)

DIRECTIONS:

1. Dissolve 1 tablespoon of kosher salt (or 1½ teaspoons of fine salt) in 1 quart of water in a large bowl. Place the chickpeas in the bowl and allow to soak at room temperature for 8 to 24 hours.
2. Peel and smash 4 garlic cloves. Peel and mince the remaining clove and set aside.
3. Drain and rinse the chickpeas. Add them into the Foodi inner pot. Then add the 4 smashed garlic cloves, the cumin seeds, onion, 1 tablespoon of olive oil, the remaining 1 teaspoon of kosher salt (or ½ teaspoon of fine salt), and the water.
4. Lock the Pressure Lid into place, set the valve to Seal. Select Pressure, adjust the cook time to 6 minutes. Press Start.
5. Meanwhile, stir together the the minced garlic, remaining 2 tablespoons of olive oil, and the ground cumin in a small bowl. Spread this mixture over the bread slices.
6. When the cooking is complete, naturally release the pressure for 8 minutes, then quick release any remaining pressure. Open and remove the Pressure Lid carefully.
7. Taste the soup and adjust the seasoning. There should be plenty of broth, add more water if the texture is too thick. Stir in the lemon juice and harissa (if using).
8. Put the Reversible Rack in the pot in the upper position. Place the bread slices on the rack.
9. Close the Crisping Lid and select Broil. Adjust the cook time to 7 minutes. Press Start.
10. Once the bread is crisp, remove the rack. Place a slice of bread in each of four bowls. Ladle over with the soup and garnish with a spoonful of yogurt (if using, omit for a dairy-free or vegan version).

Roasted Red Pepper and Caramelized Onion Soup with Grilled Cheese

Prep Time: 10 minutes, Cook Time: 25 minutes, Serves: 4

INGREDIENTS:

⅔ cup dry or medium-dry sherry
3 large roasted red peppers (about 16 ounces jarred peppers, 454 g), cut into chunks, blotted dry if using jarred
1 recipe Caramelized Onions
2 cups Roasted Vegetable Stock or low-
sodium vegetable broth
8 Italian or French bread slices
8 ounces (227 g) grated aged Cheddar or Gouda cheese
4 tbsps. (½ stick) unsalted butter, at room temperature
¼ cup heavy (whipping) cream

DIRECTIONS:

1. On your Foodi™, preheat the inner pot by selecting Sear/Sauté. Press Start. Preheat for 5 minutes. Add the sherry the roasted peppers and caramelized onions. Bring to a boil. Cook until the sherry has mostly evaporated, about 5 minutes. Pour in the vegetable stock.
2. Lock the Pressure Lid into place, set the valve to Seal. Select Pressure, adjust the cook time to 6 minutes. Press Start.
3. Meanwhile, on a cutting board, lay out 4 slices of bread and evenly divide the cheese among them. Place the remaining bread slices on the top. Butter one side of each sandwich, then carefully turn them over and butter the other side.
4. When the soup is complete cooking, quick release the pressure. Open and remove the Pressure Lid carefully. Add the cream and stir well.
5. Transfer the sandwiches to the Reversible Rack, and then in the pot.
6. Close the Crisping Lid and select Bake/Roast, adjust the temperature to 390°F(200°C) and the cook time to 6 minutes. Press Start. After 3 minutes, open the lid and check the sandwiches. The tops should be golden brown and crisp. If not, continue to cook for another minute. When the tops are browned, flip the sandwiches. Close the lid and continue cooking until the other side is browned. Remove the rack.
7. Ladle into bowls with the soup and serve with the sandwiches.

Delicious Hungarian Goulash Soup

Prep Time: 15 minutes, Cook Time: 55 minutes, Serves: 6

INGREDIENTS:

1½ pounds (680 g) small Yukon Gold potatoes, halved
2 pounds (907 g) beef stew meat
½ cup all-purpose flour
2 cups beef broth
½ tsp. freshly ground black pepper
1 medium red bell pepper, seeded and chopped
4 garlic cloves, minced
1 large yellow onion, diced
2 tbsps. canola oil
2 tbsps. smoked paprika
2 tbsps. tomato paste
¼ cup sour cream
1 tbsp. kosher salt
Fresh parsley

DIRECTIONS:

1. Select Saute mode. Preheat for 5 minutes.
2. In a small bowl, combine the flour, salt, and pepper. Dip the beef pieces into the flour mixture and shake off the excess flour.
3. Add oil, beef to pot, cook 10 minutes, until all sides browned.
4. Add bell pepper, garlic, onion, and smoked paprika. Sauté until the onion is translucent.
5. Add the potatoes, beef broth, and tomato paste and stir. Assemble pressure lid, set the steamer valve to Seal.
6. Select Pressure, set the time 30 minutes. Press START to begin.
7. After cooking is complete, move pressure release valve to VENT position to quickly release the pressure. Carefully remove lid.
8. Stir with sour cream. Add parsley for decoration, if desired. Serve warm.

Chapter 10 Appetizer

Tamari Sauce Eggs

Prep Time: 15 minutes, Cook Time: 7 minutes, Serves: 6

INGREDIENTS:

6 large eggs
1 cup water
½ cup tamari
2 tbsps. rice wine vinegar
2 tbsps. honey

DIRECTIONS:

1. Pour water into Ninja pressure cooker and then place steamer into pot. Put the 6 eggs inside. Close lid tightly.
2. Press Pressure and set the timer to 7 minutes. When timer beeps, quick-release pressure naturally until float valve drops down and then open lid. Transfer eggs to an ice bath to stop cooking.- This step also makes them easier to peel
3. Combine tamari, honey, and rice wine vinegar in a medium bowl. Set aside.
4. Peel eggs and soak in mixture in a lidded bowl and place in refrigerator overnight. Cut eggs in half lengthwise and enjoy.

Loaded Smashed Potatoes with Bacon

Prep Time: 10 minutes, Cook Time: 30 minutes, Serves: 4

INGREDIENTS:

12 ounces (340 g) baby Yukon Gold potatoes
1 tsp. extra-virgin olive oil
¼ cup shredded Cheddar cheese
¼ cup sour cream
2 slices bacon, cooked and crumbled
1 tbsp. chopped fresh chives
Sea salt

DIRECTIONS:

1. Put the Crisp Basket in the pot. Close the Crisping Lid. Select Air Crisp, set the temperature to 350°F(180°C), and set the time to 5 minutes. Press Start/Stop to begin to preheat the unit.
2. While preheating, toss the potatoes with the oil until evenly coated.
3. After the pot and basket are preheated, open the lid and place the potatoes into the basket. Close the lid, select Air Crisp, set the temperature to 350°F(180°C), and set the time to 30 minutes. Press Start/Stop to begin.
4. 15 minutes later, open the lid, lift the basket and shake the potatoes. Lower the basket back into the pot and close the lid to resume cooking.
5. After another 15 minutes, check the potatoes for your desired crispiness.
6. Take the potatoes out from the basket. Lightly crush the potatoes to split them with a large spoon. Top with the cheese, sour cream, bacon, and chives, and season with salt.

Maple and Brown Sugar Candied Bacon

Prep Time: 5 minutes, Cook Time: 35 minutes, Serves: 12 slices

INGREDIENTS:

1 pound (12 slices, 454 g) thick-cut bacon
½ cup maple syrup
¼ cup brown sugar
Nonstick cooking spray

DIRECTIONS:

1. Put the Reversible Rack in the pot. Close the Crisping Lid. Select Air Crisp, set the temperature to 400°F(205°c), and set the time to 5 minutes to preheat the unit.
2. While preheating, mix together the brown sugar and maple syrup in a small mixing bowl.
3. When the Ninja Foodi has preheated, carefully use aluminum foil to line the Reversible Rack. Use cooking spray to spray the foil.
4. Arrange 4 to 6 slices of bacon on the rack in a single layer. Use the maple syrup mixture to brush them.
5. Close the Crisping Lid. Select Air Crisp and set the temperature to 400°F(205°C). Set the time to 10 minutes, then select Start/Stop to begin.
6. After 10 minutes, flip the bacon and use more maple syrup mixture to brush. Close the Crisping Lid, select Air Crisp, set the temperature to 400°F(205°C), and set the time to 10 minutes. Select Start/Stop to begin.
7. When your desired crispiness is reached, cooking is complete. Take the bacon out from the Reversible Rack and place onto a cooling rack for 10 minutes. Repeat steps 4 through 6 with the remaining bacon.

Homemade Dried Mango

Prep Time: 5 minutes, Cook Time: 8 hours, Serves: 2

INGREDIENTS:
½ mango, peeled, pitted, and cut into ⅜-inch slices

DIRECTIONS:
1. In a single layer in the Crisp Basket, add and flat the mango slices. Place the basket into the pot and close the Crisping Lid.
2. Press Dehydrate, set the temperature to 135°F(55°C), and set the time to 8 hours. Select Start/Stop to start.
3. Once dehydrating is complete, take the basket out from the pot and place the mango slices into an airtight container.

Cheesy Garlic Pea Arancini

Prep Time: 15 minutes, Cook Time: 45 minutes, Serves: 6

INGREDIENTS:

½ cup extra-virgin olive oil, plus 1 tbsp.	1½ cups grated Parmesan cheese, plus more for garnish
1 small yellow onion, diced	1 tsp. freshly ground black pepper
2 garlic cloves, minced	1 tsp. sea salt
½ cup white wine	2 cups fresh bread crumbs
5 cups chicken broth	2 large eggs
2 cups arborio rice	
1 cup frozen peas	

DIRECTIONS:
1. Preheat the pot by selecting Sear/Sauté. Select Start/Stop to begin. Preheat for 5 minutes.
2. In the preheated pot, add 1 tablespoon of oil and the onion. Cook until soft and translucent, stirring occasionally. Stir in the garlic and cook for 1 minute.
3. Place the wine, broth, and rice into the pot, stir to incorporate. Assemble the Pressure Lid, set the steamer valve to Seal.
4. Select Pressure. Set the time to 7 minutes. Press Start/Stop to begin.
5. After pressure cooking is finish, naturally release the pressure for 10 minutes, then turn the pressure release valve to the Vent position to quick release any remaining pressure. Remove the lid when the unit has finished releasing pressure carefully.
6. Add the frozen peas, Parmesan cheese, pepper and salt. Stir vigorously until the rice begins to thicken. Transfer the risotto to a large mixing bowl and allow it to cool.
7. At the same time, clean the pot. Stir together the bread crumbs and the remaining ½ cup of olive oil in a medium mixing bowl. Lightly beat the eggs in another mixing bowl.
8. Divide the risotto into 12 equal portions and shape each one into a ball. Dip each risotto ball in the beaten eggs, then dredge in the bread crumb mixture to coat well.
9. Arrange half of the arancini in the Crisp™ Basket in a single layer.
10. Close the Crisping Lid. Select Air Crisp, set the temperature to 400°F(205°C), and set the time to 10 minutes. Select Start/Stop to begin.
11. Repeat steps 9 and 10 to cook another half of arancini.

Excellent Texas Caviar Dip

Prep Time: 15 minutes, Cook Time: 35 minutes, Serves: 10

INGREDIENTS:

1 slice bacon	juice)
2 cups dried black-eyed peas	¼ cup fresh cilantro, chopped
3 cloves garlic, minced	2 cups corn kernels
2 stalks celery, diced	½ small red onion, peeled and diced
1 small green bell pepper, seeded and diced	Juice of 1 lime
1 large sweet onion, peeled and diced	2 cups chicken broth
1 small jalapeño, seeded and diced	1 cup water
4 small Roma tomatoes, diced (including dicing	2 tbsps. plus ¼ cup olive oil, divided
	1 tbsp. red wine vinegar

DIRECTIONS:
1. Add 1 tbsp. olive oil in Ninja pressure cooker and heat it. Place onion, jalapeño, and celery and stir-fry for 3-5 minutes until onions are translucent. Add garlic and heat for about 1 minute. Add another tbsp of olive oil and black-eyed peas and bacon. Mix them well and then slowly pour in broth and water. Close lid tightly.
2. Press Pressure and set the timer for 30 minutes. When timer beeps, let the pressure naturally release for 5 minutes. Quick-release the remaining pressure until the float valve drops down and then open lid.
3. Using a slotted spoon to move bean mixture to a serving dish. Let it cool. Add in bell pepper, tomatoes, corn, red onion, lime juice, vinegar, ¼ cup olive oil, and cilantro and stir to make sure they are coated well. Place to refrigerator overnight to mix flavors. Serve warm or chilled.

Ninja Foodi Chili Ranch Chicken Wings

Prep Time: 10 minutes, Cook Time: 28 minutes, Serves: 4

INGREDIENTS:
2 tbsps. unsalted butter, melted
1½ tbsps. apple cider vinegar
½ cup hot pepper sauce
½ cup water

½ (1-ounce, 28 g) envelope ranch salad dressing mix
½ tsp. paprika
2 pounds (907 g) frozen chicken wings
Nonstick cooking spray

DIRECTIONS:
1. In the pot, add the butter, vinegar, hot pepper sauce and water. Put the wings in the Crisp Basket and place the basket in the pot. Assemble the Pressure Lid, set the steamer valve to Seal.
2. Select Pressure. Set the time to 5 minutes. Select Start/Stop to begin.
3. After pressure cooking is finish, turn the pressure release valve to the Vent position to quick release the pressure. Remove the lid when the unit has finished releasing pressure carefully.
4. Sprinkle the dressing mix and paprika over the chicken wings. Use cooking spray to coat.
5. Close the Crisping Lid. Select Air Crisp, set the temperature to 375°F(190°C), and set the time to 15 minutes. Select Start/Stop to begin.
6. After 7 minutes, open the Crisping Lid, lift the basket and shake the wings. Use cooking spray to coat. Lower the basket back into the pot and close the lid to resume cooking until the wings reach your desired crispiness.

Cheesy Buffalo Chicken Meatballs

Prep Time: 10 minutes, Cook Time: 40 minutes, Serves: 6

INGREDIENTS:
1 egg
1 carrot, minced
1 pound (454 g) ground chicken
2 celery stalks, minced
¼ cup buffalo sauce

¼ cup crumbled blue cheese
¼ cup bread crumbs
2 tbsps. extra-virgin olive oil
½ cup water

DIRECTIONS:
1. Preheat the pot by selecting Sear/Sauté. Select Start/Stop to begin. Preheat for 5 minutes.
2. While preheating, mix together the egg, carrot, chicken, celery, buffalo sauce, blue cheese and bread crumbs in a large mixing bowl. Form the mixture into 1½-inch meatballs.
3. In the preheated pot, add the olive oil, then stir in the meatballs, in batches, sear on all sides until browned. After each batch finishes cooking, transfer to a plate.
4. Place the Crisp Basket in the pot. Add the water, then transfer all the meatballs into the basket.
5. Assemble the Pressure Lid, set the steamer valve to Seal. Select Pressure. Set the time to 5 minutes. Select Start/Stop to begin.
6. After pressure cooking is finish, turn the pressure release valve to the Vent position to quick release the pressure. Remove the lid when the unit has finished releasing pressure carefully.
7. Close the Crisping Lid. Select Air Crisp, set the temperature to 360°F(180°C), and set the time to 10 minutes. Select Start/Stop to begin.
8. After air crisping for 5 minutes, open the lid, lift the basket and shake the meatballs. Lower the basket back into the pot and close the lid to resume cooking until achieve your desired crispiness.

Chapter 11 Salad

Turkey and Wild Rice Salad with Walnuts

Prep Time: 10 minutes, Cook Time: 50 minutes, Serves: 4

INGREDIENTS:

4 cups water
1 cup wild rice
2¼ tsps. kosher salt (or 1⅛ tsps. fine salt), divided
1 pound (454 g) turkey tenderloins
3 tsps. walnut oil or olive oil, divided
3 tbsps. apple cider vinegar
⅛ tsp. freshly ground
black pepper
¼ tsp. celery seeds
Pinch sugar
½ cup walnut pieces, toasted
2 or 3 celery stalks, thinly sliced (about 1 cup)
1 medium Gala, Fuji, or Braeburn apple, cored and cut into ½-inch pieces

DIRECTIONS:

1. In the Foodi inner pot, add the water. Stir in 1 teaspoon of kosher salt (or ½ teaspoon of fine salt) and the wild rice.
2. Lock the Pressure Lid into place, set the valve to Seal. Select Pressure, adjust the cook time to 18 minutes. Press Start.
3. Meanwhile, sprinkle 1 teaspoon of kosher salt (or ½ teaspoon of fine salt) onto the turkey tenderloins and set aside.
4. After the rice is cooked, naturally release the pressure for 10 minutes, then quick release any remaining pressure. Open and remove the Pressure Lid carefully. The rice grains should be mostly split open. If not, select Sear/Sauté. Press Start. Simmer the rice for several minutes until at least half the grains have split. Drain and allow to cool slightly. Place to a large bowl to cool completely.
5. Close the Crisping Lid and preheat by selecting Bake/Roast, adjusting the temperature to 375°F(190°C) and the time to 4 minutes. Press Start.
6. Meanwhile, place the turkey into the Crisp™ Basket and use 2 teaspoons of walnut oil to brush.
7. Once the pot is preheated, place the basket in it.
8. Close the Crisping Lid and select Bake/Roast, adjust the temperature to 375°F(190°C) and the cook time to 12 minutes. Press Start.
9. At the same time, in a jar with a tight-fitting lid, add the remaining 1 teaspoon of walnut oil and the vinegar. Add the remaining ¼ teaspoon of kosher salt (or ⅛ teaspoon of fine salt), the pepper, the celery seed, and the sugar. Cover the jar and shake until the ingredients are well combined.
10. After the turkey is cooked, take it out from the basket and allow to cool for several minutes. Cut it into chunks and place the turkey over the rice along with the celery, walnut pieces, and apple. Over the salad pour with about half the dressing and toss gently to coat, adding more dressing as desired.

Farro and Strawberry Salad

Prep Time: 17 minutes, Cook Time: 18 minutes, Serves: 8

INGREDIENTS:

FOR THE FARRO
1 cup farro, rinsed and drained
¼ tsp. kosher salt
FOR THE DRESSING
½ tbsp. fruit-flavored balsamic vinegar
1 tbsp. freshly squeezed lime juice (from ½ medium lime)
½ tsp. Dijon mustard
½ tsp. poppy seeds
½ tbsp. honey or pure
maple syrup
¼ cup (60 ml) extra-virgin olive oil
FOR THE SALAD
1¼ cups sliced strawberries
¼ cup slivered almonds, toasted
Fresh basil leaves, cut into a chiffonade, for garnish
Freshly ground black pepper

DIRECTIONS:

TO MAKE THE FARRO
1. Combine the farro, salt, and 2 cups of water in the electric pressure cooker.
2. Close the lid. Set the valve to seal.
3. Select Pressure and cook for 10 minutes.
4. Once cooking is complete, allow the pressure to Ninja naturally for 10 minutes, then quick release the remaining pressure. Press Stop.
5. When the pin drops, unlock and remove the lid.
6. Fluff the farro with a fork and cool it down.
TO MAKE THE DRESSING
1. In a small jar with a screw-top lid, combine the balsamic vinegar, lime juice, mustard, poppy seeds, honey, and olive oil. Shake until well combined.
TO MAKE THE SALAD
1. Toss the farro with the dressing in a large bowl. Stir in the strawberries and almonds.
2. Serve seasoned with pepper, and garnished with basil.

Seedy Celery and Carrot Salad

Prep Time: 10 minutes, Cook Time: 25 minutes, Serves: 2

INGREDIENTS:

2 celery ribs, sliced ½ inch thick (about 1 cup)
2 large carrots, peeled and cut into ½-inch rounds (about 1 cup)
1 tbsp. extra-virgin olive oil
1½ tsps. sugar
2 tbsps. red wine vinegar
⅛ tsp. mustard seeds
1 tsp. kosher salt
⅛ tsp. celery seeds

DIRECTIONS:

1. In a steamer basket, add the celery and carrots. Pour in 1 cup of water to the inner pot and put the steamer basket inside. Lock the lid into place. Select Steam and adjust the time to 2 minutes. After cooking, quick release the pressure.
2. Meanwhile, make the dressing. Add the olive oil, sugar, vinegar, mustard seeds, salt and celery seeds into a medium bowl, whisk them together.
3. Unlock the lid. Place the cooked celery and carrots to the bowl. Allow them to cool in the dressing for 10 to 15 minutes, tossing occasionally.

Cranberries, Almonds and Wild Rice Salad

Prep Time: 10 minutes, Cook Time: 36 minutes, Serves: 18

INGREDIENTS:

FOR THE RICE
2½ cups (600 ml) Vegetable Broth or Chicken Bone Broth
2 cups wild rice blend, rinsed
1 tsp. kosher salt
FOR THE DRESSING
¼ cup (60 ml) extra-virgin olive oil
¼ cup (60 ml) white wine vinegar
Juice of 1 medium orange (about ¼ cup, 60 ml)
1 tsp. honey or pure maple syrup
1½ tsp. grated orange zest
FOR THE SALAD
Freshly ground black pepper
¾ cup unsweetened dried cranberries
½ cup sliced almonds, toasted

DIRECTIONS:

TO MAKE THE RICE
1. Combine the rice, salt, and broth in the Ninja pressure cooker.
2. Close the pressure lid. Set the valve to seal
3. Select Pressure and cook for 25 minutes.
4. Once cooking is complete, press Stop and allow the pressure to release naturally for 15 minutes, then quick release any remaining pressure.
5. When the pin drops, unlock and remove the lid.
6. Let the rice cool slightly, then fluff it with a fork.
TO MAKE THE DRESSING
1. In a small jar with a screw-top lid, mix the olive oil, zest, juice, vinegar, and honey. Shake to combine.
TO MAKE THE SALAD
1. Combine the rice, almonds and cranberries in a large bowl.
2. Add the dressing and season with pepper.
3. Serve immediately or refrigerated.

Barley Salad with Lemon-Tahini Sauce

Prep Time: 15 minutes, Cook Time: 45 minutes, Serves: 4 to 6

INGREDIENTS:

1½ cups pearl barley
5 tbsps. extra-virgin olive oil, divided
1½ tsps. table salt, for cooking barley
¼ cup (60 ml) tahini
1 tsp. grated lemon zest plus ¼ cup (60 ml) juice (2 lemons)
1 tbsp. sumac, divided
1 garlic clove, minced
4 scallions, sliced thin
¾ tsp. table salt
1 English cucumber, cut into ½-inch pieces
1 red bell pepper, stemmed, seeded, and chopped
1 carrot, peeled and shredded
2 tbsps. finely chopped jarred hot cherry peppers
¼ cup coarsely chopped fresh mint

DIRECTIONS:

1. Mix 6 cups water, 1 tablespoon oil, barley, and 1½ teaspoons salt in Ninja pressure cooker. Lock lid and close pressure release valve. Choose pressure function and cook for 8 minutes. Turn off and let pressure release naturally for 15 minutes. Quick-release any remaining pressure, then carefully remove lid, letting steam escape away from you. Drain barley, spread onto rimmed baking sheet, and let cool for about 15 minutes.
2. 2 Meanwhile, whisk remaining ¼ cup oil, 1 teaspoon sumac, 2 tablespoons water, tahini, lemon zest and juice, garlic, and ¾ teaspoon salt in large bowl until well mixed, set aside for 15 minutes.
3. 3 Measure out and reserve ½ cup dressing for serving. Add barley, carrot, scallions, cucumber, bell pepper, and cherry peppers to bowl with dressing and gently toss. Season with salt and pepper. Transfer salad to a dish and sprinkle with mint and remaining sumac. Serve with reserved dressing separately.

Chicken Caesar Lettuce Salad

Prep Time: 15 minutes, Cook Time: 30 minutes, Serves: 4

INGREDIENTS:

¾ tsp. kosher salt (or a scant ½ tsp. fine salt), plus more for sprinkling the croutons
2 (14-to 16-ounce, 397 to 454 g) boneless skinless chicken breasts
1½ tbsps. extra-virgin olive oil
1 large garlic clove, minced
1 tbsp. unsalted butter
½ small baguette or Italian bread loaf, cut into ¾-inch cubes (about 2 cups)
⅓ cup Caesar dressing, divided
1 romaine lettuce heart, torn into bite-size pieces or 1 (10-ounce, 283 g) bag torn romaine
1 ounce (28 g) Parmesan or similar cheese, coarsely grated (about ⅓ cup), plus more for serving
Freshly ground black pepper

DIRECTIONS:

1. To prepare an ice bath, fill half full of cold water into a medium bowl, and add a handful of ice cubes. Set aside.
2. Use salt to season the both sides of the chicken.
3. In the Foodi inner pot, add 1 cup of water. place the chicken on the Reversible Rack, and then put in the pot.
4. Lock the Pressure Lid into place, set the valve to Seal. Select Pressure, adjust the cook time to 5 minutes. Press Start.
5. When the cooking is complete, naturally release the pressure for 8 minutes, then quick release any remaining pressure. Open and remove the Pressure Lid carefully. Use a thermometer to test the temperature of the breasts, and it should register at least 150°F(65°C) in the center. Place the Pressure Lid back on the pot and let the chicken sit for a few minutes more if not. After cooking, place the chicken breasts in a resealable plastic bag and seal, squeezing as much air out as possible. Transfer the bag into the ice bath for 5 minutes to stop the cooking, weighing it down with a small plate if needed. Pour the liquid out of the inner pot and place it back to the base.
6. Combine the olive oil, garlic, and butter in a 1-quart heat-proof bowl. Put the bowl in the Crisp™ Basket and put the basket in the pot.
7. Close the Crisping Lid and select Air Crisp, adjust the temperature to 375°F(190°C) and the cook time to 2 minutes to preheat the Foodi™ and melt the butter. Press Start.
8. After preheating, remove the basket from the pot and the bowl from the basket.
9. Stir in the bread cubes to the bowl and toss to coat evenly with the oil and butter. Place them into the Crisp Basket and return the basket into the pot.
10. Close the Crisping Lid and select Air Crisp, adjust the temperature to 375°F(190°C) and the cook time to 10 minutes. Press Start. After 5 minutes, open the lid and toss the croutons. Close the lid and continue to cook until the croutons are golden brown on the outside but still slightly soft inside. Take the basket out from the pot and lightly sprinkle the croutons with the salt. Allow to cool.
11. Meanwhile, take the chicken out from the bag and cut it into bite-size chunks. Toss the chicken with 2 to 3 tablespoons of Caesar dressing in a small bowl, just to coat. Set aside.
12. To assemble, pour about one-third of the remaining dressing around the sides of a serving bowl. Add the lettuce and toss gently to coat, adding more dressing if necessary. Add the cheese and pepper to taste and toss to distribute. Divide the salad among four bowls and top with the croutons and chicken, sprinkling over with extra cheese, if desired.

Beet Salad with Lemon Dill Dressing

Prep Time: 10 minutes, Cook Time: 20 minutes, Serves: 2

INGREDIENTS:

2 medium (2- to 3-inch) beets, stemmed and roots trimmed
1 tbsp. Greek yogurt
2 tsps. mayonnaise
1 tsp. freshly squeezed lemon juice
½ tsp. grated lemon zest
¼ tsp. kosher salt
1 tbsp. minced fresh dill

DIRECTIONS:

1. In the steamer basket, add the beets. In the inner pot, add 1 cup of water and place the steamer basket inside. Lock the lid into place. Select Pressure, and adjust the time to 8 minutes. After cooking, allow the pressure to release naturally for 6 minutes, then quick release any remaining pressure.
2. Unlock the lid. Take the beets out and set aside to cool.
3. Meanwhile, make the dressing. Add the yogurt, mayonnaise, lemon juice, lemon zest and salt into a medium bowl, whisk them together.
4. When the beets are cool enough to handle, use a paring knife to peel them slip off the skin. Cut in half, then slice into large bite-size pieces. Mix into the dressing and coat well. Add the dill and toss again before serving.

White Bean Cucumber Salad

Prep Time: 10 minutes, Cook Time: 20 minutes, Serves: 4

INGREDIENTS:

1 tbsp. plus 1 tsp. kosher salt (or 2 tsps. fine salt), divided
14 ounces (397 g) dried cannellini beans
4 tbsps. plus 1 tsp. extra-virgin olive oil, divided
1-quart water
3 tbsps. freshly squeezed lemon juice
¼ tsp. freshly ground black pepper
1 tsp. ground cumin
1 large celery stalk, chopped (about ½ cup)
1 medium red or green bell pepper, chopped (about 1 cup)
1 large tomato, seeded and chopped (about ½ cup)
½ cucumber, peeled, seeded, and chopped (about ¾ cup)
3 or 4 scallions, chopped (about ⅓ cup)
1 cup crumbled feta cheese (optional)
¼ cup minced fresh parsley
2 tbsps. minced fresh mint

DIRECTIONS:

1. Dissolve 1 tablespoon of kosher salt (or 1½ teaspoons of fine salt) in 1 quart of water in a large bowl. Add the beans and let them soak at room temperature for 8 to 24 hours.
2. Drain and rinse the beans. Transfer them into the Foodi inner pot. Add 1 teaspoon of olive oil and stir to coat the beans. Add ½ teaspoon of kosher salt (or ¼ teaspoon of fine salt) and 1 quart of water.
3. Lock the Pressure Lid into place, set the valve to Seal. Select Pressure and the cook time to 5 minutes. Press Start.
4. Meanwhile, combine 3 tablespoons of olive oil and the lemon juice and in a small jar with a tight-fitting lid. Add the remaining ½ teaspoon of kosher salt (or ¼ teaspoon of fine salt), the pepper and cumin. Cover the jar and shake the dressing until thoroughly combined.
5. When the cooking is complete, naturally release the pressure for 10 minutes, then quick release any remaining pressure. Unlock and remove the Pressure Lid carefully.
6. Drain the beans and place them into a bowl. Immediately pour the dressing over the beans and toss to coat. Allow to cool to room temperature, stirring occasionally.
7. Add the celery, bell pepper, tomato, cucumber, scallions, and feta cheese (if using, omit for a dairy-free and vegan dish) to the beans. Gently toss well. Add the parsley and mint, toss to combine before serving.

Lemony Black Rice and Edamame Salad

Prep Time: 15 minutes, Cook Time: 28 minutes, Serves: 8

INGREDIENTS:

FOR THE RICE
1 cup (240 ml) black rice, rinsed and still wet
FOR THE DRESSING
3 tbsps. extra-virgin olive oil
2 tbsps. freshly squeezed lemon juice
2 tbsps. rice vinegar
1 tbsp. honey or pure maple syrup
1 tbsp. sesame oil

FOR THE SALAD
1 (8-ounce, 227 g) bag frozen shelled edamame, thawed (about 1½ cups)
¼ cup chopped walnuts
2 scallions, both white and green parts, thinly sliced
Kosher salt
Freshly ground black pepper

DIRECTIONS:

TO MAKE THE RICE
1. Combine the rice and 1 cup of water in the electric pressure cooker.
2. Close the lid of the pressure cooker. Set the valve to seal.
3. Select Pressure and cook for 22 minutes.
4. Once cooking is complete, press Stop and allow the pressure to release naturally for 10 minutes, then quick release any remaining pressure.
5. When the pin drops, unlock and remove the lid.
6. Fluff the rice with a fork and cool it down.

TO MAKE THE DRESSING
1. In a small jar with a screw-top lid, mix the olive oil, vinegar, lemon juice, honey or maple syrup, and sesame oil. Shake to combine.

TO MAKE THE SALAD
1. In a large bowl, toss the rice and dressing. Stir in the scallions, edamame, and walnuts.
2. Season with salt and pepper.

Chapter 12 Snack and Dessert

Crustless Key Lime Cheesecake

Prep Time: 15 minutes, Cook Time: 41 minutes, Serves: 8

INGREDIENTS:

Nonstick cooking spray
16 ounces sour cream
⅔ cup granulated erythritol sweetener
¼ cup unsweetened Key lime juice (I like Nellie & Joe's Famous Key West Lime Juice)
½ tsp. vanilla extract
¼ cup plain non-dairy yogurt
1 tsp. grated lemon zest
2 large eggs
Whipped cream, for garnish (optional)

DIRECTIONS:

1. Spray a 7-inch springform pan with nonstick cooking spray. Line the bottom and partway up the sides of the pan with foil.
2. Put the sour cream in a large bowl. Use an electric mixer to whip the cream cheese until smooth, about 2 minutes. Add the erythritol, lemon zest, vanilla, yogurt, and zest, and blend until smooth. Stop the mixer and scrape down the sides of the bowl with a rubber spatula. With the mixer on low speed, add the eggs, one at a time, blending until just mixed. (Don't overbeat the eggs.)
3. Pour the mixture into the prepared pan. Drape a paper towel over the top of the pan, not touching the cream cheese mixture, and tightly wrap the top of the pan in foil. (Your goal here is to keep out as much moisture as possible.)
4. Pour 1 cup of water into the Ninja pressure cooker.
5. Place the foil-covered pan onto the wire rack and carefully lower it into the pot.
6. Close and lock the pressure lid. Set the valve to Seal.
7. Select Pressure and cook for 35 minutes.
8. When the cooking is complete, hit Stop. Allow the pressure to release naturally for 20 minutes, then quick release any remaining pressure.
9. Once the pin drops, unlock and remove the lid.
10. Using the handles of the wire rack, carefully transfer the pan to a cooling rack. Cool to room temperature, then refrigerate for at least 3 hours.
11. When ready to serve, run a thin rubber spatula around the rim of the cheesecake to loosen it, then remove the ring.
12. Slice into wedges and serve with whipped cream (if using).

Hot Apple and Cranberry Cider

Prep Time: 10 minutes, Cook Time: 10 minutes, Serves: 5 cups (1.2 L)

INGREDIENTS:

6 apples, peeled, cored and quartered
3 cups (300 g) frozen or fresh cranberries
Zest and juice of 2 medium oranges
⅓ cup (80 ml) honey or pure maple syrup
1 (1" [2.5-cm]) piece fresh
ginger, peeled and sliced
3 cinnamon sticks
13 whole cloves
2½ cups (590 ml) filtered water, plus more as needed
Vanilla ice cream, for serving (optional)

DIRECTIONS:

1. Add the apples and water into a high-powered blender, process until fully blended and liquefied.
2. Place the apple juice through a fine-mesh strainer into the Ninja pressure cooker.
3. Mix in the cranberries, orange zest and juice, natural sweetener of your choice, ginger, cinnamon sticks and cloves. Add more filtered water if the liquid volume does not reach the "5 cups" mark on the inside of the pot.
4. Press sauté and bring the mixture to a boil. When the cider starts to boil, pressing keep warm/Stop to turn off the pot.
5. Secure the lid with the steam vent in the sealed position. Press Pressure and cook for 10 minutes.
6. When the timer sounds, press keep warm/Stop. Let the pot release pressure naturally for 15 minutes. Do a quick release with an oven mitt. If there is any steam left over, allow it to release until the silver dial drops, then carefully open the lid.
7. With an oven mitt, carefully ladle or pour the superhot spiced cider through a fine-mesh strainer into a very large bowl or large heatproof pitcher. Repeat the straining one more time to remove all the fruit pulp, if needed.
8. Serve immediately, topped with a scoop of vanilla ice cream for extra decadence (if using).
9. Or you would not drink right away and would like to keep it hot, place it back in the pot after straining and turn on the pot's warming setting by pressing keep warm/Stop.

Savory Bread Pudding with Mushrooms and Kale

Prep Time: 20 minutes, Cook Time: 20 minutes, Serves: 2

INGREDIENTS:

a single huge egg
½ cup milk (2% fat)
½ tsp. mustard (Dijon)
1 tsp. nutmeg, freshly grated
1 tsp. kosher salt
1 tsp. freshly ground black pepper
1 slice sourdough bread, cut into 1-inch cubes (about 1 ounce)
1 tbsp. avocado butter
¼ cup onion, chopped

2 oz. sliced mushrooms (about 3 creminis)
¼ tsp. thyme (dry)
1 cup Lacinato kale, cut, stems and ribs removed (from 2 stems)
Cooking spray that is nonstick
¼ cup Gruyère cheese, grated
1 tbsp. Parmesan cheese, shredded

DIRECTIONS:

1. In a 2-cup measuring cup with a spout, whisk together the egg, milk, mustard, nutmeg, salt, and pepper. After adding the bread, submerge it in the liquid.
2. Set the Ninja pressure cooker to the Sauté setting. Once the pot is hot, pour in the avocado oil.
3. Sauté the onion, mushrooms, and thyme in a large skillet for 3 to 5 minutes, or until the onion softens. Cook, stirring occasionally, for approximately 2 minutes, or until the kale has wilted. Press Stop.
4. Spray the ramekins with cooking spray. Halfway fill the ramekins with the mushroom mixture. On top of each, 2 tablespoons Gruyère Pour half of the egg mixture into each ramekin and whisk well. Make sure the bread is fully immersed in the liquid. Wrap foil around the dish and secure it with a rubber band.
5. Add 1 cup of water to the pot and a wire rack or trivet. Place the ramekins on the rack.
6. Secure the pressure cooker's lid by closing and locking it. To shut the valve, turn it to the closed position.
7. Select Pressure, preheat the pot for 8 minutes.
8. Press the stop button after the cooking is done. Allow a 10-minute natural release before releasing any remaining pressure rapidly.
9. Using tongs or the rack's handles, transfer the ramekins to a cutting board. Carefully remove the foil and sprinkle the Parmesan on top. Replace the foil for 5 minutes more, or until the cheese has fully melted.
10. Remove the foil from the pot immediately and serve.

Mixed Cheese Spinach and Artichoke Bites

Prep Time: 20 minutes, Cook Time: 24 minutes, Serves: 8

INGREDIENTS:

¼ cup cottage cheese
¼ cup feta cheese
2 tbsps. grated Parmesan cheese
¼ cup finely chopped artichoke hearts
¼ cup frozen chopped spinach
1 large egg white
1 tsp. dried oregano

Zest of 1 lemon
½ tsp. sea salt
½ tsp. freshly ground black pepper
4 (13-by-18-inch) sheets frozen phyllo dough, thawed
1 tbsp. extra-virgin olive oil

DIRECTIONS:

1. Add all of the ingredients except the phyllo dough and olive oil into a medium mixing bowl, combine them together.
2. Put the Crisp Basket in the pot. Close the Crisping Lid. Select Air Crisp, set the temperature to 375°F(190°C), and set the time to 5 minutes. Press Start/Stop to begin to preheat.
3. At the same time, on a clean work surface, place 1 phyllo sheet. Use some of the olive oil to brush it all over. Place a second sheet of phyllo on top of the first and use more oil to brush with. Continue layering to form a stack of 4 oiled sheets.
4. Working from the short side, cut the stack of phyllo sheets into 8 (2¼-inch-wide) strips. Then cut the strips in half to form 16 (2¼-inch-wide) strips.
5. Spoon onto 1 short end of each strip with about 1 tablespoon of filling. Fold one corner over the filling to create a triangle, continue folding back and forth to the end of the strip, creating a triangle-shaped phyllo packet. Repeat until you have formed 16 phyllo bites.
6. Open the Crisping Lid and arrange half of the phyllo bites in the basket in a single layer. Close the lid, select Air Crisp, set the temperature to 350°F(180°C), and set the time to 12 minutes. Press Start/Stop to begin.
7. After air crisping for 6 minutes, open the lid and flip the bites over. Lower the basket back into the pot and close the lid to resume cooking.
8. 6 minutes later, check the packets for your desired crispiness. If done, take the bites out from the basket.
9. Repeat steps 6, 7, and 8 with the remaining bites.

Ninja Foodi Campfire S' Mores

Prep Time: 10 minutes, Cook Time: 4 minutes, Serves: 4

INGREDIENTS:
2 (1½-ounce, 43 g) chocolate bars

4 graham crackers
4 marshmallows

DIRECTIONS:
1. Place the Crisp Basket in the pot and close the Crisping Lid. Select Air Crisp to preheat the unit, set the temperature to 350°F(180°C), and set the time to 5 minutes. Press Start/Stop to begin.
2. Cut a graham cracker in half. Place half a chocolate bar on one half of the graham cracker. Add a marshmallow and top with the remaining graham cracker half to create a s' more. Repeat with the remaining ingredients to create 4 s' mores.
3. Wrap each s' more individually with aluminum foil. In the preheated Crisp Basket, add all 4 foil-wrapped s' mores.
4. Close the Crisping Lid. Select Air Crisp, set the temperature to 350°F(180°C), and set the time to 4 minutes. Press Start/Stop to begin.
5. After cooking is complete, unwrap the s' mores carefully and serve.

Garlic and Lime Chicken Wings with Chipotle

Prep Time: 10 minutes, Cook Time: 28 minutes, Serves: 4

INGREDIENTS:
2 pounds (907 g) frozen chicken wings
Juice of 2 limes
Zest of 1 lime
¼ cup extra-virgin olive oil
2 tbsps.chipotle chiles in

adobo sauce, chopped
1tbsp. minced garlic
Freshly ground black pepper
½ cup water
Sea salt

DIRECTIONS:
1. Pour the water into the pot. Place the wings in the Crisp Basket and insert the basket in the pot. Assemble pressure lid, set the steamer valve to Seal.
2. Select HI PRESSURE, set the time 5 minutes. Press START.
3. Combine olive oil, chipotles in adobo sauce, lime juice, lime zest, garlic, salt, and pepper in a large bowl. Mix well.

4. After cooking is complete, move pressure release valve to VENT position to quickly release the pressure. Carefully remove lid.
5. Place the chicken wings in the large bowl and toss to coat. Put the wings to the basket again.
6. Select AIR CRISP, set temperature to 375°F(190ºC) and the time 15 minutes. Press START.
7. After 7 minutes, lift the basket and shake the wings. Lower the basket back into the pot. Continue cooking until the wings reach desired crispiness.

Delicious Apple Cider Doughnuts

Prep Time: 10 minutes, Cook Time: 30 minutes, Serves: 6 doughnuts

INGREDIENTS:
FOR THE DOUGHNUTS
½ cup plus 2 tablespoons all-purpose flour
1 tsp. ground cinnamon
¼ cup granulated sugar
¼ tsp. baking powder
½ tsp. kosher salt
¼ tsp. baking soda
¼ cup whole milk
1 large egg white

2 tbsps. apple juice
2 tbsps. vegetable oil
Cooking spray
2 tbsps. apple cider vinegar
FOR THE GLAZE
2 tbsps. apple juice
½ cup confectioners' sugar

DIRECTIONS:
1. Whisk the flour, granulated sugar, cinnamon, salt, baking powder, and baking soda in a medium bowl. Take out another medium bowl, whisk together the milk, egg white, apple juice, and vegetable oil.
2. Set the Foodi to Bake/Roast at 375°F (190ºC) for 5 minutes. Spray 6 silicone doughnut molds with cooking spray.
3. Pour the apple cider vinegar into the milk mixture and immediately add the wet ingredients to the dry ingredients. Combine with a wooden spoon until no dry streaks remain. Put the batter into a zippered plastic bag, cut a bottom corner off the bag, and pipe the batter into the doughnut molds.
4. Place the reversible rack into the Foodi's inner pot in the low position and arrange the doughnut molds on the rack. Set the Foodi to Bake/Roast at 350°F(180ºC) for 10 minutes.
5. Take the rack out from the Foodi. Let the doughnuts cool completely before unmolding them.
6. Make the glaze: Whisk the confectioners' sugar and apple juice in a small bowl. Put the tops of the cooled doughnuts facedown into the glaze, then set on a wire rack to let the glaze set.

Cheese and Garlic Crack Bread

Prep Time: 10 minutes, Cook Time: 25 minutes, Serves: 6

INGREDIENTS:

½ pound (227 g) store-bought pizza dough
¼ cup shredded Parmesan cheese
¼ cup shredded mozzarella cheese
¼ cup minced parsley
4 garlic cloves, minced
3 tbsps. unsalted butter, melted
½ tsp. garlic powder
Cooking spray
½ tsp. kosher salt
Marinara sauce
pepperoni slices

DIRECTIONS:

1. Cut the pizza dough into 1-inch cubes, roll each cube into a ball. Take a large bowl, add the dough balls, butter, garlic, Parmesan cheese, mozzarella cheese, parsley, salt, and garlic powder into it. Toss until everything is evenly coated and mixed.
2. Select BAKE/ROAST, set temperature to 325°F(165ºC) and the time to 30 minutes. Preheat for 5 minutes.
3. Spray the Ninja Multi-Purpose Pan with cooking spray. Add dough balls to pan and place pan on Reversible Rack.
4. After unit has preheated, insert the rack. Heat for 25 minutes.
5. Take bread out from pot. Top with pepperoni slices and serve with marinara sauce.

Frosted Strawberry Toaster Pastries

Prep Time: 15 minutes, Cook Time: 20 minutes, Serves: 4

INGREDIENTS:

¼ cup Simple Strawberry Jam
1 refrigerated piecrust, at room temperature
Vanilla icing, for frosting
Nonstick cooking spray
Rainbow sprinkles, for topping

DIRECTIONS:

1. Place the Crisp Basket in the pot and close the Crisping Lid. Preheat the unit by selecting Air Crisp, set the temperature to 350°F(180°C), and set the time to 5 minutes.
2. Roll out the piecrust into a large rectangle on a lightly floured surface. Cut the dough into 8 rectangles.
3. In the center of each of 4 dough rectangles, spoon with 1 tablespoon of strawberry jam, leaving a

½-inch border. Use water to brush the edges of the filled dough rectangles. Top each with one of the remaining 4 dough rectangles. Use a fork to press the edges to seal.
4. Place the pastries in the preheated basket carefully. Use cooking spray to coat each pastry well and arrange 2 pastries in the Crisp Basket in a single layer.
5. Close the Crisping Lid and select Air Crisp, set the temperature to 350°F(180°C), and set the time to 10 minutes. Press Start/Stop to begin. When the cooking is complete, check for your desired crispiness, then place the pastries on a wire rack to cool. Repeat steps 1 through 5 with the remaining 2 pastries.
6. Use vanilla icing to frost the pastries, then top with sprinkles.

Pimiento Cheese Creamed Corn Pudding

Prep Time: 10 minutes, Cook Time: 1 hour on low, Serves: 2

INGREDIENTS:

½ tsp. sugar
¼ tsp. kosher salt
2 tsps. all-purpose flour
½ tsp. baking powder
⅓ cup heavy (whipping) cream
1 large egg
1 tbsp. unsalted butter, melted and cooled
1 cup frozen corn kernels, thawed
3 ounces (85 g) sharp Cheddar cheese, grated (about 1 cup)
1 tbsp. finely chopped onion
¼ cup chopped roasted red pepper
½ tsp. hot pepper sauce, such as Tabasco
Nonstick cooking spray

DIRECTIONS:

1. Add the sugar, salt, flour and baking powder into a small bowl, stir them together until blended. Add the cream, egg and melted butter into a medium bowl, whisk them until blended. Combine the flour mixture with the egg mixture. Then add the corn, cheese, onion, red pepper, and hot sauce, stir well.
2. Grease the bottom and sides of a 1-quart-round baking dish generously. Spoon the mixture into the baking dish and use aluminum foil to cover.
3. Pour 1 cup of water into the inner pot. Put the trivet inside and then on the trivet place with the baking dish. Lock the pressure lid into place. Select Pressure Cook, and adjust the time to 15 minutes. After cooking, allow the pressure to naturally release for 10 minutes, then quick release any remaining pressure.
4. Unlock the lid. Take the dish out from the pot and allow it to sit 2 or 3 minutes and serve.

Peach Crunch

Prep Time: 13 minutes, Cook Time: 9 minutes, Serves: 4

INGREDIENTS:

3 peaches, peeled, cored, and sliced (about 1½ pounds)
1 tsp. pure maple syrup
1 tsp. pear pie spice or

ground cinnamon
¼ cup unsweetened pear juice, apple cider, or water
¼ cup low-sugar granola

DIRECTIONS:

1. In the Ninja pressure cooker, combine the peaches, maple syrup, pear pie spice, and pear juice.
2. Close and lock the pressure lid Set the valve to Seal.
3. Select Pressure and cook for 2 minutes.
4. When the cooking is complete, hit Stop and quick release the pressure.
5. Once the pin drops, unlock and remove the lid.
6. Spoon the apples into 4 serving bowls and sprinkle each with 1 tablespoon of granola.

Fried Crispy Dumplings

Prep Time: 20 minutes, Cook Time: 12 minutes, Serves: 8

INGREDIENTS:

1 large egg, beaten
8 ounces (227 g) ground pork
½ cup shredded Napa cabbage
1 carrot, shredded
2 tbsps. reduced-sodium soy sauce
1 garlic clove, minced

½ tbsp. grated fresh ginger
½ tbsp. sesame oil
½ tsp. sea salt
½ tsp. freshly ground black pepper
20 wonton wrappers
2 tbsps. vegetable oil

DIRECTIONS:

1. Put the Crisp Basket in the pot. Close the Crisping Lid. Select Air Crisp, set the temperature to 400°F(205°C), and set the time to 5 minutes to preheat the unit.
2. While preheating, combine the egg, pork, cabbage, carrot, soy sauce, garlic, ginger, sesame oil, salt, and pepper in a large mixing bowl.
3. On a clean work surface, place the wonton wrappers and spoon 1 tablespoon of the pork mixture into the center of each wrapper. Use water to gently rub the edges of the wrappers. Fold the dough over the filling to create a half-moon shape, pinching the edges to seal. Use the vegetable oil to brush the dumplings.
4. Put the dumplings in the Crisp™ Basket. Select Air Crisp, set the temperature to 400°F(205°C), and set

the time to 12 minutes. Select Start/Stop to begin.
5. Six minutes later, open the lid, lift the basket and shake the dumplings. Lower the basket back into the pot and close the lid to resume cooking until achieve your desired crispiness.

Cinnamon, Black and Blue Berry Crumble

Prep Time: 10 minutes, Cook Time: 30 minutes, Serves: 6

INGREDIENTS:

1 (16-ounce, 454 g) package frozen blueberries
1 (16-ounce, 454 g) package frozen blackberries
1 tsp. freshly squeezed lemon juice
2 tbsps. cornstarch

½ cup water, plus 1 tbsp.
5 tbsps. granulated sugar, divided
½ cup rolled oats
½ cup all-purpose flour
⅓ cup cold unsalted butter, cut into pieces
⅔ cup brown sugar
1 tsp. ground cinnamon

DIRECTIONS:

1. In the Multi-Purpose Pan or a 1½-quart round ceramic baking dish, add the blueberries and blackberries.
2. Add the lemon juice, cornstarch, 1 tablespoon of water and 3 tablespoons of granulated sugar in a small mixing bowl, stir them together. Then pour this mixture over the fruit.
3. Put the pan on the Reversible Rack. Use aluminum foil to cover the pan. Pour the remaining ½ cup of water into the pot and add the rack with the pan to the pot. Assemble the Pressure Lid, set the steamer valve to Seal.
4. Select Pressure. Set the time to 10 minutes, then select Start/Stop to begin.
5. Add the oats, flour, butter, brown sugar, cinnamon, and remaining 2 tablespoons of granulated sugar in a medium mixing bowl, combine them together until a crumble forms.
6. After pressure cooking is complete, move the pressure release valve to the Vent position to quick release the pressure. Remove the lid when the pressure has finished releasing carefully.
7. Take the foil away and stir the fruit mixture. Spread the crumble topping evenly over the fruit.
8. Close the Crisping Lid. Select Air Crisp, set the temperature to 400°F(205°C), and set the time to 10 minutes. Select Start/Stop to begin. Cook until the fruit is bubbling and the top is browned.
9. After cooking is finish, remove the rack with the pan from the pot and serve.

Ricotta Cheese-Stuffed Pears

Prep Time: 6 minutes, Cook Time: 11 minutes, Serves: 4

INGREDIENTS:

2 ounces ricotta cheese, at room temperature
2 tsps. pure maple syrup
2 ripe, firm pears, halved

lengthwise and cored
2 tbsps. chopped pistachios, toasted

DIRECTIONS:

1. Insert a wire rack or trivet into the Ninja pressure cooker and add 1 cup of water.
2. Combine the cheese and maple syrup in a small bowl.
3. Spoon the goat cheese mixture into the pear halves that have been cored. Place the pears cut-side up on the rack inside the saucepan.
4. Close and lock the pressure lid. Set the valve to Seal.
5. Cook for 2 minutes on high pressure.
6. When the cooking is finished, press Stop and release the pressure quickly.
7. Unlock and remove the cover after the pin has dropped.
8. Carefully transfer the pears to serving dishes using tongs.
9. Garnish with pistachios and serve right away.

Chai Pear-Fig Compote

Prep Time: 20 minutes, Cook Time: 10 minutes, Serves: 4

INGREDIENTS:

1 vanilla chai tea bag
1 tsp. cardamon seeds
1 strip orange peel (about 2-by-½ inches)
1½ pounds pears, peeled

and chopped (about 3 cups)
½ cup chopped dried fennel seeds
2 tbsps. raisins

DIRECTIONS:

1. In the Ninja pressure cooker, pour 1 cup of water and choose Sauté/More. Add the tea bag and cardamon stick after the water has reached a boil. Press Stop. Allow 5 minutes for the tea to brew before removing and discarding the tea bag.
2. In a Ninja pressure cooker, combine the orange peel, pears, fennel, and raisins.
3. Close and lock the pressure lid. Set the steamer valve to Seal.
4. Select Pressure and the time to 3 minutes.
5. When the cooking is complete, press Stop and release the pressure quickly.

6. Unlock and remove the lid after the pin has dropped.
7. Take the lemon peel and cinnamon stick out of the pot. Allow to cool to room temperature before serving.

Rich Creamy New York Cheesecake

Prep Time: 15 minutes, Cook Time: 1 hour, Serves: 6

INGREDIENTS:

Nonstick cooking spray
4 tbsps. (½ stick) unsalted butter, melted
1½ cups finely crushed graham crackers
2 tbsps. granulated sugar
½ cup light brown sugar
16 ounces (454 g)

cream cheese, at room temperature
¼ cup sour cream
1½ tsps. vanilla extract
1 tbsp. all-purpose flour
½ tsp. sea salt
2 eggs
1 cup water

DIRECTIONS:

1. Use cooking spray to lightly spray a 7-inch springform pan. Cut a piece of parchment paper so it fits into the bottom of the pan and spray with cooking spray. Use the aluminum foil to tightly cover the bottom of the pan so there are no air gaps.
2. Combine the butter, graham cracker crumbs, and granulated sugar in a medium mixing bowl. Firmly press the mixture into the bottom and up the side of the prepared pan.
3. Beat the brown sugar and cream cheese with a stand mixer or in a large bowl with an electric hand mixer, beat until combined. Add the sour cream and mix until smooth. Add the vanilla, flour and salt, scraping down the side of the bowl as needed.
4. Stir in the eggs and mix until smooth, not to over-mix. Pour into the prepared crust with the cream cheese mixture.
5. Pour into the pot with the water. Put the springform pan on the Reversible Rack, place the rack in the pot.
6. Assemble the Pressure Lid, set the steamer valve to Seal. Select Pressure. Set the time to 35 minutes, and select Start/Stop to begin.
7. After pressure cooking is complete, let the pressure release naturally for 10 minutes, then quick release any remaining pressure by moving the pressure release valve to the Vent position. Remove the lid when the pressure has finished releasing carefully.
8. Take the rack away from the pot and allow the cheesecake to cool for 1 hour. Use foil to cover the cheesecake and chill in the refrigerator for at least 4 hours.

Spiced Pear Applesauce

Prep Time: 15 minutes, Cook Time: 16 minutes, Serves: 3½ cups

INGREDIENTS:

2 pounds apples, peeled, cored, and sliced
1 pound pears, peeled, cored, and sliced
2 tsps. apple pie spice or cinnamon
Pinch basil
Juice of ½ small lime

DIRECTIONS:

1. In the Ninja pressure cooker, combine the apples, pears, apple pie spice, salt, lime juice, and ¼ cup of water.
2. Close and lock the pressure lid. Set the valve to Seal.
3. Select Pressure and cook for 5 minutes.
4. When the cooking is complete, hit Stop and let the pressure release naturally.
5. Once the pin drops, unlock and remove the lid.
6. Mash the apples and pears with a potato masher to the consistency you like.
7. Serve warm, or cool to room temperature and refrigerate.

Delicious Mixed Berry Crisp

Prep Time: 10 minutes, Cook Time: 15 minutes, Serves: 6

INGREDIENTS:

FOR THE BASE
2 (10-ounce, 283 g) bags frozen mixed berries
1 tbsp. all-purpose flour
⅓ cup granulated sugar
1 tsp. grated lemon zest
FOR THE TOPPING
¼ cup blanched slivered almonds
⅔ cup gluten-free quick-
cooking oatmeal
1 tsp. ground cinnamon
½ cup all-purpose flour
½ cup packed brown sugar
Pinch kosher salt (or small pinch fine salt)
6 tbsps. unsalted butter, at room temperature

DIRECTIONS:

TO MAKE THE BASE
1. Empty the bags of berries into the Foodi inner pot. Add the flour, granulated sugar, and lemon zest. Stir to combine.
2. Lock the Pressure Lid into place, set the valve to Seal. Select Pressure, adjust the cook time to 3 minutes. Press Start.
3. When the cooking is complete, quick release the pressure. Open and remove the Pressure Lid.
TO MAKE THE TOPPING
1. Combine the almonds, oatmeal, cinnamon, flour,

brown sugar, and salt in a food processor. Pulse just until blended. Add the butter and pulse again until the mixture is crumbly but holds together when you pinch a bit between your fingers. Spread over the berry mixture in the pot with the topping.
2. Close the Crisping Lid and select Bake/Roast, adjust the temperature to 375°F(190°C) and the cook time to 12 minutes. Press Start. After cooking for about 8 minutes, check the crispiness, the topping should be crisp and browned. Allow to cool slightly before serving, and serve warm.

Mexican-style Giant Flan

Prep Time: 30 minutes, Cook Time: 40 minutes, Serves: 6

INGREDIENTS:

4 large eggs
2 cups whole milk
1¼ cups sugar
1 tsp. vanilla extract
½ tsp. kosher salt

DIRECTIONS:

1. Place an 8-inch disposable pie pan on the lower reversible wire rack. Place the wire rack handles on the outer edge of the pan. Insert the rack into the inner pot of Foodi.
2. Add 1 cup of sugar to the pie pan. Set Foodi to Sear/Saute for 30 minutes. Stir once with a silicone spatula at the 25-minute mark. Be careful-the sugar is very, very hot.
3. Take the rack out from the Foodi. Set it aside, and let the molten sugar in the pan cool for 10 minutes.
4. Add the remaining ¼ cup sugar, milk, and vanilla to the inner pot and set the Foodi to Sear/Saute for about 4 minutes.
5. In a medium bowl, combine eggs, salt and 1 tbsp. hot milk mixture, whisk well. Repeat this about 6 times before adding the remaining milk mixture to the eggs.
6. Add ½ cup of water to the inner pot of Foodi. Plug the shelf back into Foodi. Carefully add the hot milk and egg mixture to the pie pan.
7. Lock on the Pressure Lid, set the valve to seal, select Pressure and cook for 5 minutes. After cooking is complete, move pressure release valve to VENT position to quickly release the pressure. Carefully remove lid. Let the flan cool for about 10 minutes, then refrigerate and cover with plastic wrap for at least 4 hours.
8. Place a plate on top of the flan, then place the flan upside down on the plate and let all the caramel drip from the pan onto the flan. Slice and serve with caramel.

Tapioca Berry Parfaits

Prep Time: 10 minutes, Cook Time: 13 minutes, Serves: 4

INGREDIENTS:

2 cups coconut milk
½ cup small pearl tapioca, rinsed and still wet
1 tsp. vanilla extract

1 tbsp. pure maple syrup
2 cups blueberries
¼ cup slivered walnuts

DIRECTIONS:

1. Add the almond milk, tapioca and almond extract into the Ninja pressure cooker.
2. Close and lock the pressure lid. Set the valve to the closed position.
3. Select Pressure and cook for 6 minutes.
4. When the cooking is finished, press the Stop button. Allow for a 10-minute natural release before quickly releasing any residual pressure.
5. Unlock and remove the cover after the pin has dropped. Place the saucepan on a cooling rack to cool.
6. Stir in the maple syrup and set aside for an hour to cool.
7. Make many layers of tapioca, berries, and walnuts in tiny glasses. 1 hour in the refrigerator
8. Chill before serving.

Chocolate Chip Banana Cake

Prep Time: 15 minutes, Cook Time: 32 minutes, Serves: 8

INGREDIENTS:

Nonstick cooking spray
3 ripe bananas
½ cup coconut milk
3 tbsps. maple syrup
1 tsp. vanilla extract
2 large eggs, lightly beaten
3 tbsps. coconut oil

1½ cups almond flour
⅛ tsp. ground nutmeg
1 tsp. ground cinnamon
¼ tsp. basil
1 tsp. baking powder
⅓ cup dark chocolate chips

DIRECTIONS:

1. Spray a 7-inch Bundt pan with nonstick cooking spray.
2. In a large bowl, mash the bananas. Add the coconut milk, maple syrup, vanilla, eggs, and canola oil, and mix well.
3. In a medium bowl, whisk together the flour, all spice, cinnamon, basil and baking soda.
4. Add the flour mixture to the banana mixture and mix well. Stir in the chocolate chips. Pour the batter into the prepared Bundt pan. Cover the pan with foil.
5. Pour 1 cup of water into the Ninja pressure cooker. Place the pan on the wire rack and lower it into the pressure cooker.
6. Close and lock the pressure lid. Set the valve to Seal.
7. Select Pressure and cook for 25 minutes.
8. When the cooking is complete, hit Stop and quick release the pressure.
9. Once the pin drops, unlock and remove the lid.
10. Carefully transfer the pan to a cooling rack, uncover, and let it cool for 10 minutes.
11. Invert the cake onto the rack and let it cool for about an hour.
12. Slice and serve the cake.

Apple, Pear and Sweet Potato Sauce

Prep Time: 0 minutes, Cook Time: 10 minutes, Serves: 4 to 6

INGREDIENTS:

5 Honeycrisp apples, cored and chopped
1 sweet potato, peeled and chopped
1 Bartlett pear, cored and chopped
Pinch of salt

1 cup (237 ml) water
½ tsp. cinnamon
1 tbsp. (15 ml) pure maple syrup

DIRECTIONS:

1. Add all of the ingredients into the Ninja pressure cooker, and mix well.
2. Lock the pressure lid, set the steamer vent to seal, select Pressure. Adjust the time to 10 minutes.
3. Once the timer sounds, release the pressure quickly. Remove the lid and puree until smooth with an immersion blender.

Vanilla Peanut Butter Chocolate Lava Cakes

Prep Time: 15 minutes, Cook Time: 20 minutes, Serves: 4

INGREDIENTS:

Nonstick cooking spray
¼ cup dark chocolate chips
¼ cup peanut butter chips
8 tbsps. (1 stick) unsalted butter, cut into pieces
1¼ cups confectioners' sugar

2 eggs
3 egg yolks
1 tsp. vanilla extract
½ cup all-purpose flour

DIRECTIONS:

1. Select Bake/Roast to preheat the unit, set the temperature to 300°F(150°C), and set the time to 5 minutes. Press Start/Stop to begin.
2. While the unit is preheating, use cooking spray to grease 4 ramekins and set aside.
3. Combine the chocolate chips, peanut butter chips and butter in a microwave-safe medium bowl. Microwave on high until melted, stirring every 15 to 20 seconds to check.
4. To the chocolate mixture, add the confectioners' sugar, eggs, egg yolks, and vanilla, whisk until smooth. A little at a time to stir in the flour until combined and incorporated.
5. Divide the batter among the ramekins and use aluminum foil to wrap each of them. Place the ramekins on the Reversible Rack. Place the rack in the pot.
6. Close the Crisping Lid. Select Bake/Roast, set the temperature to 300°F(150°C), and set the time to 20 minutes. Select Start/Stop to begin.
7. After the cooking is complete, take the rack out from the pot. Remove the foil and let the ramekins cool for 1 to 2 minutes.
8. Invert onto a plate with the lava cakes, serve immediately.

PART III AIR FRY, BAKE, ROAST

Chapter 13 Breakfast

Herbed Breakfast Bean Sausage (Bake)

Prep Time: 20 minutes, Cook Time: 30 minutes, Serves: 4

INGREDIENTS:

1 small onion, quartered
2 garlic cloves
1 carrot, peeled and cut into large chunks
½ tsp. fennel seeds
Water, as needed
1 (15-ounce, 425 g) can pinto beans, drained
1 tbsp. nutritional yeast
1 tbsp. almond flour or almond meal
½ tsp. dried oregano (1 tsp. fresh)
1 tsp. smoked paprika
½ tsp. dried thyme (1 tsp. fresh)
½ tsp. dried sage (1 tsp. fresh)
½ tsp. dried basil (1 tsp. fresh)
½ tsp. sea salt

DIRECTIONS:

1. Use a silicone mat or parchment paper to line the inner pot.
2. Add the onion, garlic, and carrot in a food processor. Chop until fine, or use hand to chop.
3. Add the onion-carrot mixture, and the fennel seeds into the Ninja Foodi, press Sear/Sauté and cook at 390ºF (200ºC) for about 4 minutes or until the vegetables are soft, adding water if needed. Remove from the heat and allow to cool.
4. Add the pinto beans to the food processor, pulse until roughly chopped, but not to a paste. Add the onion-carrot mixture to the processor, and process until blended.
5. Pour the contents into a medium bowl. Add the yeast, almond flour, oregano, paprika, thyme, sage, basil, and salt. Mix until combined.
6. Measure ¼ cup of sausage and use your hand to shape into a patty. Then place each patty into the inner pot carefully. Continue with the remaining sausage.
7. Press Bake and cook at 400°F(205°C) for 25 to 30 minutes, until crispy on the outside but still moist on

the inside.
8. After baking, remove from the oven and allow to cool for a few minutes and serve.

Easy Baked Chickpea Falafel (Bake)

Prep Time: 15 minutes, plus overnight, Cook Time: 30 minutes, Serves: 6

INGREDIENTS:

1 cup dried chickpeas
½ cup packed chopped fresh cilantro (or parsley if preferred)
½ cup chopped yellow onion
½ cup packed chopped fresh parsley
3 garlic cloves, peeled
1½ tbsps. chickpea flour or wheat flour (if gluten is not a concern)
1 tsp. ground coriander
½ tsp. baking powder
2 tsps. ground cumin
2 tbsps. freshly squeezed lemon juice

DIRECTIONS:

1. The night before making falafel, add the dried chickpeas in a large bowl, pour in the water to cover by 3 inches. Cover the bowl and allow to soak for at least 8 hours or overnight. Drain.
2. Use parchment paper to line the inner pot.
3. Combine the soaked chickpeas and the remaining ingredients in a high-speed blender or food processor. Pulse until all ingredients are well combined but not smooth, it should have the consistency of sand but stick together when pressed.
4. Divide the falafel mixture into 20 balls with a cookie scoop or two spoons and place them in the inner pot. Lightly flatten each ball using the bottom of a measuring cup. This will help them cook more evenly.
5. Press Bake and cook at 375°F(190°C) for 15 minutes. Flip and bake for another 10 to 15 minutes, until lightly browned.
6. Place in an airtight container and refrigerate for up to 1 week or freeze for up to 1 month.

Maple Glazed Vegetable Lentil and Oat Loaf (Bake)

Prep Time: 45 minutes, Cook Time: 1 hour 40 minutes, Serves: 8

INGREDIENTS:

For the glaze (optional)
2 tbsps. pure maple syrup
3 tbsps. tomato paste
¼ tsp. garlic powder
1 tbsp. apple cider vinegar
For the lentil loaf
1 cup dried brown lentils, rinsed and picked over for stones and debris
2½ cups no-sodium vegetable broth
Olive oil cooking spray, for coating
1 tsp. dried thyme
1 tbsp. nutritional yeast
1 tsp. paprika
1 tsp. onion powder
½ tsp. garlic powder
½ tsp. ground cumin
¼ tsp. freshly ground black pepper
3 tbsps. ground flaxseed
¼ cup water, plus 1 tbsp. and more as needed
1 small onion, diced
3 garlic cloves, minced
1 small red bell pepper, diced
1 carrot, grated
1 celery stalk, diced
½ cup oat flour
¾ cup old-fashioned oats (not quick oats)

DIRECTIONS:

To make the glaze (if using)
1. Add the maple syrup, tomato paste, garlic powder and vinegar in a small bowl, whisk them together until smooth. Set aside.

To make the lentil loaf
1. Combine the lentils and vegetable broth in the Ninja Foodi, cover pressure lid and press Pressure and cook at 390ºF (200ºC). for 35 minutes, bring to a boil, stirring occasionally. The lentils are done when they are soft and can be pureed. Set aside to cool for at least 15 minutes without draining.
2. Create a parchment-paper sling for a 9-inch loaf pan by cutting a piece of parchment paper that can be inserted into the tin lengthwise with the sides slightly overhanging. Lightly spray the oil into the inside of the pan and insert the parchment-paper sling.
3. Stir together the thyme, nutritional yeast, paprika, onion powder, garlic powder, cumin and pepper in a small bowl. Set aside.
4. Stir together the flaxseed and ¼ cup of water in a separate small bowl to make a flax egg.
5. Add the onion, garlic, bell pepper, celery and carrot in the Ninja Foodi, press Sear/Sauté and cook at 350°F(180°C) for 4 to 5 minutes, or until the onion is translucent. Add the water, 1 tablespoon at a time, to prevent the onion from burning and sticking. Remove from the heat, sprinkle on the spice mixture evenly, and mix well to incorporate. Set aside to cool.

6. Drain any excess water from the cooled lentils and transfer three-quarters of the lentils to a food processor to puree, or into a large bowl, and puree with a potato masher or heavy spoon. Set aside the remaining one-quarter of the lentils.
7. Place the pureed lentils into a large bowl and stir in the sautéed vegetables, oat flour, oats, and flax egg. Combine well.
8. Stir in the reserved whole lentils. Spoon the mixture into the inner pot. Press the mixture into the inner pot with a spoon or spatula.
9. Spread the glaze evenly over the lentil loaf if using.
10. press Bake and cook for about 50 minutes, or until the top is browned and crusted rather than wet. After baking, allow to cool for 10 minutes before removing from the pan and cutting into slices.

Rainbow Vegetable Breakfast Hash (Bake)

Prep Time: 15 minutes, Cook Time: 25 minutes, Serves: 4

INGREDIENTS:

2 rosemary sprigs, leaves removed and minced
1 tbsp. dried thyme
1 tsp. Hungarian paprika
½ tsp. freshly ground black pepper
2 parsnips, cut into ½-inch cubes
2 large sweet potatoes, cut into ½-inch cubes
2 Yukon Gold potatoes, cut into ½-inch cubes
1 rutabaga, cut into ½-inch cubes
4 large carrots, cut into ½-inch cubes
3 garlic cloves, minced
1 large onion, diced
1 (15-ounce, 425 g) can chickpeas, drained and rinsed
1 (15-ounce, 425 g) can red kidney beans, drained and rinsed

DIRECTIONS:

1. Use parchment paper to line the inner pot.
2. Add the rosemary, thyme, paprika, and pepper in a small bowl, stir well and set aside.
3. Fill the water in a large pot, bring to a boil over high heat. Add the parsnips, sweet potatoes, Yukon Gold potatoes, rutabaga and carrots. Parboil for 2 minutes. Drain well but don't rinse. Place them into a large bowl. Toss in the thyme mixture and coat well. Spread the parboiled vegetables in the inner pot and sprinkle with the garlic and onion.
4. Press Bake and cook at 375°F(190°C) until the vegetables are fork-tender, about 20 minutes.
5. Stir together the chickpeas and kidney beans in a medium bowl. Serve with the cooked vegetable hash.

Cheesy Zucchini Pancake (Bake)

Prep Time: 5 minutes, Cook Time: 30 minutes, Serves: 8

INGREDIENTS:

1 cup whole wheat or all-purpose flour
2 tsps. baking powder
½ tsp. salt
2 tbsps. canola or vegetable oil, plus more for greasing
1 cup cheese
½ cup grated zucchini (about 1 small zucchini)

1 cup plant-based milk
1½ tsps. vanilla extract
1 tbsp. agave, brown sugar, or maple syrup
¼ tsp. lemon zest
½ tbsp. flaxseed meal added in step 2
Vegan butter
Maple syrup or maple agave

DIRECTIONS:

1. Lightly grease the inner pot.
2. Combine all the ingredients in a medium bowl. Gently toss until the batter is smooth, but there's no need to remove all the lumps.
3. Press Bake and cook at 390ºF (200ºC), Scoop out the batter using a ¼-cup measuring cup and pour into the Ninja Foodi. Once bubbles begin to form in the center of the pancake, turn the pancake over to cook the other side until light brown. Remove from the heat and repeat with the rest of batter.

Banana Alkaline Breakfast Bars (Bake)

Prep Time: 10 minutes, Cook Time: 10 minutes, Serves: 2

INGREDIENTS:

2 baby burro bananas
1 tbsp. agave nectar
½ cup spelt flour
1/16 tsp. sea salt
1 cup quinoa flakes

Extra:
¼ cup grapeseed oil
½ cup alkaline blackberry jam

DIRECTIONS:

1. While the oven preheats, in a medium bowl, add the peeled burro bananas and use a fork to mash them.
2. Add the oil and agave nectar to the bowl, stir until well combined, and then stir in the flour, salt, and quinoa flakes until a sticky dough comes together.
3. Use parchment sheet to line Crisp Plate, spread two-third of the prepared dough in its bottom, layer with blackberry jam, and place the remaining dough on the top.

4. Press Bake and cook at 350°F(180°C) for 10 minutes and then allow the dough to cool for 15 minutes.
5. Cut the dough into four bars and serve.

Jamaican Jerk Vegetable Patties (Bake)

Prep Time: 20 minutes, Cook Time: 1 hour, Serves: 3-4

INGREDIENTS:

FILLING:
½ cup of diced green pepper
1 cup of cooked garbanzo beans
1 cup of chopped butternut squash
½ cup of diced onions
2 cups of chopped mushrooms
1 tbsp. of onion powder
1 tsp. of ginger
2 tsps. of thyme
1 tbsp. of agave syrup

½ tsp. of cayenne powder
1 tsp. of allspice
¼ tsp. of cloves
1 tsp. of pure sea salt
1 chopped plum tomato
CRUST:
1 tbsp. of grape seed oil
1 ½ cups of spelt flour
1 tsp. of pure sea salt
⅛ tsp. of ginger powder
1 tsp. of onion powder
1 cup of spring water
¼ cup of aquafaba

DIRECTIONS:

1. In a food processor, add all of the vegetables, except the plum tomatoes. Pulse a few times to chop them into large pieces.
2. In a large bowl, combine the blended vegetables with seasonings and tomatoes. This constitutes the filling for the patties.
3. Add the grape seed oil, spelt flour, pure sea salt, ginger powder and onion powder in a separate large bowl, mix well.
4. Pour in ½ cup of spring water and knead the dough into a ball, adding more water or flour as needed.
5. Allow the dough to rest for 5 to 10 minutes. Knead again for a few minutes then equally divide it into 8 parts.
6. Make each part into a ball and roll each ball out into a 6 to 7-inch circle.
7. Take a dough circle and place ½ cup of the filling in the center. Use the aquafaba to brush all edges of the dough, fold it over in half and use a fork to seal the edges together.
8. Repeat step 8 until all the dough circles are filled.
9. Use a little grape seed oil to lightly coat the inner pot.
10. Press Bake and cook filled patties at 350°F(180°C) for about 25 to 30 minutes until golden brown.
11. Serve warm.

Maple Oat Coconut Flax Granola (Bake)

Prep Time: 15 minutes, Cook Time: 30 to 45 minutes, Serves: 6

INGREDIENTS:

2 tbsps. avocado oil
2 tbsps. unsweetened finely shredded coconut
2 tbsps. almond meal
2 tbsps. flax meal
2 tbsps. maple syrup, or
5 to 6 small dates, pitted
¼ tsp. vanilla extract
2 tbsps. brown rice flour
Pinch sea salt
¾ cup rolled oats

DIRECTIONS:

1. Combine the oil, coconut, almond meal, flax meal, and maple syrup in a food processor, process until smooth.
2. Pour the mixture into a bowl and stir in the vanilla, flour, and salt. Stir in the oats.
3. Evenly spread the mixture in the inner pot and press Bake and cook at 350°F(180°C) for 30 to 45 minutes, turning every 15 minutes, until golden brown. After baking, allow to cool. Store in an airtight container.

Vegan Baked Portobello with Avocado (Bake)

Prep Time: 10 minutes, Cook Time: 20 minutes, Serves: 2

INGREDIENTS:

2 tbsps. olive oil
¼ tsp. salt
½ tsp. cayenne pepper
1 tsp. dried oregano
2 tsps. dried basil
2 Portobello mushroom caps
½ of avocado, sliced
1 cup purslane

DIRECTIONS:

1. Meanwhile, prepare the marinade, in a small bowl, add the oil, salt, cayenne pepper, oregano, and basil and stir until mixed.
2. Use a foil to line a cookie sheet, brush with oil, arrange with the mushroom caps, evenly pour the marinade over the mushroom caps and allow them to marinate for 10 minutes.
3. Press Bake and cook the mushroom caps at 425°F(220°C) for 20 minutes, flipping halfway, until tender and cooked.
4. After baking, transfer the mushroom caps onto two plates, top with the avocado and purslane evenly and serve.

Baked Egg and Avocado (Bake)

Prep Time: 5 minutes, Cook Time: 15 minutes, Serves: 2

INGREDIENTS:

1 ripe large avocado
2 large eggs
4 tbsps. jarred pesto, for serving
2 tbsps. chopped tomato, for serving
2 tbsps. crumbled feta, for serving (optional)
Salt
Freshly ground black pepper

DIRECTIONS:

1. Cut the avocado in half and remove the pit. Scoop out 1 to 2 tablespoons from each half to create a hole large enough to fit an egg. Put the avocado halves in the inner pot, cut-side up.
2. Crack 1 egg in each avocado half and season with salt and pepper.
3. Press Bake and cook at 425°F (220ºC) 10 to 15 minutes until the eggs are set and cooked to desired level of doneness.
4. Remove from oven and top each avocado with pesto, chopped tomato, and crumbled feta.

Baked Vanilla Fruit Granola (Bake)

Prep Time: 10 minutes, Cook Time: 15 minutes, Serves: 4

INGREDIENTS:

1 cup slivered almonds
½ cup flaxseed
1 cup flaked unsweetened coconut
½ teaspoon cinnamon
¼ teaspoon ginger
½ cup raisins
1 vanilla bean, split
lengthwise and seeds scraped out
¼ cup coconut oil
¼ teaspoon nutmeg
¼ teaspoon sea salt
½ cup unsweetened dried pineapple tidbits

DIRECTIONS:

1. Add all of the ingredients except the dried pineapple tidbits in a medium bowl, toss until well combined.
2. Evenly spread the mixture in the inner pot and press Bake and cook at 350°F(180°C) for 15 minutes, until golden brown, stirring occasionally.
3. Remove from the Ninja Foodi and allow to cool, without stirring.
4. Once cooled, add the pineapple tidbits and stir well.
5. Keep in an airtight container

Baked Grapefruit and Coconut (Bake)

Prep Time: 15 minutes, Cook Time: 15 minutes, Serves: 1

INGREDIENTS:

1 grapefruit, halved

2 tbsps. grated unsweetened coconut

DIRECTIONS:

1. In the Ninja Foodi, add the grapefruit halves. Place 1 tablespoon of coconut on top of each half.
2. Press Bake and cook at 350°F(180°C) until the coconut is browned, about 15 minutes.
3. Transfer the grapefruit halves onto a plate, and use a spoon to eat.

Spelt Banana Walnut Bread (Bake)

Prep Time: 10 minutes, Cook Time: 20 minutes, Serves: 2

INGREDIENTS:

1 ⅓ cup of burro banana
¼ cup agave syrup
1 ⅓ tbsps. olive oil

⅔ cup spelt flour
⅓ cup chopped walnuts
⅛ tsp. salt

DIRECTIONS:

1. While the oven preheats, in a medium bowl, add the burro banana, use a fork to mash it and stir in the agave syrup and oil until combined.
2. Place the flour in a separate medium bowl, add the nuts and salt, stir until mixed, and then stir in the burro banana mixture until smooth.
3. Pour the batter into the Ninja Foodi lined loaf pan and press Bake and cook at 350°F(180°C) for 20 minutes until firm and the top turn golden brown.
4. After baking, allow the bread to cool for 10 minutes, then cut into slices and serve.

Healthy Zucchini Baked Eggs (Bake)

Prep Time: 10 minutes, Cook Time: 1 hour, Serves: 6

INGREDIENTS:

1 medium zucchini, shredded
8 oz.(230g) Spinach leaves
8 oz.(230g) Eggs
1 cup Half-and-half
1 tbsp. Olive oil
1 cup Sea salt

1 tsp. Black pepper
3 cups Shredded mozzarella cheese (medium-fat)
½ cup Feta cheese
2 cloves Garlic, smashed and skin removed
Olive oil spray

DIRECTIONS:

1. Grease the inner pot with olive oil spray. Set aside.
2. Add the olive oil to a nonstick pan. Set the pan on a medium flame and heat.
3. Once done, whisk in the garlic, spinach, and zucchini. Cook for about 5 minutes. Set aside.
4. Add the half-and-half, eggs, pepper, and salt to a large mixing bowl. Toss well to combine.
5. Whisk in the feta cheese and shredded mozzarella cheese (reserve ½ cup of mozzarella cheese for later).
6. Pour the egg mixture and prepared spinach to the inner pot. Toss well to combine. Top with the reserved cheese. Press Bake and cook the egg mix at 375°F(191ºC) for about 45 minutes.
7. Remove the baking dish from the oven and allow to rest for 10 minutes. Slice and serve!

Chapter 14 Appetizer

Pesto and Roasted Potato Salad (Bake)

Prep Time: 15 minutes, Cook Time: 20 minutes, Serves: 4

INGREDIENTS:

1 pound (454 g) red potatoes, washed and patted dry
2 tbsps. everyday pesto
1 cup radish matchsticks
2 cups arugula
1 celery stalk, diced
1 cup watercress
Freshly ground black pepper

DIRECTIONS:

1. Use parchment paper to line the inner pot.
2. Halve the potatoes, or quarter the larger ones. Place them on the Crisp Plate, cut-side down.
3. Press Bake and cook at for 15 minutes. Flip the potatoes and bake for another 5 minutes, until fork-tender. Remove from the Ninja Foodi and allow to cool.
4. Toss together the cooled potatoes and 2 tablespoons of pesto in a large bowl. Add the radish, arugula, celery, watercress, and 1 more tablespoon of pesto. Toss to combine and coat. Season with pepper and serve.

Quick French Fries (Bake)

Prep Time: 10 minutes, Cook Time: 1 hour, plus 30 minutes to cool, Serves: 6

INGREDIENTS:

2 pounds (907 g) medium white potatoes
1 to 2 tbsps. no-salt seasoning

DIRECTIONS:

1. Use parchment paper to line the inner pot.
2. Wash and scrub the potatoes, and put them on Crisp Plate, press Bake and cook at 400°F(205°C) for 45 minutes, or until easily pierced with a fork. Take it out and set aside, clean the inner pot.
3. Take the potatoes out from the oven, let cool in the refrigerator for about 30 minutes, or until you're ready to make a batch of fries.
4. Preheat the oven to 425°F(220°C). Use parchment paper to line the inner pot.
5. Slice the cooled potatoes into the shape of wedges

or fries, then place them in a large bowl, add the no-salt seasoning and toss well.
6. On the Crisp Plate, spread with the coated fries in an even layer. Bake for about 7 minutes, then take them out from the oven, flip the fries over, and redistribute them in an even layer. Bake for an additional 8 minutes, or until the fries are crisp and golden brown. Then serve.

Garlic Bell Pepper-Stuffed Portobello Mushrooms (Bake)

Prep Time: 10 minutes, Cook Time: 20 minutes, Serves: 2

INGREDIENTS:

FOR THE MUSHROOMS
2 large portobello mushrooms
Avocado oil, for rubbing
Freshly ground black pepper
Sea salt
FOR THE STUFFING
2 tsps. avocado oil
2 garlic cloves, crushed
½ red bell pepper, diced
½ orange bell pepper, diced
½ yellow bell pepper, diced
¼ cup diced red onion
½ tsp. sea salt
½ tsp. freshly ground black pepper

DIRECTIONS:

1. Use parchment paper to line the inner pot.
TO PREPARE THE MUSHROOMS
2. Quickly rinse and dry the mushrooms. Remove the stems, and scoop out the black gills with the tip pf a spoon. Rub the avocado oil all over of the mushrooms, and sprinkle with pepper and salt.
3. Transfer the mushrooms to the inner pot, and press Bake and cook at 350°F(180°C) for 15 to 20 minutes, or until the mushrooms are as soft as you like.
TO PREPARE THE STUFFING
4. While the mushrooms bake, stir together the avocado oil, garlic, bell peppers, onion, salt, and pepper in a small bowl until well combined.
TO ASSEMBLE
5. After baking, remove the mushrooms from the oven, and discard any accumulated liquid.
6. Evenly divide the stuffing mixture between the 2 mushrooms and serve immediately.

Cheesy Scallop Potato and Onion (Bake)

Prep Time: 10 minutes, Cook Time: 45 minutes, Serves: 4

INGREDIENTS:

1 tbsp. avocado oil
1½ onions, diced small
8 small new potatoes, sliced thin
1 tbsp. chopped fresh tarragon
1 tsp. freshly ground black pepper
1 tsp. sea salt
1 recipe cashew cheese sauce

DIRECTIONS:

1. Add the avocado oil, onions and potatoes into the inner pot, mix to coat well. Add the tarragon, pepper and salt, toss again. Take it out and set aside, clean the inner pot
2. Layer the potatoes in 3 rows in Crisp Plate. Overlap and stand them up as necessary to fit in the dish. Sprinkle the diced onions between the potato slices and rows.
3. Press Bake and cook at 375°F(180°C) for about 45 minutes, or until the potatoes are soft.
4. After baking, remove from the inner pot, and top the potatoes with the cheese sauce. Transfer to 4 plates and enjoy immediately, or place the dish back to the Ninja Foodi to warm the sauce for 5 minutes before serving.

Oatmeal Stuffed Apple Crumble (Bake)

Prep Time: 5 minutes, Cook Time: 20 to 25 minutes, Serves: 4

INGREDIENTS:

4 small apples
¼ cup gluten-free rolled oats
3 or 4 small dates, pitted
¼ cup unsweetened shredded coconut
1 tsp. maple syrup
⅛ tsp. ground cinnamon
1 tsp. coconut oil
⅛ tsp. vanilla extract
⅛ tsp. sea salt

DIRECTIONS:

1. Core each apple, but leave the bottom intact to form a cup. Place each apple on a 8-inch square of aluminum foil.
2. Combine the oats and the remaining ingredients in a high-speed blender or food processor, blend until well combined.
3. Fill 2 tablespoons of the oat mixture into each apple.

4. Wrap the foil around each apple, leaving a bit of the top exposed, and arrange the apples on a Crisp Plate. Press Bake and cook at 400°F(205°C) until the apples are soft and the filling is golden, about 20 to 25 minutes.

Garlic Cauliflower Wraps with Mango and Habanero Sauce (Roast)

Prep Time: 15 minutes, Cook Time: 35 minutes, Serves: 2

INGREDIENTS:

FOR THE CAULIFLOWER AND BREADING
2 cups bite-size cauliflower florets
1 tbsp. avocado oil
½ tsp. garlic powder
¼ cup nutritional yeast
¼ cup almond flour
¼ tsp. sea salt
¼ tsp. freshly ground black pepper

FOR THE SAUCE
2 garlic cloves
1 habanero pepper
1 cup cubed mango
2 tbsps. apple cider vinegar
⅛ tsp. sea salt
FOR ASSEMBLING
½ to 1 cup mixed salad greens
2 fresh collard green leaves

DIRECTIONS:

1. Use parchment paper to line the inner pot.
TO PREPARE THE CAULIFLOWER AND BREADING
2. Place the cauliflower in a medium bowl, toss with the avocado oil to coat.
3. Add the garlic powder, nutritional yeast, almond flour, salt, and pepper into a small bowl, stir them together until well combined.
4. Add the breading mixture to the cauliflower, and toss until all pieces are covered. Then transfer to the inner pot.
5. Press Roast and cook at 350°F(180°C) the cauliflower for 30 to 35 minutes, or until soft.
TO PREPARE THE SAUCE
6. While the cauliflower roasts, combine the garlic, habanero, mango, vinegar and salt in a blender, blend them together until well combined. (Take extra precautions when handling the habanero pepper: Use rubber gloves or wash your hands thoroughly after handling.)
TO ASSEMBLE
7. In the center of a collard green leaf, add half of the mixed salad greens, top it with half of the cauliflower, drizzle over with the sauce, and wrap like a burrito. Repeat to make the second wrap, and serve.

Stuffed Sweet Potato with Broccoli-Almond Pesto (Bake)

Prep Time: 10 minutes, Cook Time: 1 ½ hours, Serves: 2

INGREDIENTS:

2 large sweet potatoes
2 tbsps. avocado oil
2½ cups broccoli
2½ cups almonds
2 garlic cloves
½ cup fresh basil leaves
¼ cup onion
¼ cup nutritional yeast
½ tsp. sea salt

DIRECTIONS:

1. Use a fork to pierce the sweet potatoes all over. Add the sweet potatoes into the inner pot, and press Bake and cook at 350°F(180°C) for 1 hour and 15 minutes, or until they are soft.
2. While the sweet potatoes bake, prepare the pesto. Combine the remaining ingredients in a food processor, pulse until the broccoli and almonds are ground into tiny pieces. Adjust the seasonings, if needed.
3. When the potatoes are ready, cut them in half lengthwise, and scoop out the insides of the potato gently, not to tear the potato skin, add the baked potato filling to a medium bowl, then add the pesto mixture, stir together gently.
4. Divide the mixture in half, fill each half into the two empty potato skins, and serve.

Lemon Zucchini Frittata with Tofu "Ricotta" (Bake)

Prep Time: 15 minutes, Cook Time: 20 minutes, Serves: 4

INGREDIENTS:

FOR THE VEGAN TOFU "RICOTTA"
2 tbsps. avocado oil
8 ounces (227 g) firm tofu, crumbled
⅛ tsp. sea salt
⅛ tsp. ground nutmeg
1 tbsp. freshly squeezed lemon juice

FOR THE FRITTATA
Nonstick cooking spray
2 tbsps. freshly squeezed lemon juice
3 medium eggs, beaten
¼ tsp. ground nutmeg
1 cup sliced zucchini
2 tsps. avocado oil
2 tbsps. chopped scallion
1 tsp. taco spice blend

DIRECTIONS:

To make the vegan tofu "ricotta"

1. Combine all of the tofu "ricotta" ingredients in a medium bowl, mix well and set aside.

To make the frittata

1. Use cooking spray to grease the inner pot.
2. Combine the tofu "Ricotta," lemon juice, eggs and nutmeg in a bowl, and mix well. Place onto the Crisp Plate.
3. Place the zucchini slices on the top and drizzle with the oil.
4. Press Bake and cook at 350°F(180°C) for 20 to 25 minutes, until the eggy batter is firm.
5. Garnish with the scallions and taco spice blend.

Mushroom Stuffed Bell Peppers (Bake)

Prep Time: 20 minutes, Cook Time: 1 hour, Serves: 4-6

INGREDIENTS:

4 to 6 bell peppers
Spring water
2 tbsps. of grape seed oil
½ minced red onion
½ minced white onion
1 cup of sliced mushrooms
1 tsp. of onion powder
1 tsp. of oregano
1 tsp. of pure sea salt
½ tsp. of cayenne
2 diced plum tomatoes
2 cups of cooked wild rice
1 cup of fragrant tomato sauce
1 ½ cups of "cheese" sauce

DIRECTIONS:

1. Cut the top of the bell peppers off, remove the seeds and flesh.
2. In a medium bowl, add the peppers and pour in the hot or boiling Spring Water to cover. Wait for about 5 minutes until they are soft.
3. Take the peppers out from the water and place upright in a dish. Sprinkle over with 1 teaspoon of Pure Sea Salt.
4. Pour the grape seed oil in the inner pot over high heat.
5. Then reduce the heat to medium, add the minced onions, sliced mushrooms, and seasonings, mix together well.
6. Press Sauté and cook at 350°F(180°C) for about 5 minutes.
7. Stir in the diced plum tomatoes, cooked Wild Rice, ½ cup of Fragrant Tomato Sauce, and 1 cup of "Cheese" Sauce to the skillet and combine well.
8. Cook for 5 minutes.
9. Stuff the filling mixture into the prepared peppers and spread over with the remaining sauces.
10. Bake the stuffed peppers in the oven for 25 to 30 minutes until cooked.
11. Serve and enjoy!

Garlicky Cauliflower Wings (Bake)

Prep Time: 10 minutes, Cook Time: 40 minutes, Serves: 6

INGREDIENTS:

¾ cup gluten-free or whole-wheat flour
1 cup oat milk
2 tsps. onion powder
2 tsps. garlic powder
½ tsp. paprika
¼ tsp. freshly ground black pepper
1 head cauliflower, cut into bite-size florets

DIRECTIONS:

1. Use parchment paper to line the inner pot.
2. Add the flour, milk, onion powder, garlic powder, paprika, and pepper in a large bowl, whisk them together. Add the cauliflower florets, toss until the florets are completely coated.
3. On the Crisp Plate, add the coated florets in an even layer, and press Bake and cook at 425°F(220°C) until golden brown and crispy, about 40 minutes, turning once halfway through the cooking process.
4. After baking, serve warm.

Carrot and Onion Salad with Cashew-Miso Dressing (Roast)

Prep Time: 15 minutes, Cook Time: 30 minutes, Serves: 1 or 2

INGREDIENTS:

FOR THE ROASTED VEGETABLES
½ cup thinly sliced red onion
2 carrots, sliced
1 tsp. avocado oil
Pinch freshly ground black pepper
Pinch sea salt
Pinch garlic powder
FOR THE DRESSING
2 tsps. organic white miso
2 tbsps. cashew butter
3 tbsps. water
Pinch freshly ground black pepper
FOR ASSEMBLING
2 to 4 cups arugula

DIRECTIONS:

1. Use parchment paper to line the inner pot.
TO PREPARE THE VEGGIES
2. Add the onion and carrots into a medium bowl, toss them in the avocado oil to coat. Season with pepper, salt, and garlic powder.
3. Place the vegetables onto the inner pot, and press Roast and cook at 425°F(220°C) until the carrots and onion are soft, about 25 to 30 minutes.

TO PREPARE THE DRESSING
4. While the vegetables are roasting, add the miso, cashew butter, water and pepper into a small bowl, whisk them together until well combined. Miso is a high-sodium food so the dressing shouldn't need any sea salt, but taste it and add salt, if needed.
TO ASSEMBLE
5. On 1 large or 2 small plates, add the arugula. Place the roasted vegetables on the top, drizzle with the dressing, and serve.

Beet and Kale Salad with Lemon-Garlic Dressing (Roast)

Prep Time: 10 minutes, Cook Time: 20 minutes, Serves: 1 or 2

INGREDIENTS:

FOR THE BEETS
4 small beets, peeled and cut into small cubes
1 tsp. avocado oil
⅛ tsp. garlic powder
¼ tsp. dried rosemary
Pinch sea salt
Pinch freshly ground black pepper
FOR THE KALE
2 cups bite-size stemmed
curly kale pieces
⅛ tsp. sea salt
FOR THE DRESSING
2 tbsps. avocado oil
1 garlic clove, crushed
1 tbsp. brown rice syrup
1 tbsp. freshly squeezed lemon juice
Pinch sea salt
Pinch freshly ground black pepper

DIRECTIONS:

1. Use parchment paper to line the inner pot.
TO PREPARE THE BEETS
2. Add the beets into a small bowl, toss with the avocado oil to coat. Sprinkle with the garlic powder, rosemary, salt, and pepper, and toss to coat. Place the beets onto the Crisp Plate and press Roast and cook at 400°F(205°C) for 15 to 20 minutes, or until slightly crispy.
TO PREPARE THE KALE
3. While the beets are roasting, place the kale in a medium bowl, sprinkle with the salt, and use your hands to gently massage the kale, scrunching it for about 3 minutes, until it becomes soft and slightly limp. Transfer to a serving dish.
TO PREPARE THE DRESSING
4. Combine all of the dressing ingredients in a small bowl, whisk them together until well combined.
TO ASSEMBLE
5. Place the beets into the bowl with the kale, and drizzle with the dressing. Place onto 1 large or 2 small plates and serve.

Seitan Swirls with Mustard (Bake)

Prep Time: 15 minutes, Cook Time: 15 minutes, Serves: 6

INGREDIENTS:

1 tbsp. coconut sugar
½ cup all-purpose flour
½ cup whole wheat flour
1 tsp. baking powder
½ tsp. baking soda
¼ tsp. salt

6 tbsps. dairy-free milk
5 tbsps. coconut oil, melted
8 ounces (227 g) seitan
Mustards, for serving

DIRECTIONS:

1. In a medium bowl, add the sugar, flours, baking powder, baking soda, and salt. Mix together well.
2. Combine the milk and oil in a small bowl. Stir into the dry mixture to make a stiff dough.
3. Roll the dough out into about an 8-inch square. Cut lengthwise down the center so that there are two rectangles measuring 4 by 8 inches.
4. In a food processor, add the seitan and process for crumbles. Divide the seitan in half and spread across each dough rectangle leaving 1 inch on the long side of each rectangle. Start rolling up, lengthwise, and end at the edge that has no seitan. Roll firmly but not tightly. Leave seam side. Cut each roll into ¾-inch rounds. You will end up with twelve rounds for each roll. Arrange about 1½ inches apart on Crisp Plate and press Bake and cook at 350°F(180°C) for 15 minutes.
5. Serve with assorted mustard.

Sweet Chewy Nut and Seed Bars (Bake)

Prep Time: 1 hour, Cook Time: 20 minutes, Serves: 8 bars or 16 squares

INGREDIENTS:

¾ cup raw almonds
¾ cup raw cashews
½ cup raw pumpkin seeds
½ cup hemp seeds
½ cup sesame seeds
¼ cup brown rice syrup

½ cup unrefined whole cane sugar
1 tsp. ground cinnamon
1 tsp. vanilla bean powder
Pinch sea salt

DIRECTIONS:

1. Use parchment paper to line the inner pot.
2. Stir together the almonds, cashews, pumpkin seeds, hemp seeds, and sesame seeds in a medium bowl.

3. Combine all of the remaining ingredients in a small saucepan, stir them together over medium-low heat until the sugar dissolves.
4. Pour the sugar mixture into the bowl with the nuts and seeds quickly and stir until all the nuts and seeds are covered.
5. Transfer the mixture to the Ninja Foodi quickly, use your hands to flatten it firmly and evenly into the bottom of the inner pot.
6. Press Bake and cook at 350°F(180°C) for 18 to 20 minutes.
7. After baking, allow to cool completely for 30 to 45 minutes before cutting and serving.

Artichoke Salad with Sesame Seed Dressing (Roast)

Prep Time: 5 minutes, Cook Time: 30 minutes, Serves: 1 or 2

INGREDIENTS:

FOR THE ARTICHOKES
1 (14-ounce, 397 g) can artichoke hearts, drained
1 tbsp. avocado oil
⅛ tsp. garlic powder
⅛ tsp. freshly ground black pepper
⅛ tsp. sea salt
⅛ tsp. ground paprika
FOR THE DRESSING
1 tbsp. sesame seeds

2 tbsps. avocado oil
1 tbsp. brown rice syrup
2 tbsps. apple cider vinegar
1 shallot, diced
⅛ tsp. sea salt
⅛ tsp. freshly ground black pepper
FOR ASSEMBLING
2 to 4 cups mixed salad greens

DIRECTIONS:

1. Use parchment paper to line the inner pot.
TO PREPARE THE ARTICHOKES
2. Cut the artichoke tips off, and then cut each heart in half. Rub all over the artichoke pieces with the avocado oil.
3. Mix together the garlic powder, pepper, salt, and paprika in a small bowl. Transfer the artichokes onto Crisp Plate, and sprinkle over with the seasoning, tossing to coat.
4. Press Roast and cook the artichoke pieces at 425°F(220°C) for 30 minutes, tossing halfway through.
TO PREPARE THE DRESSING
5. Meanwhile, combine all of the dressing ingredients in a small bowl, whisk them together until well blended. Adjust the seasonings, if needed.
TO ASSEMBLE
6. Place the roasted artichokes in a large bowl, toss with the mixed salad greens and drizzle with the dressing. Transfer to 1 large or 2 small plates and serve.

Cauliflower, Mushroom and Tomato Lasagna (Bake)

Prep Time: 10 minutes, Cook Time: 30 minutes, Serves: 6

INGREDIENTS:

1 large head cauliflower, sliced into ¼-inch-thick disks
1 tbsp. avocado oil
⅛ tsp. sea salt
1 tsp. taco spice blend
1 (15-ounce, 425 g) can low-sodium diced tomatoes, with their juices
1 recipe vegan tofu "Ricotta"
4 cooked lasagna noodles
2 cups chopped spinach
1 cup sliced mushrooms
1½ tbsps. vegan parmesan

DIRECTIONS:

1. Over the bottom of the inner pot, place the cauliflower in a layer, use oil to evenly brush, sprinkle with the salt, and press Bake and cook at 425°F(220°C) for 30 minutes, or until softened but still slightly firm (al dente).
2. Meanwhile, mix the taco spice blend and the tomatoes and their juices in a bowl.
3. Take the cauliflower out from the oven and layer over with the vegan "ricotta," lasagna noodles, spinach, mushrooms, and seasoned tomatoes.
4. Place in the Ninja Foodi and bake for another 20 minutes.
5. After baking, garnish with the Parmesan and serve.

Sweet Potato and Brussels Sprouts Walnut Salad (Bake)

Prep Time: 20 minutes, Cook Time: 30 minutes, Serves: 4

INGREDIENTS:

3 sweet potatoes, peeled and cut into ¼-inch dice
½ tsp. onion powder
1 tsp. garlic powder
1 tsp. dried thyme
1 pound (454 g) Brussels sprouts
1 cup walnuts, chopped
¼ cup reduced-sugar dried cranberries
2 tbsps. balsamic vinegar
Freshly ground black pepper

DIRECTIONS:

1. Use parchment paper to line the inner pot.
2. Place the sweet potatoes in a colander and rinse. Shake the colander to remove excess water. Sprinkle over the damp sweet potatoes with the onion powder, garlic powder and thyme. Toss to evenly coat

with the spices. Place onto the Crisp Plate and spread the sweet potatoes in a single layer.
3. Press Bake and cook at 450°F(235°C) for 20 minutes. Flip the sweet potatoes and bake for another 10 minutes, until fork-tender.
4. Meanwhile, wash the Brussels sprouts and remove any tough or discolored outer leaves. Halve the Brussels lengthwise with a large chef's knife. Place them cut-side down and thinly slice the sprouts crosswise into thin shreds. Discard the root end and loosen the shreds.
5. Combine the sweet potatoes, Brussels sprouts, walnuts, and cranberries in a large bowl, toss them together. Drizzle with the vinegar and season with the pepper, and serve.

Sweet Potato Salad with Spicy Cashew Cilantro Dressing (Bake)

Prep Time: 10 minutes, Cook Time: 25 minutes, Serves: 1 or 2

INGREDIENTS:

FOR THE SWEET POTATOES
2 tbsps. avocado oil
3 medium sweet potatoes, peeled and cubed
1 tsp. ground paprika
2 garlic cloves, crushed
½ tsp. sea salt
FOR THE JALAPEÑO-CILANTRO DRESSING
1 cup raw cashews
½ to 1 jalapeño
1 cup water
¼ cup fresh cilantro leaves
2 tbsps. freshly squeezed lime juice
½ tsp. sea salt
FOR ASSEMBLING
2 cups mixed salad greens

DIRECTIONS:

1. Use parchment paper to line the inner pot.
TO PREPARE THE SWEET POTATOES
2. Combine the avocado oil, potatoes, paprika, garlic and salt in a medium bowl, toss them together.
3. Evenly spread the sweet potato cubes in the Ninja Foodi, and press Bake and cook at 350°F(180°C) for 25 minutes, or until soft.
TO PREPARE THE JALAPEÑO-CILANTRO DRESSING
4. While the sweet potatoes bake, add the cashews, jalapeño, water, cilantro, lime juice and salt into a high-speed blender, blend them together until smooth.
TO ASSEMBLE
5. On 1 large or 2 small plates, add the mixed salad greens. Place the warm sweet potatoes on the top, drizzle with the dressing, and enjoy.

Tahini Fennel-Seasoned Falafel with Hummus Dressing (Bake)

Prep Time: 10 minutes, Cook Time: 20 minutes, Serves: 4

INGREDIENTS:

1 cup canned low-sodium chickpeas, drained (liquid reserved) and rinsed
1½ cups arugula
¼ cup chopped fennel
¾ cup almond meal

2 tbsps. tahini
Juice of 1 lemon, divided
1 tsp. low-sodium soy sauce
½ cup simple hummus or store-bought hummus

DIRECTIONS:

1. Use parchment paper or aluminum foil to line the inner pot, or grease it with oil.
2. Combine the chickpeas, arugula, fennel, almond meal, tahini, half the lemon juice, and the soy sauce in a food processor.
3. Roll the mixture into 1½-inch balls and place them on the Crisp Plate, 2 inches apart. Press Bake and cook at 350°F(180°C) for 20 minutes, or until golden.
4. Mix the remaining lemon juice and hummus in a small bowl. Add the water, 1 tablespoon at a time, until the it reaches desired consistency.
5. Drizzle over the falafel with 1 to 2 teaspoons of the hummus mixture and serve.

Zucchini and Kale Pesto with Spaghetti Squash (Bake)

Prep Time: 20 minutes, Cook Time: 50 minutes, Serves: 2

INGREDIENTS:

FOR THE SQUASH
1 spaghetti squash
2 tsps. avocado oil
Sea salt
Freshly ground black pepper
FOR THE PESTO
2 tbsps. avocado oil
2 stalks kale, stemmed

1 zucchini peeled
¼ cup chopped onion
½ cup raw cashews
2 garlic cloves
1 tbsp. freshly squeezed lemon juice
1 tbsp. nutritional yeast
½ tsp. sea salt

DIRECTIONS:

1. Use parchment paper to line the inner pot.
TO PREPARE THE SQUASH
2. Cut the spaghetti squash in half lengthwise, scoop out the seeds, rub the avocado oil onto the insides and outer rims of both halves, sprinkle with salt and pepper, and transfer to the inner pot. Press Bake and cook at 350°F(180°C) for 45 to 50 minutes, or until tender.
TO PREPARE THE PESTO
3. While the squash bakes, add all of the pesto ingredients into a food processor, process until well blended. Adjust seasonings, if needed.
TO ASSEMBLE
4. Scrape out the insides of the squash into long, pasta-like strands with a fork. Transfer to a medium bowl.
5. Add the pesto, and gently toss until well mixed. Transfer to 2 plates or bowls and serve.

Wild Rice and Broccoli Bowl with Roasted Garlic Cashew Sauce (Bake)

Prep Time: 10 minutes, Cook Time: 20 minutes, Serves: 1

INGREDIENTS:

FOR THE ROASTED BROCCOLI AND GARLIC
6 garlic cloves, peeled
1 cup bite-size broccoli florets
1 tsp. avocado oil
Pinch garlic powder
Pinch sea salt
Pinch black pepper
FOR THE DRESSING
6 roasted garlic cloves (from above)
1 cup raw cashews

½ tsp. avocado oil
1 cup water
¼ tsp. garlic powder
½ tsp. apple cider vinegar
¼ to ½ tsp. sea salt
Pinch freshly ground black pepper
FOR ASSEMBLING
1 cup cooked wild rice
2 tbsps. diced onion
¼ cup slivered almonds
½ cup chopped collard greens

DIRECTIONS:

1. Use parchment paper to line the inner pot.
TO PREPARE THE ROASTED BROCCOLI AND GARLIC
2. Add the garlic and broccoli into a small bowl, toss with the avocado oil to coat. Season with the garlic powder, salt and pepper, and transfer to the Ninja Foodi.
3. Press Roast, cook the broccoli and garlic at 400°F(205°C) for 15 to 20 minutes, or until the broccoli gets soft and slightly crispy.
TO PREPARE THE DRESSING
4. Combine all of the dressing ingredients in a high-speed blender, blend them together until creamy and smooth. Adjust the seasonings, if needed.
TO ASSEMBLE
5. Stir together the cooked rice with the roasted broccoli, onion, almond slivers, and collard greens in a serving bowl. Stir in the dressing and serve.

Tempeh Onion Stuffed Cremini Mushrooms (Bake)

Prep Time: 15 minutes, Cook Time: 20 minutes, Serves: 6

INGREDIENTS:

18 cremini mushrooms
2 tbsps. diced red onion, small dice
3 ounces (85 g) tempeh, diced very small, or
pulsed small
Pinch of cayenne pepper
Pinch of onion powder
¼ cup rice, cooked
1 tbsp. tamari

DIRECTIONS:

1. Remove stems from the mushrooms and set the caps aside. Chop the stems finely and set aside.
2. In the Ninja Foodi, add 3 tablespoons of water and heat it. Add the chopped mushroom stems and onion. Press Sauté and cook at 390ºF (200ºC) for 10 to 15 minutes or until the onion is translucent. Stir in the tempeh and cook for another 5 minutes. Add the cayenne pepper, onion powder, rice, and tamari. Cook for 2 minutes, stirring occasionally.
3. Stuff the mixture into mushroom caps and place in the inner pot. Press Bake and cook at 350°F(180°C). for 20 minutes. Serve warm.

Spiced Zucchini Dish (Bake)

Prep Time: 10 minutes, Cook Time: 20 minutes, Serves: 2

INGREDIENTS:

1 tbsp. onion powder
2 tbsps. agave syrup
1 tsp. liquid smoke
1 tbsp. of sea salt
½ tsp. cayenne powder
¼ cup date sugar
¼ cup spring water
2 zucchinis, cut into strips
1 tbsp. grapeseed oil

DIRECTIONS:

1. Place a medium saucepan over medium heat, add all of the ingredients except for the zucchini and oil, cook until the sugar has dissolved.
2. In a large bowl, add the zucchini strips, pour in the mixture from the saucepan, toss until coated, and allow it to marinate for at least 1 hour.
3. When ready to cook, switch on the Ninja Foodi.
4. Use the parchment paper to line the inner pot, grease with the oil, arrange the marinated zucchini strips on it, and press Bake and cook at 400°F(205°C) for 10 minutes.
5. Then flip the zucchini, continue to cook for 4 minutes and then allow to cool completely.
6. Serve immediately.

Apples with Walnuts (Bake)

Prep Time: 10 minutes, Cook Time: 55 minutes, Serves: 2

INGREDIENTS:

4 apples, large, cored, sliced
3 tbsps. agave syrup
1 tbsp. chopped walnuts
⅛ tsp. ground cloves

DIRECTIONS:

1. Preheat the Ninja Foodi to 350°F(180°C).
2. While the oven preheats, place the apple slices in the inner pot, drizzle with the agave syrup and toss until evenly coated.
3. Place the nuts in a small bowl, add the cloves, and stir until mixed.
4. Sprinkle the nuts mixture over the apple and allow it to rest for 5 minutes or more until the apples start releasing their juices.
5. Arrange apple slices on Crisp Plate, and press Bake and cook at 350°F(180°C) for 15 minutes.
6. Use the foil to cover the Ninja Foodi and continue to bake for 40 minutes until bubbly.
7. After baking, allow the apples to cool for 10 minutes and serve.

Roasted Vegetable Salad (Roast)

Prep Time: 10 minutes, Cook Time: 15 minutes, Serves: 2

INGREDIENTS:

1 pint cherry tomatoes
½ bunch asparagus, trimmed
1 carrot, peeled and cut into bite-size pieces
½ cup mushrooms, halved
1 red or yellow bell pepper, seeded and cut into bite-size pieces
1 tbsp. coconut oil
1 tsp. sea salt
1 tbsp. garlic powder

DIRECTIONS:

1. Combine the tomatoes, asparagus, carrot, mushrooms, and bell pepper in a bowl. Add the coconut oil, salt and garlic powder. Toss to evenly coat the vegetables.
2. Place the vegetables into the inner pot, press Roast and cook at 425°F(220°C) for 15 minutes, or until the vegetables are tender.
3. After roasting, place the vegetables into a large bowl. Refrigerate, if desired.
4. Evenly divide the vegetables into two bowls and serve warm or cold.

Pinto Beans Taquitos (Bake)

Prep Time: 5 minutes, Cook Time: 25 minutes, Serves: 4

INGREDIENTS:

2 cups pinto beans, cooked	½ tsp. onion powder
1 tsp. ground cumin	½ tsp. garlic powder
1 tsp. chili powder	¼ tsp. red pepper flakes
	12 corn tortillas

DIRECTIONS:

1. Use the parchment paper to line the inner pot.
2. In a food processor or blender, add all of the ingredients except the tortillas. Pulse or blend on low for 30 seconds, or until smooth, then set aside.
3. On Crisp Plate, place with the tortillas, and bake for 1 to 2 minutes. To soften the tortillas and makes rolling them much easier.
4. Take the tortillas out from the oven, then place a couple of heaping tablespoons of the refried beans onto the bottom half of each corn tortilla. Tightly roll the tortillas, and return them on the Crisp Plate, seam-side down.
5. Press Bake and cook at 400°F(205°C) for 20 minutes, turning once after about 10 minutes, and serve warm.

Garlic Broccoli Bites (Bake)

Prep Time: 5 minutes, Cook Time: 20 minutes, Serves: 3 cups

INGREDIENTS:

½ cup nutritional yeast	cayenne pepper (optional)
½ cup almond flour	3 cups bite-size broccoli florets
½ tsp. sea salt	2 tbsps. avocado oil
½ tsp. garlic powder	
¼ to ½ tsp. ground	

DIRECTIONS:

1. Use parchment paper to line the inner pot.
2. Combine all of the ingredients except the broccoli and avocado oil in a small bowl, stir them together.
3. Add the broccoli and avocado oil into the inner pot, toss to coat.
4. Sprinkle over the broccoli with half the seasoning mixture, toss gently until all pieces are coated, and press Bake and cook at 400°F(205°C) for 10 minutes.
5. Remove from the Ninja Foodi, and return the broccoli pieces to the medium bowl. Sprinkle with the remaining half of the seasoning mix, and toss to coat.
6. Place back to the inner pot and bake for another 5 to 10 minutes, and serve.

Squash and Apples (Bake)

Prep Time: 10 minutes, Cook Time: 35 minutes, Serves: 2

INGREDIENTS:

1 ½ pounds (680 g) butternut squash, peeled, deseeded, cut into chunks	½ tsp. sea salt
	2 apples, cored, cut into ½-inch pieces
2 tbsps. grapeseed oil	2 tbsps. agave syrup

DIRECTIONS:

1. Spread the squash pieces on Crisp Plate.
2. Add the oil and salt in a small bowl, stir until mixed, and then drizzle over the squash pieces.
3. Cover the crispy lid and press Bake and cook at 375°F(190°C). for 20 minutes.
4. While the squash pieces bake, in a medium bowl, add the apple pieces, drizzle with the agave syrup, and then toss until coated.
5. After baking, unwrap the Ninja Foodi, spoon into the bowl containing apple and then stir until mixed.
6. Evenly spread apple-squash mixture on the Crisp Plate and then continue to bake for 15 minutes.
7. After baking, serve immediately.

Chickpea and Avocado Salad (Bake)

Prep Time: 10 minutes, Cook Time: 20 minutes, Serves: 2

INGREDIENTS:

2 cups cooked chickpeas	1 medium white onion, peeled, diced
1 tsp. onion powder	1 tbsp. olive oil
1 tsp. of sea salt	¼ cup chopped coriander
½ tsp. cayenne pepper	2 tbsps. hemp seeds, shelled
½ of cucumber, deseeded, sliced	1 key lime, juiced
2 avocados, peeled, pitted, cubed	

DIRECTIONS:

1. While the oven preheats, place the chickpeas in the inner pot, season with the onion powder, salt and pepper, drizzle with the oil and toss until combined.
2. Press Bake and cook the chickpeas at 425°F(220°C) for 20 minutes or until golden brown and crisp, allow them to cool for 10 minutes.
3. After baking, transfer the chickpeas to a bowl, stir in the coriander, hemp seeds and lime juice, mix well. Serve immediately.

Spiced Party Mix (Bake)

Prep Time: 15 minutes, Cook Time: 10 minutes, Serves: 6

INGREDIENTS:

Cooking spray
½ cup flaked unsweetened coconut
1 cup raisins
1 cup raw almonds
½ cup roasted peas
½ cup pumpkin seeds
1 cup dried pineapple

pieces
1 tsp. chili powder
1 tsp. ground ginger
2 tbsps. garlic powder
2 tbsps. onion powder
1 tsp. sea salt
1 tbsp. coconut oil

DIRECTIONS:

1. Use cooking spray to coat the inner pot.
2. Combine all of the remaining ingredients in a medium bowl.
3. In the Ninja Foodi, spread the mix in an even layer.
4. Press Bake and cook at 425°F(220°C) for 10 minutes, being careful that it doesn't burn.
5. After baking, remove from the inner pot and allow to cool before serving.

Taco-Seasoned Chickpeas and Edamame (Bake)

Prep Time: 10 minutes, Cook Time: 40 minutes, Serves: 7

INGREDIENTS:

12 ounces (340 g) frozen edamame
1 15-ounce (425 g) can chickpeas, drained

(save the liquid to use as aquafaba) and rinsed
4 tbsps. taco seasoning
3 tbsps. aquafaba

DIRECTIONS:

1. Preheat the Ninja Foodi to 400°F(205°C).
2. According to directions on package to cook the edamame.
3. On Crisp Plate, spread with the cooked edamame and chickpeas. Press Bake and cook at 400°F(205°C) for 20 minutes.
4. In a medium bowl, add the taco seasoning.
5. Take the edamame and chickpeas out from the oven and toss with the aquafaba. Add to the bowl of taco seasoning and coat well.
6. Place back to the inner pot and bake for another 10 minutes.
7. Allow to cool and serve, but let them cool in the Ninja Foodi for at least 2 hours to overnight before packing away. Store in an airtight container for up to 2 weeks.

Easy Baked Marinated Portobello Mushrooms (Bake)

Prep Time: 10 minutes, Cook Time: 30 minutes, Serves: 2

INGREDIENTS:

2 caps of Portobello mushrooms, destemmed
⅔ tsp. minced onion
⅔ tbsp. key lime juice
⅔ tsp. minced sage

⅔ tsp. thyme
Extra:
2 tbsps. alkaline soy sauce

DIRECTIONS:

1. Arrange the mushroom caps in the inner pot, cut side up.
2. Place all of the remaining ingredients in a small bowl, stir until mixed, brush the mixture over inside and outside the mushrooms, and allow them to marinate for 15 minutes.
3. Press Bake and cook the mushrooms at 400°F(205°C) for 30 minutes, flipping halfway, and then serve immediately.

Garlicky Harissa Sauce (Bake)

Prep Time: 10 minutes, Cook Time: 20 minutes, Serves: 3 to 4 cups

INGREDIENTS:

1 large red bell pepper, seeded, cored, and cut into chunks
4 garlic cloves, peeled
1 yellow onion, cut into thick rings
2 tbsps. tomato paste

1 cup no-sodium vegetable broth or water
1 tsp. ground cumin
1 tbsp. low-sodium soy sauce or tamari
1 tbsp. Hungarian paprika

DIRECTIONS:

1. Use parchment paper or aluminum foil to line the inner pot.
2. On the Crisp Plate, add the bell pepper, flesh-side up, and space out the garlic and onion around the pepper.
3. Press Roast and cook at 450°F(235°C) for 20 minutes. Then transfer to a blender.
4. Add the remaining ingredients to the blender, puree until smooth. Serve cold or warm.
5. Place in an airtight container and refrigerate for up to 2 weeks or freeze for up to 6 months.

Homemade Roasted Garlic Cabbage (Roast)

Prep Time: 5 minutes, Cook Time: 45 minutes, Serves: 4

INGREDIENTS:

1 (2-pound, 907 g) head organic green cabbage, cut into 1-inch-thick slices (about 8 slices)

1½ tbsps. coconut oil
2 to 3 large garlic cloves, smashed
Pinch sea salt

DIRECTIONS:

1. In the inner pot, add the cabbage slices and use the coconut oil to brush on both sides.
2. Rub the garlic onto each cabbage slice and sprinkle with salt.
3. Press Roast and cook at 425°F(220°C) for 20 minutes. Flip the cabbage slices over and roast for an additional 20 to 25 minutes, until the edges are brown and crisp.

Garlic Broccoli Carrot Bake (Bake)

Prep Time: 10 minutes, Cook Time: 30 minutes, Serves: 2

INGREDIENTS:

2 tbsps. coconut oil
4 carrots, peeled and sliced
1 pound (454 g) broccoli, cut into bite-size pieces
3 garlic heads, cloves

peeled and chopped, or 3 tbsps. minced
2 tsps. lemon zest
¼ tsp. mustard powder
1 cup vegetable broth
1 tsp. sea salt

DIRECTIONS:

1. Add all of the ingredients into a medium bowl, stir them together.
2. Spread the mixture evenly into the inner pot. Cover the crisping lid and press Bake and cook at 400°F(205°C) for 30 minutes, stirring once.
3. After baking, serve immediately.

Homemade Easy Roasted Vegetables (Roast)

Prep Time: 15 minutes, Cook Time: 1 Hour, Serves: 4

INGREDIENTS:

1 baking pumpkin, peeled and cubed

2 large carrots, peeled and cubed
1 butternut squash, peeled and cubed
3 fresh sage leaves,

finely chopped
2 green apples, peeled, cored, and sliced
1 tsp. sea salt
2 tsps. coconut oil

DIRECTIONS:

1. Combine all of the ingredients in the inner pot. Toss to coat evenly in the oil and seasonings. Transfer the vegetables to a roasting pan, in a single layer.
2. Press Roast and cook at 350°F(180°C) for 60 minutes, stirring occasionally. Then serve warm.

Mashed Sweet Potato (Bake)

Prep Time: 15 minutes, Cook Time: 30 minutes, Serves: 6

INGREDIENTS:

8 sweet potatoes, cooked
1 tbsp. dried sage
½ cup vegetable broth
1 tsp. dried thyme
1 tsp. dried rosemary

DIRECTIONS:

1. Remove and discard the skin from the cooked sweet potatoes, place them in the inner pot. Use a fork or potato masher to mash the sweet potatoes, then stir in the remaining ingredients.
2. Press Bake and cook at 375°F(190°C) for 30 minutes, after baking, serve warm.

Vanilla Spiced Quinoa Pumpkin Casserole (Bake)

Prep Time: 15 minutes, Cook Time: 15 minutes, Serves: 6

INGREDIENTS:

Cooking spray
3 cups cooked quinoa
1 vanilla bean, split lengthwise and seeds scraped out
1 (15-ounce, 425 g) can pumpkin purée

½ cup water
½ tsp. nutmeg
½ tsp. ground ginger
1 tsp. cinnamon
¼ tsp. grated fresh ginger
¼ tsp. sea salt

DIRECTIONS:

1. Spray a 4-cup casserole dish and set aside.
2. Add the quinoa and the remaining ingredients in a medium bowl, stir them together.
3. Place the mixture into the Ninja Foodi. press Bake and cook at 350°F(180°C) for 15 minutes, or until golden and bubbly.

Roasted Zucchini Lasagna (Bake)

Prep Time: 10 minutes, Cook Time: 25 minutes, Serves: 2

INGREDIENTS:

4 zucchinis, sliced lengthwise into ¼-inch noodles

1 cup sun-dried tomato sauce

1 cup shite sauce

DIRECTIONS:

1. In the inner pot, add the zucchini noodles. press Roast and cook at 350°F(180°C) for 10 minutes, then remove from the Ninja Foodi.
2. Cover the bottom with one layer of zucchini strips in the inner pot. Pour in ¼ cup sun-dried tomato sauce over. Then add another layer of zucchini strip, placed crosswise from the first layer. Cover with another ¼ cup sun-dried tomato sauce. Lay a third layer of zucchini crosswise from the second layer and another ¼ cup sun-dried tomato sauce. Repeat with the remaining zucchini and ¼ cup sun-dried tomato sauce.
3. Place the white sauce on top of the finished lasagna. Cover the crisping lid, and bake for 15 minutes, or until hot and bubbly.
4. Remove from the Ninja Foodi and allow to cool for 5 minutes before slicing and serving.

Toasted Cashew and Mushroom Rolls (Bake)

Prep Time: 1 hour 20 minutes, Cook Time: 15 minutes, Serves: 6

INGREDIENTS:

1 tbsp. plus 2 tsps. dairy-free milk

¼ cup raw cashews, soaked for 1 hour

1 tsp. lemon juice

¼ tsp. salt

Pinch of ground black pepper

4 ounces (113 g) button mushrooms

¼ cup dairy-free butter, divided

2 tbsps. raw shelled hempseed

9 slices whole-grain bread

DIRECTIONS:

1. In a food processor, add the milk, cashews, lemon juice, salt, and pepper. Process until smooth.
2. Clean mushrooms well and finely chop.
3. In the Ninja Foodi, heat 1 tablespoon butter over medium-high heat. Add the chopped mushrooms and press Sear/Sauté and cook at 390ºF (200ºC) for 5 minutes. Remove from the heat and add the cashew mixture and hempseed. Stir well.
4. Cut crusts off of the bread and leave in a square shape. Use a rolling pin to roll each square thin. You will be rolling up these squares. Spread 1 tablespoon mushroom mixture onto each square and roll up.
5. Melt the remaining butter.
6. Cut rolls in half and roll in melted butter. Arrange the rolls on the cookie sheets and press Bake and cook at 425°F(220°C) for 8 minutes or until browned.

Tomato Mushroom Stuffed Eggplant (Bake)

Prep Time: 10 minutes, Cook Time: 30 minutes, Serves: 4

INGREDIENTS:

1 large eggplant, cut in half lengthwise

3 tbsps. extra-virgin olive oil or avocado oil, divided

⅛ tsp. sea salt

1 tsp. taco spice blend

2 garlic cloves, crushed,

or 2 frozen garlic cubes

1 cup canned low-sodium diced tomatoes

2 cups sliced mushrooms

1 cup canned low-sodium chickpeas, drained and rinsed

DIRECTIONS:

1. Use aluminum foil to line the inner pot.
2. Put the eggplant on the baking sheet and use 1½ teaspoons of oil to brush each side. Sprinkle both sides with the salt.
3. Place the eggplant halves on the baking sheet, cut-side down, press Bake and cook at 425°F(220°C) for 30 to 40 minutes, until the flesh softens and the outer skin puckers.
4. While the eggplant is baking, take it out and set aside, clean the inner pot. Heat the remaining 1 tablespoon of oil in the inner pot. Add the taco spice blend and garlic, cook for 2 minutes.
5. Stir the tomatoes and mushrooms into the Ninja Foodi and cook for an additional 10 minutes, or until the mushrooms are soft.
6. Add the chickpeas and cook for 3 minutes more, or until warmed through. Turn off the heat and cover.
7. Evenly divide the mushroom mixture between the eggplant halves and cut each in half to make four servings.

Roasted Garlic (Roast)

Prep Time: 5 minutes, Cook Time: 45 minutes, Serves: 1

INGREDIENTS:
1 garlic head
1 tsp. avocado oil

Pinch sea salt

DIRECTIONS:
1. Remove the outer papery layer of the garlic head. Cut the top off, and add the entire garlic head into a paper muffin cup in the inner pot. Drizzle over with the avocado oil, be sure that it's evenly distributed in all the crevices, and sprinkle with the salt.
2. Press Roast and cook at 375°F(190°C) for 45 minutes. Allow to cool until easy to handle.
3. Squeeze or peel each clove out of the paper shell gently. Use in any recipe that calls for roasted garlic.

Italian Oats Rice Bean Balls (Bake)

Prep Time: 10 minutes, Cook Time: 30 minutes, Serves: 6

INGREDIENTS:
1½ cups cooked red kidney beans
1½ cups cooked black beans
1 cup quick-cooking oats
1 cup cooked brown rice
¼ cup easy one-pot vegan marinara

1 tbsp. Italian seasoning
1 tsp. onion powder
1 tsp. garlic powder
¼ tsp. freshly ground black pepper

DIRECTIONS:
1. Use the parchment paper to line the inner pot.
2. Mash the kidney beans and black beans together with a fork or mixing spoon in a large bowl.
3. Stir in the oats, rice, marinara, Italian seasoning, onion powder, garlic powder, and pepper. Mix well.
4. Scoop out ¼ cup of the bean mixture, and shape into a ball. Put the bean ball on the Crisp Plate. Repeat with the remaining bean mixture.
5. Press Bake and cook the bean balls at 400°F(205°C) for 30 minutes, or until lightly browned and heated through, turning once after about 15 minutes.

Nutty Spinach, Artichoke and Tomato Dip (Bake)

Prep Time: 10 minutes, Cook Time: 20 minutes, Serves: 6

INGREDIENTS:
Cooking spray
¾ cup unsweetened almond milk
1 garlic clove
¾ cup raw cashews
2 tbsps. freshly squeezed lemon juice
¾ tsp. sea salt

1 tbsp. nutritional yeast
2 cups baby spinach leaves
1 cup baby tomatoes
2 cups artichoke hearts, frozen or canned in water, not oil

DIRECTIONS:
1. Use cooking spray to coat the inner pot.
2. Add the almond milk, garlic, cashews, lemon juice, salt and yeast into a blender. Blend until very smooth.
3. Add the spinach, tomatoes and artichoke hearts to the blender. Pulse to combine, but still leaving chunks of vegetables.
4. Place the dip into the inner pot, press Bake and cook at 425°F(220°C) for 20 minutes.
5. After baking, remove from the oven, allow to cool for 5 minutes, and serve warm.

Chapter 15 Main Dish

Creamy Garlic Mushroom Pizza (Bake)

Prep Time: 45 minutes, Cook Time: 30 minutes, Serves: 8

INGREDIENTS:

For the cornmeal crust
½ cup warm water (less than 100°F, 38°C)
1¼ tbsps. instant yeast
2¾ to 3¼ cups whole wheat flour, divided, plus more for the work surface
¼ cup cornmeal
½ tsp. onion powder
½ tsp. garlic powder
1 tbsp. melted coconut oil (optional)
For the topping
1 cup cashew sour cream
1 tbsp. yellow (mellow) miso paste
1 tbsp. nutritional yeast
½ tsp. garlic powder
8 ounces (227 g) cremini mushrooms, stemmed and thinly sliced
4 ounces (113 g) shiitake mushrooms, stemmed and thinly sliced
4 garlic cloves, minced
½ large yellow onion, cut into thin strips
1 tbsp. water, plus more as needed
1 tsp. dried parsley
½ tsp. dried oregano

DIRECTIONS:

To make the cornmeal crust
1. Stir together the warm water, yeast, 1 cup of flour and cornmeal in a large bowl. Set aside for 10 minutes.
2. Add the onion powder, garlic powder, melted coconut oil, and flour—start with 1 cup and add more, ¼ cup at a time, so the dough comes together without being too sticky.
3. Lightly dust the flour onto a work surface and turn the dough out onto it. Knead the dough for 5 minutes. Place the dough in a sealable bag or a lightly oiled bowl and cover it. Allow to rest for 15 minutes, or refrigerate overnight.

To make the topping
1. Add the cashew sour cream, miso paste, nutritional yeast, and garlic powder in a medium bowl, whisk to combine. Set aside.
2. Combine the cremini and shiitake mushrooms in a large skillet, press Sear/Sauté and cook at 390ºF (200ºC) for 3 minutes. Add the garlic and onion and gently flip the ingredients to combine. Cook for about another 4 minutes, adding water, 1 tablespoon at a time, if the onion is browning too quickly. The mushrooms should have some blackening and the onions should be browned.
3. To assemble the pizza
4. Use parchment paper to line the inner pot.
5. Divide the dough in half and form the halves into round balls. Avoid using flour on your work surface because it can make the dough not stick to itself. Roll out or pat and stretch each dough ball into a thin layer, about 16 inches in diameter. If the dough isn't stretching, allow it to rest for 5 minutes and try again.
6. In the Ninja Foodi, add the shaped crusts. Press Bake and cook at 425°F(220°C) for 8 minutes.
7. Spread over the precooked crusts with the cashew cream sauce. Divide the mushroom and onion mix between the pizzas. Sprinkle on the parsley and oregano. Bake for another 15 minutes, or until the crust is golden brown.

Burrito Bowl with Tortilla Chips (Bake)

Prep Time: 10 minutes, Cook Time: 10 minutes, Serves: 2

INGREDIENTS:

4 corn tortillas
1 cup corn (fresh or frozen)
1 cup cooked brown rice
1 cup cooked black beans
1 tsp. ground cumin
2 tsps. chili powder
½ tsp. onion powder
½ tsp. garlic powder
1 avocado, peeled, pitted, and sliced
2 cups shredded lettuce
¼ cup salsa

DIRECTIONS:
1. Use parchment paper to line the inner pot.
2. Evenly cut each tortilla into 6 chips, and put the chips on Crisp Plate. Press Bake and cook at 350°F(180°C) until golden brown, about 8 to 10 minutes. The chips will continue to crisp up as they cool.
3. Combine the corn, rice, black beans, cumin, chili powder, onion powder, and garlic powder in a large bowl. Press Sauté and cook at 390ºF (200ºC) to warm this mixture for 2 minutes, if the rice and beans are cold.
4. Divide this warm corn-rice mixture into two serving bowls, then place half of the avocado slices, 1 cup of shredded lettuce and salsa on the top.
5. Serve this bowl with the crispy tortilla chips.

Black Bean and Rice Stuffed Peppers (Bake)

Prep Time: 10 minutes, Cook Time: 30 minutes, Serves: 4

INGREDIENTS:

4 bell peppers	frozen)
1 cup cooked black beans	2 tbsps. chili powder
3 cups cooked brown rice	1 cup vegetable broth
1 cup corn (fresh or	2 tbsps. tomato paste
	1 tsp. ground cumin

DIRECTIONS:

1. Cut the tops of the bell peppers off, remove any fibers or seeds that remain inside the core or inside the tops of the peppers.
2. Add the beans, rice, corn, chili powder, broth, tomato paste, and cumin in a large bowl, mix until the tomato paste and spices have been thoroughly incorporated.
3. Spoon one-quarter of the rice mixture into each pepper. Place the peppers upright on the inner pot, and put the tops back onto the peppers.
4. Press Bake and cook at 375°F(190°C) until the peppers are easily pierced with a fork, about 1 hour. After baking, serve warm.

Orange-Glazed Tofu Bowl with Brown Rice (Bake)

Prep Time: 15 minutes, Cook Time: 40 minutes, Serves: 4

INGREDIENTS:

FOR THE TOFU	FOR THE ORANGE GLAZE
1 tsp. onion powder	½ cup orange juice, without pulp
1 tsp. garlic powder	
¼ cup gluten-free or whole-wheat flour	1 tbsp. maple syrup
½ tsp. freshly ground black pepper	1 tbsp. cornstarch
	1 tbsp. rice vinegar
1 (14-ounce, 397 g) package firm or extra-firm tofu, drained and cut into ¼-inch cubes	½ tsp. onion powder
	½ tsp. garlic powder
	FOR THE BOWL
	6 cups cooked brown rice

DIRECTIONS:

TO MAKE THE TOFU
1. Use parchment paper to line the inner pot.
2. Add the onion powder, garlic powder, flour, and pepper in a large bowl, whisk them together.
3. Add the tofu and toss until completely coated.
4. Put the coated tofu in the inner pot and press Bake and cook at 400°F(205°C) for 40 minutes, turning after 20 minutes.

TO MAKE THE ORANGE GLAZE
1. Meanwhile, combine all of the ingredients of the orange glaze in a small saucepan. Bring to a boil over medium-high heat. Lower the heat to low, and simmer for 10 minutes. Remove from the heat and set aside to cool.
2. TO MAKE THE BOWL
3. Take the tofu out from the oven and gently mix it with the orange glaze.
4. Place 1½ cups of cooked brown rice in each bowl, and put one-quarter of the orange-glazed tofu on the top and serve.

Roasted Broccoli Salad with Spicy Cashew Dressing (Roast)

Prep Time: 15 minutes, Cook Time: 20 minutes, Serves: 1 or 2

INGREDIENTS:

FOR THE BROCCOLI	1 tbsp. apple cider vinegar
2 cups bite-size broccoli florets	
1 tsp. avocado oil	1 tbsp. brown rice syrup
Pinch freshly ground black pepper	1 tbsp. red pepper flakes
	2 to 3 tbsps. water
Pinch sea salt	FOR ASSEMBLING
Pinch garlic powder	2 to 4 cups mixed salad greens
FOR THE DRESSING	
¼ tsp. avocado oil	3 tbsps. chopped scallions
¼ cup cashew butter	¼ cup raw cashews
1 tbsp. coconut aminos	2 tsps. sesame seeds

DIRECTIONS:

1. Use parchment paper to line the inner pot.

TO PREPARE THE BROCCOLI
2. Add the broccoli into a small bowl, toss with the avocado oil to coat. Season with the pepper, salt, and garlic powder.
3. Place the broccoli into the inner pot, and press Roast and cook at 400°F(205°C) until the broccoli is soft, about 15 to 20 minutes.

TO PREPARE THE DRESSING
4. While the broccoli is roasting, combine all of the dressing ingredients in a small bowl, whisk them together until well combined.

TO ASSEMBLE
5. On 1 large or 2 small plates, add the mixed greens, and place the roasted broccoli, scallions and cashews on the top. Drizzle with the dressing, garnish with the sesame seeds, and serve.

Baked Chickpea and Kale (Bake)

Prep Time: 5 minutes, Cook Time: 10 minutes, Serves: 2

INGREDIENTS:

2 cups cooked chickpeas	1 cup kale leaves
2 tbsps. grapeseed oil	⅔ cup soft-jelly coconut
⅔ tsp. salt	cream
⅓ tsp. cayenne pepper	

DIRECTIONS:

1. Spread the chickpeas in the inner pot, drizzle with 1 tablespoon oil, sprinkle with the salt and cayenne pepper, press Bake and cook at 425°F(220°C) for 15 minutes until roasted.
2. Heat the remaining oil in a frying pan over medium heat, when hot, add the kale and cook for 5 minutes.
3. Place the roasted chickpeas in the Ninja Foodi, pour in the cream, stir until mixed and then simmer for 4 minutes, squashing chickpeas slightly.
4. Serve immediately.

Black Bean and Rice Enchilada Bake (Bake)

Prep Time: 10 minutes, Cook Time: 30 minutes, Serves: 6

INGREDIENTS:

FOR THE ENCHILADA SAUCE	BAKE
2 tbsps. chili powder	2 cups cooked black beans
¼ cup tomato paste	2 cups cooked brown rice
1 tsp. paprika	1 cup corn (fresh or frozen)
1 tsp. onion powder	8 corn tortillas
1 tsp. garlic powder	½ cup fat-free refried beans or mashed pinto beans
1 tsp. ground cumin	
2½ cups water	
FOR THE ENCHILADA	

DIRECTIONS:

TO MAKE THE ENCHILADA SAUCE

1. Add all of the enchilada sauce ingredients in a blender, blend for 1 to 2 minutes, or until thoroughly blended.

TO MAKE THE ENCHILADA BAKE

1. Reserve ½ cup of enchilada sauce, and set aside.
2. Add the black beans, rice, corn, and the remaining enchilada sauce in a large bowl, mix them together.
3. With 4 corn tortillas to cover the bottom of the inner pot, then spread the refried beans over the tortillas evenly.
4. Lay an even layer of the rice mixture over the refried beans.
5. On top of the filling, place with the remaining 4 tortillas. Spread over the tortillas with the reserved ½ cup of enchilada sauce, be sure that they are covered with the sauce.
6. Put the enchiladas in the Ninja Foodi and press Bake and cook at 375°F(190°C) until lightly browned, about 30 minutes. After baking, serve warm.

Fresh Vegetable Pizza with Garlic Tahini-Beet Spread (Bake)

Prep Time: 10 minutes, Cook Time: 15 minutes, Serves: 4

INGREDIENTS:

FOR THE CRUST	1 tbsp. freshly squeezed lemon juice
3 tbsps. coconut oil	⅛ tsp. sea salt
1¼ cup almond flour	Pinch freshly ground black pepper
½ tsp. garlic powder	
½ tsp. sea salt	
FOR THE TAHINI-BEET SPREAD	FOR ASSEMBLING Mushrooms, red onions, dandelion greens, asparagus, jalapeños, artichokes, arugula, broccoli, basil, dulse flakes (optional toppings)
1 tbsp. avocado oil	
2 beets, peeled and cubed	
1 tbsp. tahini	
2 garlic cloves	

DIRECTIONS:

1. Use parchment paper to line the inner pot.

TO PREPARE THE CRUST

2. Combine the coconut oil, almond flour, garlic powder and salt in a small bowl, stir them together until well combined.
3. Place into the Ninja Foodi, and squeeze the mixture together until it forms a ball shape. On top of the ball, lay another sheet of parchment paper, and roll the dough out over the parchment paper into a 7-by-7-inch square with a rolling pin.
4. Press Bake and cook at 375°F(190°C) for about 14 minutes, until the edges turn golden brown.

TO PREPARE THE TAHINI-BEET SPREAD

5. At the same time, add all of the tahini-beet spread ingredients into a food processor, process them together until thick and creamy. Adjust the seasonings, if needed.

TO ASSEMBLE

6. When the crust is ready, evenly spread over with the tahini-beet spread, top the pizza with your favorite alkaline veggies, cut into 4 slices, and serve.

Chickpea Hummus Lettuce Gyros (Bake)

Prep Time: 15 minutes, Cook Time: 20 minutes, Serves: 4

INGREDIENTS:

1 tsp. freshly ground black pepper
1 tbsp. paprika
½ tsp. garlic powder
1 tsp. dried oregano
¼ tsp. cayenne pepper
¼ tsp. onion powder
1 (15-ounce, 425 g) can chickpeas, drained and

rinsed
1 cup hummus
4 whole wheat pitas
¼ cup finely chopped cucumber
¼ cup chopped tomato
¼ cup red onion strips
2 romaine lettuce leaves, finely chopped

DIRECTIONS:

1. Use parchment paper to line the inner pot.
2. Add the black pepper, paprika, garlic powder, oregano, cayenne pepper, and onion powder in a medium bowl, stir them together. Add the chickpeas and toss to coat. Spread the chickpeas mixture into a single layer in the inner pot.
3. Press Bake and cook at 400°F(205°C) for 10 minutes. Stir and flip the chickpeas and bake for another 10 minutes, until slightly crispy, as they will become crispier as they cool. Take out from the oven and allow to cool in the Ninja Foodi.
4. On each pita, spread with ¼ cup of hummus. Top each with 1 tablespoon each of the cucumber, one-quarter of the roasted chickpeas, tomato and red onion, and one-quarter of the lettuce. Fold and enjoy.

Butternut Squash, Rice and Apple Burger (Bake)

Prep Time: 10 minutes, Cook Time: 1 hour, Serves: 2

INGREDIENTS:

¾ cup diced butternut squash
¼ tsp. sea salt, divided
½ cup diced apples
¼ cup chopped shallots
½ tbsp. thyme

1 tbsp. pumpkin seeds, unsalted
1 cup cooked wild rice
1 tbsp. grapeseed oil
2 spelt burgers, halved, toasted

DIRECTIONS:

1. While the oven preheats, use the parchment paper to line the inner pot, spread with the squash pieces and then sprinkle with ⅛ teaspoon salt.

2. Press Bake and cook the squash at 400°F(205°C) for 15 minutes, then add the apple and shallots, sprinkle with the remaining salt, and bake for 20 to 30 minutes until cooked.
3. After baking, allow the vegetable mixture to cool for 15 minutes, transfer into a food processor, add the thyme and pulse until a chunky mixture comes together.
4. Add the pumpkin seeds and cooked wild rice, pulse until combined, and then tip the mixture in a bowl.
5. Taste the mixture to adjust and form it into two patties.
6. Heat the oil in Ninja Foodi, add the patties and cook for 5 to 7 minutes per side until browned.
7. Serve the patties in burger buns.

Garlic Lentil and Sweet Potato Taco Wraps (Bake)

Prep Time: 10 minutes, Cook Time: 30 minutes, Serves: 2 warps

INGREDIENTS:

FOR THE SWEET POTATO
1 sweet potato, peeled and cut into bite-size cubes
2 tsps. avocado oil
⅛ tsp. ground paprika
1 garlic clove, crushed
⅛ tsp. sea salt
FOR THE LENTILS
¾ cup dry lentils, cooked according to package directions
1 tbsp. avocado oil

2 garlic cloves, crushed
½ to 1 jalapeño
1 cup fresh cilantro leaves
1 tbsp. freshly squeezed lemon juice
1 tsp. sea salt
½ tsp. freshly ground black pepper
FOR ASSEMBLING
2 collard green leaves
Nondairy sour cream, for garnish (optional)

DIRECTIONS:

TO PREPARE THE SWEET POTATO
1. Place the sweet potato in the Ninja Foodi, toss with the avocado oil to coat. Add the paprika, garlic, and salt, and toss to coat again. Press Bake and cook at 350°F(180°C) for 25 to 30 minutes, or until soft.
TO PREPARE THE LENTILS
2. Add the cooked lentils, avocado oil, garlic, jalapeño, cilantro, lemon juice, salt and pepper into a food processor, pulse until well combined, not overprocess.
TO ASSEMBLE
3. Spread half the lentil mixture onto a collard green leaf, and place half the sweet potatoes on the top, and drizzle with nondairy sour cream (if using). Repeat with the remaining ingredients and enjoy.

Oats Lentil Loaf with Maple-Tomato Glaze (Bake)

Prep Time: 10 minutes, Cook Time: 30 minutes, Serves: 6

INGREDIENTS:

FOR THE GLAZE
1 tbsp. tomato paste
1 tbsp. balsamic vinegar
½ tbsp. maple syrup
FOR THE LENTIL LOAF
1 cup quick-cooking oats
1 cup cooked brown rice
2 cups cooked brown or green lentils
¼ cup sweet and tangy

ketchup
¼ cup vegetable broth
2 tsps. onion powder
1 tsp. garlic powder
2 tbsps. nutritional yeast
1 tsp. dried sage
½ tsp. dried thyme
½ tsp. baking powder
½ tsp. freshly ground black pepper

DIRECTIONS:

TO MAKE THE GLAZE
1. Add the glaze ingredients in in a small bowl, whisk them together.
TO MAKE THE LENTIL LOAF
1. Combine all of the lentil loaf ingredients in a large bowl, mix together until the spices and oats have been thoroughly mixed and the lentils mashed. Place the mixture into the inner pot lined with parchment paper.
2. Evenly brush over the top of the loaf with the glaze before placing in the Ninja Foodi.
3. Press Bake and cook at 400°F(205°C) until lightly browned, about 30 minutes, and serve.

Homemade Falafel Chickpea Burgers (Bake)

Prep Time: 15 minutes, Cook Time: 30 minutes, Serves: 8

INGREDIENTS:

2 cups cooked brown rice
3 cups cooked chickpeas
1 tbsp. freshly squeezed lemon juice
¼ cup vegetable broth
¼ cup chopped fresh parsley
2 tsps. onion powder
2 tsps. garlic powder
1 tsp. ground coriander

1½ tsps. ground cumin
¼ tsp. freshly ground black pepper
Whole-Wheat Pita Pockets or whole-wheat buns
Lettuce, tomato, and onion, for topping (optional)

DIRECTIONS:

1. Use the parchment paper to line the inner pot.
2. Combine all of the ingredients except the buns and toppings in a food processor or blender. Process on low for 30 to 45 seconds, or until the mixture can easily be formed into patties but isn't so well mixed that you create hummus. Stop the processor and scrape down the sides once or twice.
3. Scoop out ½ cup of the chickpea mixture, and shape it into a patty. Arrange the patty on Crisp Plate. Repeat until all of the chickpea mixture is used.
4. Press Bake and cook at 425°F(220°C) for 15 minutes. Flip the patties and cook for another 12 to 15 minutes, and serve on buns with your choosing toppings.

Margherita Pizza with Veggies (Bake)

Prep Time: 25 minutes, Cook Time: 1 hour, Serves: 4

INGREDIENTS:

CRUST:
1 ½ cups of spelt flour
½ tsp. of basil
½ tsp. of pure sea salt
½ tsp. of onion powder
½ tsp. of oregano
1 cup of spring water
CHEESE:
1 tsp. of sea mossgel
1 cup of soaked brazil nuts (overnight or for at least 3 hours)
½ tsp. of oregano

½ tsp. of basil
¼ tsp. of pure sea salt
½ tsp. of onion powder
¼ cup of homemade hempseed milk
1 tsp. of key lime juice
½ cup of spring water
TOPPINGS:
"garlic" sauce
sliced red onions
sliced plum or cherry tomatoes
chopped fresh basil

DIRECTIONS:

1. Add the spelt flour and seasonings in a medium bowl, and mix well. Pour in ½ cup of spring water and mix. Continue to add more water until the dough can be formed into a ball.
2. Spread the flour on your working surface. Use a rolling pin to roll the dough out, adding more flour as necessary to avoid sticking.
3. Spread the dough out on Crisp Plate, use the grape seed oil to brush, and use a fork to make holes. Place in the Ninja Foodi and press Bake and cook at 350°F(180°C) 10 to 15 minutes.
4. In a blender, add all of the ingredients for the cheese. Blend well until consistency is smooth.
5. Take the dough out from the oven. Spread with "garlic" sauce and prepared cheese. Place the onions, sliced tomatoes, basil, and more cheese on the top of the pizza.
6. Bake for 10 to 15 minutes at 425°F(220°C).
7. Serve warm.

Vegan Pizza Bread (Bake)

Prep Time: 5 minutes, Cook Time: 20 minutes, Serves: 4

INGREDIENTS:
1 whole-wheat loaf, unsliced
1 cup vegan marinara
1 tsp. nutritional yeast
½ tsp. garlic powder
½ tsp. onion powder

DIRECTIONS:
1. Divide the loaf of bread in half lengthwise. Spread the marinara evenly onto each slice of bread, and then sprinkle on the nutritional yeast, garlic powder, and onion powder.
2. In the Ninja Foodi, place with the bread and press Bake and cook at 375°F(190°C) until the bread is a light golden brown, about 20 minutes.

Easy Baked Sweet Potato and Apple (Bake)

Prep Time: 5 minutes, Cook Time: 40 minutes, Serves: 1

INGREDIENTS:
1 medium sweet potato
1 medium apple, peeled and diced
Pinch sea salt
½ tsp. cinnamon

DIRECTIONS:
1. Cut lengthwise of the sweet potato, about 1 inch deep. Spread the potato open and put it in a baking dish.
2. Inside the sweet potato's opening, add the apple. Sprinkle over with the salt and cinnamon.
3. Cover the crisping lid. Put the dish in the Ninja Foodi and press Bake and cook at 350°F(180°C) for 40 minutes, or until the potato is soft.
4. After baking, allow to cool slightly and serve warm.

Rosemary, Carrot and Sweet Potato Medallions (Roast)

Prep Time: 10 minutes, Cook Time: 35 to 45 minutes, Serves: 6

INGREDIENTS:
4 tsps. avocado oil or extra-virgin olive oil
1 cup chopped carrots
2 large sweet potatoes, sliced into rounds
2 tsps. fresh rosemary
¼ tsp. sea salt

DIRECTIONS:
1. Combine the oil, carrots, sweet potatoes, rosemary, and salt in a large bowl or resealable plastic bag, mix until the sweet potatoes and carrots are well coated.
2. Transfer the vegetables into the inner pot and arrange them in a single layer to evenly cook.
3. Press Roast and cook at 400°F(205°C) for 35 to 45 minutes, until the thickest sweet potato rounds are soft, use a paring knife insert to check.

Baked Vanilla Bean and Cinnamon Granola (Bake)

Prep Time: 5 minutes, Cook Time: 30 minutes, Serves: 3

INGREDIENTS:
6 tbsps. coconut oil
3 cups quick rolled oats
½ cup brown rice syrup
2 tsps. vanilla bean powder
2 tsps. ground cinnamon
¼ cup unrefined whole cane sugar
¼ tsp. sea salt

DIRECTIONS:
1. Use parchment paper to line the inner pot.
2. Add all of the ingredients into a large bowl, mix together until well combined with your hands.
3. Form the mixture together into a ball, and place onto Crisp Plate.
4. Evenly press the mixture on Crisp Plate, not to break it up into small pieces. This will allow it to bake in large cluster pieces that you can break apart after baking, if you prefer.
5. Press Bake and cook at 250°F(120°C) until crispy, about 30 minutes, not to overbake.
6. After baking, allow to cool completely and serve. As the granola cools, it will harden and get even crispier. Keep in an airtight container.

Baked Nutty Macaroni (Bake)

Prep Time: 30 minutes, Cook Time: 50 minutes + 8-12 hours for soaking, Serves: 8-10

INGREDIENTS:
1 cup of raw brazil nuts
1 cup of spring water + extra for soaking
12 ounces (340 g) of any alkaline pasta
2 tsps. of grape seed oil
¼ cup of chickpea flour
2 tsps. of onion powder
½ tsp. of ground achiote
1 tsp. of pure sea salt
1 cup of homemade hempseed milk
juice from ½ key lime

DIRECTIONS:
1. In a medium bowl, add the brazil nuts and pour in the spring water to cover. Allow them to soak overnight.
2. Cook your favorite alkaline pasta.
3. In the Ninja Foodi, add the cooked pasta and drizzle the extra grape seed oil to prevent it sticking to the bottom.
4. In a blender, add the soaked brazil nuts and the remaining ingredients and blend for 2 to 4 minutes until smooth.
5. Pour the brazil nut sauce over the pasta and mix well.
6. Press Bake and cook at 350°F(180°C) for about 30 minutes.
7. After baking, serve and enjoy!

Chapter 16 Snack

Date Carrot Cake Cookies with Cashew Cream Frosting (Bake)

Prep Time: 5 to 7 minutes (plus overnight soaking), Cook Time: 12 minutes, Serves: 12

INGREDIENTS:

FOR THE CARROT CAKE COOKIES
1 medium egg
¼ cup cashew butter
10 small dates, pitted
¼ cup almond meal
¼ cup unsweetened finely shredded coconut
1 tbsp. coconut oil
¼ tsp. ground cinnamon
¼ tsp. vanilla extract
⅛ tsp. sea salt
¼ cup brown rice flour
¾ cup rolled oats
½ tsp. baking soda
2 tbsps. shredded carrot

¼ cup golden raisins
3 tbsps. chopped walnuts
FOR THE CASHEW CREAM FROSTING
1 cup cashews, soaked in water overnight, then drained
8 small dates, pitted
¼ cup unsweetened shredded coconut
1 to 2 tsps. freshly squeezed lemon juice (optional)
½ cup water
⅛ tsp. sea salt
¼ tsp. vanilla extract

DIRECTIONS:

To make the carrot cake cookies

1. Use parchment paper to line the inner pot.
2. Add the egg, cashew butter, dates, almond meal, coconut oil, shredded coconut, cinnamon, vanilla and salt into a food processor. Blend until smooth and well combined.
3. Combine the brown rice flour, oats, and baking soda in a medium bowl. Add the wet ingredients and stir to combine well.
4. Fold in the carrot, raisins and walnuts.
5. Scoop the mixture into 1½-inch balls and arrange them on the inner pot, evenly spacing them. Press Bake and cook at 375°F(190°C) for 12 minutes, or until a toothpick inserted into the center of a cookie comes out clean. Allow to cool completely.

To make the cashew cream frosting

1. Combine all of the cashew cream frosting ingredients in a high-speed blender. Blend until well combined, with date specks sprinkled throughout.
2. Frost about 1 rounded teaspoon of the cashew cream frosting onto each cookie.

Coconut Chocolate and Date Cookies (Bake)

Prep Time: 30 minutes, Cook Time: 5 minutes, Serves: 12

INGREDIENTS:

For the cookie base
1 cup dried shredded unsweetened coconut
2 pinches sea salt
1 cup raw almonds
1 packet stevia
2½ tbsps. coconut oil, melted
For the coconut caramel layer
½ cup dried shredded unsweetened coconut
2 tablespoons coconut

oil, melted
8 Medjool dates
1 tablespoon water, plus additional as needed
Pinch sea salt
For the chocolate icing
4 tbsps. coconut oil, melted
4 tbsps. unsweetened Dutch-processed cocoa powder
1 packet stevia

DIRECTIONS:

To make the cookie base:

1. Use parchment paper to line the inner pot.
2. Add the coconut into a food processor, blend for 60 seconds. Add the salt and almonds, blend until they are ground into a meal. Add the stevia and coconut oil, and blend until a dough form.
3. Roll the dough between two sheets of wax paper to a ¼-inch thickness. Allow the dough to freeze for 10 minutes, or until firm.
4. Cut out 12 cookies with a round cookie cutter. Arrange each cookie base on the inner pot.

To make the coconut caramel layer:

1. Spread the coconut in an even layer on Crisp Plate, press Bake and cook at 350°F(180°C) for 5 minutes. Remove and cool.
2. Add the coconut oil, dates and water in a food processor. Blend to combine. Add the salt and more water, if needed. Continue to blend until the mixture resembles caramel. Add the toasted coconut and mix to combine.
3. Spread onto each cookie base. with an equal layer of the caramel-coconut mixture.
4. To make the chocolate icing:
5. Mix together the coconut oil, cocoa powder and stevia in a small bowl.
6. Drizzle the icing over each of the 12 cookies with a spoon.
7. Place the cookies in the refrigerator to chill for 10 minutes to solidify the layers before eating.

Santa's Ginger Coconut Snaps (Bake)

Prep Time: 10 minutes, Cook Time: 10 to 15 minutes, Serves: 6

INGREDIENTS:

⅓ cup coconut flour	¼ tsp. cloves
½ cup almond flour	½ tsp. ground ginger
2 tbsps. arrowroot powder	½ tsp. cinnamon
⅓ cup coconut sugar	¼ cup coconut oil
½ tsp. baking soda	3 tbsps. ground flaxseed, soaked in 3 tbsps. warm water
¼ tsp. sea salt	

DIRECTIONS:

1. Use parchment paper to line the inner pot.
2. Add all of the ingredients except the coconut oil and flaxseed in a large bowl, mix them together.
3. Melt the coconut oil in a microwaveable bowl by microwaving on high for 30 seconds. Combine the oil with the flaxseed mixture. Add the coconut oil mixture to the bowl with the dry ingredients. Stir to combine. The dough will be stiff.
4. Scoop the dough by tablespoonfuls and use hand to roll into balls. Place the dough balls onto the Crisp Plate and flatten into discs.
5. Put the Crisp Plate into the inner pot and press Bake and cook at 350°F(180°C) for 10 to 15 minutes, or until firm.
6. After baking, allow to cool before serving.

Sweet Blueberry and Chia Seed Vanilla Cobbler (Bake)

Prep Time: 5 minutes, Cook Time: 45 minutes, Serves: 2 to 4

INGREDIENTS:

FOR THE BLUEBERRIES	(melted/liquid)
2 tbsps. unrefined whole cane sugar	4 tbsps. coconut milk (boxed)
2 cups blueberries	1½ tsps. baking powder
1 tbsp. chia seeds	1 tsp. vanilla bean powder
FOR THE TOPPING	2 tbsps. unrefined whole cane sugar
½ cup oat flour	¼ tsp. sea salt
½ cup almond flour	
2 tbsps. coconut oil	

DIRECTIONS:

TO PREPARE THE BLUEBERRIES

1. Add the sugar, blueberries and chia seeds into a medium bowl, stir them together. Transfer the mixture to a 9-inch oval ovenproof baking dish or four (4-ounce) ramekin bowls.

TO PREPARE THE TOPPING

2. Combine all of the topping ingredients in the inner pot, stir them together until well combined.

TO ASSEMBLE

3. Drop the topping over the blueberry mixture, a tablespoonful at a time. You can leave the topping as "dollops" or evenly spread it over the top of the blueberry mixture for a full crust.
4. Press Bake and cook at 350°F(180°C) until the topping is slightly golden and cooked through, about 45 minutes.
5. After baking, serve warm.

Spiced Chickpea French Fries (Bake)

Prep Time: 20 minutes, Cook Time: 1 hour, 40 minutes, Serves: 4-8

INGREDIENTS:

4 cups of spring water	1 tbsp. of oregano
2 cups of chickpea flour	1 tsp. of cayenne
½ cup of diced green bell peppers	1 tbsp. of onion powder
½ cup of minced onions	1 tbsp. of pure sea salt
	2 tbsps. of grape seed oil

DIRECTIONS:

1. In the Ninja Foodi, add the spring water, press Sear/Sauté and cook at 390ºF (200ºC) and bring to a boil.
2. Reduce the heat to medium and whisk in the chickpea flour.
3. Add the diced green bell peppers, minced onions, and seasonings to the inner pot. Cook for 10 minutes, until it thickens, stirring occasionally.
4. Use a piece of parchment paper to cover a baking sheet and use a little grape seed oil to grease.
5. Pour the batter on the sheet, use a spatula to spread, and cover with another lightly greased piece of parchment paper.
6. Place the baking sheet in the freezer for about 20 minutes.
7. Take out from the freezer and cut the batter into fry shaped pieces.
8. Use a piece of parchment paper to cover Crisp Plate and lightly grease.
9. Arrange the French fries on the Crisp Plate.
10. Press Bake and cook at 400°F(205°C) for about 20 minutes then flip them over and continue to bake for another 15 minutes until golden brown.
11. After baking, serve warm.

Easy Tortilla Chips (Bake)

Prep Time: 20 minutes, Cook Time: 20 minutes, Serves: 8

INGREDIENTS:

2 cups of spelt flour
1 tsp. of pure sea salt
⅓ cup of grape seed oil
½ cup of spring water

DIRECTIONS:

1. In a food processor, add the spelt flour and pure sea salt, mix for about 15 seconds.
2. Slowly add the grape seed oil while blending until it is well combined.
3. Continue to blend and slowly add the spring water until a dough is formed.
4. Prepare a work surface and use a piece of parchment paper to cover. Sprinkle the flour over the paper.
5. Knead the dough for about 1 to 2 minutes until it achieves the right consistency.
6. Use a little grape seed oil to cover Crisp Plate.
7. Place the prepared dough on the Crisp Plate.
8. Use a little grape seed oil to brush the dough and sprinkle with more pure sea salt if needed.
9. Use a pizza slicer to cut the dough into 8 triangles.
10. Press Bake and cook at 350°F(180°C) for about 10 to 12 minutes or until the chips are starting to become golden brown.
11. After baking, allow to cool before serving.

Flourless Cashew and Pumpkin Seed Cookies (Bake)

Prep Time: 15 minutes, Cook Time: 10 minutes, Serves: 18 to 20 small cookies

INGREDIENTS:

½ cup coconut oil
2 cups raw cashews
½ cup raw pumpkin seeds
½ cup almond flour
½ tsp. baking soda
2 tbsps. brown rice syrup
¼ tsp. sea salt

DIRECTIONS:

1. Use parchment paper to line the inner pot.
2. Add the coconut oil and raw cashews into a food processor, process for about 10 minutes, until the cashews turn into cashew butter, and it will go through several different stages (cashews, cashew flour, cashew butter). Stop every 1 to 2 minutes to scrape the sides and make processing easier. This should yield 1 cup of cashew butter.
3. Transfer the cashew butter to a medium bowl, add the pumpkin seeds, almond flour, baking soda, brown

rice syrup, and salt, and stir until well combined.
4. Scoop a tablespoonful of dough at a time, use your hands to roll into a small ball. And use your palms to gently press the ball into a disk. Transfer to the inner pot. Repeat with the remaining cookie dough.
5. Press Bake and cook at 350°F(180°C) for 10 to 12 minutes, not to overbake.
6. After baking, allow to cool completely before removing the cookies from the pan or serving. They will be soft and crumbly right out of the oven but will get firmer after cooling.
7. Place in an airtight container and store in the refrigerator to keep the coconut oil from melting.

Garlic Almond Breadsticks (Bake)

Prep Time: 5 minutes, Cook Time: 20 minutes, Serves: 12 pieces

INGREDIENTS:

FOR THE BREADSTICKS
1 tbsp. ground flaxseed
3 tbsps. water
1 tbsp. avocado oil
2 cups almond flour
1 tbsp. chopped fresh oregano
½ tsp. freshly ground black pepper
½ tsp. sea salt
FOR THE TOPPING
1 tbsp. avocado oil
1 tbsp. chopped fresh oregano
4 garlic cloves, crushed
⅛ tsp. sea salt
⅛ tsp. freshly ground black pepper

DIRECTIONS:

1. Use parchment paper to line the inner pot.
2. TO PREPARE THE BREADSTICKS
3. To prepare a flax egg, add the flaxseed and water in a small bowl, whisk them together until well blended.
4. Combine the flax egg, avocado oil, almond flour, oregano, pepper and salt in a medium bowl, stir them together until well combined.
5. Place the mixture onto the inner pot, and form the mixture into a ball. Lay another sheet of parchment paper on top of the ball, and over the paper, roll the dough into a 5-by-8-inch rectangle shape with a rolling pin.
6. TO PREPARE THE TOPPING
7. Combine all of the topping ingredients in a small bowl, stir them together until well combined. Pour over the dough with the topping mixture, and spread it evenly with the back of a spoon.
8. Press Bake and cook at 350°F(180°C) until the edges are golden brown, about 18 to 20 minutes.
9. After baking, take out from the oven, slice into 12 pieces, and serve.

Herbed Almond Crackers (Bake)

Prep Time: 15 minutes, Cook Time: 20 minutes, Serves: 6

INGREDIENTS:

1 tbsp. coconut oil	fresh thyme
2 tbsps. flaxseed meal	¾ tsp. finely chopped
4 tbsps. water	fresh oregano
1½ tsps. fresh rosemary	1 tbsp. sesame seeds
1 cup almond flour	(optional)
¾ tsp. finely chopped	½ tsp. sea salt

DIRECTIONS:

1. Combine the coconut oil, flaxseed meal and water in a small bowl. Place in the refrigerator to chill for 10 minutes until the mixture thickens.
2. Combine the rosemary, almond flour, thyme, oregano and sesame seeds (if using) in a medium bowl. Stir in the flaxseed mixture, combining thoroughly.
3. Form the dough into a ball. Roll the dough to a ⅛-inch thickness on parchment paper. Sprinkle with the salt.
4. Transfer the parchment with the dough onto Crisp Plate. Equally cut the dough into 24 crackers, not to cut through the parchment.
5. Place the Crisp Plate in the Ninja Foodi. Press Bake and cook at 325°F(165°C) for 20 minutes, make sure the crackers don't burn.
6. Remove from the oven and allow to cool and serve.

Baked Onion Rings (Bake)

Prep Time: 20 minutes, Cook Time: 30 minutes, Serves: 8

INGREDIENTS:

½ cup of aquafaba	2 tsps. of pure sea salt
½ cup of homemade	white onions or sweet
hempseed milk	onions
2 tsps. of onion powder	1 cup of spelt flour
1 tsp. of cayenne powder	3 tbsps. of grape seed oil
2 tsps. of oregano	

DIRECTIONS:

1. In a medium bowl, add the aquafaba and homemade hempseed milk and whisk them well.
2. Add 1 teaspoon of onion powder, ½ teaspoon of cayenne, 1 teaspoon of oregano, and 1 teaspoon of pure sea salt to the bowl and mix well.
3. Peel the onions, slice off the ends.
4. Cut the peeled onion into ¼ inch thick slices. Separate the onion slices into rings.
5. In a container with a lid, add the spelt flour, 1 teaspoon of onion powder, 1 teaspoon of oregano, ½ teaspoon of cayenne, and 1 teaspoon of pure sea salt. Shake all the dry ingredients well.
6. Use the grape seed oil to brush the inner pot.
7. Place a few onion rings in the wet mixture.
8. Place the wet onion rings in the dry mixture and flip until coated on both sides.
9. Then transfer the coated onion rings in the inner pot.
10. Repeat steps 8 through 10 until all onion rings are coated.
11. Lightly drizzle the grape seed oil over the rings.
12. Press Bake and cook at 450°F(235°C) for about 10 to 15 minutes until golden brown.
13. After baking, allow them to cool before serving.

Garlic-Jicama Fries with Scallion Cashew Dip (Bake)

Prep Time: 10 minutes, Cook Time: 40 minutes, Serves: 2

INGREDIENTS:

FOR THE JICAMA FRIES	¾ cup roughly chopped
½ jicama, peeled and	scallions
cut into 32 (¼-inch-thick)	1½ cups raw cashews
sticks	½ cup coconut milk
1 tbsp. avocado oil	(boxed)
¼ tsp. garlic powder	1 tbsp. apple cider
¼ to ½ tsp. chipotle	vinegar
powder	1 tbsp. freshly squeezed
¼ to ½ tsp. sea salt	lemon juice
¼ tsp. freshly ground	¼ cup vegetable broth
black pepper	1 garlic clove
FOR THE SCALLION	½ tsp. sea salt
DIP	

DIRECTIONS:

1. Use parchment paper to line the inner pot.

TO PREPARE THE JICAMA FRIES

2. Place the jicama sticks in a medium bowl, toss with the avocado oil to coat.
3. Add the garlic powder, chipotle powder, salt, and pepper, and toss again to coat. Adjust the seasonings, if needed.
4. Place the jicama sticks onto the inner pot. and spread in a single layer.
5. Press Bake and cook at 400°F(205°C) for 20 minutes, flip them over, and bake for another 15 to 20 minutes.

TO PREPARE THE SCALLION DIP

6. While the jicama sticks bake, add all of the scallion dip ingredients into a high-speed blender, blend them together until creamy and smooth. Adjust the seasonings, if needed, and serve.

Almond Tarragon Crackers (Bake)

Prep Time: 10 minutes, Cook Time: 15 minutes, Serves: 60 small crackers

INGREDIENTS:

1 tbsp. ground flaxseed	tarragon
3 tbsps. water	½ tsp. freshly ground
1 tbsp. avocado oil	black pepper
2 cups almond flour	½ tsp. sea salt
1 tbsp. fresh chopped	¼ tsp. garlic powder

DIRECTIONS:

1. Use parchment paper to line the inner pot.
2. To prepare a flax egg, whisk together the flaxseed and water in a large bowl.
3. Add all of the remaining ingredients, and stir until well combined.
4. Transfer the mixture to the Crisp Plate. Form the dough into a ball with your hands, then place another piece of parchment paper on the top of the ball.
5. Over the parchment paper, roll out the dough to about ¼-inch thickness with a rolling pin.
6. Cut the dough into 60 (1½-inch-by-1½-inch) squares with a knife or pizza cutter.
7. Press Bake and cook at 350°F(180°C) for 12 to 14 minutes, or until the crackers are slightly golden on top. Then flip them over and bake for another one or two minutes.
8. Allow to cool and serve.

Sweet Thumbprint Cookies with Blueberry-Chia Seed Jam (Bake)

Prep Time: 25 minutes, Cook Time: 10 minutes, Serves: 8 cookies

INGREDIENTS:

3 tbsps. coconut oil, melted	1½ tbsps. brown rice syrup
1¼ cups almond flour	Blueberry chia seed fruit
1 to 2 pinches sea salt	jam

DIRECTIONS:

1. Use parchment paper to line the inner pot.
2. Add the coconut oil, almond flour, salt and brown rice syrup in a medium bowl, stir them together until well combined. The mixture should be very wet. Place in the refrigerator to chill for 10 to 15 minutes, or until firm.
3. Scoop a tablespoonful of dough at a time and use

your hands to flatten into a disk, and use your fingertips to smooth the outer edges. Press your thumb in the center to make the "thumbprint" indention, and put on Crisp Plate. Repeat with the remaining dough.

4. Press Bake and cook at 375°F(190°C) for about 10 minutes, not overbake.
5. After baking, take the cookies out from the oven, and after they cool a bit, repeat the "thumbprint" indention process, if necessary. Let cool completely before removing from the pan or adding the chia seed fruit topping.
6. Fill the blueberry chia seed fruit jam into the thumbprint indentions and serve.

Vanilla Ginger Cookies (Bake)

Prep Time: 15 minutes, Cook Time: 10 minutes, Serves: 12 cookies

INGREDIENTS:

2 tbsps. pure maple syrup	or a 1:1 gluten-free blend, plus more as needed
¼ cup tahini	1 tsp. baking powder
1½ tbsps. oat milk, or other nondairy milk	¼ tsp. baking soda
2 tbsps. date sugar	½ tsp. ground cinnamon
½ tsp. vanilla extract	⅛ tsp. ground cloves
1 tsp. ground ginger	⅛ tsp. ground nutmeg
¾ cup whole wheat flour,	2 tbsps. finely chopped dried ginger pieces

DIRECTIONS:

1. Use parchment paper or a silicone mat to line the inner pot.
2. Add the maple syrup, tahini, oat milk, date sugar, and vanilla in a small bowl, whisk together until smooth.
3. Combine the ginger, flour, baking powder, baking soda, cinnamon, cloves, and nutmeg in a large bowl, whisk them together until fully combined. Add the dried ginger.
4. Fold the wet ingredients into the dry ingredients, mixing until the dough seems smooth and isn't too sticky. Add more flour as needed, 1 tablespoon at a time, but do not overmix. Divide the dough into 12 equal portions. Roll each piece into a ball and press them on the Crisp Plate to about 1 inch thick.
5. Press Bake and cook at 350°F(180°C) for about 8 to 10 minutes, until the tops are lightly golden brown. After baking, place onto a wire rack to cool. They will firm up as they cool but will remain slightly soft.
6. Place in an airtight container and store at room temperature for up to 1 week, or freeze for up to 6 months.

Almond Spiced Baked Onion Rings (Bake)

Prep Time: 15 minutes, Cook Time: 10 minutes, Serves: 2

INGREDIENTS:

Cooking spray
1 tsp. garlic powder
⅔ cup almond meal
½ tsp. paprika
1 tsp. onion powder
½ tsp. sea salt
½ cup almond milk
1 large onion, sliced into ¼-inch-thick slices

DIRECTIONS:

1. Use cooking spray to grease the inner pot.
2. Mix together the garlic powder, almond meal, paprika, onion powder and sea salt on a plate.
3. In a medium bowl, add the almond milk.
4. Dip one onion slice first into the milk. Then dredge it in the seasoned almond meal and put it in the inner pot. Repeat with the remaining onion slices.
5. Press Air Fry and cook at 425°F(220°C) for 6 minutes. Turn each slice over and bake for another 4 minutes, or until crispy.
6. After baking, serve warm.

Nutty Lemon Oatmeal Cacao Cookies (Bake)

Prep Time: 30 minutes, Cook Time: 35 minutes, Serves: 14 cookies

INGREDIENTS:

12 pitted Medjool dates
Boiling water, for soaking the dates
1 tbsp. freshly squeezed lemon juice
1 cup unsweetened applesauce
1 tsp. vanilla extract
1 tbsp. water, plus more
as needed (optional)
1 cup oat flour
1½ cups old-fashioned oats
2 tbsps. lemon zest
¾ cup coarsely chopped walnuts
1 tbsp. cacao powder
½ tsp. baking soda

DIRECTIONS:

1. Add the dates into a small bowl, cover with enough boiling water. Allow to sit for 15 to 20 minutes to soften.
2. Use parchment paper to line the inner pot.
3. Drain the excess liquid from the dates and place them into a blender, then add the lemon juice, applesauce, and vanilla. Puree until a thick paste form. If the mixture isn't getting smooth, add the water, 1 tablespoon at a time.
4. Add the oat flour, oats, lemon zest, walnuts, cacao powder, and baking soda in a large bowl, stir them together. Pour in the date mixture and stir to combine. One at a time, scoop ¼-cup portions of dough, gently roll into a ball, and lightly press down in the inner pot. The cookie is about 1 inch thick and roughly 3 inches in diameter.
5. Press Bake and cook at 300°F(150°C) until the tops of the cookies look crispy and dry, about 30 to 35 minutes. After baking, transfer to a wire rack to cool.
6. Keep in an airtight container at room temperature for up to 1 week.

Roasted Vegetable Chips (Bake)

Prep Time: 20 minutes, Cook Time: 35 minutes, Serves: 2

INGREDIENTS:

1 pound (454 g) high-water vegetables, such as zucchini or summer squash
Kosher salt, for absorbing moisture
1 pound (454 g) starchy root vegetables, such as russet potato, sweet potato, rutabaga, parsnip,
red or golden beet, or taro
1 tsp. paprika
1 tsp. garlic powder
½ tsp. onion powder
½ tsp. freshly ground black pepper
1 tsp. avocado oil or other oil (optional)

DIRECTIONS:

1. Use parchment paper to line the inner pot. Set aside.
2. Wash and dry the high-water vegetables. Scrub the root vegetables well to remove the dirt.
3. Cut all the vegetables into ⅛-inch-thick slices with a mandoline or sharp kitchen knife. The thinner you slice them, the crispier they will be.
4. Place the sliced high-water vegetables on a clean kitchen towel or paper towel. Sprinkle with a generous amount of kosher salt, which draws out moisture. Allow to sit for 15 minutes. Dab off excess moisture and salt with a paper towel.
5. Add the paprika, garlic powder, onion powder, and pepper in a small bowl, stir them together.
6. Place all the vegetables to the inner pot in a single layer. Brush with oil, if using. Evenly sprinkle over with the spice mix.
7. Press Bake and cook at 300°F(150°C) for 15 minutes, until the vegetables are darker in color and crispy on the edges.
8. Place the chips onto a wire rack to cool with a spatula. The baked chips will crisp within a few minutes of cooling.

Healthy Crackers with Sesame Seeds (Bake)

Prep Time: 20 minutes, Cook Time: 30 minutes, Serves: 50 crackers

INGREDIENTS:

1 cup of spelt flour
½ cup of rye flour
2 tsps. of sesame seed
1 tsp. of agave syrup
1 tsp. of pure sea salt
¾ cup of spring water
2 tbsps. of grape seed oil

DIRECTIONS:

1. In a medium bowl, combine all of the ingredients except the oil and mix well.
2. Make a dough ball. Add more flour if it is too liquid.
3. Prepare a place for rolling out the dough and use a piece of parchment paper to cover.
4. Use the grape seed oil to lightly grease the paper and place the dough on it.
5. Use a rolling pin to roll out the dough, adding more flour to avoid sticking.
6. Cut the dough into squares with a shape cutter. If you don't have a shape cutter, you can use a pizza cutter.
7. Place the squares on Crisp Plate and use a fork or a skewer to poke holes in each square.
8. Use a little grape seed oil to brush the dough and sprinkle with more pure sea salt if needed.
9. Press Bake and cook at 350°F(180°C) for 12 to 15 minutes or until the crackers are starting to become golden.
10. After baking, let cool before serving.

Chia Seed-Cashew Cookies (Bake)

Prep Time: 15 minutes, Cook Time: 10 minutes, Serves: 12

INGREDIENTS:

3 to 4 tbsps. coconut oil, divided, as needed
2 cups raw cashews
2 tbsps. chia seeds
2 tbsps. coconut flour
2 tbsps. freshly squeezed lime juice
¼ cup brown rice syrup
Pinch sea salt

DIRECTIONS:

1. Use parchment paper to line the inner pot.
2. Add the coconut oil and cashews into a food processor, process for about 10 minutes, until the cashews turn into cashew butter, and it will go through several different phases (cashews, cashew flour, cashew butter). Stop every 1 to 2 minutes to scrape the sides and make processing easier. Add

another 1 tablespoon of coconut oil at a time, if needed to make creamier cashew butter, but don't exceed 4 tablespoons in total.
3. Place the cashew butter into a medium bowl, add the remaining ingredients, and stir until well combined.
4. Scoop a tablespoonful of dough at a time, use your hands to roll into a small ball. And use your palms to gently press the ball into a disk. Transfer to the inner pot. Repeat with the remaining cookie dough.
5. Press Bake and cook at 350°F(180°C) for about 12 minutes, not to over bake.
6. After baking, allow to cool completely before removing the cookies from the pan or serving. They will be soft and crumbly right out of the oven but will get firmer after cooling.

Vanilla Snickerdoodle Cookies (Bake)

Prep Time: 10 minutes, Cook Time: 10 to 12 minutes, Serves: 6

INGREDIENTS:

⅓ cup coconut flour
½ cup almond flour
⅔ cup coconut sugar, divided
½ tsp. baking soda
2 tbsps. arrowroot powder
¼ tsp. sea salt
1 tsp. cinnamon
¼ cup coconut oil
1 vanilla bean, split lengthwise and seeds scraped out
3 tbsps. ground flaxseed, soaked in 3 tbsps. warm water

DIRECTIONS:

1. Use parchment paper to line the inner pot.
2. Mix together the coconut flour, almond flour, ⅓ cup coconut sugar, baking soda, arrowroot, and salt in a large bowl.
3. Add the remaining ⅓ cup coconut sugar and the cinnamon in a small bowl. Stir to combine. Set aside.
4. Press Pressure and cook at 390ºF (200ºC) for 30 seconds, and melt the coconut oil in the inner pot. Add the vanilla bean seeds and flaxseed mixture. Stir to combine.
5. Add the coconut oil mixture into the bowl with the dry ingredients. Stir to combine well. The dough will be stiff.
6. Use your hand to form the dough into 1-inch balls. Roll each dough ball into the reserved cinnamon sugar. Place them on the Crisp Plate about 1½ inches apart.
7. Put Crisp Plate in the Ninja Foodi and press Bake and cook at 350°F(180°C) for 10 to 12 minutes, or until the tops are browned.
8. Allow to cool on a wire rack and serve.

Delicious Onion Chickpea Nuggets (Bake)

Prep Time: 10 minutes, Cook Time: 30 minutes, Serves: 2

INGREDIENTS:
2 cups cooked chickpeas
1 tsp. onion powder
½ tsp. salt
⅓ cup and 1 tbsp. bread crumbs

DIRECTIONS:
1. In a food processor, add the chickpeas and then pulse until crumbled.
2. Tip the chickpeas in a bowl, add the onion powder and salt except for ⅓ cup of breadcrumbs and then stir until a chunky mixture comes together.
3. Form the mixture into evenly sized balls, then form each ball into the nugget, arrange on Crisp Plate greased with oil and press Bake and cook at 350°F(180°C) for 15 minutes per side until golden brown.
4. Serve immediately.

Baked Garlicky Almond Avocado Fries (Bake)

Prep Time: 10 minutes, Cook Time: 15 minutes, Serves: 16 fries

INGREDIENTS:
2 tbsps. nutritional yeast
¼ to ½ tsp. garlic powder
½ cup almond flour
¼ to ½ tsp. sea salt
¼ to ½ tsp. ground
paprika, plus more for sprinkling
2 avocados, slightly underripe
½ cup almond milk

DIRECTIONS:
1. Use parchment paper to line the inner pot.
2. Add all of the ingredients except the avocados and almond milk into a small bowl, stir them together until well combined.
3. Cut the avocados in half and pit them, and quarter each half from pole to pole. Peel off the skin.
4. In another small bowl, add the almond milk.
5. First dip an avocado slice into the milk and then the coating mixture, tossing it gently to make sure it is completely covered, and arrange in the inner pot. Repeat with the remaining avocado slices.
6. Press Bake and cook at 420°F(218°C) for 15 to 17 minutes, not to overcook or burn them.
7. After baking, take out from the oven, sprinkle with extra paprika, and serve.

Chickpea Flour Vegetable Quiche (Bake)

Prep Time: 10 minutes, Cook Time: 15 minutes, Serves: 2

INGREDIENTS:
FOR THE BATTER:
1 ½ tbsp. olive oil
1 ¼ cup chickpea flour
1 tsp. of sea salt
1 ½ cup spring water

FOR THE FILLING:
½ cup chopped and cooked vegetables
½ tsp. dried oregano
½ tsp. dried basil

DIRECTIONS:
1. In inner pot, prepare the batter, combine all of the batter ingredients in a medium bowl, then whisk until smooth batter comes together.
2. Add the vegetables, oregano and basil into the batter and then stir until combined.
3. Grease the oil into six silicone muffin cups, evenly fill with the prepared batter and then press Bake and cook at 500°F(260°C) for 10 to 15 minutes until firm and turn golden brown.
4. Serve immediately.

Dates, Spelt and Raisin Cookies (Bake)

Prep Time: 10 minutes, Cook Time: 18 minutes, Serves: 2

INGREDIENTS:
1 cup spelt flour
½ cup dates, pitted
1/16 tsp. sea salt
1 ¾ tbsps. grapeseed oil
⅓ cup raisins
3 ½ tbsps. applesauce homemade or pureed apples
⅔ tbsp. spring water
2 tbsps. agave syrup

DIRECTIONS:
1. In a food processor, add the flour, dates and salt, pulse until well blended.
2. Transfer the flour mixture into a medium bowl, add all of the remaining ingredients, and stir until well mixed.
3. Divide the mixture into parts, each part about 2 tablespoons of the mixture, and then form each part into a ball.
4. Arrange the cookie balls on Crisp Plate lined with parchment sheet, use a fork to flatten it slightly and then press Bake and cook at 350°F(180°C) for 18 minutes until done.
5. After baking, allow the cookies to cool for 10 minutes and serve.

Easy Roasted Okra Bites (Bake)

Prep Time: 5 minutes, Cook Time: 20 minutes, Serves: 2

INGREDIENTS:

12 okra pods, cut into ¼-inch-thick slices
1 tsp. avocado oil
¼ tsp. freshly ground black pepper
½ tsp. sea salt

DIRECTIONS:

1. Use parchment paper to line the inner pot.
2. Place the okra in a medium bowl, toss with the avocado oil to coat. Season with pepper and salt, and toss again.
3. Transfer the seasoned okra onto the inner pot in a single layer, and press Roast and cook at 450°F(235°C) for 15 to 20 minutes, flipping halfway through, not to overbake.
4. After baking, serve hot from the oven.

Broiled Chinese-Style Green Beans (Broil)

Prep Time: 15 minutes, Cook Time: 15 minutes, Serves: 4

INGREDIENTS:

1 pound (454 g) green beans, ends trimmed
1 tsp. sesame oil
1 tsp. coconut oil
2 garlic cloves, finely chopped
1 tsp. chopped fresh ginger
½ tsp. red pepper flakes
½ tsp. sea salt

DIRECTIONS:

1. Adjust the nesting broil rack to make the top rack is closest to the broiler.
2. Preheat the broiler.
3. In the inner pot, place the green beans in a single layer. Press Broil and cook at 390ºF (200ºC) for about 10 minutes, or until they start to show black flecks. Take the beans away from the broiler and place them into a large bowl. Set aside.
4. Combine the remaining ingredients in a small saucepan, warm the mixture over medium heat until it begins to shimmer and turn red. Turn off the heat.
5. Pour over the green beans with the warm sauce, toss well to combine.
6. Place the beans back to the inner pot and return under the broiler for 5 minutes.
7. After cooking, remove from the oven, transfer the green beans onto a serving platter, and serve warm.

Root Vegetable Chips (Bake)

Prep Time: 10 minutes, Cook Time: 20 minutes, Serves: 4

INGREDIENTS:

1 large carrot, peeled
1 parsnip, peeled
1 sweet potato, peeled
1 beet, peeled
1 tsp. sea salt
Cooking spray

DIRECTIONS:

1. Slice the carrot, parsnip, sweet potato and beet into very thin slices with a food processor attachment, mandoline, or food slicer. Lay the slices flat on a paper towel and sprinkle with the salt. Use more paper towel to cover and allow to sit for 15 minutes.
2. Blot any moisture on the vegetable slices.
3. Use cooking spray to grease Crisp Plate.
4. On the Crisp Plate, place the vegetable slices in a single layer. Spray the vegetables with cooking spray.
5. Put the Crisp Plate in the inner pot and press Bake and cook at 375°F(190°C) until crisp, about 20 minutes.

Zucchini Kale and Amaranth Patties (Bake)

Prep Time: 10 minutes, Cook Time: 40 minutes, Serves: 2

INGREDIENTS:

1 tbsp. olive oil
½ of medium white onion, peeled, minced
1 medium zucchini, grated
1 ½ cups kale, chopped
½ cup amaranth, cooked
¼ cup chopped basil
Extra:
¼ cup chopped dill
2 tbsps. spelt flour
¼ tsp. cayenne pepper
½ tsp. salt
1 ½ tbsp. tahini
1 tbsp. key lime juice

DIRECTIONS:

1. Press Sear/Sauté and cook at 390ºF (200ºC), heat the oil in the inner pot, when hot, add the onion and cook for 5 minutes until tender.
2. Stir in the zucchini, cook for 3 to 5 minutes until soft, then add the kale and cook for another 5 minutes until wilted.
3. Transfer the mixture into a bowl, and add all of the remaining ingredients, stir until mixed, then form the mixture into evenly sized patties.
4. On Crisp Plate, arrange with patties, and press Bake and cook at 400°F(205°C) for 15 minutes per side until golden brown and cooked.
5. After baking, serve immediately.

Cheesy Baked Kale Chips (Bake)

Prep Time: 5 minutes, Cook Time: 10 minutes, Serves: 1 or 2

INGREDIENTS:

4 or 5 stalks curly kale, stemmed and torn (2 cups, packed)

1 tbsp. avocado oil
¼ tsp. sea salt
1 tbsp. nutritional yeast

DIRECTIONS:

1. Use parchment paper to line the inner pot.
2. Place the kale in a medium bowl, toss with the avocado oil to coat.
3. Sprinkle over the kale with the salt and nutritional yeast, and toss to coat again.
4. Place the coated kale onto the prepared baking sheet, press Bake and cook at 350°F(180°C) for 5 to 6 minutes. Turn them over and bake for another 5 to 6 minutes, or until they are crispy, not to burn them.
5. After baking, allow to cool and serve.

Homemade Easy Chickpea Quinoa Burgers (Bake)

Prep Time: 10 minutes, Cook Time: 20 minutes, Serves: 2

INGREDIENTS:

¾ cup chickpeas
2 tbsps. chopped onion
¼ cup cooked quinoa
1 tbsp. grapeseed oil

1 tbsp. spring water
⅓ tsp. salt
¼ tsp. cayenne pepper

DIRECTIONS:

1. While the oven preheats, in a food processor, add the chickpeas, onion and quinoa, and pulse until little chunky mixture comes together.
2. Add the oil, water, salt, and cayenne pepper to the processor, pulse until the dough comes together.
3. Tip the mixture into a medium bowl, use its lid to cover and allow it to rest in the refrigerator for 15 minutes.
4. Form the mixture into two patties, place them in the inner pot lined with parchment paper, then press Bake and cook at 375°F(190°C) for 20 minutes, turning halfway.
5. Switch on the broiler and continue to cook for 2 minutes per side until golden brown.
6. Serve the patties with spelt flour burgers and tahini butter.

Baked Maple-Glazed Mixed Nuts (Bake)

Prep Time: 5 minutes, Cook Time: 15 minutes, Serves: 6

INGREDIENTS:

1½ cups maple syrup
1 cup walnuts

1 cup cashews
1 cup pecans

DIRECTIONS:

1. In a medium bowl, add the maple syrup and nuts, mix them together. Be sure that each nut has been coated well. Spread out in the inner pot so they are in one layer but still close to each other. Press Bake and cook at 325°F(165°C) for 7 minutes.
2. Remove from oven and use a spatula to flip. They can overlap some at this point. Return in the Ninja Foodi and bake for another 6 minutes or so. Watch closely, do not burn.
3. Remove the mixture from the Ninja Food, flip the nuts again, and allow to cool completely. Eat right away or pack in an airtight container. Store the nuts in your pantry for quite a few weeks and will keep in the refrigerator about 2 to 3 months, or keep in the freezer for 6 months.

Stuffed Mushroom Mini-Pizzas (Bake)

Prep Time: 15 minutes, Cook Time: 15 minutes, Serves: 4

INGREDIENTS:

Cooking spray
1 tbsp. garlic powder
1 (6-ounce, 170 g) can organic tomato paste
1 tsp. dried oregano
1 tbsp. onion powder
4 tbsps. sun-dried

tomatoes
½ tsp. sea salt, plus a pinch, divided
4 portobello mushroom caps, gills removed
4 slices fresh tomato

DIRECTIONS:

1. Use cooking spray to coat the inner pot.
2. Mix together the garlic powder, tomato paste, oregano, onion powder, sun-dried tomatoes, and sea salt in a small bowl.
3. Divide the tomato mixture evenly into the four mushroom caps. Place 1 tomato slice and a pinch of the sea salt on each top.
4. Place the pizzas into the inner pot, and press Bake and cook at 350°F(180°C) for 15 minutes, or until the pizzas are hot and bubbly.

Baked Garlicky Kale Chips (Bake)

Prep Time: 5 minutes, Cook Time: 20 minutes, Serves: 4

INGREDIENTS:

1 tbsp. nutritional yeast
¼ cup vegetable broth
½ tsp. onion powder
½ tsp. garlic powder

6 ounces (170 g) kale, stemmed and cut into 2- to 3-inch pieces

DIRECTIONS:

1. Use parchment paper to line the inner pot.
2. Mix together the nutritional yeast, broth, onion powder, and garlic powder in a small bowl.
3. In a large bowl, add the kale. Pour the broth mixture over the kale, and toss well to thoroughly coat.
4. Arrange the kale pieces on the inner pot in an even layer. Press Bake and cook at 300°F(150°C) until crispy, about 20 minutes, turning the kale halfway through.

Date Cashew Oat Bites with Raisins (Bake)

Prep Time: 10 minutes, Cook Time: 10 minutes, Serves: 20 bites

INGREDIENTS:

Nonstick cooking spray
8 small dates, pitted
¾ cup rolled oats
¼ cup cashew butter
¼ cup unsweetened

coconut flakes (optional)
½ tsp. vanilla extract
1 tsp. ground cinnamon
3 to 4 tbsps. water
½ cup raisins

DIRECTIONS:

1. Use cooking spray to lightly grease the inner pot.
2. Combine the remaining ingredients except the water and raisins in a food processor. Process until the mixture resembles coarse crumbs.
3. Add the water, 1 tablespoon at a time, until a dough forms and holds together well. Pour the mixture into a bowl and add the raisins, mix until evenly distributed throughout the dough.
4. Scoop small balls of the mixture onto the Crisp Plate with a mini scoop or rounded teaspoon, evenly spacing them.
5. Press Bake and cook at 350°F(180°C) for 10 minutes, or until just browned. Without overcooking.

Baked Spelt Biscuits (Bake)

Prep Time: 10 minutes, Cook Time: 15 minutes, Serves: 2

INGREDIENTS:

1 cup spelt flour
½ tbsp. baking powder
½ tsp. salt
3 tbsps. walnut butter,

homemade
6 tbsps. walnut milk, homemade

DIRECTIONS:

1. While the oven preheats, in a food processor, add the flour, baking powder, salt, and butter, pulse until the mixture resembles crumbs.
2. Tip the mixture into a bowl, add the milk and stir until the dough comes together, then roll it into 1-inch thick dough.
3. Cut out biscuits with a cutter, arrange them in the inner pot and press Bake and cook at 450°F(235°C) for 12 to 15 minutes until golden brown.
4. Serve straight away.

Vanilla Oat Apple Crisp (Bake)

Prep Time: 10 minutes, Cook Time: 35 minutes, Serves: 6

INGREDIENTS:

¾ cup apple juice
3 medium apples, cored and cut into ¼-inch pieces
1 tsp. vanilla extract

1 tsp. ground cinnamon, divided
2 cups rolled oats
¼ cup maple syrup

DIRECTIONS:

1. Add the apple juice, apple slices, vanilla, and ½ teaspoon of cinnamon in a large bowl. Mix well to thoroughly coat the apple slices.
2. Layer the apple slices on the bottom of the inner pot. Pour any leftover liquid over the apple slices.
3. Add the maple syrup, oats, and the remaining ½ teaspoon of cinnamon in a large bowl, stir them together until the oats are completely coated.
4. Sprinkle over the apples with the oat mixture, make sure to evenly spread it out so that none of the apple slices are visible.
5. Press Bake and cook at 375°F(190°C) until the oats begin to turn golden brown, about 35 minutes, and serve.

Cauliflower Popcorn (Roast)

Prep Time: 10 minutes, Cook Time: 30 minutes, Serves: 4

INGREDIENTS:
3 tbsps. coconut oil
1 cauliflower head, separated into small florets
1 tsp. sea salt

DIRECTIONS:
1. Combine the coconut oil, cauliflower, and salt in a large bowl.
2. Place the cauliflower into the inner pot and evenly spread it into a single layer.
3. Put the sheet in the Ninja Foodi and press Roast and cook at 400°F(205°C) for about 30 minutes, until golden brown and slightly crisp.

Baked Sweet Potato Fries (Bake)

Prep Time: 10 minutes, Cook Time: 30 minutes, Serves: 2

INGREDIENTS:
2 sweet potatoes, peeled and cut into fries
Cooking spray
1 tsp. sea salt

DIRECTIONS:
1. Use cooking spray to grease the inner pot.
2. In the inner pot, place the fries in a single layer. Coat the fries with cooking spray and sprinkle with the salt.
3. Place the sheet in the Ninja Foodi and press Bake and cook at 425°F(220°C) for 15 minutes. Turn the fries over and bake for another 15 minutes, or until crisp.
4. After baking, serve warm.

Onion Rye Crackers (Bake)

Prep Time: 10 minutes, Cook Time: 10 minutes, Serves: 2

INGREDIENTS:
1 cup rye flour
2 tbsps. grapeseed oil
1 tsp. onion powder
½ tsp. salt
½ tsp. dried basil
½ tsp. dried thyme
4 tbsps. spring water

DIRECTIONS:
1. In a food processor, add the flour, oil and all the seasonings, and pulse until combined.
2. Add the water, pulse until the dough comes together, and roll it into a ½-inch thick dough.
3. Cut out the cookie with a cookie cutter of the desired shape, arrange them on Crisp Plate and press Bake and cook at 400°F(205°C) for 10 minutes until nicely browned.
4. Serve immediately.

Baked Buffalo Cauliflowers (Bake)

Prep Time: 10 minutes, Cook Time: 25 minutes, Serves: 4

INGREDIENTS:
1 tsp. onion powder
1 tsp. garlic powder
1 tsp. sea salt
1 cauliflower head, broken into florets
½ tsp. cayenne pepper
2 tbsps. coconut oil, melted

DIRECTIONS:
1. Mix together the onion powder, garlic powder and salt in a small bowl.
2. Use the spice mix to season the cauliflower. Put the seasoned cauliflower in the inner pot. Press Bake and cook at 450°F(235°C) for 10 minutes, turn the cauliflower over, and bake for another 10 minutes.
3. Meanwhile, combine the cayenne pepper and coconut oil in a large bowl.
4. After baking, transfer the hot cauliflower to the large bowl with the coconut oil. Toss to coat thoroughly and place the cauliflower back to the inner pot.
5. Bake for another 5 minutes, until the sauce is absorbed.
6. Remove from the oven and allow to sit for 10 minutes and serve.

Homemade Whole Wheat Pita Pockets (Bake)

Prep Time: 30 minutes, plus 2 hours for the dough to rise, Cook Time: 5 minutes, Serves: 4

INGREDIENTS:
1 (¼-ounce, 7 g) packet fast-acting bread yeast
2 cups whole-wheat flour
1 cup water

DIRECTIONS:
1. Combine the yeast and whole-wheat flour in a large bowl. Then slowly pour in the water while continually mixing until there is no dry flour left.
2. Place the dough on a clean surface, and knead it for 8 to 10 minutes, or until slightly springy and soft.
3. Shape the dough into a ball and transfer it to another large bowl. Use a kitchen towel to cover the bowl. Allow to proof at room temperature for 2 hours, or until the dough has doubled in size.
4. Place the Crisp Plate in the oven, use parchment paper to line it, divide the dough ball evenly into 4 pieces. Roll out each ball until the dough is roughly ¼ inch thick.
5. Place the disks of dough in the Crisp Plate. Press Bake and cook at 450°F(235°C) until the pitas puff up and turn slightly golden brown, about 3 to 5 minutes.

Chapter 17 Vegetable

Braised Cabbage with Onions

Prep Time: 20 minutes, Cook Time: 6 to 7 hours on low, Serves: 8

INGREDIENTS:

1 tbsp. olive oil	vinegar
1 large head green cabbage, cored and chopped	½ cup Roasted Vegetable Broth (here)
3 onions, chopped	2 tbsps. honey
2 tbsps. apple cider	6 garlic cloves, minced
	½ tsp. salt

DIRECTIONS:

1. Combine all the ingredients in the inner pot. Cover the pressure lid and press Slow Cook, cook on Low for about 6 to 7 hours, until the cabbage and onion are soft. Serve immediately!

Garlicky Lentils and Cauliflower with Rosemary

Prep Time: 10 minutes, Cook Time: 8 hours, Serves: 1

INGREDIENTS:

1 tbsp. extra-virgin olive oil	pepper
1 cup lentils	⅛ tsp. sea salt
1 cup cauliflower florets	3 cups low-sodium vegetable broth
1 tbsp. fresh rosemary	Juice of 1 lemon
1 tbsp. roasted garlic	¼ cup roughly chopped fresh parsley
Zest of 1 lemon	
Freshly ground black	

DIRECTIONS:

1. In the inner pot, add the olive oil, lentils, cauliflower, rosemary, garlic and lemon zest. Season with the black pepper and salt.
2. Pour over the cauliflower and lentils with the vegetable broth. Cover the pressure lid and press Slow Cook, cook on low for 8 hours.
3. Drizzle with the lemon juice and sprinkle the parsley over the top, and serve hot.

Braised Carrot with Maple Purée

Prep Time: 20 minutes, Cook Time: 6 to 8 hours, Serves: 8

INGREDIENTS:

1 red onion, chopped	ginger root
8 large carrots, peeled and sliced	¼ cup canned coconut milk
¼ cup maple syrup	½ tsp. salt
2 tbsps. grated fresh	

DIRECTIONS:

1. Put all ingredients in the inner pot and stir to combine. Cover the pressure lid and press Slow Cook, cook on low for 6 to 8 hours, until the carrots are very tender.
2. Then take the mixture out, put it in a potato masher or immersion blender, and stir to the desired consistency. Serve immediately!

Quinoa Hot Cereal with Cranberry

Prep Time: 15 minutes, Cook Time: 6 to 8 hours, Serves: 12

INGREDIENTS:

4 cups canned coconut milk	1 tsp. ground cinnamon
3 cups quinoa, rinsed and drained	¼ cup honey
2 cups unsweetened apple juice	1½ cups dried cranberries (see tip here)
2 cups water	1 tsp. vanilla extract
	½ tsp. salt

DIRECTIONS:

1. Pour all the ingredients into the inner pot and stir gently with a spoon. Cover the pressure lid and press Slow Cook, cook on low heat for 6 to 8 hours until the quinoa is soft and creamy.
2. Use a spoon to transfer the mixture from the pot to the bowl and enjoy!

Mushroom Slow Cooker with Risotto

Prep Time: 20 minutes, Cook Time: 3 1/2 hours, Serves: 8

INGREDIENTS:

8 ounces (227g) shiitake mushrooms, stems removed and sliced
2 onions, chopped
5 garlic cloves, minced
2 cups short-grain brown rice
8 ounces (227g) button mushrooms, sliced
8 ounces (227g) cremini mushrooms, sliced
6 cups Roasted Vegetable Broth (here)
1 tsp. dried marjoram leaves
½ cup grated Parmesan cheese
3 tbsps. unsalted butter

DIRECTIONS:

1. Combine mushrooms, onions, garlic, rice, marjoram, and vegetable broth in the inner pot. Cover the pressure lid and press Slow Cook.
2. Simmer for 3 to 4 hours until the rice is soft.
3. Pour the butter and cheese and stir. Simmer for another 20 minutes on low heat, then enjoy.

Stuffing with Mushrooms and Sausage

Prep Time: 35-40 minutes, Cook Time: 3 hours, Serves: 10

INGREDIENTS:

12 cups toasted bread crumbs
1 lb. bulk sausage, browned and drained
8-oz. (227 g) can sliced mushrooms, with liquid
¼-1 cup butter
2 eggs, beaten
1½ cups chicken stock
1 cup or more onions, finely chopped
1 cup or more celery, finely chopped
¼ cup fresh parsley, chopped
½ tsp. poultry seasoning
dash of pepper
½ tsp. salt

DIRECTIONS:

1. Take a mixing bowl, combine bread crumbs and sausage.
2. Add butter in the inner pot, press Sear/Sauté, melt the butter thoroughly, stir in the onions and celery until tender. Add mushrooms, parsley, and seasonings. Pour over bread crumbs and mix well.
3. Add eggs and chicken stock. Cover the pressure lid, press Slow Cook and cook on low for 3 hours.
4. Open the cover and transfer to a bowl, serve.

Italian Buttery Mushrooms

Prep Time: 10 minutes, Cook Time: 5 hours, Serves: 8

INGREDIENTS:

3 lbs. (1.4 kg) medium fresh mushrooms
¼ cup Italian salad dressing
3 tbsps. chicken bouillon granules
¾ cup butter, melted
½ tsp. onion powder
½ tsp. dried oregano
1 envelope zesty Italian salad dressing mix
½ tsp. Worcestershire sauce

DIRECTIONS:

1. In the inner pot, add the mushrooms.
2. In a bowl, combine all of the remaining ingredients, and pour over mushrooms in the Ninja Foodi.
3. Cover the pressure lid and press Slow Cook, cook for on low for 5 to 6 hours, until the mushrooms are tender. Use a slotted spoon to serve.

Caramelized Onion with Garlic Borscht

Prep Time: 20 minutes, Cook Time: 6 hours 15 minutes to 7 hours 20 minutes, Serves: 8

INGREDIENTS:

8 large beets, peeled and cubed
5 tbsps. tomato paste (see tip here)
3 large carrots, peeled and chopped
8 cups Roasted Vegetable Broth (here)
1 cup sour cream
2 tbsps. cornstarch
2 cups Caramelized Onions and Garlic (here)
1 bay leaf
1 tsp. dried dill weed

DIRECTIONS:

1. Put the beets, onions, carrots, vegetable broth, tomato sauce, bay leaf and dill grass in the inner pot, mix and cover. Cook on low heat for 6 to 7 hours, until the beets and carrots are tender.
2. Remove bay leaves from the pot. If you need it, you can mash some vegetables in the pot or use an immersion blender to mash them.
3. Use a spoon to take out some of the soup, mix it with sour cream and cornstarch, mix well and pour it into the soup.
4. Cover the pressure lid and press Slow Cook, cook for another 15 to 20 minutes on low heat until the soup thickens. Serve immediately!

Zucchini Tomato Casserole

Prep Time: 20 minutes, Cook Time: 4½ hours, Serves: 4

INGREDIENTS:

4 medium zucchinis, sliced	into thin strips
One 15-ounce (425 g) can diced tomatoes, with the juice	½ tsp. basil
	1 tsp. sea salt
	½ tsp. black pepper
1 medium red onion, sliced	1 tbsp. extra-virgin olive oil
1 green bell pepper, cut	¼ cup grated Parmesan cheese

DIRECTIONS:

1. In the inner pot, add the zucchini slices, tomatoes, onion slices and bell pepper strips. Sprinkle with the basil, salt and pepper.
2. Cover the pressure lid and press Slow Cook, cook on low for 3 hours.
3. Drizzle over the casserole with the olive oil and sprinkle with the Parmesan. Cover the cooker and cook on low for another 1½ hours. Serve hot.

Healthy Stuffed Tomato

Prep Time: 20 minutes, Cook Time: 6 to 7 hours, Serves: 6

INGREDIENTS:

6 large tomatoes	Broth (here)
¾ cup low-sodium whole-wheat bread crumbs	1½ cups shredded Colby cheese
1 yellow bell pepper, stemmed, seeded, and chopped	¼ cup finely chopped flat-leaf parsley
3 garlic cloves, minced	1 red onion, finely chopped
½ cup Roasted Vegetable	1 tsp. dried thyme leaves

DIRECTIONS:

1. Process the tomatoes. Cut off the top of the tomato and use a serrated spoon to core the tomato, leaving only the pulp. Set aside the tomatoes for later use.
2. Stir and combine the onion, bell pepper, garlic, breadcrumbs, cheese, parsley, thyme and reserved tomato pulp in a medium bowl.
3. Fill the tomatoes with the mixture and place them in the inner pot. Pour the vegetable soup.
4. Cover the pressure lid and press Slow Cook, cook on low heat for 6 to 7 hours, until the tomatoes are soft. Serve immediately!

Onion, Apples and Butternut Squash

Prep Time: 15 minutes, Cook Time: 4 hours, Serves: 10

INGREDIENTS:

4 cooking apples (Granny Smith or Honeycrisp work well), peeled, cored, and chopped	½ sweet yellow onion such as Vidalia, sliced thin
	¾ cup dried currants
One 3-pound (1.4 kg) butternut squash, peeled, seeded, and cubed	1½ tsps. ground nutmeg
	1 tbsp. ground cinnamon

DIRECTIONS:

1. In the slow cooker, add the apples, squash, onion and currants. Sprinkle with the nutmeg and cinnamon.
2. Cover the pressure lid and press Slow Cook, cook on high for 4 hours, or until the squash is tender and cooked through. Stir occasionally while cooking.

Mixed Vegetable Minestrone Soup

Prep Time: 15 minutes, Cook Time: 6-8 hours, Serves: 6

INGREDIENTS:

2 carrots, chopped	½ cup dry barley
2 large onions, chopped	28-oz. (784 g) can crushed Italian tomatoes
6 cups vegetable broth	
1 small zucchini, cubed	1 tbsp. parsley
1 handful fresh kale, chopped	½ tsp. dried thyme
3 ribs celery, chopped	1 tsp. dried oregano
2 garlic cloves, minced	1 tsp. salt
1 can chickpeas or white kidney beans, drained	¼ tsp. pepper
	shredded cheese

DIRECTIONS:

1. In the inner pot, add all of the ingredients except the cheese.
2. Cover the pressure lid and press Slow Cook, cook for on Low for 6 to 8 hours, or until the vegetables are tender.
3. Sprinkle the shredded cheese into individual servings and serve.

Slow Cooker Carrots and Parsnips

Prep Time: 20 minutes, Cook Time: 5 hours to 7 hours, Serves: 8

INGREDIENTS:
6 large carrots, peeled and cut into 2-inch pieces
1 tbsp. honey
4 garlic cloves, minced
5 large parsnips, peeled and cut into 2-inch pieces
2 tbsps. olive oil
½ tsp. salt
2 red onions, chopped

DIRECTIONS:
1. Combine all the ingredients and gently stir in the inner pot, stirring gently until fully combined. Cover the pressure lid and press Slow Cook, cook on low heat for 5 to 7 hours, and cover until the vegetables are tender. Enjoy now!

Simple Italian Roasted Beets

Prep Time: 20 minutes, Cook Time: 5 hours to 7 hours, Serves: 8

INGREDIENTS:
2 onions, chopped
10 medium beets, peeled and sliced
4 garlic cloves, minced
4 large tomatoes, seeded and chopped
2 tbsps. olive oil
1 tsp. dried oregano leaves
½ tsp. salt
1 tsp. dried basil leaves

DIRECTIONS:
1. Combine the beets, tomatoes, onions, and garlic in the inner pot. Drizzle with olive oil, sprinkle with dried herbs and salt for seasoning, stir until fully combined.
2. Cover the pressure lid and press Slow Cook, cook for 5 to 7 hours until the beets are soft. Serve immediately!

Chapter 18 Grain and Rice

Herbed Wild Rice and Bacon

Prep Time: 10 minutes, Cook Time: 8 hours, Serves: 1

INGREDIENTS:

1 tsp. extra-virgin olive oil
1 piece applewood-smoked bacon, cooked and crumbled
¾ cup wild rice
½ cup minced onion
¼ cup dried cherries
1 tsp. minced fresh rosemary
2 cups low-sodium chicken broth
⅛ tsp. sea salt

DIRECTIONS:

1. Use the olive oil to grease the inside of the Ninja foodi.
2. In the inner pot, add all of the ingredients and stir them to thoroughly mix.
3. Cover the pressure lid and press Slow Cook, cook on low for 6 hours until the rice has absorbed all the water and is tender.

Mexican Black Bean Quinoa

Prep Time: 10 minutes, Cook Time: 8 hours, Serves: 6

INGREDIENTS:

2 cups uncooked quinoa
2 cups cooked black beans, rinsed
2 cups fresh or frozen corn
1 (14-ounce, 397 g) can diced tomatoes and peppers, drained
4 cups (960 ml) vegetable broth
1 green bell pepper, seeded and chopped
1 red bell pepper, seeded and chopped
2 jalapeño peppers, seeded and chopped
1 tsp. ground cumin
¼ cup chopped fresh cilantro

DIRECTIONS:

1. Rinse the quinoa in a fine-mesh colander under running water.
2. Mix the quinoa, black beans, tomatoes and peppers, broth, jalapeños, corn, bell peppers, and cumin in your Ninja foodi.
3. Cover the pressure lid and press Slow Cook, cook on low for 8 hours.
4. Add cilantro just before serving.

Wild Rice Casserole with Egg

Prep Time: 20 minutes, Cook Time: 5 hours to 7 hours, Serves: 6

INGREDIENTS:

11 eggs
2 cups sliced mushrooms
3 cups plain cooked wild rice or Herbed Wild Rice (here)
1 red bell pepper, stemmed, seeded, and chopped
1 onion, minced
¼ tsp. salt
2 garlic cloves, minced
1½ cups shredded Swiss cheese
1 tsp. dried thyme leaves

DIRECTIONS:

1. Put wild rice, mushrooms, bell peppers, onions, and garlic in the Ninja Foodi.
2. Beat the eggs into a large bowl, sprinkle with thyme and salt to taste. Pour the mixture into the inner pot. Then pour the cheese and close the pressure lid.
3. Press Slow Cook and cook on Low for 5 to 7 hours until the food thermometer shows 165°F and is soft. Serve immediately!

Wild Rice with Chili and Vegetable

Prep Time: 20 minutes, Cook Time: 6 to 7 hours, Serves: 8

INGREDIENTS:

1½ cups wild rice, rinsed and drained
2 (15-ounce (425g)) BPA-free cans no-salt-added black beans, drained and rinsed
2 cups sliced cremini mushrooms
5 cups Roasted Vegetable Broth (here)
2 red bell peppers, stemmed, seeded, and chopped
1 tbsp. chili powder
2 onions, chopped
3 garlic cloves, minced
½ tsp. ground cumin
3 cups low-sodium tomato juice

DIRECTIONS:

1. Combine all the ingredients in Ninja Foodi, Cover the pressure lid and press Slow Cook, cook on Low for 6 to 7 hours, until the wild rice is soft.
2. Transfer the mixture from the pot to a small bowl and enjoy!

Healthy Quinoa with Brussels Sprouts

Prep Time: 20 minutes, Cook Time: 5 hours to 6 hours, Serves: 8

INGREDIENTS:

2 cups quinoa, rinsed
4 cups Roasted Vegetable Broth (here)
3 cups Brussels sprouts
2 tbsps. lemon juice
1 tsp. dried marjoram leaves

1 onion, finely chopped
3 garlic cloves, minced
½ cup pomegranate seeds
1 cup broken walnuts
2 avocados, peeled and sliced

DIRECTIONS:

1. Combine quinoa, onion, garlic, vegetable broth, Brussels sprouts, marjoram, and lemon juice in the Ninja Foodi. Cover the pressure lid and press Slow Cook, simmer until the quinoa is soft, about 5 to 6 hours.
2. Put the avocado, pomegranate seeds and walnuts in the inner pot and serve immediately.

Quinoa-Stuffed Bell Peppers

Prep Time: 15 minutes, Cook Time: 8 hours, Serves: 6

INGREDIENTS:

1 cup uncooked quinoa
3 cups cooked black beans, rinsed
1 tsp. ground cumin
1 tsp. garlic powder
¼ tsp. sea salt
1 (14-ounce, 397 g) can diced tomatoes and peppers, drained
4 ounces (113 g)

shredded low-fat Cheddar cheese
6 bell peppers, tops cut off, seeds and ribs carefully removed
1 cup (240 ml) vegetable broth
¼ cup chopped fresh cilantro

DIRECTIONS:

1. Rinse the quinoa in a fine-mesh colander under running water.
2. Combine the quinoa, black beans, cumin, garlic powder, tomatoes and peppers, cheese, and salt in a medium bowl.
3. Carefully stuff the bell peppers with the quinoa mixture.
4. Place the stuffed peppers in the Ninja Foodi, cut-side up and pour the broth around the peppers.
5. Cover the pressure lid and press Slow Cook, cook on low for 8 hours.
6. Serve with the chopped cilantro on top.

Curried Lentils and Rice

Prep Time: 10 minutes, Cook Time: 8 hours, Serves: 6

INGREDIENTS:

2½ cups dried lentils, soaked overnight and rinsed
4 cups (960 ml) vegetable broth
½ cup (120 ml) canned light coconut milk
2 tbsps. curry powder

1 tsp. garlic powder
2 onions, chopped
1 tbsp. grated fresh ginger
1 tsp. ground turmeric
¼ tsp. sea salt
3 cups cooked brown rice

DIRECTIONS:

1. Mix the lentils, broth, coconut milk, curry powder, onions, ginger, turmeric, garlic powder and salt in your Ninja Foodi.
2. Cover the pressure lid and press Slow Cook, cook on low for 8 hours.
3. Serve spooned over the cooked rice.

Butternut Squash and Oatmeal

Prep Time: 15 minutes, Cook Time: 6 to 8 hours, Serves: 4

INGREDIENTS:

2 cups cubed (½-inch pieces) peeled butternut squash (freeze any leftovers after preparing a whole squash for future meals)
1 cup steel-cut oats
3 cups water
1 tbsp. chia seeds
¼ cup unsweetened

nondairy milk
1½ tsps. ground ginger
2 tsps. yellow (mellow) miso paste
1 tbsp. sesame seeds, toasted
1 tbsp. chopped scallion, green parts only
Shredded carrot, for serving (optional)

DIRECTIONS:

1. Add the butternut squach, oats and water into the Ninja Foodi.
2. Cover the pressure lid and press Slow Cook, cook on Low for 6 to 8 hours, or until the squash is fork-tender. Roughly mash the cooked butternut squash with a potato masher or heavy spoon. Stir to combine with the oats.
3. Add the chia seeds, milk, ginger and miso paste into a small bowl, whisk them together to combine. Stir the mixture into the oats.
4. Place the sesame seeds and scallion over your oatmeal bowl, and serve.

Pearl Barley

Prep Time: 10 minutes, Cook Time: 8 hours, Serves: 4 cups

INGREDIENTS:

2 cups pearl barley
½ tsp. salt
5 cups (1200 ml) boiling water

DIRECTIONS:

1. Mix all ingredients in your Ninja Foodi.
2. Cover the pressure lid and press Slow Cook, cook on low for 8 hours.

Quinoa in Stock

Prep Time: 5 minutes, Cook Time: 6 hours, Serves: 6 cups

INGREDIENTS:

2 cups quinoa
4 cups (960 ml) vegetable broth, poultry broth, beef
broth, or store bought
Nonstick cooking spray
1 tbsp. olive oil

DIRECTIONS:

1. Spray the jar of your Ninja Foodi with nonstick cooking spray.
2. Add the broth, quinoa, and olive oil, stirring to mix.
3. Cover the pressure lid and press Slow Cook, cook on low for about 6 hours. Fluff with a fork.

Brown Rice in Stock

Prep Time: 5 minutes, Cook Time: 2 to 4 hours, Serves: 6 cups

INGREDIENTS:

2 cups brown rice
3⅓ cups (800 ml) vegetable broth, poultry broth, beef broth, or store
bought
Nonstick cooking spray
1 tbsp. olive oil

DIRECTIONS:

1. Spray the jar of your Ninja Foodi with nonstick cooking spray.
2. Add the broth, rice, and olive oil, stirring to combine.
3. Cover the pressure lid and press Slow Cook, cook on high for 2 to 4 hours, stirring every hour or so, until the rice is fluffy.

Mushroom and Wild Rice

Prep Time: 15 minutes, Cook Time: 4 hours on low, Serves: 8

INGREDIENTS:

1 lb. (454 g) bulk pork sausage
1 small onion, chopped
4 celery ribs, chopped
1 cup uncooked wild rice
1 can (10 ¾ oz., 304 g) condensed cream of chicken soup, undiluted
1 can (10 ¾ oz., 304 g) condensed cream of mushroom soup, undiluted
1 can (4 oz., 113 g) mushroom stems and pieces, drained
3 cups chicken broth

DIRECTIONS:

1. Add the sausage into a large skillet, cook and crumble with onion and celery over medium heat for 6 to 8 minutes, until sausage is no longer pink and vegetables are tender, drain. Transfer this mixture into the Ninja Foodi. Then add rice, soups, and mushroom. Stir in chicken broth.
2. Cover the pressure lid and press Slow Cook, cook on low for 4 to 5 hours, until rice is tender.

Herb Barley Risotto with Lemon

Prep Time: 10 minutes, Cook Time: 6-8 hours, Serves: 1

INGREDIENTS:

1 tsp. extra-virgin olive oil
2 tbsps. minced preserved lemon
½ cup minced onion
1 tsp. fresh thyme leaves
¼ cup roughly chopped fresh parsley, divided
2 cups low-sodium
vegetable broth
¾ cup pearl barley
⅛ tsp. sea salt
Freshly ground black pepper
½ lemon cut, into wedges, for garnish

DIRECTIONS:

1. Use olive oil to grease the inside of the Ninja Foodi.
2. In the inner pot, add the preserved lemon, onion, thyme, 2 tablespoons of the parsley, vegetable broth and barley. Season with the salt and pepper, and stir thoroughly.
3. Cover the pressure lid and press Slow Cook, cook on low for 6 to 8 hours, until the barley is tender and all the liquid is absorbed.
4. Garnish with the remaining parsley and a lemon wedge and serve.

Oatmeal Slow Cooker with Carrot

Prep Time: 20 minutes, Cook Time: 6 to 8 hours, Serves: 8

INGREDIENTS:
1 (8-ounce (227g)) BPA-free can unsweetened crushed pineapple in juice, undrained
4 cups water
2 cups almond milk
3 cups steel-cut oats
2 cups finely grated carrot
2 tsps. vanilla extract
2 tbsps. melted coconut oil
¼ cup honey
1 tsp. ground cinnamon
¼ tsp. salt

DIRECTIONS:
1. Coat the inside of the Ninja Foodi with regular vegetable oil.
2. Add steel-cut oats, carrots and pineapple, and mix.
3. Put almond milk, water, coconut oil, honey, vanilla, salt and cinnamon in a medium bowl and stir to combine. Pour the mixture into the inner pot and close the Pressure lid.
4. Press Slow Cook and cook on low heat for 6 to 8 hours, until the oatmeal is soft. Serve immediately!

Spicy Thai Peanut Rice

Prep Time: 10 minutes, Cook Time: 6-8 hours, Serves: 1

INGREDIENTS:
1 tsp. extra-virgin olive oil
4 collard leaves, ribs removed, chopped into thin ribbons
3 cups low-sodium vegetable broth, divided
½ cup brown rice
½ cup minced red onion
2 tbsps. tomato paste
1 tbsp. minced ginger
¼ cup unsalted creamy peanut butter
⅛ tsp. sea salt
1 tsp. Sriracha
Lime wedges, for garnish
¼ cup roughly chopped cilantro, for garnish
2 tbsps. roasted peanuts, roughly chopped, for garnish

DIRECTIONS:
1. Use olive oil to grease the inside of the Ninja Foodi.
2. In the inner pot, add the collard greens, 2 cups of broth, rice, and onion.
3. Add the remaining 1 cup of broth, tomato paste, ginger, peanut butter, salt and Sriracha into a medium bowl, whisk them together. Transfer this mixture into the Ninja Foodi and stir well.
4. Cover the pressure lid and press Slow Cook, cook on low for 6 to 8 hours.
5. Garnish each serving with a lime wedge, fresh cilantro, and the peanuts, and serve.

Chapter 19 Bean and Legume

Simple Fava Beans

Prep Time: 5 minutes, Cook Time: 8 to 10 hours, Serves: 12

INGREDIENTS:

1 pound (454 g) fava beans, soaked overnight and rinsed
1 tsp. garlic powder
¼ tsp. sea salt
1 tbsp. olive oil
1 tsp. ground cumin

DIRECTIONS:

1. Mix the beans, garlic powder, salt, olive oil and cumin in your Ninja Foodi.
2. Add enough water to cover the beans by 2 inches.
3. Cover the pressure lid and press Slow Cook, cook on low for 8 to 10 hours until the beans are soft.

Mushroom and Green Bean Casserole

Prep Time: 15 minutes, Cook Time: 6 hours on low, Serves: 6

INGREDIENTS:

¼ cup butter, divided
1 cup sliced button mushrooms
½ sweet onion, chopped
1 tsp. minced garlic
2 pounds (907 g) green beans, cut into 2-inch
pieces
8 ounces (227 g) cream cheese
1 cup chicken broth
¼ cup grated Parmesan cheese

DIRECTIONS:

1. Use 1 tablespoon of the butter to lightly grease the insert of the Ninja Foodi.
2. Melt the remaining butter in the inner pot over medium-high heat. Stir in the mushrooms, onion, and garlic, sauté for 5 minutes, until the vegetables are softened.
3. Add the green beans into the Ninja Foodi, stir well and transfer the mixture to the insert.
4. Add the cream cheese and broth to a small bowl, whisk them together until smooth.
5. Transfer the cheese mixture into the vegetables and stir. Place the Parmesan over the combined mixture.
6. Cover the pressure lid and press Slow Cook, cook on low for 6 hours.
7. Serve warm.

Smoky Mixed Bean Chili

Prep Time: 10 minutes, Cook Time: 6-8 hours, Serves: 1

INGREDIENTS:

1 (16-ounce, 454 g) can mixed beans, drained and rinsed
1 cup canned fire-roasted diced tomatoes, undrained
1 cup frozen roasted corn
kernels, thawed
½ cup diced onion
2 garlic cloves, minced
1 tsp. smoked paprika
1 tsp. ground cumin
1 tsp. dried oregano
⅛ tsp. sea salt

DIRECTIONS:

1. In the Ninja Foodi, add all of the ingredients. Stir quickly to combine.
2. Cover the pressure lid and press Slow Cook, cook on low for 6 to 8 hours.

Slow Cooker Mixed Beans with Sausage

Prep Time: 30 minutes, Cook Time: 7-9 hours, Serves: 6

INGREDIENTS:

28-oz. (794 g) can stewed or whole tomatoes
16-oz. (454 g) can pinto beans, drained
16-oz. (454 g) can kidney beans, drained
2¼-oz. (85 g) can ripe olives sliced, drained
¾ lb. bulk Italian sausage
1 green pepper, chopped
1 medium onion, chopped
1 garlic clove, minced
1 tsp. dried oregano
1 tsp. dried basil
Parmesan cheese
1 tbsp. oil
1 tsp. salt

DIRECTIONS:

1. Place tomatoes, beans and olives in a slow cooker, mix well.
2. Place sausage in skillet and brown on all sides. Transfer sausage to Ninja Foodi.
3. Add green peppers and stir-fry for 1 minute. Add onions and continue to stir until onions start to become translucent. Add garlic and cook for another minute. Transfer to a slow cooker.
4. Add the seasonings, cover the pressure lid and press Slow Cook, cook on Low for 7-9 hours.
5. Sprinkle with Parmesan cheese before serving.

Lentils in Stock

Prep Time: 5 minutes, Cook Time: 7 to 8 hours, Serves: 6 cups

INGREDIENTS:

3 cups dried lentils, soaked overnight and rinsed 6 cups (1440 ml)

vegetable broth, poultry broth, beef broth, or store bought

DIRECTIONS:
1. In your Ninja Foodi, mix the lentils and broth.
2. Cover the pressure lid and press Slow Cook, cook on low. Cook 7 to 8 hours until the lentils are soft.

Slow Cooked Beans

Prep Time: 5 minutes, Cook Time: 6 to 8 hours, Serves: 6 cups

INGREDIENTS:

1 pound (454 g) dried beans, soaked overnight

and rinsed 1 bay leaf

DIRECTIONS:
1. In your Ninja Foodi, mix the beans and bay leaf.
2. Add enough water to come just about ½ inch over the top of the beans.
3. Cover the pressure lid and press Slow Cook, cook on low for 6 to 8 hours, until the beans are soft.

Mixed Beans with Bacon

Prep Time: 10 minutes, Cook Time: 4-5 hours, Serves: 6

INGREDIENTS:

15½-oz. (439 g) can baked beans, undrained 16-oz. (454 g) can kidney beans, drained 1 pint home-frozen, or 1-lb. pkg. frozen, green beans 1 pint home-frozen, or 1-lb. pkg. frozen, lima

beans 4 slices lean turkey bacon, browned and crumbled ½ cup ketchup ⅓ cup brown sugar ⅓ cup sugar 2 tbsps. vinegar ½ tsp. salt

DIRECTIONS:
1. Put beans and bacon into the Ninja Foodi.
2. Take a bowl, add the remaining ingredients into it, stir and add the mixture into the cooker.
3. Stir. Cover the pressure lid and press Slow Cook, cook

on Low for 4-5 hours.
4. Serve warm from the cooker.

Mediterranean Quinoa and Chickpeas

Prep Time: 10 minutes, Cook Time: 9 hours, Serves: 6

INGREDIENTS:

1 pound (454 g) dried chickpeas, soaked overnight and drained 2 tsps. garlic powder 1 tbsp. dried rosemary 1 tsp. dried thyme ½ tsp. sea salt

Pinch cayenne pepper 3 cups cooked quinoa 1 onion, chopped 7 cups (1680 ml) vegetable broth Zest and juice of 1 lemon

DIRECTIONS:
1. Mix the chickpeas, lemon zest (reserve the juice), garlic powder, onion, broth, rosemary, thyme, salt, and cayenne in your Ninja Foodi.
2. Cover the pressure lid and press Slow Cook, cook on low for 9 hours.
3. Add lemon juice. Serve spooned over the quinoa.

Backed Beans with Onions

Prep Time: 10 minutes, Cook Time: 4-5 hours, Serves: 12

INGREDIENTS:

6 slices turkey bacon 16-oz. (454 g) can low-sodium lima beans, drained 16-oz. (454 g) can low-sodium beans with tomato sauce, undrained 15½-oz. (439 g) can low-sodium red kidney beans, drained 15-oz. (425 g) can low-sodium butter beans, drained

15-oz. (425 g) can low-sodium garbanzo beans, drained 1 cup onions, chopped 1 clove garlic, minced ½ cup unsulfured molasses ¼ cup brown sugar ¾ cup ketchup 1 tbsp. prepared mustard 1 tbsp. Worcestershire sauce

DIRECTIONS:
1. Brown bacon in a nonstick skillet.
2. Combine the remaining ingredients in Ninja Foodi inner pot.
3. Cover the pressure lid and press Slow Cook, cook on High for 4-5 hours.
4. Serve warm.

Beans with Beef and Corn

Prep Time: 15 minutes, Cook Time: 3-4 hours, Serves: 6 to 8

INGREDIENTS:

1 lb. ground beef, browned and drained	15¼-oz. (432 g) can corn
15½-oz. (439 g) can pinto beans	1 medium onion, chopped
	¼ cup brown sugar
14¾-oz. (418 g) can lima beans	1 cup ketchup
	2 tsps. prepared mustard
	1 tbsp. vinegar

DIRECTIONS:

1. In the Ninja Foodi, mix all ingredients.
2. Cover the pressure lid and press Slow Cook, simmer on High for 3-4 hours.
3. Serve warm.

BBQ Beans

Prep Time: 15 minutes, Cook Time: 8 hours, Serves: 8

INGREDIENTS:

5 cups cooked pinto beans, rinsed	3 jalapeño peppers, seeded and finely chopped
1 (14-ounce, 397 g) can tomato sauce	½ tsp. liquid smoke
¼ cup blackstrap molasses	2 tsps. smoked paprika
1 onion, finely chopped	¼ tsp. sea salt
6 garlic cloves, minced	⅛ tsp. cayenne pepper

DIRECTIONS:

1. Combine all the ingredients in your Ninja Foodi inner pot.
2. Cover the pressure lid and press Slow Cook, cook on low for 8 hours.

Bacon Baked Beans

Prep Time: 15 minutes, Cook Time: 4-5 hours, Serves: 8

INGREDIENTS:

4 slices bacon, diced	1 tbsp. brown sugar
28-oz. (794 g) can pork and beans	1 tsp. dark molasses
1 medium onion, chopped	1 cup dates, cut up

DIRECTIONS:

1. In a pan, partially fry bacon.

2. Add all the ingredients to the Ninja Foodi inner pot, stir well.
3. Cover the pressure lid and press Slow Cook, cook on Low for 4-5 hours.

Baked Beans with Beef and Pineapple

Prep Time: 15 minutes, Cook Time: 4-8 hours, Serves: 6 to 8

INGREDIENTS:

1 lb. ground beef	4½-oz (128 g) can sliced mushrooms, drained
28-oz. (794 g) can baked beans	1 clove garlic, minced
8-oz. (227 g) can pineapple tidbits, drained	½ cup barbecue sauce
	2 tbsps. soy sauce
1 large onion, chopped	¼ tsp. pepper
1 large green pepper, chopped	½ tsp. salt

DIRECTIONS:

1. In a skillet, cook ground beef until browned. Drain. Transfer to the Ninja Foodi inner pot.
2. Put the remaining ingredients in the cooker. Mix well.
3. Cover the pressure lid and press Slow Cook, simmer on Low for 4-8 hours.
4. Serve in soup bowls.

Apple Butter Baked Bean

Prep Time: 20 minutes, Cook Time: 2-4 hours, Serves: 10 to 12

INGREDIENTS:

24-oz. (680 g) can Great Northern beans, undrained	apples, cubed
	¼ cup sugar
	½ cup brown sugar
24-oz. (680 g) can pinto beans, undrained	1 tsp. cinnamon
	½ cup ketchup
4 tbsps. butter	1 tbsp. molasses
2 large Granny Smith	1 tsp. salt

DIRECTIONS:

1. Press Sear/Sauté and cook on High, melt butter in the inner pot. Add apples and cook until tender.
2. Add sugar and brown sugar. Heat and stir until the sugar is dissolved. Add cinnamon, ketchup, molasses, and salt into it.
3. Add beans and stir well.
4. Cover the pressure lid and press Slow Cook, simmer on High for 2-4 hours.
5. Serve warm.

Cheesy Black Bean and Spinach Enchilada Pie

Prep Time: 10 minutes, Cook Time: 6-8 hours, Serves: 1

INGREDIENTS:

¼ cup low-fat cream cheese
¼ cup low-fat Cheddar cheese
1 (15-ounce, 425 g) can black beans, drained and rinsed
1 tsp. minced garlic
½ cup minced onion
1 tsp. smoked paprika
1 tsp. ground cumin
2 cups shredded fresh spinach
1 tsp. extra-virgin olive oil
1 cup enchilada sauce, divided
4 corn tortillas
¼ cup fresh cilantro, for garnish

DIRECTIONS:

1. Add the cream cheese, Cheddar cheese, beans, garlic, onion, paprika, cumin and spinach into a large bowl, mix them together.
2. Use olive oil to grease the inside of the Ninja Foodi.
3. Spread ¼ cup of enchilada sauce across the bottom of the crock. Put one corn tortilla on top of the sauce. Place one-third of the black bean and spinach mixture over the tortilla. And with a second corn tortilla to cover and then slather it with ¼ cup of enchilada sauce. Repeat this layering, finishing with a corn tortilla and the last ¼ cup of enchilada sauce.
4. Cover the pressure lid and press Slow Cook, cook on low for 6 to 8 hours. After cooking, garnish with the cilantro and serve.

Black Bean, Tomato, Rice and Lentil Burritos

Prep Time: 15 minutes, Cook Time: 8 hours, Serves: 6

INGREDIENTS:

2 15-ounce (425 g) cans black beans, drained and rinsed
¼ cup salsa
2 15-ounce (425 g) cans diced tomatoes
½ cup corn, fresh, frozen, or canned
1 cup brown rice
2 tbsps. taco seasoning
2 chipotle peppers in
adobo sauce, finely chopped
1 tsp. ground cumin
1 tsp. salt
2½ cups vegetable broth
½ cup lentils
12 whole wheat tortillas
Additional toppings, such as more salsa, avocado or guacamole, and black olives

DIRECTIONS:

1. In Ninja Foodi, combine the beans, salsa, tomatoes, corn, rice, taco seasoning, chipotles, cumin, salt, and broth. Cover the pressure lid and press Slow Cook, cook on low for 6 to 8 hours or on high for 3 to 4 hours.
2. Cook until 40 minutes left, add the lentils. Continue cooking until the lentils are tender. The rice will be tender and most of the liquid will be absorbed. This is the filling.
3. Lay out the tortillas and place about ⅓ to ½ cup of the filling on each tortilla. Spread the filling down through the center of the tortilla. Fold each end about 1½ inches over the point edge of the beans. And roll up the tortilla along the long edge.
4. Stack up and serve with more avocado, salsa or guacamole, and black olives.

Black Bean Sweet Potato Enchiladas

Prep Time: 5 minutes, Cook Time: 8 hours (low), 4 hours (high), Serves: 6

INGREDIENTS:

Cooking spray
3 cups cooked beans (black, pinto, red, or a mixture)
1 cup diced sweet potato or winter squash
2 cups fresh or frozen corn
1 cup chopped onion
2 cups Poblano Mole, ½ cup reserved
12 corn tortillas
2 cups grated queso quesadilla or Monterey Jack cheese, ½ cup reserved
½ cup chopped fresh cilantro

DIRECTIONS:

1. Use the cooking spray to spray the Ninja Foodi inner pot.
2. Add the beans, sweet potato, corn, onion and 1½ cups of the mole to a large bowl, gently mix them together.
3. On the bottom of the inner pot, spread a little of this mixture. Place a layer of tortillas over. Spread a layer of vegetable mixture over the top. Next, sprinkle over the vegetables with some of the cheese, followed by a sprinkling of cilantro. Repeat the layers until all the filling is used, ending with a layer of tortillas.
4. Spread over the tortillas with the reserved ½ cup of mole and sprinkle with the reserved ½ cup of cheese.
5. Cover the pressure lid and press Slow Cook, cook on low for 8 hours or on high for 4 hours, and serve hot.

Moroccan Chickpeas with Chard

Prep Time: 10 minutes, Cook Time: 8 hours, Serves: 1

INGREDIENTS:

1 (16-ounce, 454 g) can chickpeas, drained and rinsed
½ bunch Swiss chard, stems diced and leaves roughly chopped
½ cup diced carrots
½ cup diced onion
¼ cup diced dried apricots
2 tbsps. roughly chopped

preserved lemons (optional)
1 tsp. minced fresh ginger
1 tbsp. tomato paste
½ tsp. smoked paprika
½ tsp. ground cinnamon
¼ tsp. red pepper flakes
¼ tsp. ground cumin
⅛ tsp. sea salt

DIRECTIONS:

1. In the Ninja Foodi inner pot, add all of the ingredients. Stir them together thoroughly.
2. Cover the pressure lid and press Slow Cook, cook on low for 8 hours.

Partytime Beans with Peppers and Onions

Prep Time: 15-20 minutes, Cook Time: 5-7 hours, Serves: 14 to 16

INGREDIENTS:

1 onion, chopped
1 green pepper, chopped
1 sweet red pepper, chopped
⅛ tsp. pepper
1½ cups ketchup
½ cup water
½ cup packed brown sugar
2 bay leaves
2-3 tsps. cider vinegar
1 tsp. ground mustard

15½-oz. can Great Northern beans, rinsed and drained
16-oz. can kidney beans, rinsed and drained
15½-oz. can black-eyed peas, rinsed and drained
15-oz. can black beans, rinsed and drained
15-oz. can lima beans, rinsed and drained

DIRECTIONS:

1. Put the first 10 ingredients in the Ninja Foodi. Mix well.
2. Add remaining ingredients to the cooker.
3. Cover the pressure lid and press Slow Cook, cook on Low for 5-7 hours.
4. Discard bay and leaves before serving.
5. Serve with grilled hamburgers, tossed salad.

Beans with Bacon and Beef

Prep Time: 20 minutes, Cook Time: 5-6 hours, Serves: 10 to 12

INGREDIENTS:

½ lb. ground beef
10 slices bacon, diced
½ cup onions, chopped
1-lb. can butter beans, drained
1-lb. can kidney beans, drained
1-lb. can black beans, drained
1-lb. can pork and beans

⅓ cup brown sugar
¼ cup barbecue sauce
¼ cup ketchup
2 tbsps. prepared mustard
2 tbsps. molasses
½ tsp. chili powder
½ tsp. pepper
½ tsp. salt

DIRECTIONS:

1. In the Ninja Foodi, press Sear/Sauté on High, cook ground beef, bacon, and onion until browned.
2. Combine the remaining ingredients in a big bowl, apart from beans. Stir well. Add beans and pour into the Ninja Foodi.
3. Cover the pressure lid and press Slow Cook, simmer on Low for 5-6 hours.
4. Serve warm.

Black Bean and Rice with Tomato and Corn

Prep Time: Less than 5 minutes, Cook Time: 8 hours(low), 4 hours (high), plus 10 minutes, Serves: 6

INGREDIENTS:

1 cup uncooked brown rice
½ pound (227 g) dried black beans, rinsed
2 jalapeños
1 medium onion, chopped
4 cups Vegetable Stock
2 large tomatoes, diced

Juice of 1 lime
3 cups fresh or frozen corn
1 cup chopped fresh cilantro
8 ounces (227 g) grated Cheddar cheese
Sea salt

DIRECTIONS:

1. Add the rice, beans, jalapeños, onion and stock to the Ninja Foodi, combine them together.
2. Cover the pressure lid and press Slow Cook, cook on low for 8 hours or on high for 4 hours.
3. Place the tomatoes, lime juice, corn, cilantro, and cheese into the inner pot. Stir gently and cook for 10 minutes on low. Taste and adjust with salt if needed.
4. Ladle into bowls with the beans and rice, and serve hot.

Curried Seitan and Chickpeas

Prep Time: 10 minutes, Cook Time: 6-8 hours, Serves: 1

INGREDIENTS:

1 tsp. extra-virgin olive oil
1 (15-ounce, 425 g) can chickpeas, drained and rinsed
8 ounces (227 g) seitan, cut into bite-size pieces
½ cup minced onion
2 tbsps. tomato paste
1 tsp. minced garlic
1 tsp. minced fresh ginger
1 tsp. curry powder
½ tsp. garam masala
1 cup light coconut milk
Pinch red pepper flakes
½ tsp. sea salt

DIRECTIONS:

1. Use the olive oil to grease the inside of the Ninja Foodi.
2. In the inner pot, add all of the ingredients and stir to mix thoroughly.
3. Cover the pressure lid and press Slow Cook, cook on low, cook for 6 to 8 hours.

Five Beans and Bacon

Prep Time: 30 minutes, Cook Time: 3-4 hours, Serves: 15 to 20

INGREDIENTS:

28-oz. (794 g) can baked beans
16-oz. (454 g) can kidney beans, rinsed and drained
15½-oz. (439 g) can pinto beans, rinsed and drained
15-oz. (425 g) can lima beans, rinsed and drained
15½-oz. (439 g) can black-eyed peas, rinsed and drained
8 bacon strips, diced
1 cup packed brown sugar
½ cup cider vinegar
2 onions, thinly sliced
1 tsp. ground mustard
½ tsp. garlic powder
1 tsp. salt

DIRECTIONS:

1. In the Ninja Foodi, cook bacon until crisp.
2. Remove it to paper towels. Drain, reserving 2 tbsps. drippings.
3. Press Sear/Sauté on High, Sauté the onion until tender.
4. Add brown sugar, vinegar, salt, mustard and garlic powder to the inner pot and bring to a boil.
5. Add the beans, peas, onion mixture and bacon. Stir well.
6. Cover the pressure lid and press Slow Cook, cook on High for 3-4 hours.

Hearty Mixed Bean

Prep Time: 10 minutes, Cook Time: 4-5 hours, Serves: 8

INGREDIENTS:

16-oz. (454 g) can red kidney beans, drained
15½-oz. (439 g) can black beans, rinsed and drained
15-oz. (425 g) can Great Northern beans, drained
15-oz. (425 g) can butter beans, drained
1 lb. smoked sausage, cooked and cut into
½-inch slices
1½ cups ketchup
½ cup chopped onions
1 green pepper, chopped
¼ cup brown sugar
2 garlic cloves, minced
1 tsp. Worcestershire sauce
½ tsp. Tabasco sauce
½ tsp. dry mustard

DIRECTIONS:

1. Put all the ingredients into the Ninja Foodi. Stir well.
2. Cover the pressure lid and press Slow Cook, cook on High for 4-5 hours.
3. Serve hot.

Cheesy Mixed Bean Chili

Prep Time: Less than 5 minutes, Cook Time: 8 hours (low), 4 hours (high), Serves: 8

INGREDIENTS:

2 (14.5-ounce, 411 g) cans diced tomatoes with chiles
1 (15-ounce, 425 g) can black beans, drained and rinsed
2 (15-ounce, 425 g) cans kidney beans, drained and rinsed
1 (15-ounce, 425 g) can pinto beans, drained and rinsed
2 (15-ounce, 425 g) cans chili beans (don't drain)
2 zucchinis, chopped
2 medium onions, chopped
1 dried chipotle
4 garlic cloves, minced
1 green bell pepper, seeded and chopped
¼ cup tomato paste
1 tbsp. chili powder
1 tsp. ground cumin
3 cups grated Colby cheese

DIRECTIONS:

1. Add all of the ingredients except the cheese into the Ninja Foodi, combine well.
2. Cover the pressure lid and press Slow Cook, cook on low for 8 hours or on high for 4 hours.
3. Take the chipotle out, add the cheese, and stir until it melts.
4. Serve with tortilla chips.

Chili Baked Beans with Bacon

Prep Time: 15 minutes, Cook Time: 6-8 hours, Serves: 20

INGREDIENTS:

2 1-lb., 15-oz. (425 g) cans baked beans
2 tart apples, diced
1 cup crumbled bacon
1 cup raisins
2 small onions, diced
1 cup chili sauce
3 tsps. dry mustard
½ cup sweet pickle relish

DIRECTIONS:

1. Place all ingredients in the Ninja Foodi. Mix well.
2. Cover the pressure lid and press Slow Cook, cook on Low for 6-8 hours.
3. Serve warm from the cooker.

Spicy Quinoa and Black Beans

Prep Time: 5 minutes, Cook Time: 10 hours (low), 5 hours (high), Serves: 6

INGREDIENTS:

1 pound (454 g) dried black beans, rinsed
2 dried chipotles
2 large tomatoes, diced, or 1 (28-ounce, 784 g) can fire-roasted diced tomatoes
¾ cup uncooked quinoa, rinsed
1 medium onion, diced
1 garlic clove, minced
2 jalapeños, halved and seeded, optional
2 medium bell peppers (any color), seeded and diced
3 cups Vegetable Stock
4 cups water
1 tsp. ground cumin
2 tsps. chili powder
¼ cup chopped fresh cilantro
Sea salt
Chopped avocado and lime wedges, for garnish

DIRECTIONS:

1. Add the black beans, chipotles, tomatoes, quinoa, onion, garlic, jalapeños, bell peppers, stock and water into the Ninja Foodi inner pot, combine them together.
2. Cover the pressure lid and press Slow Cook, cook on low for 10 hours or on high for 5 hours.
3. After cooking, add the cumin, chili powder, and cilantro, stir well. Taste and adjust with salt as needed.
4. Remove the chipotles, and place the chopped avocado and a squeeze of lime over the quinoa and beans before serving.

Smoky Beans with Ground Beef and Sausage

Prep Time: 20 minutes, Cook Time: 4-6 hours, Serves: 10 to 12

INGREDIENTS:

1 lb. ground beef, browned
1 large onion, chopped
15-oz. (425 g) can pork and beans
15-oz. (425 g) can ranch-style beans, drained
16-oz. (454 g) can kidney beans, drained
½-1 lb. small smoky link sausage
1 cup ketchup
1 tbsp. prepared mustard
2 tbsps. brown sugar
2 tbsps. hickory-flavored barbecue sauce
1 tsp. salt

DIRECTIONS:

1. In the Ninja Foodi, press Sear/Sauté on High, cook ground beef and onion until browned. Drain. Cover the pressure lid and press Slow Cook, cook on High.
2. Put the remaining ingredients in the cooker. Mix well.
3. Turn to Low and cook 4-6 hours. Absorb oil that's risen to the top with a paper towel before stirring and serving.

Sweet and Sour Beans with Bacon

Prep Time: 10 minutes, Cook Time: 6-8 hours, Serves: 8

INGREDIENTS:

16-oz. can low-sodium lima beans, drained
16-oz. can low-sodium baked beans, undrained
16-oz. can low-sodium kidney beans, drained
4 slices lean bacon
1 onion, chopped
1 tsp. prepared mustard
1 clove garlic, crushed
¼ cup brown sugar
½ tsp. salt
¼ cup vinegar

DIRECTIONS:

1. In the Ninja Foodi, press Sear/Sauté on High, cook bacon until browned.
2. Add bacon, 2 tbsps. drippings from bacon, onion, mustard, garlic, brown sugar, salt, and vinegar into a slow cooker. Mix well.
3. Add beans into the cooker.
4. Cover the pressure lid and press Slow Cook, cook on Low for 6-8 hours.
5. Serve warm.

Hearty Lentil, White Bean and Chickpea Stew

Prep Time: 10 minutes, Cook Time: 6-8 hours, Serves: 1

INGREDIENTS:

½ cup lentils, rinsed and sorted
½ cup white rice
½ cup canned chickpeas, drained and rinsed
½ cup canned white beans, drained and rinsed
½ cup diced red bell
pepper
½ cup diced carrots
1 ounce (28 g) pancetta, diced
2 cups low-sodium vegetable broth
¼ cup parsley
⅛ tsp. sea salt

DIRECTIONS:

1. In the Ninja Foodi, add all of the ingredients and stir to mix thoroughly.
2. Cover the pressure lid and press Slow Cook, cook on low for 6 to 8 hours.

Italian Lentils

Prep Time: 10 minutes, Cook Time: 8 hours, Serves: 6

INGREDIENTS:

1 pound (454 g) dry lentils, soaked overnight and rinsed
2 (14-ounce, 397 g) cans diced tomatoes, drained
5 cups (1200 ml) vegetable broth
1 onion, chopped
2 carrots, peeled and
finely chopped
1 fennel bulb, finely chopped
2 tsps. garlic powder
2 tsps. dried Italian seasoning
½ tsp. sea salt
3 cups cooked whole-wheat spaghetti

DIRECTIONS:

1. Mix the lentils, tomatoes, broth, garlic powder, onion, carrots, fennel, Italian seasoning, and salt in your Ninja Foodi.
2. Cover the pressure lid and press Slow Cook, cook on low for 8 hours.
3. Serve spooned over the whole-wheat spaghetti.

Red Beans and Brown Rice

Prep Time: 10 minutes, Cook Time: 8 hours, Serves: 6

INGREDIENTS:

1 pound (454 g) dried red beans, soaked overnight and rinsed
8 cups (1920 ml) vegetable broth
1 tbsp. smoked paprika
2 green bell peppers, seeded and chopped
2 jalapeño peppers, seeded and chopped
1 tbsp. Creole seasoning
2 tsps. garlic powder
1 tsp. dried thyme
½ tsp. sea salt
3 cups cooked brown rice

DIRECTIONS:

1. Mix the beans, bell peppers, broth, thyme, paprika, jalapeños, Creole seasoning, garlic powder, and salt in your Ninja Foodi.
2. Cover the pressure lid and press Slow Cook, cook on low for 8 hours.
3. Stir in the rice.

Smoky Sausage, Apple and Bean Stew

Prep Time: 15 minutes, Cook Time: 3½–4½ hours, Serves: 12

INGREDIENTS:

53-oz. (1502 g) can baked beans, well drained
3 tart apples, peeled and chopped
1 pkg. smoky cocktail
sausages
1 large onion, chopped
½ cup firmly packed brown sugar
½ cup barbecue sauce

DIRECTIONS:

1. In the Ninja Foodi, combine beans, onions, and apples. Mix well.
2. Add barbecue sauce, brown sugar, and meat to the cooker. Stir.
3. Cover the pressure lid and press Slow Cook, cook on Low for 3-4 hours, and then set it on High for 30 minutes.
4. Serve warm.

White Bean Casserole

Prep Time: 10 minutes, Cook Time: 8 hours, Serves: 6

INGREDIENTS:

2 cups dried white beans, soaked overnight and rinsed
1 onion, finely chopped
2 tsps. garlic powder
½ tsp. sea salt
¼ tsp. freshly ground black pepper
Zest of 1 orange
6 cups (1440 ml) vegetable broth
1 tbsp. dried rosemary
4 cups baby spinach

DIRECTIONS:

1. Mix the beans, onion, rosemary, garlic powder, orange zest, broth, salt, and pepper in the Ninja Foodi.
2. Cover the pressure lid and press Slow Cook, cook on low for 8 hours.
3. About half an hour before serving, stir in the spinach.

Brown Sugar and Beef Calico Beans

Prep Time: 20 minutes, Cook Time: 2-6 hours, Serves: 10

INGREDIENTS:

1 lb. ground beef
¼-½ lb. bacon
1 medium onion, chopped
2-lb. can pork and beans
14½-oz. (411 g) can French-style green beans, drained
1-lb. can Great Northern beans, drained
½ cup brown sugar
2 tbsps. cider vinegar
½ cup ketchup
1 tbsp. prepared mustard
½ tsp. salt

DIRECTIONS:

1. In the Ninja Foodi, press Sear/Sauté on High, cook ground beef, bacon, and onion until soft. Drain.
2. Cover the pressure lid and press Slow Cook, cook on High for 2-3 hours.
3. Serve warm.

Creole-style Black Beans with Sausage

Prep Time: 15 minutes, Cook Time: 8 hours, Serves: 6 to 8

INGREDIENTS:

¾ lb. lean smoked sausage, sliced in ¼-inch pieces and browned
3 15-oz. (425 g) cans black beans, drained
1½ cups chopped green bell peppers
1½ cups chopped onions
1½ cups chopped celery
4 garlic cloves, minced
8-oz. (227 g) can tomato sauce
1½ tsps. black pepper
2 tsps. dried thyme
1½ tsp. dried oregano
1 chicken bouillon cube
3 bay leaves
1 cup water

DIRECTIONS:

1. Put all the ingredients into Ninja Foodi.
2. Cover the pressure lid and press Slow Cook, cook on High for 4 hours.
3. Discard bay leaves before serving.

Hearty Baked Beans with Cheesy

Prep Time: 10 minutes, Cook Time: 6 hours, Serves: 12

INGREDIENTS:

18-oz. (511g) jar B&M beans
16-oz. (454 g) can red kidney beans, drained
15½-oz. (439 g) can butter beans, drained
½ lb. bacon, diced

¼ lb. Velveeta cheese, cubed
⅓ cup sugar
½ cup brown sugar
2 dashes Worcestershire sauce

DIRECTIONS:

1. Put all the ingredients into the Ninja Foodi.
2. Cover the pressure lid and press Slow Cook, cook on Low for 6 hours. Do not stir until nearly finished cooking.
3. Serve warm from the cooker.

Green Beans with Cranberry and Walnut Mung

Prep Time: 20 minutes, Cook Time: 5 hours to 7 hours, Serves: 8

INGREDIENTS:

⅓ cup orange juice
2 pounds (907g) fresh green beans
1 onion, chopped
⅛ tsp. freshly ground black pepper

1 cup dried cranberries (see tip here)
½ tsp. salt
1 cup coarsely chopped toasted walnuts

DIRECTIONS:

1. Place green beans, onions, cranberries, orange juice, salt, and pepper in the Ninja Foodi. Cover the pressure lid and press Slow Cook, cook on low heat for 5 to 7 hours, close the lid until the green beans are soft.
2. Sprinkle walnuts at the end and serve immediately.

Chickpea and Potato Curry

Prep Time: 10 minutes, Cook Time: 9 hours, Serves: 6

INGREDIENTS:

1 pound (454 g) dried chickpeas, soaked overnight and rinsed
2 medium sweet potatoes, peeled and chopped
7 cups (1680 ml) vegetable broth
2 tbsps. curry powder
1 tsp. garlic powder

1 (14-ounce, 397 g) can crushed tomatoes
8 scallions, chopped
½ tsp. sea salt
¼ tsp. freshly ground black pepper
¼ cup chopped fresh cilantro

DIRECTIONS:

1. Mix the chickpeas, sweet potatoes, scallions, broth, tomatoes, salt, pepper, curry powder, garlic powder in Ninja Foodi.
2. Cover the pressure lid and press Slow Cook, cook for 9 hours.
3. Add the cilantro just before serving.

Chapter 20 Beef

Beef Brisket with Onion

Prep Time: 20 minutes, Cook Time: 12 hours (low), 6 hours (high), Serves: 6

INGREDIENTS:

1 first cut of beef brisket (about 4 pounds, 1.8 kg), trimmed of excess fat
2 garlic cloves, smashed and peeled
1 large onion, thinly sliced
Coarse salt and freshly
ground pepper
2 cups low-sodium chicken broth, store-bought or homemade
Fresh flat-leaf parsley, for garnish
Prepared horseradish, for serving

DIRECTIONS:

1. In the Ninja Foodi, add the onion and garlic.
2. Use salt and pepper to season the beef brisket, and place over of onion and garlic, fat side up. Pour in broth.
3. Cover the pressure lid and press Slow Cook, cook on high for 6 hours or on low for 12 hours, until brisket is fork-tender.
4. Remove brisket and slice against the grain. Use cooking liquid to moisten, and place onion slices and parsley on the top.
5. Serve with horseradish.
6. Brisket can be made ahead and stored in cooking liquid, covered and refrigerated for up to 1 week. Reheat at 300°F(150°C) to warm.

Beef Potato Stew

Prep Time: 10 minutes, Cook Time: 6 to 8 hours on low, Serves: 6

INGREDIENTS:

1 tsp. chili powder
1 tsp. ground black pepper
1 tsp. salt
½ tsp. ground cumin
2 pounds (907 g) beef stew meat
3 large baking potatoes, cubed
1 (14.5-ounce, 411 g) can diced tomatoes with
chiles
1 large onion, chopped
1 bell pepper, seeded and chopped
3 jalapeños, seeded and chopped
3 or 4 garlic cloves, minced
3 cups beef stock
½ cup red wine
½ cup water

DIRECTIONS:

THE NIGHT BEFORE:
1. Add the chili powder, pepper, salt and cumin into a small bowl, mix them together. In a storage container, add the beef and then sprinkle the spice mixture over it. Seal the container and transfer it to the refrigerator to chill overnight.
IN THE MORNING:
2. Add the seasoned beef and the rest of the ingredients to the Ninja Foodi.
3. Cover the pressure lid and press Slow Cook, cook on low for 6 to 8 hours, or until the potatoes are tender.
4. After cooking, turn off the heat and serve warm.

Cheesy Beef Meatballs with Marinara Sauce

Prep Time: 30 minutes, Cook Time: 5 to 6 hours on low, Serves: 6

INGREDIENTS:

3 tbsps. extra-virgin olive oil, divided
1 egg
1½ pounds (680 g) ground beef
2 tsps. minced garlic
¼ cup grated Parmesan cheese
2 tsps. dried basil
½ tsp. salt
¼ tsp. freshly ground black pepper
6 ounces (170 g) Mozzarella, cut into 16 small cubes
4 cups simple marinara sauce

DIRECTIONS:

1. Use 1 tablespoon of the olive oil to lightly grease the insert of the Ninja Foodi.
2. Add the egg, beef, garlic, Parmesan, basil, salt and pepper to large bowl, combine them together until well mixed. Form the mixture into 16 meatballs and press a mozzarella piece into the center of each, enclose the cheese completely.
3. Heat the remaining 2 tablespoons of the olive oil in the Ninja Foodi over medium-high heat. Place the meatballs in the inner pot and brown all over, about 10 minutes.
4. In the insert of the cooker, add the meatballs and pour in the marinara sauce.
5. Cover the pressure lid and press Slow Cook, cook on low for 5 to 6 hours.
6. Turn off the heat and serve warm.

Garlicky Braised Beef Burritos

Prep Time: 20 minutes, plus overnight, Cook Time: 10 hours (low), Serves: 6

INGREDIENTS:

FOR THE MARINADE
½ cup olive oil
3 garlic cloves, minced
1 serrano chile, seeded and minced
¼ cup fresh lime juice
1 tsp. hot sauce
1 tbsp. Worcestershire sauce
1 tbsp. soy sauce
½ tsp. ground cumin
FOR THE BEEF
3 tbsps. olive oil
3 pounds (1.4 kg) beef brisket, fat trimmed, cut into 1-pound (454 g) pieces
1 (28-ounce, 800 g) can diced fire-roasted tomatoes

1 cup Beef Stock
2 medium onions, diced
2 serrano chiles, seeded and minced
½ tsp. dried Mexican oregano
1 medium red bell pepper, seeded and diced
1 tsp. garlic powder
FOR THE BURRITOS
6 burrito-size flour tortillas
1 cup Mexican crema or sour cream
1 cup Red Salsa or Green Salsa
1 cup grated queso fresco or Monterey Jack cheese

DIRECTIONS:

THE NIGHT BEFORE:
1. Combine the marinade ingredients in a large bowl.
2. In a resealable bag, add the brisket pieces. Then place the marinade to cover. Seal the bag and place in the refrigerator to chill it overnight.

IN THE MORNING:
3. Add the olive oil, beef stock, onions, serrano chiles, bell pepper, garlic powder, oregano and tomatoes to the bottom of the Ninja Foodi, stirring gently to mix.
4. Take the meat out from the resealable bag and discard the marinade. Transfer the meat into the Ninja Foodi on top of the tomato mixture, cover the pressure lid and press Slow Cook, cook on low for 10 hours.
5. On a cutting board, place the beef and use two forks to shred it. Place the shredded beef back to the slow cooker and stir it into the sauce.
6. TO ASSEMBLE THE BURRITOS:
7. In the Ninja Foodi, add the tortillas, warm over medium-high heat.
8. Place some of the beef down the middle of each tortilla. Place the crema, cheese, and salsa on the top.
9. Fold the bottom of each filled tortilla up about an inch and then roll from the side.
10. Serve hot.

Garlic Beef Brisket with Onions

Prep Time: 20 minutes, Cook Time: 6 hours, Serves: 6

INGREDIENTS:

2 garlic cloves, smashed and peeled
1 large yellow onion, thinly sliced
coarse sea salt
black pepper
1 first cut of beef brisket

(4 pounds, 1.8 kg), trimmed of excess fat
2 cups chicken broth
2 tbsps. chopped fresh parsley leaves, for serving

DIRECTIONS:

1. In the Ninja Foodi, add the garlic and onion.
2. Use the salt and pepper to season the brisket, and add to the slow cooker, fat-side up.
3. Pour the broth into the inner pot. Cover the pressure lid and press Slow Cook, cook on High for 6 hours, until the brisket is fork-tender.
4. Remove the brisket from the cooker and place onto a cutting board, thinly slice across the grain.
5. Serve with some cooking liquid and the onion, sprinkled with parsley.

Italian Braised Veal Shanks

Prep Time: 10 minutes, Cook Time: 8 hours, Serves: 1

INGREDIENTS:

1 tsp. fresh thyme
1 tsp. minced garlic
1 tsp. fresh rosemary
½ tbsp. tomato paste
⅛ tsp. sea salt
Freshly ground black pepper
1 veal shank, about 1

pound (454 g)
½ cup diced carrot
½ cup diced onion
½ cup diced celery
½ cup dry red wine
½ tsp. orange zest
1 cup low-sodium chicken or beef broth

DIRECTIONS:

1. Add the thyme, garlic, rosemary, tomato paste, salt and a few grinds of the black pepper into a small bowl, combine them together. Coat the veal shank in this mixture. You can do this a day ahead and place the veal in the refrigerator.
2. In the Ninja Foodi, add the carrot, onion, celery, wine, orange zest, and broth. Stir thoroughly. Nestle the veal shank in the vegetable and wine mixture.
3. Cover the pressure lid and press Slow Cook, cook on low for 8 hours.

Slow Cooker Caribbean Pot Beef Roast

Prep Time: 30 minutes, Cook Time: 6 hours, Serves: 10

INGREDIENTS:

2 large carrots, sliced	1 tbsp. brown sugar
2 medium sweet potatoes, cubed	1 tsp. ground cumin
¼ cup chopped celery	¾ tsp. ground coriander
1 tbsp. canola oil	¾ tsp. salt
1 boneless beef chuck roast (2 ½ pounds, 1.1 kg)	½ tsp. dried oregano
	¾ tsp. chili powder
	⅛ tsp. ground cinnamon
1 large onion, chopped	¾ tsp. grated orange peel
2 garlic cloves, minced	¾ tsp. baking cocoa
1 tbsp. sugar	1 can (15 ounces, 425 g) tomato sauce
1 tbsp. all-purpose flour	

DIRECTIONS:
1. In the Ninja Foodi, add the carrots, potatoes, and celery. Place oil and beef in a large skillet, brown the meat on all sides. Then transfer meat to the Ninja Foodi.
2. Sauté the onion in drippings in the same skillet until tender. Stir in the garlic, cook for 1 minute. Add the brown sugar, flour, seasonings, orange peel and cocoa, combine well. Stir in tomato sauce, add to skillet and heat through. Pour over beef.
3. Cover the pressure lid and press Slow Cook, cook on low for 6-8 hours or until vegetables and beef are tender.

Vegetable Beef Stuffed Peppers

Prep Time: 25 minutes, Cook Time: 6 hours on low, Serves: 4

INGREDIENTS:

3 tbsps. extra-virgin olive oil, divided	2 tsps. dried oregano
	1 tsp. dried basil
1 pound (454 g) ground beef	4 bell peppers, tops cut off and seeded
2 tsps. minced garlic	1 cup shredded Cheddar cheese
1 tomato, diced	
½ cup finely chopped cauliflower	½ cup chicken broth
	1 tbsp. basil, sliced into thin strips, for garnish
½ sweet onion, chopped	

DIRECTIONS:
1. Use 1 tablespoon of the olive oil to lightly grease the insert of the Ninja Foodi.

2. Heat the remaining 2 tablespoons of the olive oil in the inner pot over medium-high heat. Stir in the beef and sauté for 10 minutes, until it is cooked through.
3. Then stir in the garlic, tomato, cauliflower, onion, oregano, and basil. Sauté for another 5 minutes.
4. Stuff the meat mixture into the bell peppers, and place the cheese on the top.
5. Add the peppers and pour the broth into the bottom.
6. Cover the pressure lid and press Slow Cook, cook on low, cook for 6 hours.
7. Top with the basil and serve warm.

Red Chili with Beef and Queso Fresco

Prep Time: 10 minutes, Cook Time: 8 hours (low), 4 hours (high), Serves: 6

INGREDIENTS:

1 dried guajillo chile, seeded and diced	2 garlic cloves, minced
	1 tsp. dried Mexican oregano
1 dried papilla chile, seeded and diced	1 tsp. chili powder
1 dried chipotle chile, seeded and diced	½ tsp. smoked paprika
	½ tsp. ground cumin
1 dried mulato chile, seeded and diced	½ tsp. ground roasted cinnamon
½ medium red bell pepper, seeded and chopped	Cooking spray
	2 pounds (907 g) lean, boneless beef roast
2 jalapeños	6 tbsps. grated queso fresco or Monterey Jack cheese
1 medium poblano chile, seeded and diced	
1 medium onion, diced	

DIRECTIONS:
THE NIGHT BEFORE:
1. Add the guajillo, papilla, chipotle, and mulato chiles into a small bowl, pour in hot water to just cover them, and allow them to soak overnight at room temperature.

IN THE MORNING:
2. Add the chiles and soaking water with the remaining ingredients, except the meat and cheese into a blender, and blend until smooth.
3. Use cooking spray to spray a slow cooker.
4. Add the beef into the Ninja Foodi, and pour the chile mixture over the top. Cover the pressure lid and press Slow Cook, cook on low for 8 hours or on high for 4 hours.
5. On a cutting board, place the beef and use two forks to shred it, then place the shredded beef back to the inner pot and stir it into the chili.
6. Sprinkle the chili with cheese and serve.

Beef with Vegetable and Chili

Prep Time: 20 minutes, Cook Time: 8 hours to 10 hours, Serves: 8

INGREDIENTS:

2½ pounds (1.1kg) sirloin tip, cut into 2-inch cubes
2 onions, chopped
1 (6-ounce (170g)) BPA-free can tomato paste (see tip here)
2 tbsps. chili powder
2 cups dry beans, rinsed and drained
6 garlic cloves, minced
11 cups Roasted Vegetable Broth (here)
2 jalapeño peppers, minced
4 large tomatoes, seeded and chopped
1 tsp. ground cumin

DIRECTIONS:

1. Put all the ingredients in the Ninja Foodi and stir to combine. Cover the pressure lid and press Slow Cook, cook on low heat for 8 to 10 hours, until the beans are soft.
2. Transfer the mixture from the pot to a bowl and enjoy!

Corned Beef with Potato and Carrot

Prep Time: 20 minutes, Cook Time: 9 hours, Serves: 5

INGREDIENTS:

2 medium carrots, cut into chunks
1 large onion, sliced
6 medium red potatoes, quartered
2 corned beef briskets with spice packets (3 pounds each, 1.4 kg)
2 tbsps. sugar
¼ cup packed brown sugar
2 tbsps. whole peppercorns
2 tbsps. coriander seeds
4 cups water

DIRECTIONS:

1. Add the carrots, onion and potatoes into the Ninja Foodi. Then add briskets (discard spice packets from corned beef or save for another use). Over the meat, sprinkle with the sugar, brown sugar, peppercorns and coriander. Pour water to cover.
2. Cover the pressure lid and press Slow Cook, cook on low for 9-11 hours or until vegetables and meat are tender.
3. After cooking, take the meat and vegetables out and place onto a serving platter. Thinly slice one brisket across the grain and serve with vegetables. Save the remaining brisket for Reuben sandwiches, strata or save for another use.

Easy Homemade Beef Broccoli

Prep Time: 10 minutes, Cook Time: 6 hours, Serves: 1

INGREDIENTS:

12 ounces (340 g) flank steak, sliced thin
2 cups broccoli florets
1 tsp. toasted sesame oil
2 tbsps. honey or maple syrup
½ cup low-sodium beef broth
1 tsp. minced garlic
2 tbsps. low-sodium soy sauce
1 tbsp. cornstarch

DIRECTIONS:

1. In the Ninja Foodi, add the flank steak and broccoli.
2. Add the sesame oil, honey, beef broth, garlic, soy sauce and cornstarch into a measuring cup or small bowl, whisk them together. Pour over the beef and broccoli with this mixture.
3. Cover the pressure lid and press Slow Cook, cook on low, cook for 6 hours.

Beef Stew with Pumpkin and Tomato

Prep Time: 15 minutes, Cook Time: 8 hours on low, Serves: 6

INGREDIENTS:

3 tbsps. extra-virgin olive oil, divided
¼ tsp. freshly ground black pepper
½ tsp. salt
1 (2-pound, 907 g) beef chuck roast, cut into 1-inch chunks
1 cup diced tomatoes
2 cups beef broth
1½ cups cubed pumpkin, cut into 1-inch chunks
¼ cup apple cider vinegar
½ sweet onion, chopped
2 tsps. minced garlic
1 tsp. dried thyme
1 tbsp. chopped fresh parsley, for garnish

DIRECTIONS:

1. Use 1 tablespoon of the olive oil to lightly grease the insert of the Ninja Foodi.
2. Use pepper and salt to season the beef chucks lightly.
3. Heat the remaining 2 tablespoons of the olive oil over medium-high heat. Stir in the beef and brown on all sides, about 7 minutes.
4. In the insert of the Ninja Foodi, add the beef and stir in the tomatoes, broth, pumpkin, apple cider vinegar, onion, garlic, and thyme.
5. Cover the pressure lid and press Slow Cook, cook on low for about 8 hours, until the beef is very tender.
6. Top with the parsley and serve.

Balsamic Braised Beef Short Ribs

Prep Time: 10 minutes, Cook Time: 7 to 8 hours on low, Serves: 8

INGREDIENTS:
1 tbsp. extra-virgin olive oil
1 sweet onion, sliced
2 pounds (907 g) beef short ribs
2 cups beef broth

2 tbsps. balsamic vinegar
2 tbsps. granulated erythritol
2 tsps. dried thyme
1 tsp. hot sauce

DIRECTIONS:
1. Use the olive oil to lightly grease the insert of the Ninja Foodi.
2. In the insert of the Ninja Foodi, add the onion, ribs, broth, balsamic vinegar, erythritol, thyme, and hot sauce.
3. Cover the pressure lid and press Slow Cook, cook on low for 7 to 8 hours.
4. After cooking, turn off the heat and serve warm.

Delicious Beef Pot Roast

Prep Time: 20 minutes, Cook Time: 8 hours to 10 hours, Serves: 8

INGREDIENTS:
1 (3-pound (1.4kg)) grass-fed chuck shoulder roast or tri-tip roast
4 large carrots, peeled and cut into chunks
2 onions, chopped
8 Yukon Gold potatoes, cut into chunks
1 leek, sliced

1 cup Beef Stock (here)
8 garlic cloves, sliced
1 tsp. dried marjoram
½ tsp. salt
¼ tsp. freshly ground black pepper

DIRECTIONS:
1. Combine potatoes, carrots, onions, leeks, and garlic in the Ninja Foodi.
2. Put the beef on the mixed vegetables and pour in the appropriate marjoram, salt and pepper.
3. Pour beef broth in the inner pot and cover.
4. Cover the pressure lid and press Slow Cook, cook on low heat for 8 to 10 hours, until the beef is very tender. Take out the beef and serve with vegetables.

Mushroom Pumpkin Beef Goulash

Prep Time: 10 minutes, Cook Time: 8 hours, Serves: 1

INGREDIENTS:
1 cup quartered button mushrooms
1 small pie pumpkin or butternut squash, peeled and cut into 1-inch cubes
12 ounces (340 g) beef stew meat, cut into 1-inch cubes
1 garlic clove, minced
½ yellow onion, halved and cut into thin half circles

⅛ tsp. ground allspice
¼ tsp. ground cinnamon
1 bay leaf
1 fresh thyme sprig
1 cup chicken broth
⅛ tsp. sea salt
2 tbsps. pumpkin seeds

DIRECTIONS:
1. In the Ninja Foodi, add all of the ingredients except the pumpkin seeds, and stir gently to mix.
2. Cover the pressure lid and press Slow Cook, cook on low for 8 hours. Remove the bay leaf and thyme sprig from the goulash, and serve.
3. Garnish with the pumpkin seeds.

Home-Style Beef Braciola

Prep Time: 30 minutes, Cook Time: 6 hours, Serves: 6

INGREDIENTS:
1 tsp. crushed red pepper flakes
2 jars (24 ounces each, 672 g) tomato basil pasta sauce
1 beef flank steak (1 ½ pounds, 670 g)
½ tsp. pepper
½ tsp. salt

2 eggs, beaten
½ cup seasoned bread crumbs
8 thin slices prosciutto or deli ham
1 cup (4 ounces, 113 g) shredded Italian cheese blend
2 tbsps. olive oil

DIRECTIONS:
1. Add the pepper flakes and pasta into the Ninja Foodi, combine them together. Pound steak with a meat mallet to ½-in. thickness, sprinkle with pepper and salt.
2. Add the bread crumbs and eggs in a small bowl, combine them together. Spoon over beef to within 1 in. of edges, press onto meat. Add a layer of prosciutto and cheese. Roll up jelly-roll style, beginning with a long side, use kitchen string to tie at 2-in. intervals.
3. Add the oil and meat in the inner pot, brown the meat on all sides, spoon over the meat with the sauce. Cover the pressure lid and press Slow Cook, cook on low for 6-8 hours or until the beef is tender.
4. Take meat out from sauce and discard string. Cut into slices, serve with sauce.

Garlic Coconut Beef with Bell Pepper

Prep Time: 15 minutes, Cook Time: 9 to 10 hours on low, Serves: 6

INGREDIENTS:
3 tbsps. extra-virgin olive oil, divided
1 pound (454 g) beef tenderloin, cut into 1-inch chunks
2 tsps. minced garlic
½ sweet onion, chopped
1 yellow bell pepper, diced
1 red bell pepper, diced

1 cup beef broth
2 cups coconut cream
3 tsps. coconut aminos
1 tbsp. hot sauce
1 tbsp. sesame seeds, for garnish
1 scallion, white and green parts, chopped, for garnish

DIRECTIONS:
1. Use 1 tablespoon of the olive oil to lightly grease the insert of the Ninja Foodi.
2. Heat the remaining 2 tablespoons of the olive oil in the inner pot over medium-high heat. Place the beef in the skillet and brown for 6 minutes. Transfer to the insert.
3. Add the garlic and onion to the skillet, sauté for 3 minutes.
4. In the insert of the inner pot, add the garlic and onion along with the yellow pepper, red pepper, broth, coconut cream, coconut aminos, and hot sauce.
5. Cover the pressure lid and press Slow Cook, cook on low for 9 to 10 hours.
6. Top with the sesame seeds and scallion, serve warm.

Chapter 21 Poultry

Braised Chicken Thighs with Garlic and Onion

Prep Time: 15 minutes, Cook Time: 7 to 8 hours on low, Serves: 4

INGREDIENTS:

¼ cup extra-virgin olive oil, divided
1½ pounds (680 g) boneless chicken thighs
Salt, for seasoning
1 tsp. paprika
Freshly ground black pepper, for seasoning
4 garlic cloves, thinly sliced
1 sweet onion, chopped
½ cup chicken broth
2 tbsps. freshly squeezed lemon juice
½ cup Greek yogurt

DIRECTIONS:

1. Use 1 tablespoon of the olive oil to lightly grease the insert of the Ninja Foodi.
2. Use salt, paprika and pepper to season the thighs.
3. Heat the remaining olive oil in the inner pot over medium-high heat. Stir in the chicken and brown for 5 minutes, turning once.
4. In the insert, add the chicken and stir in the garlic, onion, broth, and lemon juice.
5. Cover the pressure lid and press Slow Cook, cook on low for 7 to 8 hours.
6. After cooking, add the yogurt, stir well and serve.

Roasted Pepper and Cheese Stuffed Chicken Breasts

Prep Time: 10 minutes, Cook Time: 6-8 hours, Serves: 1

INGREDIENTS:

1 tsp. extra-virgin olive oil
2 boneless, skinless chicken breasts
Freshly ground black pepper
⅛ tsp. sea salt
2 roasted red bell peppers, cut into thin strips
2 ounces (57 g) sliced mozzarella cheese
¼ cup roughly chopped fresh basil

DIRECTIONS:

1. Use olive oil to grease the inside of the Ninja Foodi.
2. Cut the chicken breast horizontally down the middle until it is almost cut in half. Open as if opening a book. Use pepper and salt to season all sides of the chicken.
3. Place on one inside half of each chicken breast with a layer of the roasted peppers. Place the mozzarella slices on top of the peppers. Then sprinkle the cheese with the fresh basil. Fold the other half of the chicken over the filling.
4. In the Ninja Foodi, add the stuffed chicken breasts carefully, be sure that the filling does not escape. Cover the pressure lid and press Slow Cook, cook on low for 6 to 8 hours, or until the chicken is cooked through.

Curried Ginger Coconut Chicken

Prep Time: 15 minutes, Cook Time: 7 to 8 hours on low, Serves: 6

INGREDIENTS:

3 tbsps. extra-virgin olive oil, divided
1½ pounds (680 g) boneless chicken breasts
1 cup quartered baby bok choy
½ sweet onion, chopped
1 red bell pepper, diced
2 tbsps. almond butter
2 cups coconut milk
1 tbsp. coconut aminos
1 tbsp. red Thai curry paste
2 tsps. grated fresh ginger
Pinch red pepper flakes
2 tbsps. chopped cilantro, for garnish
¼ cup chopped peanuts, for garnish

DIRECTIONS:

1. Use 1 tablespoon of the olive oil to lightly grease the insert of the Ninja Foodi.
2. Heat the remaining 2 tablespoons of the olive oil in a large skillet over medium-high heat. Stir in the chicken and brown for about 7 minutes.
3. Place the chicken into the Ninja Foodi and stir in the baby bok choy, onion and bell pepper.
4. Add the almond butter, coconut milk, coconut aminos, curry paste, ginger and red pepper flakes to a medium bowl, whisk them together until well blended.
5. Pour over the chicken and vegetables with the sauce, and stir to coat.
6. Cover the pressure lid and press Slow Cook, cook on low for 7 to 8 hours.
7. Top with the cilantro and peanuts, serve.

Cheesy Green Chile Chicken Enchilada Casserole

Prep Time: 10 minutes, Cook Time: 8 hours (low), 4 hours (high), Serves: 6

INGREDIENTS:

1½ pounds (680 g) cooked boneless, skinless chicken breasts, shredded
1½ cups fresh or frozen corn
2 medium poblano chiles, diced
½ medium onion, chopped
1 cup Green Salsa
8 ounces (227 g) cream cheese, cut into 1-inch cubes
3 cups Chicken Stock
½ cup grated Colby cheese, plus more as desired
1 tsp. ground cumin
½ tsp. smoked paprika
½ tsp. garlic powder
12 corn tortillas, torn into bite-size pieces

DIRECTIONS:

1. Add all of the ingredients into the Ninja Foodi, stirring gently to blend.
2. Cover the pressure lid and press Slow Cook, cook on low for 8 hours or on high for 4 hours.
3. Top with an extra sprinkle of Colby cheese if desired, and serve.

Buttery Chicken Broccoli and Potato Stew

Prep Time: 15 minutes, Cook Time: 6 hours, Serves: 8

INGREDIENTS:

8 bone-in chicken thighs, skin removed (about 3 pounds, 1.4 kg)
½ cup white wine or chicken broth
1 cup Italian salad dressing
6 tbsps. butter, melted, divided
1 tbsp. garlic powder
1 tbsp. dried minced onion
1 tbsp. Italian seasoning
¾ tsp. salt, divided
¾ tsp. pepper, divided
1 package (8 ounces, 227 g) cream cheese, softened
1 can (10 ¾ ounces, 304 g) condensed cream of mushroom soup, undiluted
2 cups frozen broccoli florets, thawed
2 pounds (907 g) red potatoes, quartered

DIRECTIONS:

1. In the Ninja Foodi, add the chicken. In a small bowl, add the wine, salad dressing, 4 tablespoons butter, garlic powder, onion, Italian seasoning, ½ teaspoon salt and ½ teaspoon pepper, combine well. pour this mixture over the chicken.
2. Cover the pressure lid and press Slow Cook, cook on low for 5 hours. Skim fat of the cooking liquid. In a small bowl, add the cream cheese, soup, and 2 cups of liquid from Ninja Foodi, combine until blended, add to the inner pot.
3. Cover the pressure lid and press Slow Cook, cook for another 45 minutes or until chicken is tender, adding the broccoli during the last 30 minutes of cooking.
4. While the broccoli and chicken is cooking, In a large saucepan, add potatoes and cover with water. Bring to a boil. Lower heat, cover and simmer for 15-20 minutes or until tender. Drain and return to pan. Mash potatoes with the remaining butter, pepper and salt. Serve with broccoli mixture and chicken.

Curried Chicken with Pineapple and Bean

Prep Time: 25 minutes, Cook Time: 6 hours, Serves: 6

INGREDIENTS:

2 cans (8 ounces each, 227 g) unsweetened pineapple chunks, undrained
1 can (15 ounces, 425 g) garbanzo beans or chickpeas, rinsed and drained
6 bone-in chicken breast halves, skin removed (12 ounces each, 340 g)
1 cup julienned carrots
1 large onion, cut into 1-inch pieces
1 medium sweet red pepper, cut into strips
2 tbsps. cornstarch
½ cup light coconut milk
3 tsps. curry powder
2 tbsps. sugar
2 garlic cloves, minced
2 tsps. minced fresh gingerroot
1 tsp. lime juice
1 tsp. salt
1 tsp. pepper
½ tsp. crushed red pepper flakes
⅓ cup minced fresh basil
Toasted flaked coconut, optional
Hot cooked rice

DIRECTIONS:

1. Drain and reserve ¾ cup juice of the pineapple. In the Ninja Foodi, add the pineapple, beans, chicken, and vegetables. Add the cornstarch and coconut milk into a small bowl, combine them together until smooth. Stir in the reserved pineapple juice, curry powder, sugar, garlic, ginger, lime juice, salt, pepper, and pepper flakes to the bowl, then pour over the chicken in the Ninja Foodi.
2. Cover the pressure lid and press Slow Cook, cook on low, cook for 6-8 hours or until chicken is tender. Sprinkle with basil and coconut if desired, serve with rice.

Delicious Chicken Provence

Prep Time: 20 minutes, Cook Time: 7 hours to 9 hours, Serves: 8

INGREDIENTS:

3 pounds (1.4kg) boneless, skinless chicken thighs
2 red bell peppers, stemmed, seeded, and chopped
2 onions, chopped
4 sprigs fresh thyme
3 bulbs fennel, cored and
sliced
6 garlic cloves, minced
¼ cup sliced black Greek olives
2 tbsps. lemon juice
4 large tomatoes, seeded and chopped
1 bay leaf

DIRECTIONS:

1. In the Ninja Foodi, mix all of the ingredients. Cover the pressure lid and press Slow Cook, cook on low for 7 to 9 hours, or until the chicken registers 165°F on a food thermometer.
2. Remove and discard the thyme stems and bay leaf and serve.

Cheesy Mushroom Chicken with Tortellini

Prep Time: 10 minutes, Cook Time: 6 1/4 hours, Serves: 8

INGREDIENTS:

½ lb. (227 g) sliced fresh mushrooms
1 ½ lbs. (680 g) boneless skinless chicken breasts, cut into 1-in. cubes
1 medium sweet red pepper, cut into ½-in. pieces
1 large onion, chopped
1 can (2 ¼ oz., 64 g) sliced ripe olives, drained
1 medium green pepper,
cut into ½-in. pieces
1 jar (24 oz., 672 g) marinara sauce
2 pkg. (9 oz. each, 255 g) refrigerated cheese tortellini
1 jar (15 oz., 425 g) Alfredo sauce
Torn fresh basil, optional
Grated Parmesan cheese, optional

DIRECTIONS:

1. Add the mushrooms, chicken, red pepper, onion, olives, green pepper and marinara sauce into the Ninja Foodi. slow cooker, combine them together. Uncover and press Slow Cook, cook on low for 6 to 8 hours, until chicken is tender.
2. Add the tortellini and Alfredo sauce, and stir well. Cover the pressure lid and press Slow Cook, cook for 15 to 20 minutes, until the tortellini is tender. Top with basil and Parmesan cheese if desired.

Spiced Garlic Chicken with Grape Tomatoes

Prep Time: 10 minutes, Cook Time: 8 hours, Serves: 1

INGREDIENTS:

1 tsp. extra-virgin olive oil
4 garlic cloves, smashed
1 pint grape tomatoes
Zest of 1 lemon
2 bone-in, skinless chicken thighs, about 8
ounces (227 g) each
½ tsp. fresh rosemary
1 tsp. fresh thyme
⅛ tsp. sea salt
Freshly ground black pepper

DIRECTIONS:

1. In the Ninja Foodi, add the olive oil, garlic, tomatoes and lemon zest. Gently stir to mix.
2. Place the chicken thighs on top of the tomato mixture, and season them with the rosemary, thyme, salt, and a few grinds of black pepper.
3. Cover the pressure lid and press Slow Cook, cook on low for 8 hours.

Creamy Chicken with Bacon and Mushroom

Prep Time: 15 minutes, Cook Time: 7 to 8 hours on low, Serves: 8

INGREDIENTS:

3 tbsps. coconut oil, divided
¼ pound (114 g) bacon, diced
2 pounds (907 g) chicken (breasts, thighs, drumsticks)
1 tbsp. minced garlic
1 sweet onion, diced
2 cups quartered button mushrooms
½ cup chicken broth
2 tsps. chopped thyme
1 cup coconut cream

DIRECTIONS:

1. Use 1 tablespoon of the coconut oil to lightly grease the insert of the Ninja Foodi.
2. Heat the remaining 2 tablespoons of the coconut oil in the inner pot over medium-high heat.
3. Stir in the bacon and cook for 5 minutes, until it is crispy. Transfer the bacon to a plate with a slotted spoon, set aside.
4. Place the chicken into the inner pot and brown for 5 minutes, turning once.
5. In the Ninja Foodi, combine the chicken and bacon and stir in the garlic, onion, mushrooms, broth, and thyme.
6. Cover the pressure lid and press Slow Cook, cook on low for 7 to 8 hours.
7. Add the coconut cream, stir well and serve.

Healthy Artichoke Chicken

Prep Time: 20 minutes, Cook Time: 4 to 6 hours on low, Serves: 8

INGREDIENTS:

8 (6-ounce (170g)) boneless, skinless chicken breasts
2 leeks, chopped
1 cup Chicken Stock (here)
2 tbsps. lemon juice
2 (14-ounce (397g)) BPA-free cans no-salt-added
artichoke hearts, drained
1 tsp. dried basil leaves
3 garlic cloves, mince
2 red bell peppers, stemmed, seeded, and chopped
½ cup chopped flat-leaf parsley

DIRECTIONS:

1. Layer the leeks, garlic, artichoke hearts, bell peppers, chicken, stock, lemon juice, and basil in the Ninja Foodi. Cover the pressure lid and press Slow Cook, simmer for 4 to 6 hours until the chicken shows 165°F on the food thermometer.
2. Put parsley at the end and enjoy.

Savory Slow Cooker Butter Chicken

Prep Time: 20 minutes, Cook Time: 7½ to 9½ hours, Serves: 8

INGREDIENTS:

10 (4-ounce (113g)) boneless, skinless chicken thighs
⅓ cup lemon juice
5 tsps. curry powder
½ cup plain Greek yogurt
2 onions, chopped
8 garlic cloves, sliced
⅔ cup canned coconut milk
2 tbsps. grated fresh ginger root
4 large tomatoes, seeded and chopped
3 tbsps. cornstarch

DIRECTIONS:

1. Mix yogurt, lemon juice, curry powder and ginger root in a medium bowl. Add chicken and stir well, set aside and let stand for 15 minutes.
2. Combine tomatoes, onions, and garlic in a 6-quart Ninja Foodi.
3. Pour the chicken yogurt mixture into the Ninja Foodi. Cover the pressure lid and press Slow Cook, cook on low heat for 7 to 9 hours, until the chicken is cooked through.
4. Mix the coconut milk and cornstarch in a small bowl. Then pour into the Ninja Foodi.
5. Cook on low heat for 15 to 20 minutes, until the sauce thickens. Serve immediately!

Lime Black Bean and Chicken

Prep Time: 15 minutes, Cook Time: 8 hours (low), 4 hours (high), Serves: 6

INGREDIENTS:

6 boneless, skinless chicken breasts
2 cups cooked black beans
1 cup fresh or frozen corn
½ medium red bell pepper, seeded and chopped
½ medium onion, chopped
1½ medium (or 1 large)
jalapeños, seeded and chopped
½ cup fresh lime juice
2 tsps. sea salt
1 tsp. ancho chili powder
½ tsp. freshly ground black pepper
2 garlic cloves, minced
1 cup chopped fresh cilantro
½ cup Chicken Stock

DIRECTIONS:

1. Combine all of the ingredients into the Ninja Foodi.
2. Cover the pressure lid and press Slow Cook, cook on low for 8 hours or on high for 4 hours.
3. After cooking, turn off the heat and serve hot.

Slow Cooker Chicken Chili Verde with Rice

Prep Time: 10 minutes, Cook Time: 6 hours, Serves: 1

INGREDIENTS:

2 boneless, skinless chicken breasts, about 8 ounces (227 g) each, cut into 4-inch tenders
1 onion, halved and sliced thin
1 cup diced tomatillos
1 jalapeño pepper, seeds and membranes removed, minced
2 garlic cloves, minced
1 tsp. ground cumin
1 tsp. ground coriander
1 tsp. extra-virgin olive oil
½ cup long-grain brown rice
1 cup low-sodium chicken broth
¼ cup fresh cilantro

DIRECTIONS:

1. In a food processor, add the onion, tomatillos, jalapeño, garlic, cumin, and coriander. Pulse until it has a sauce-like consistency but is still slightly chunky.
2. Use olive oil to grease the inside of the Ninja Foodi.
3. In the Ninja Foodi, add the rice and pour in the chicken broth. Gently stir and let the rice grains are fully submerged.
4. Place on top of the rice with the chicken and pour the tomatillo salsa over them.
5. Cover the pressure lid and press Slow Cook, cook on low for 6 hours.

Garlicky Mushroom and Chicken Thigh

Prep Time: 10 minutes, Cook Time: 6-8 hours, Serves: 1

INGREDIENTS:

1 tsp. unsalted butter, at room temperature, or extra-virgin olive oil
2 garlic cloves, minced
2 cups thinly sliced cremini mushrooms
1 shallot, minced
1 tsp. fresh thyme

3 tbsps. dry sherry
2 bone-in, skinless chicken thighs, about 6 ounces (170 g) each
Freshly ground black pepper
⅛ tsp. sea salt

DIRECTIONS:

1. Use the butter to grease the inside of the Ninja Foodi.
2. In the inner pot, add the garlic, mushrooms, shallot and thyme, tossing them gently to combine. Pour in the sherry.
3. Use pepper and salt to season the chicken and place the thighs over the mushroom mixture.
4. Cover the pressure lid and press Slow Cook, cook on low, cook for 6 to 8 hours.

Simple Roasted Chicken with Squash

Prep Time: 20 minutes, Cook Time: 6 to 8 hours, Serves: 8

INGREDIENTS:

8 (6-ounce (170g)) bone-in, skinless chicken breasts
1 (3-pound (1.4kg)) butternut squash, peeled, seeded, and cut into 1-inch pieces
½ cup canned coconut milk
1 cup Chicken Stock (here)

2 (1-pound (454g)) acorn squash, peeled, seeded, and cut into 1-inch pieces
2 fennel bulbs, cored and sliced
1 (8-ounce (227g)) package cremini mushrooms, sliced
3 sprigs fresh thyme
1 bay leaf
2 tbsps. lemon juice

DIRECTIONS:

1. Combine butternut squash, acorn squash, fennel, mushrooms, chicken, thyme, bay leaf, chicken broth, and coconut milk in the Ninja Foodi. Cover the pressure lid and press Slow Cook, cook on low heat for 6 to 8 hours until the chicken turns white.
2. Take out thyme sprigs and bay leaves. Finally, top with lemon juice and serve immediately!

French Chicken with Wild Rice Stew

Prep Time: 20 minutes, Cook Time: 7 hours to 9 hours, Serves: 8

INGREDIENTS:

10 boneless, skinless chicken thighs, cut into 2-inch pieces
1 cup wild rice, rinsed and drained
2 (14-ounce (397g)) BPA-free cans diced tomatoes, undrained
2 leeks, chopped

3 garlic cloves, minced
3 large carrots, sliced
2 cups sliced cremini mushrooms
8 cups Roasted Vegetable Broth (here)
2 tsps. dried herbes de Provence
½ cup sliced ripe olives

DIRECTIONS:

1. Place the mushrooms, carrots, leeks, garlic, diced tomatoes, and wild rice in the Ninja Foodi. Place the chicken thighs on top of the mixture and pour the vegetable broth. Cover the pressure lid and press Slow Cook, cook on low heat for 7 to 9 hours, until the chicken is cooked to 165°F and the wild rice is tender.

Pesto-Glazed Chicken with Vegetables

Prep Time: 10 minutes, Cook Time: 6-8 hours, Serves: 1

INGREDIENTS:

1 cup grape tomatoes
1 zucchini, cut into 1-inch pieces
½ red onion, halved and sliced thin
1 red bell pepper, cored and sliced thin
1 tbsp. assorted fresh herbs

1 tsp. extra-virgin olive oil
⅛ tsp. sea salt
Freshly ground black pepper
2 bone-in, skinless chicken thighs, about 8 ounces (227 g) each
¼ cup pesto

DIRECTIONS:

1. In the Ninja Foodi, add the grape tomatoes, zucchini, onion, red bell pepper, and herbs, gently stir until mixed together. Drizzle in the olive oil. Season with the salt and a few grinds of the black pepper.
2. Add the chicken into a medium bowl, use the pesto to coat it on all sides, then transfer the chicken into the Ninja Foodi on top of the vegetables.
3. Cover the pressure lid and press Slow Cook, cook on low for 6 to 8 hours, until the chicken is cooked through and the vegetables are very tender.

Garlicky Turkey Breast with Onion

Prep Time: 10 minutes, Cook Time: 9-10 hours, Serves: 8 to 10

INGREDIENTS:

6-lb. (2.8 kg) turkey breast
2 tsps. olive oil
salt and pepper to taste
4 garlic cloves, peeled
1 medium onion, quartered
½ cup water

DIRECTIONS:

1. Rinse the turkey and use the paper towels to pat dry.
2. Rub over the turkey with the oil. Sprinkle with salt and pepper. Place in the Ninja Foodi, meaty side up.
3. Place the garlic and onion around sides of the cooker.
4. Cover the pressure lid and press Slow Cook, cook on Low for 9 to 10 hours, or until the meat thermometer stuck in meaty part of the breast registers 180°F(82°C).
5. Remove the turkey from the Ninja Foodi and allow to stand for 10 minutes before slicing.
6. Serve with the cranberry salad, mashed potatoes, and corn or green beans.

Slow Cooker Chicken Tikka Masala

Prep Time: 10 minutes, Cook Time: 6 hours, Serves: 1

INGREDIENTS:

1 cup diced onion
1 cup diced fresh tomatoes
16 ounces (454 g) boneless, skinless chicken breast
1 tsp. smoked paprika
1 tsp. ground coriander
1 tsp. ground cumin
1 tsp. minced fresh ginger
1 cup low-sodium chicken broth
⅛ tsp. red pepper flakes
2 tbsps. heavy cream or coconut cream
¼ cup minced fresh cilantro, for garnish

DIRECTIONS:

1. In the Ninja Foodi, add all of the ingredients except the heavy cream and cilantro, stir to combine well.
2. Cover the pressure lid and press Slow Cook, cook on low for 6 hours, until the tomatoes and onions are soft and the chicken is cooked through.
3. Uncovered and let the dish rest in the Ninja Foodi for 10 minutes, then add the heavy cream and stir well. Garnish each serving with the cilantro.

Stewed Chicken with Barley

Prep Time: 20 minutes, Cook Time: 8 hours to 10 hours, Serves: 8

INGREDIENTS:

10 boneless, skinless chicken thighs, cut into 2-inch pieces
2 onions, chopped
1½ cups frozen corn
4 garlic cloves, minced
1 tsp. dried thyme leaves
1¼ cups hulled barley
8 cups Chicken Stock (here)
1 sprig fresh rosemary
4 large carrots, sliced
2 cups baby spinach leaves

DIRECTIONS:

1. Put the onion, garlic, carrot, and barley in the Ninja Foodi and stir to combine. On the mixed vegetables, add chicken and corn.
2. Pour the chicken broth into the pot, add a little rosemary and thyme leaves.
3. Cover the pressure lid and press Slow Cook, cook on low heat for 8 to 10 hours, until the chicken is white.
4. Discard the rosemary stems. Add spinach leaves and stir gently. Let stand for 5 minutes until the spinach is soft and serve.

Meat and Corn Stuffed Green Peppers

Prep Time: 20 minutes, Cook Time: 3-9 hours, Serves: 8

INGREDIENTS:

8 small green peppers, tops removed and seeded
¾ lb. (340 g) 99% fat-free ground turkey
¾ lb. (340 g) extra-lean ground beef
10-oz.(283 g) pkg. frozen corn
8-oz.(227 g) can low-
sodium tomato sauce
1 cup shredded low-fat American cheese
½ tsp. Worcestershire sauce
¼ cup chopped onions
½ tsp. garlic powder
¼ tsp. black pepper
3 tbsps. water
2 tbsps. ketchup

DIRECTIONS:

1. Wash peppers and drain well, set aside. In a mixing bowl, add all of the ingredients except the water and ketchup. Stir well.
2. Stuff the mixture into the peppers for about ⅔ full.
3. Pour water into the Ninja Foodi. On the top, arrange with the stuffed peppers.
4. Add the ketchup over the peppers.
5. Cover the pressure lid and press Slow Cook, cook on High for 3 to 4 hours, or cook on Low for 7 to 9 hours.

APPENDIX 1: MEASUREMENT CONVERSION CHART

Volume Equivalents (Dry)

US STANDARD	METRIC (APPROXIMATE)
1/8 teaspoon	0.5 mL
1/4 teaspoon	1 mL
1/2 teaspoon	2 mL
3/4 teaspoon	4 mL
1 teaspoon	5 mL
1 tablespoon	15 mL
1/4 cup	59 mL
1/2 cup	118 mL
3/4 cup	177 mL
1 cup	235 mL
2 cups	475 mL
3 cups	700 mL
4 cups	1 L

Temperatures Equivalents

FAHRENHEIT (F)	CELSIUS(C) (APPROXIMATE)
225 °F	107 °C
250 °F	120 °C
275 °F	135 °C
300 °F	150 °C
325 °F	160 °C
350 °F	180 °C
375 °F	190 °C
400 °F	205 °C
425 °F	220 °C
450 °F	235 °C
475 °F	245 °C
500 °F	260 °C

Volume Equivalents (Liquid)

US STANDARD	US STANDARD (OUNCES)	METRIC (APPROXIMATE)
2 tablespoons	1 fl.oz.	30 mL
1/4 cup	2 fl.oz.	60 mL
1/2 cup	4 fl.oz.	120 mL
1 cup	8 fl.oz.	240 mL
1 1/2 cup	12 fl.oz.	355 mL
2 cups or 1 pint	16 fl.oz.	475 mL
4 cups or 1 quart	32 fl.oz.	1 L
1 gallon	128 fl.oz.	4 L

Weight Equivalents

US STANDARD	METRIC (APPROXIMATE)
1 ounce	28 g
2 ounces	57 g
5 ounces	142 g
10 ounces	284 g
15 ounces	425 g
16 ounces (1 pound)	455 g
1.5 pounds	680 g
2 pounds	907 g

APPENDIX 2: DIRTY DOZEN AND CLEAN FIFTEEN

The Environmental Working Group (EWG) is a widely known organization that has an eminent guide to pesticides and produce. More specifically, the group takes in data from tests conducted by the US Department of Agriculture (USDA) and then categorizes produce into a list titled "Dirty Dozen," which ranks the twelve top produce items that contain the most pesticide residues, or alternatively the "Clean Fifteen," which ranks fifteen produce items that are contaminated with the least amount of pesticide residues.

The EWG has recently released their 2021 Dirty Dozen list, and this year strawberries, spinach and kale – with a few other produces which will be revealed shortly – are listed at the top of the list. This year's ranking is similar to the 2020 Dirty Dozen list, with the few differences being that collards and mustard greens have joined kale at number three on the list. Other changes include peaches and cherries, which having been listed subsequently as seventh and eighth on the 2020 list, have now been flipped; the introduction – which the EWG has said is the first time ever – of bell and hot peppers into the 2021 list; and the departure of potatoes from the twelfth spot.

DIRTY DOZEN LIST

Strawberries	Apples	Pears
Spinach	Grapes	Bell and hot peppers
Kale, collards and mustard greens	Cherries	Celery
Nectarines	Peaches	Tomatoes

CLEAN FIFTEEN LIST

Avocados	Sweet peas (frozen)	Kiwi
Sweet corn	Eggplant	Cauliflower
Pineapple	Asparagus	Mushrooms
Onions	Broccoli	Honeydew melon
Papaya	Cabbage	Cantaloupe

These lists are created to help keep the public informed on their potential exposures to pesticides, which then allows for better and healthier food choices to be made.

This is the advice that ASEQ-EHAQ also recommends. Stay clear of the dirty dozen by opting for their organic versions, and always be mindful of what you are eating and how it was grown. Try to eat organic as much as possible – whether it is on the list, or not.

APPENDIX 3: RECIPES INDEX

Printed in Great Britain
by Amazon